P9-AOA-350

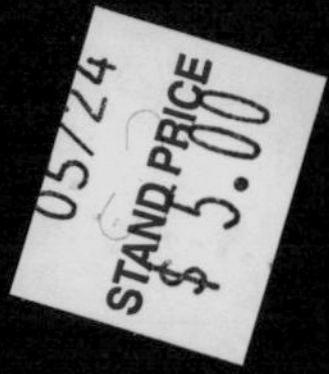
STAND PRICE

THE NEO-PRIMITIVIST TURN:
CRITICAL REFLECTIONS ON ALTERITY, CULTURE,
AND MODERNITY

VICTOR LI

The Neo-primitivist Turn

Critical Reflections on Alterity, Culture, and Modernity

UNIVERSITY OF TORONTO PRESS
Toronto Buffalo London

Toronto Buffalo London
Printed in Canada

ISBN 10: 0-8020-9111-3
ISBN 13: 978-0-8020-9111-6

Printed on acid-free paper

Library and Archives Canada Cataloguing in Publication

Li, Victor, 1952–
The neo-primitivist turn : critical reflections on alterity, culture, and modernity / Victor Li.

Includes bibliographical references and index.
ISBN 0-8020-9111-3

1. Primitive societies. 2. Primitivism. I. Title.

GN316.L52 2006 306 C2006-900655-5

University of Toronto Press acknowledges the financial assistance to its publishing program of the Canada Council for the Arts and the Ontario Arts Council.

This book has been published with the help of a grant from the Canadian Federation for the Humanities and Social Sciences, through the Aid to Scholarly Publications Programme, using funds provided by the Social Sciences and Humanities Research Council of Canada.

University of Toronto Press acknowledges the financial support for its publishing activities of the Government of Canada through the Book Publishing Industry Development Program (BPIDP).

Contents

Preface

Knowing as we do today that there have never existed peoples untouched by history, why do we continue to believe that such groups of people, by-passed by modern history, still exist? Why do we still believe in the idea of the primitive when the term 'primitive' itself has been increasingly withdrawn from circulation? Why still harp on the primitive when we have been made aware that primitive society was an invention of the modern West? These questions insistently frame the example that follows. In the summer of 2003, the Canadian newspaper the *Globe and Mail* featured in its book review section a photograph of 'an Aboriginal group in Australia ... doing a traditional dance. Leaves are attached to their ankles and emu plumes adorn their headdresses.' Exoticism visually established, a brief entry under the photograph summarized the contents of the book under review: 'As the world becomes increasingly globalized and as McDonald's [*sic*] sprouts on seemingly every corner, there are still small pockets where individual cultures and ethnic groups survive. In *Living Tribes,* Colin Prior gives a spectacular photographic record of fifteen such peoples, from the Inuit to the Padaung of Thailand to the Turkana of the Kenyan desert.'[1] We will no doubt notice, especially in these politically enlightened times, that the word 'primitive' does not appear in the description. Instead, acceptable terms like 'individual cultures,' 'ethnic groups,' or 'living tribes' are used. But even though the denigration implied by evolutionary ranking is lifted when the word 'primitive' is studiously avoided, it is less easy to avoid the suspicion that 'individual cultures' or 'ethnic groups' may just be euphemisms inasmuch as they are still employed as concepts opposed, as 'primitive' once was, to a globalizing modernity. In other words, terminological replacements for 'primitive' remain mere euphemisms if they continue to function conceptually and rhetorically as endangered antitheses to the modern West.

To be sure, unlike 'primitive,' which is burdened by a history of derogation, the new terms are greeted positively as expressions of cultural resistance against the threat of a homogenizing modernity, the coming of a monocultural McWorld. But the avoidance of the word 'primitive,' far from signifying a complete rejection of primitivism, represents instead primitivism's transmutation into the liberal creed of multiculturalism, the preservation of cultural diversity in the age of globalization. Politically acceptable terms like 'individual culture' and 'ethnic group' may appear to oppose evolutionary narratives of primitive inferiority, but they still fall into the 'savage slot' that primitivism has always reserved for the Other of Euro-American modernity.[2] We should also note that the 'primitive,' as a chronopolitical concept, is related to terms such as the 'premodern,' the 'archaic,' and 'traditional' or 'tribal' societies. These terms may have different temporal inflections than 'primitive,' but they are often used as equivalents of the latter, especially in their perceived common opposition to the concept of modernity. Like Orientalism, primitivism functions as a grab-bag concept into which everything that is seen as opposed to the modern West is gathered. As such, any study of primitivism (and mine is no different) must acknowledge that the term 'primitive' lacks singular definition and possesses protean, multiple identities. The 'primitive' is not an ontological entity; it is a relational concept that expresses various 'modern' needs.

The story of the 'savage slot' and its related manifestations is well known and has been critically analysed in such notable works as Johannes Fabian's *Time and the Other*, Adam Kuper's *The Invention of Primitive Society*, Bernard McGrane's *Beyond Anthropology*, Marianna Torgovnick's *Gone Primitive*, Micaela di Leonardo's *Exotics at Home*, Shelly Errington's *The Death of Authentic Primitive Art and Other Tales of Progress*, Elazar Barkan and Ronald Bush's collection *Prehistories of the Future*, Helen Carr's *Inventing the American Primitive*, Sieglinde Lemke's *Primitivist Modernism*, Peter Fitzpatrick's *The Mythology of Modern Law*, and Nicholas Thomas's *Colonialism's Culture*.[3] A new perspective can, nonetheless, be introduced to complicate this familiar story. Our awareness of the chronopolitics and geopolitics of primitivism, an awareness we owe in large part to the studies mentioned above, has not led to the disappearance of primitivism but to its deeper imbrication in contemporary theoretical discourses that appear to be anti-primitivist and politically progressive.[4] This book seeks to understand why primitivism keeps reappearing *even after* it has been uncovered as a myth, a projection, or a construction necessary for establishing the modernity of the West. It examines the ways in which a deconstructed primitivism is replaced by 'neo-primitivism.'

By 'neo-primitivism' I mean the conceptual move through which the rejection of primitivism allows it to reappear in new, more acceptable forms. Neo-primitivism is a contemporary version of primitivism in which the critical repudiation of earlier primitivist discourses paradoxically enables their re-introduction, under different names and configurations to be sure, as cultural, political, ethical, and aesthetic alternatives to Western modernity. Neo-primitivist discourses, as we will see, ignore or forget their own repeated warnings against the pitfalls of earlier forms of primitivism, thereby reproducing the very same problems they have warned us against. Neo-primitivism can thus be characterized as an anti-primitivist primitivism that simultaneously disavows and reinscribes the primitive.

Neo-primitivism has become an attractive theoretical option precisely at a time when 'primitives,' defined as belonging to authentic, primordial cultures yet untouched or uncontaminated by modernity, can no longer be called upon to act as pure forms of otherness. Nevertheless, the 'primitive,' as the ultimate sign of alterity, still seems to serve a useful theoretical function, though it is now conceptualized as a regulative ideal rather than as an actuality. Neo-primitivism can thus be seen as a primitivism without primitives insofar as it forwards a concept of the primitive so pure that no empirical referent or actual primitive can contradict or refute it. Though neo-primitivism questions the use of terms like 'primitive' and 'primitivism,' it continues to exhibit a deep primitivist logic that lurks in displaced but related concepts like 'alterity,' 'culture,' and, surprisingly, 'modernity.'

This book examines how neo-primitivism as an anti-primitivist primitivism without primitives functions as an important theoretical concept in the writings of postmodernist theorists Jean Baudrillard and Jean-François Lyotard, the literary and cultural studies scholar Marianna Torgovnick, the cultural anthropologist Marshall Sahlins, and the champion of philosophical modernity Jürgen Habermas. I have chosen to study theorists and thinkers who are normally considered to be anti-primitivist in order to show the continuing power and persistence of primitivism even in works that are critical of it. I want to argue that though greater critical awareness has allowed us to put scare quotes (or to retain the trace of scare quotes even when we dispense with them) around the word 'primitive' to indicate its invented or culturally con-

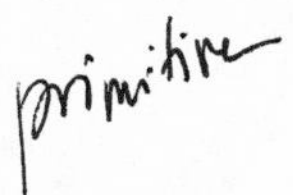

structed nature or, even better, to drop the word altogether from our theoretical vocabulary, primitivism, nonetheless, continues to thrive in concepts that are not usually thought of as primitivist in orientation.

The book's organization attempts to reflect just such a vanishing recurrence by describing how the term 'primitive' has gradually disappeared, only to be revived under such acceptable or neutral names as 'alterity,' culture,' and 'modernity.' As the book proceeds, we will notice that the latter terms move increasingly to the foreground even as the former recedes. The book's title, *The Neo-primitivist Turn: Critical Reflections on Alterity, Culture, and Modernity,* can therefore be seen as recording both the persistence and lability of primitivism, its remarkable ability to take on different new names while maintaining its structural force. Primitivism's ability to change itself while remaining the same is what I have termed 'the neo-primitivist turn.' I should add that in the book's title, 'turn' does not merely describe a determined progression or direction to the argument (the insistence on a singular focus), but also refers to the emergence of tropes or figures of speech, metaphorical shifts in which words cross and re-cross each other (an acknowledgment of the dispersion and diversity of focus). The mobility or diversity of neo-primitivism, reflected in the book's study of different authors from different disciplines (continental philosophy, literary and cultural studies, anthropology, and critical social theory), testifies to primitivism's strength, its ability to transform itself and survive even as its very logic is rigorously questioned. The book concludes by warning us that such a persistent primitivism requires, turn for turn, an equally unending critical vigilance and reflexivity on our part.

Acknowledgments

I wish to thank Karyn Ball, Rodolphe Gasché, David Johnson, Scott Michaelsen, Gananath Obeysekere, Michael O'Driscoll, and Tilottama Rajan for reading and commenting on various chapters of my book. Two anonymous readers for the University of Toronto Press read the entire manuscript and provided insightful criticisms and constructive suggestions for revision. I have benefited immensely from the comments of all these readers, even if I have not always followed their advice.

Two fine institutions have provided me with the collegial support and intellectual stimulation necessary for critical thought: the English Department at Dalhousie University (where I taught for many years) and the English Department at the University of Toronto (where I currently teach). I have been blessed with many colleagues, friends, and students who have encouraged my work and enriched my thinking. If I have not named them individually it is because the list would be far too long. They know who they are and they have my deep gratitude.

I am grateful to Siobhan McMenemy at the University of Toronto Press for steering my manuscript to publication with the kind of grace and efficiency only the best editors are capable of demonstrating. I must also thank Frances Mundy and John St James for their careful copyediting of my manuscript; the latter's sharp eye saved me from many errors and verbal infelicities.

A version of chapter 3 originally appeared as 'Marshall Sahlins and the Apotheosis of Culture,' in *CR: The New Centennial Review* 1, no. 3 (2001), published by Michigan State University Press. Part of chapter 2 was first published as 'The Premodern Condition: Neo-primitivism in Baudrillard and Lyotard,' in *After Poststructuralism: Writing the Intellectual History of Theory*, edited by Tilottama Rajan and Michael O'Driscoll (University of

Toronto Press, 2002). A section of chapter 4 appeared as 'Rationality and Loss: Habermas and the Recovery of the Pre-modern Other,' in *Parallax* 11, no. 3 (2005), published by Routledge Journals, an imprint of Taylor and Francis Group Ltd. (http://www.tandf.col.uk). A few paragraphs in chapter 4 are from 'Habermas and the Ethnocentric Discourse of Modernity,' in *Constructive Criticism: The Human Sciences in the Age of Theory*, edited by Martin Kreiswirth and Thomas Carmichael (University of Toronto Press, 1995). My thanks to the publishers for their permission to reprint these articles in revised form.

My deepest gratitude goes to my family. My late father and my mother have always given their unstinting support to all my endeavours. My sons Nick and Simon have helped me balance the abstractions of philosophical thought with the pulse of contemporary culture; my daughter Allanah went beyond the call of family loyalty to type the bulk of my manuscript, in the course of which she managed to 'invent' a new theorist named 'Bortangle' (a transcription generated out of my handwritten scrawl of the name 'Bataille'). Tania knows how much the book's existence owes to her. I have been inspired by her critical scholarship and buoyed by her love and support. She has always been there for me in all aspects of our life together.

There has been a beautiful moment of culture ... [I]t is between the seventeenth and the nineteenth centuries. Here we find exchange, cultures bump into each other, and considering also the irruption of primitive cultures, it is a very interesting moment. But today, with globalization, all differences are annulled, or else it is a game of differences, but there is no longer a real clash, an alterity of cultures ... But there can't be identity without alterity; if there is no other, there is no self. Today one does not know where the other is, because with globalization there is no other.

Jean Baudrillard, 'An Interview with Jean Baudrillard'

As the predominant sign of traditional culture can no longer monopolize signification ... fantasies of an origin arise. These fantasies are played out through a *generic* realm of associations, typically having to do with the animal, the savage, the countryside, the indigenous, the people, and so forth, which *stand in* for that 'original' something that has been lost ... The primitive defined in these terms provides a way for thinking about the *unthinkable* – as that which is at once basic, universal, and transparent to us all, *and* that which is outside time and language. Because it is only in this imaginary space that the primitive is located, the primitive is phantasmagoric and, literally, ex-otic.

Rey Chow, *Primitive Passions*

1 The Neo-primitivist Turn

From the 'Savage Slot' to the Critique of Modernity

The passage from primitivism to neo-primitivism generally follows the trajectory of Western thought from nineteenth-century evolutionism and the belief in universal histories of progress to twentieth-century cultural relativism and the so-called postmodern incredulity towards modern universalist narratives. We need to examine this trajectory briefly in order to understand how primitivism was dismissed as a Eurocentric myth only to have neo-primitivism end up rescuing and renewing the Western subject of knowledge. We need to understand what the critics and theorists we will be studying reject in Western forms of primitivism, and what aspects of the repudiated primitivist forms they paradoxically continue to reproduce.

It can be argued that primitivism was an invention of the nineteenth century, coterminous with the theory of social evolution. In his brilliant, if somewhat condensed, Foucaultian study of Western conceptions of the Other, Bernard McGrane contends that it was in the nineteenth century that 'evolutionary time ... came between the European and the non-European Other' and gave rise to an anthropology that 'first ... transformed difference into *historical* difference, and then ... transformed history into evolution (progressive evolution).'[1] Before the nineteenth century and its discovery of evolutionary time, the Other in the Renaissance was the non-Christian and, as such, was perceived in terms of *demonology*; during the Enlightenment 'it was *ignorance* that came between the European and the Other.'[2] Though McGrane's periodization may be a little too blunt and totalizing, his observations provide a general insight into pre-nineteenth-century *epistemes* within which the non-European Other was conceptualized. The Other's difference before the nineteenth century was not conceived in terms of evolutionary time that allowed for *comparison* between the modern present and the primitive past. Before the nineteenth century, the Other's difference was ideological, and spatial or geographical; the Other was 'exotic,' regarded as the demonic or ignorant 'outside' to the Christian or Enlightenment world view. By the late eighteenth century and into the nineteenth century, the Other's difference was located at one end of a linear-temporal, evolutionary scale; the Other was no longer the 'exotic,' but the 'primitive.' Unlike 'exoticism,' which has 'more to do with difference and strangeness,' we have arrived at 'primitivism,' which has more to do with temporal comparison and measure, thus serving 'an antithetical relation to modernity.'[3] It should be noted, of course, that the distinction between 'primitive' and 'exotic' is hard to maintain, since the 'primitive,' as modernity's Other, is also seen as 'exotic,' and the 'exotic' to modern eyes often exists in areas of the world that are considered backward or 'primitive.' The two terms thus often shade into one another in modern usage, though the temporal politics of primitivism cannot be ignored.

Opposed to the medieval Christian 'Time of Salvation,' the nineteenth century's concept of time was based on an evolutionary scale founded on an ideology of progress.[4] Popular versions of nineteenth-century evolutionism advocated what A.O. Lovejoy famously described as 'the temporalization of the Chain of Being.'[5] Time now provided the measure of value for both Nature and Man. As a fledgling discipline in the nineteenth century, anthropology relied on evolutionary time to come up with its own hierarchical classification of human beings and their societies. Noting anthropology's contribution to 'the intellectual justification of the colonial enterprise,' Johannes Fabian points out that it 'gave to politics and economics ... a firm belief in "natural," i.e., evolutionary Time. It promoted a scheme in terms of which not only past cultures, but all living societies were irrevocably placed on a temporal slope, a stream of Time – some upstream, others downstream.'[6] Nineteenth-century anthropology was able to transform spatial or geographical differences into 'differences residing in developmental historical time.'[7] Differences between peoples and societies could now be measured and ranked according to a temporal scale of progress or development. This temporal scale allowed nineteenth-century evolutionary anthropology to collapse 'all of the dimensions of human variation onto a single axis ... [and made it] possible to rank all of the members of a single population and all of the societies that had ever existed.'[8] The scale's unitary standard of measure and value was of course firmly based on evolutionism's idea of progress. The idea of progress allowed nineteenth century evolutionary anthropology not only to justify European civilization's position at the top of the temporal scale, but also to place other societies at the bottom, marking them out as savage or primitive.

E.B. Tylor, the first Professor of Anthropology at Oxford (1896) and dubbed by some 'the Father of Anthropology,'[9] had recourse to such an evolutionary scale of progress in his influential book *Primitive Culture* (1871), when he wrote:

> Civilization actually existing among mankind in different grades, we are enabled to estimate and compare it by positive examples. The educated world of Europe and America practically settles a standard by simply placing its own nations at one end of the social series and savage tribes at the other, arranging the rest of mankind between these limits according as they correspond more closely to savage or cultured life. The principal criteria of classification are the absence or presence, high or low development, of the industrial arts ... the extent of scientific knowledge, the definiteness of moral principles, the condition of religious belief and ceremony, the degree of social and political organization, and so forth. Thus, on the definite basis of compared facts, ethnographers are able to set up at least a rough scale of civilization. Few would dispute that the following races are arranged rightly in order of culture: Australian [Aboriginal], Tahitian, Aztec, Chinese, Italian.[10]

Though Tylor believed in the psychic unity of mankind and argued that primitive 'survivals' in civilized societies proved that savages, like our archaic ancestors, are not absolutely different from us, there was never any doubt in his mind that civilized Europeans were to be considered superior to savages or primitives, contemporary or historical.[11] Thus he could strongly assert: 'That any known savage tribe would not be improved by judicious civilization, is a proposition which no moralist would dare to make; while the general tenor of the evidence goes far to justify the view that on the whole the civilized man is not only wiser and more capable than the savage, but also *better* and *happier*.'[12]

Written at the height of British imperial expansion, and published six years before Queen Victoria was crowned Empress of India, Tylor's *Primitive Culture* was perhaps the most influential of many anthropological studies that indirectly helped to justify colonialism in the name of a universal, teleological narrative of progress.[13] Indeed, Tylor saw anthropology as 'essentially a reformer's science.'[14] Encouraged by colonial success and influenced by ideas of reform and progress, nineteenth-century Europeans began to see history, in Shelly Errington's words, as 'a story of Man's climb from a low and tribal existence to his culmination in European civilization.' 'The idea of progress,' she adds, 'was a brilliant solution to the problem of the Other.'[15] Progress solved the problem of the Other by turning the Other into the primitive whose historical or temporal backwardness legitimized the 'civilizing mission' of the West. McGrane, in his usual pithy way, cogently describes how the primitive was an invention necessary to sustain the nineteenth century's belief in progress:

> Without our whole sensibilities being formed and informed by the concept of progress, being organized and ordered by the historical a priori of progress, we would have never, in encountering and confronting difference, experienced 'primitiveness,' experienced our advance over their backwardness, our linear growth over their linear fossilization. The resource of 'progress' authorized the transformation of the 'different' into the 'primitive' ... The 'factual' existence of 'primitive peoples' – 'primitive peoples' are not a fact, but an interpretation – did not slowly, gradually, yet inevitably reveal to the European the reality of progress; rather the invention and institutionalization of progress in the mode of anthropological discourse created 'primitive peoples.' Progress produces primitives; primitives do not prove progress.[16]

Nineteenth-century evolutionary primitivism can therefore be defined as the modern West's representation of itself as the telos of progress, with the primitive as the temporal or historical past from which it has evolved.

Evolutionary primitivism's legitimization of the West often required the denigration of so-called primitive peoples. If modern Europeans are considered 'advanced' and at the 'top' of the evolutionary scale, then primitives, as earlier specimens of humanity, must be 'less developed' and occupy the 'lower' end of the scale. But what may appear to be descriptive, positional terms soon take on the qualitative values of 'inferiority' and 'superiority.' As Ashley Montagu has noted, 'The notion of "lowness" in the evolutionary "scale" of development is ... extended to mean "lowness" in the intellectual and moral as well as the physical character of the individual or group defined as primitive.'[17] Thus, John Lubbock could write in his *Prehistoric Times, as Illustrated by Ancient Remains, and the Manners and Customs of Modern Savages* (1865) that 'the true savage is neither free nor noble; he is a slave to his own wants, his own passions; imperfectly protected from the weather, he suffers from the cold by night and the heat of sun by day; ignorant of agriculture, living by the chase, and improvident in success, hunger always stares him in the face, and often drives him to the dreadful alternative of cannibalism.'[18] The same generic denigration of the savage or primitive can be found in American anthropologist Lewis Henry Morgan's *Ancient Society* (1877), which describes the 'inferiority of savage man in the mental and moral scale, undeveloped, inexperienced, and held down by his low animal appetites and passions,' and in Tylor's *Anthropology* (1891), which asserts that savages can be compared to children 'as fairly as to their moral as to their intellectual condition' and that 'the better savage social life seems in but unstable equilibrium, liable to be easily upset by a touch of distress, temptation, or violence, and then it becomes the worse savage life, which we know by so many dismal and hideous examples.'[19] What started off as an ostensibly ethnological classification according to evolutionary principles of sociocultural differences between human groups became an insidious Victorian racism that imputed not just cultural, but also biological or organic, inferiority to primitive Others. As George Stocking Jr has noted: 'Darwinian evolution, evolutionary ethnology, and polygenist race ... interacted to support a raciocultural hierarchy in terms of which civilized men, the highest products of social evolution, were large-brained white men, and only large-brained white men, the highest products of organic evolution, were fully civilized.'[20] The psychic unity of mankind, a central tenet of Tylor's evolutionary anthropology, seemed to fade as European colonial power and technological supremacy encouraged polygenist beliefs in a racial hierarchy. Evolutionary anthropology's drift into a dangerous racial taxonomy that not only denigrated primitive Others, but also called for their 'replacement' can be seen clearly in this chilling passage from Karl Pearson's *The Grammar of Science* (1900):

> It is a false view of human solidarity, a weak humanitarianism, not a true humanism, which regrets that a capable and stalwart race of white men should replace a dark-skinned tribe which can neither utilize its land for the full benefit of mankind, nor contribute its quota to the common stock of human knowledge ... This sentence must not be taken to justify a brutalizing destruction of human life ... At the same time, there is cause for human satisfaction in the replacement of the aborigines throughout America and Australia by white races of far higher civilization.[21]

But if primitivism, in its evolutionary version, can be used to support a raciocultural hierarchy in which the West occupies the apex and the savage cannot but submit to progress and either disappear or assimilate, it is also the case that the cultural relativism implied by primitivism can be employed to critique the problems generated by Western modernity. Historians of British and American anthropology like George W. Stocking Jr and Henrika Kuklick have argued that a significant change in anthropological attitude towards so-called primitive peoples occurred after the First World War. Stocking notes that the horror of witnessing the civilized nations of the West employing their superior technology in mutual slaughter forced many intellectuals to question their belief in progress and improvement and to seek a 'regenerative relativity,' 'some alternative to the values of what Ezra Pound called "a botched civilization."'[22] Kuklick points out that 'postwar anthropology became a vehicle for liberal criticism of Western society in general and colonialism in particular' and that anthropologists 'stressed the negative features of high civilization,' no longer assuming 'that the most technologically advanced and politically organized societies would adhere to the highest moral standards.'[23] The functionalist Meyer Fortes, for example, attributed the social harmony of the Tallensi to the lack of both economic differentiation and inequality and the absence of capital accumulation and technological advance in their society.[24] Reacting similarly to evolutionist triumphalism, A.M. Hocart argued that though primitive societies 'cannot form big nations, maintain disciplined armies, lay networks of roads and railways, or suffer economic crises on a colossal scale, ... they can exist, and quite successfully too, if success consists in surviving with happiness.'[25]

Not only anthropologists, but writers and artists as well, turned to the primitive as an alternative to modernity's malaise. Helen Carr's study of American literary primitivism shows how 'modernists in America, as elsewhere, drew on "primitive" art as a critique of bourgeois philistine modernity.'[26] She cites, for example, the art critic Edgar Holger Cahill's 1922 article entitled 'America Has Its "Primitives,"' in which he writes that the Indian is not a ferocious, indolent savage but a peaceful 'child of nature, close to the soil from which he wins his living, cultivating the earth with a rough hoe, hunting wild creatures, and living with his tribe in free democratic association.' Cahill goes on to remind his white American readers that '[w]e great Machine People, who have carried ugliness well-nigh to apotheosis in the fairest of lands, ... may forgo the conqueror's pride and learn wisdom from our humble brother of the

Pueblos, who has made the desert bloom with beauty.'[27] The contrast between the beauty, harmony, and happiness of primitive society and the discontents of modern industrial civilization is most famously expressed, however, in Edward Sapir's essay 'Culture, Genuine and Spurious' (1924), a seminal statement on 'regenerative relativity' that praised the American Indian's 'genuine culture' and opposed it to the 'spurious culture' of modern day America:

> The great cultural fallacy of industrialism ... is that in harnessing machines to our uses it has not known how to avoid the harnessing of the majority of mankind to its machines. The telephone girl who lends her capacities, during the greater part of the living day, to the manipulation of a technical routine that has an eventually high efficiency value but that answers to no spiritual needs of her own is an appalling sacrifice to civilization. As a solution of the problem of culture she is a failure ... As with the telephone girl, so, it is to be feared, with the great majority of us, slave-stokers to fires that burn for demons we would destroy, were it not that they appear in the guise of our benefactors. The American Indian who solves the economic problem with salmon-spear and rabbit-snare operates on a relatively low level of civilization, but he represents an incomparably higher solution than our telephone girl of the questions that culture has to ask of economics. There is here no question of the immediate utility, of the effective directness, of economic effort, nor of any sentimentalizing regrets as to the passing of the 'natural man.' The Indian's salmon-spearing is a culturally higher type of activity than that of the telephone girl or mill hand simply because there is normally no sense of spiritual frustration during its prosecution, no feeling of subservience to tyrannous yet largely inchoate demands, because it works in naturally with all the rest of the Indian's activities instead of standing out as a desert patch of merely economic effort in the whole life.[28]

Thus, to the intelligentsia of the interwar years the concept of the primitive could no longer support the progressive, evolutionary narrative of modern Western civilization; it provided instead a critique of that civilization's sense of superiority and faith in progress. Though a whiff of the eighteenth century's 'noble savagery' is present in these affirmative discourses of primitivism, sentimental nostalgia for the passing of the 'natural man' is, as Sapir's pronouncement reminds us, restrained by a more pressing concern with self-critique, with criticism of one's own ignoble society. Native Americans or the Tallensi are figures less to be idealized (though idealization occurs nevertheless) than to be regarded as critical alternatives to modern industrial civilization. The American Indian's salmon-spearing may be admired, but it is admired less for its own indigenous skill than for its representative status in Euro-America as an organic antithesis to the mechanical slavery of the telephone girl. The primitivism of a Sapir or a Cahill is thus not so much a nostalgic primitivism as a primitivism *in the service of the West's own self-criticism.*

Twentieth-century European primitivism has generally followed the self-critical agenda set by anthropologists like Sapir. In the late 1930s, just before the Second World War, the Collège de Sociologie, an informal Parisian intellectual circle, whose most prominent members were Georges Bataille, Roger Caillois, and Michel Leiris, adopted Émile Durkheim and Marcel Mauss's sociological method, which urged an 'ethnographic detour' in order to understand one's own society. In her astute study of the College's debt to Durkheim and Mauss, Michèle Richman points out that the College's writings belong squarely in a French intellectual history that regards ethnographic evidence as 'providing a privileged vantage point from which to examine one's own cultural practices or to look at oneself through the eyes of the other.'[29] Discussing more specifically the College's aims, Richman argues that its ethnographic detour into other 'archaic' cultures was seen as a way of proving that modern society had not superseded the archaic or primitive, but had forgotten or repressed it to sustain its identity.[30] To the College, the task of post-Durkheimian sociology is to look to 'exotic representations derived from ... ethnography'[31] in order to understand better the crises and discontents of modern civilization:

> The archaeological perspective directed by *archaic* (the preferred replacement for 'primitive') examples extends the ethnographic revolution into an even more explicit form of self-scrutiny, since it explores phenomena that have been segregated, devalued, or even actively repressed. With its willingness to excavate relatively obscure phenomena of social life, sociology counters the occultation of archaic social forms and brings to the fore of consciousness collective representations banished from the social imagination.[32]

Not a member of the Collège de Sociologie, but influenced by Mauss, Claude Lévi-Strauss similarly viewed the ethnography of primitive societies as an opportunity to question his own. Maurice Blanchot, in a perceptive review of Lévi-Strauss's *Tristes Tropiques* (1955), notes that the deepest impulse of anthropology is the search for an origin or point zero, however hypothetical or fictive, which would provide a theoretical model of an originary society that would 'help us to see clearly into the complexities of existing societies.'[33] Lévi-Strauss is aware that his search for mankind's beginning may be misinterpreted as a nostalgia for the 'natural man.' Citing Rousseau and, in the process, rescuing him from the charge of 'noble savagery,' Lévi-Strauss stresses methodology over utopian longing:

> The study of ... savages leads to something other than the revelation of a Utopian state of nature or the discovery of the perfect society in the depths of the forest; it helps us to build a theoretical model of human society, which does not correspond to any observable reality, but with the aid of which we may succeed in distinguishing between [in Rousseau's words] 'what is primordial and what is artificial in man's present nature and in obtaining a good knowledge of a state which no longer exists, which has perhaps never existed, and which will probably never exist in the future, but of which it is nevertheless essential to have a sound conception in order to pass valid judgement on our present state.'[34]

Lévi-Strauss seems to be suggesting in the above passage that even if primitive society never existed it would have to be invented in order to provide us with an original model against which our present society can be compared and judged. A better understanding of other societies, even if they are less than pristinely primordial, enables us, according to Lévi-Strauss, to

> detach ourselves from our own society. Not that our own society is peculiarly or absolutely bad. But it is the only one from which we have a duty to free ourselves ... We thus put ourselves in a position to embark on the second stage, which consists ... [of elucidating] principles of social life that we can apply in reforming our own customs ... Enthusiastic partisans of the idea of progress are in danger of failing to recognize – because they set so little store by them – the immense riches accumulated by the human race on either side of the narrow furrow on which they keep their eyes fixed; by underrating the achievements of the past, they devalue all those which still remain to be accomplished.[35]

By holding out the possibility of alternative values, primitive societies help the powerful West to free itself from its ethnocentric views. The study of savage societies, Lévi-Strauss tells us, 'removes from our own customs that air of inherent rightness which they so easily have for anyone unacquainted with other customs, or whose knowledge is partial and biased.'[36] Lévi-Strauss's lament for the disappearance of the 'sad tropics' is thus ultimately self-interested, even ethnocentric; it is a lament for the passing of a primitive otherness *whose importance lies in the fact that it has enabled the West to be self-critical, to free itself from itself.*

Arguing, in the turbulent sixties, for a politically committed, Marxist-inspired dialectical anthropology, Stanley Diamond criticized Lévi-Strauss rather polemically, for being a 'mathematician' operating with mental abstractions or for assuming the role of 'the cold poet of a formalist esthetics.'[37] But, more like Lévi-Strauss than he cares to admit, Diamond too seeks in the primitive a critical alternative to modern Western society. Just as Lévi-Strauss questions his society for its ethnocentric belief in progress and ignorance of the 'immense riches' of primitive societies, so too does Diamond criticize his society by turning to the primitive for what Eric Wolf in his foreword to Diamond's book calls 'a vision, a sense of a life once led by all men and still led by some, a life richer and more intricately human than our own.'[38] Again like Lévi-Strauss, Diamond denies the accusation that anthropology displays a nostalgic yearning for the 'noble savage': 'It is not a question of regaining lost paradises or savage nobility, neither of which ever existed in the manner imputed to their authors.' Instead, Diamond argues, anthropology assumes 'a comprehensively critical role, based on our respect for and knowledge of human nature and the "irreducibly" human, I would say the primitive, past – the past that we have reduced to the past by the imperial machines that civilizations are, most particularly those of the Euro-American world of the last 500 years.'[39] Anthropology thus conducts a critique of Euro-American society through the antithetical vision of primitive life. In Diamond's words:

> If the fulfillment and delineation of the human person within a social, natural and supernatural (transcendent) setting is a universally valid measure for the evaluation of culture, primitive societies are our primitive superiors ... What I mean is that in the basic and essential respects ... primitive societies illuminate, *by contrast,* the dark side of a world civilization which is in chronic crisis.[40]

Note, however, that primitive society's superiority is a superiority achieved only through its role as a *contrast,* an *antithesis* to what is Diamond's primary interest: the chronic crisis of Western civilization. The primitive, precisely because he is not the problem, is ultimately not the main concern of critical anthropology. Diamond recognizes this and his confession reminds us that anthropology is a Western discipline that cannot escape its own ethnocentric, epistemic needs:

> In this anthropological 'experiment' which we initiate, it is not they [primitives] who are the ultimate objects but ourselves. We study men, that is, we reflect on ourselves studying others, because we must, because man in civilization is the problem. Primitive peoples do not study man. It is unnecessary; the subject is given. They say this or that about behavior (who has not been impressed by the wisdom of his informants?); they engage in ritual, they celebrate, but they are not compelled to objectify. We, on the contrary, are engaged in a complex search for the subject in history, as the precondition for a minimal definition of humanity and, therefore, of self-knowledge as the ground for self-criticism. The questions we bring to history come out of our own need.[41]

Primitives have no need for anthropological thinking because, at home in being, they have no need for objectification or self-reflection, unlike the anthropologist's own culture. The latter, chronically in crisis and suffering from alienation within and without, requires the study of others in order to gain 'self-knowledge as the ground for self-criticism.' In this, Diamond finds himself, like Lévi-Strauss, advocating a self-critical, reflexive Western thought that paradoxically depends on its opposite – on primitives who have no need to think about others or themselves. In his illuminating study of Lévi-Strauss, Marcel Hénaff draws our attention to just this asymmetry of thought:

> What is this savage thought with respect to ours, which Lévi-Strauss defines as domesticated [domesticated thought is instrumental or utilitarian thought that seeks to control Nature for the purpose of yielding a return]? Ricoeur characterizes it as a 'thought which does not think itself,' thus indicating its insufficiency and marking as an indirect consequence the fundamental requirement of Western thought that, since Greek philosophy, has unceasingly formalized its own approaches. It is certain that when Lévi-Strauss analyzes the operations of savage thought, he does so using thought that thinks itself. But it is precisely to recognize that the one that does not think itself ... is no less wholly thought. It does not state what it does, yet it does it: this innocence is the source of its beauty – like an art that does not know itself as art – and perhaps it is no less the source of its fragility.[42]

'Like an art that does not know itself as art,' the primitive is an innocent who does not know that he thinks. But this lack of self-consciousness which is admired is also a weakness, 'the source of its fragility.' For in his innocence the primitive lacks what the Western thinker possesses – knowledge of others that leads to self-knowledge. Since the primitive has no need for thought that thinks itself, he can become that which is thought by a culture that prizes reflexive thinking. To both Diamond and Lévi-Strauss, the concept of the primitive is absolutely necessary, but it is necessary not for itself but for what it can do for Western self-knowledge and self-criticism. The primitive is needed by the West because the primitive is good to think with. As we shall see, this is a characteristic shared by primitivisms old and new.

Closer to our own time, George Marcus and Michael Fischer in their 1986 book *Anthropology as Cultural Critique* see anthropology's task, much in the same light as Diamond and Lévi-Strauss, as providing 'cultural critique which plays off other cultural realities against our own in order to gain a more adequate knowledge of them all.'[43] 'In using portraits of other cultural patterns to reflect self-critically on our own ways,' they write, 'anthropology disrupts common sense and makes us reexamine our taken-for-granted assumptions.'[44] By studying cultural difference, anthropology delivers the West from ethnocentrism. To be sure, Marcus and Fischer acknowledge that in the 1980s primitivism starts to lose its critical allure as it becomes accepted as just another aesthetic style:

> [T]he resources of anthropology, as traditionally presented, no longer seem to have their critical, reflective appeal. One recent sign of this, for example, is the much discussed retrospective at New York's Museum of Modern Art, '"Primitivism" in 20th Century Art: Affinity of the Tribal and the Modern.' The exotic other inspired avant-garde artists during the 1920s and 1930s, but now this source of innovation and critique has lost its shock value; this show marks the definitive assimilation of the primitive into the history of Western art.[45]

But if primitivism has lost its 'shock value' and the homogenizing spread of modernization has to be acknowledged, can anthropology still provide a cultural critique of our society? Marcus and Fischer say yes. If we can no longer employ accounts of difference from primitives abroad, we can still find differences among 'exotics at home' (to refer to the resonant title of Micaela di Leonardo's book).[46] In Marcus and Fischer's words: 'In purely domestic terms, the role of the exotic has been displaced by other descriptive domains for posing important differences within and alternatives to mainstream American life.' The foreign primitive is replaced by domestic exotics like the poor, women, blacks, and gays, who contribute 'frameworks for the consideration of alternative realities.'[47] Thus, in a sense, Marcus and Fischer's 'repatriated ethnography' can be seen as repeating Diamond's and Lévi-Strauss's call for a deliverance from Western society's ethnocentrism, the only difference being that the primitive Other is no longer without but is within the anthropologists' own culture. Moreover, the accounts of difference, internal or external, that Marcus and Fischer see as necessary for cultural critique, disturb mainstream American society's ethnocentrism only so that cultural difference and cultural richness can be used 'for self-reflection and self-growth.'[48] In Marcus and Fischer's view, American society is questioned by anthropology so that it can become a better society. Anthropology, they state, promises 'on the basis of reliable knowledge of cultural alternatives to critique and suggest *reform* in the way *we* live.'[49] The differences offered by primitives abroad or exotics at home matter ultimately only in relation to what they can do to reform the way mainstream America lives. The foreign or domestic Other remains in the service of reforming what is still a recognizably American way of life.

To summarize our discussion so far, we have examined how nineteenth-century primitivism, which relied generally on evolutionary arguments to legitimize European superiority (and European colonialism), gave way to a twentieth-century primitivism that used the concept of the primitive to critique a Western civilization seemingly mired in chronic crisis. In the earlier primitivism, the primitive is regarded as inferior and justifiably superseded by modern civilization, whereas in the later version the primitive is seen as a corrective to the malaise of Western modernity. But in both cases the primitive is known, given a value, and exists only as an antithesis to the modern West, which not only remains the central point of reference but also is the source from which the idea of the primitive emerged in the first place. In both forms of primitivism, the primitive does not exist in itself but only in relation to and for the West.

We are not surprised, therefore, to hear from Marcus and Fischer that through long familiarity the primitive has lost its 'shock value' and has been assimilated into Western history. Primitivism it seems has lost its critical power, its subversive edge, and turned, ironically, into its opposite; we have called on the savage mind far too often and, as a consequence, have domesticated it, turned it into a Western product. Even a critical primitivism that seeks to free the West from itself remains, as we have seen, trapped in a kind of self-regard, its critique merely affirming the West's capacity for 'self-reflection and self-growth,' in Marcus and Fischer's words. Primitivism, in both its nineteenth-century evolutionary and twentieth-century critical forms, can thus be accused of ethnocentrism, of projecting its fears and desires onto the figure of the primitive Other. As Marianna Torgovnick has perceptively noted:

> The needs of the present determine the value and nature of the primitive. The primitive does what we ask it to do. Voiceless, it lets us speak for it. It is our ventriloquist's dummy – or so we like to think ... The real secret of the primitive in this century has often been the same secret as always: the primitive can be – has been, will be (?) – whatever Euro-Americans want it to be. It tells us what we want it to tell us.[50]

But what if the Euro-American voice were to confess that the all-too-familiar primitive 'dummy' no longer serves its desire? What if, like Torgovnick herself, the Euro-American voice were to turn critical and resolve that the primitive should no longer be its ventriloquist's dummy and that the primitive be allowed to speak otherwise, in its own voice? What if the primitive can be uncoupled from Western ethnocentric needs to become a truly autonomous Other? New, radical forms of otherness are clearly needed to challenge the hegemony of Western primitivism. It is from a deconstructive questioning of primitivism, such as Torgovnick's, that neo-primitivism emerges offering a more 'authentic' primitive, a radical otherness displacing its older, ethnocentrically compromised precursors.

Anti-primitivist Primitivism

A good example of what one might call the neo-primitivist turn occurs in Hal Foster's astute critique of the same MOMA exhibition that Marcus and Fischer described as confirmation of primitivism's assimilation into Western art history. According to Foster, the problem with '"Primitivism" in 20th Century Art: Affinity of the Tribal and the Modern' can be attributed to the word 'affinity' in the exhibition's subtitle. The show's curators, William Rubin and Kirk Varnedoe, promote the concept of 'affinity' in order to link the primitive Other to our (modern) humanity and to narrow the gap that evolutionary theory had imposed between 'us' and 'them.' But, Foster argues, '[h]owever progressive once, this election to *our* humanity is now thoroughly ideological, for if evolutionism subordinated the primitive to western history, affinity-ism recoups it under the sign of western universality ... In this recognition difference is discovered only to be fetishistically disavowed, and in the celebration of "human creativity" the dissolution of specific cultures is carried out: the Museum of Modern Art played host to the Musée de l'Homme indeed.'[51] To Foster, then, both evolutionism and affinity-ism presume that the difference of the primitive can be assimilated into the universal sameness of the West. If in nineteenth-century evolutionary primitivism difference is seen as just so many steps in a progressive march towards the same universal end (that is, Western civilization), then the affinity-ism promoted by the twentieth-century 'Primitivism' exhibition recognizes difference, but only as part of a more inclusive, universal humanity. Foster argues that historically the primitive has been 'articulated by the west in deprivative or supplemental terms'; the primitive is either inferior in evolutionary terms or he embodies certain vital values the West lacks. In either case, the primitive has been 'domesticated' and 'is thus constructive, not disruptive, of the binary *ratio* of the west; fixed as a structural opposite or a dialectical other to be incorporated, it assists in the establishment of a western identity, center, norm and name.' To be sure, in the critical version of twentieth-century primitivism, the primitive acts as the antithetical figure that questions and threatens Western modernity. Foster acknowledges that in modernist primitivism 'the primitive may appear transgressive ... but it still serves as a limit: projected within and without, the primitive becomes a figure of our unconscious and outside (a figure constructed in modern art as well as in psychoanalysis and anthropology in the privileged triad of the primitive, the child and the insane).'[52] In short, modernist primitivism's critique of Western modernity will still remain within the ethnocentric limits of that modernity, so long as the primitive is conceived not as an absolute rupture but as an oppositional or dialectical other, not as radical, incommensurable alterity but as recognizable, recuperable difference. Foster, therefore, advocates a 'counterprimitivism,' or what I call 'neo-primitivism,' which challenges an ethnocentric, 'domesticated' primitivism by insisting on the absolute rupture and transgression of the primitive rather than its affinity to or dialectical complicity with modern Western regimes of knowledge. Praising dissident surrealists like Georges Bataille for their 'counterprimitivism,' which shows how 'the primitive might be thought disruptively, not recuperated abstractly,' Foster writes: 'Rather than seek to master the primitive – or, alternatively, to fetishize its difference into opposition or identity – these primitivists welcomed "the unclassified, unsought Other."'[53] The epistemic rupture of counterprimitivism emerges as a response to the dialectical, incorporative understanding of primitivism; in the latter, the primitive is known and its difference is fetishized, whereas in the former, the primitive is unclassifiable and incommensurable, and its difference therefore cannot be recuperated. The emergence of counterprimitivism is, moreover, periodized by Foster as a shift from the modern to the postmodern, from the modernist management of the primitive to the primitive's disruptive return in postmodern theory:

> On the one hand, then the primitive is a modern problem, a crisis in cultural identity, which the west moves to resolve: hence the modernist construction 'primitivism,' the fetishisitic recognition – and – disavowal of the primitive difference. This ideological resolution renders it a 'nonproblem' for us. On the other hand, this resolution is only a repression: delayed into our political unconscious, the primitive returns uncannily at the moment of its potential eclipse. The rupture of the primitive, managed by the moderns, becomes our postmodern event.[54]

To support his argument about the rupture of the primitive as a postmodern event, Foster cites Jean Baudrillard's sarcastic criticism of Lévi-Strauss's incorporation of savage thought 'under the sign of the universality of the human mind': 'This harmonious vision of two thought processes renders their *confrontation* perfectly inoffensive, by denying the difference of the primitives as an element of rupture with and subversion of (our) "objectified thought and its mechanisms."'[55] Postmodernist counterprimitivism is therefore not really a repudiation of primitivism or of the primitive Other; rather it is a critique of modernist primitivism for not being primitive enough, that is, for not allowing the primitive Other to be radically and truly Other. As such, Foster's description of postmodern counterprimitivism is a good example of what I call neo-primitivism, an anti-primitivist primitivism. Primitivism is questioned for its adherence to a Eurocentric universalism that fetishistically recognizes and disavows primitive difference; but in its place a neo-primitivism is installed that guards the primitive Other from dialectical appropriation. Opposing the assimilative impulse of identity logic and the ethnocentrism that sees difference only on its own terms, neo-primitivism emphasizes absolute difference or radical alterity. But in doing so it produces unintended consequences that return ironically as the very problems it had set out to avoid in the first place. Foster's essay itself is an illuminating example of just such an ironic reversal; its categorical rejection of MOMA's ethnocentric incorporation of the primitive, and its insistence on the primitive as absolute rupture result in the primitive acting as the Other that guarantees the integrity of the Western subject by marking its limits. In other words, the critique of Western ethnocentrism via the affirmation of the primitive's radical alterity is also the rehabilitation and renewal of the Western subject. Once again, the Western subject finds that it needs the absolute difference of the primitive in order to achieve the non-ethnocentric, critically reflexive, ethical stance it aspires to. Foster's essay ends with this declaration: '[T]he other remains – indeed, as the very field of difference in which the subject emerges – to challenge western pretenses of sovereignty, supremacy and self-creation.'[56] There is some ambiguity in the syntax as to who the subject is. Who is this emergent subject? If 'the other remains ... as the very field of difference,' then it appears that the subject that emerges from the difference is the *subject* made possible by the Other, that is to say, the Western subject. The primitive Other not only ensures the self-deconstruction of the modern Western subject, but also enables the subject to rise phoenix-like out of its own self-critical immolation.

Though it challenges primitivism's ethnocentric projection and incorporation of the primitive by valorizing the latter's radical and unassimilable otherness, neo-primitivism ends up much like its precursor in that its solicitude for the primitive Other also allows it to capitalize on the opportunity the Other presents for self-critique *and* self-validation. Foster's vigilant anti-ethnocentrism is related to what one can call an ethics of alterity, in which the denial of the Cartesian subject enables both sensitivity and openness to radical otherness. At the same time, however, as we have seen in Foster's essay, such an ethics of alterity may run up against an unintended consequence, namely, that the critical reduction of the subject in the presence of the Other is also the subject's ethico-cognitive expansion, its *new awareness* of its own limitation and finitude and of its infinite responsibility to the Other. Robert Bernasconi has provided an illuminating analysis of how an ethics of alterity, as described by perhaps its most rigorous advocate, Emmanuel Levinas, can harbour in the asymmetrical generosity it shows to the Other an antithetical claim to an asymmetrical epistemic superiority over the Other. Bernasconi cites a passage from Levinas's essay 'Meaning and Sense' in which Levinas moves from a generous acknowledgment of otherness, of 'the abstract man in men,' to a recognition of the specific cultural location of this generosity:

> It [Platonism] is overcome in the name of the generosity of Western thought itself, which, catching sight of the *abstract* man in men, proclaimed the absolute value of the person, and then encompassed in the respect it bears in the cultures in which these persons stand or in which they express themselves. Platonism is overcome with the very means which the universal thought issued from Plato supplied. It is overcome by this so disparaged Western civilization, which was able to understand the particular cultures, which never understood themselves.[57]

Bernasconi suggests that Levinas's account of the West's self-critical generosity to the Other is also an attribution of a certain superiority to itself:

> The superiority would seem to lie in [the West's] capacity to understand. Indeed, Levinas seems to be suggesting that it would lie in its ability to understand other cultures better than they understood themselves. Could the 'end of eurocentrism' be 'the ultimate wisdom of Europe'? The 'generosity' of Western thought, which at first sight seems to be an illustration of the one-way direction of ethics in favor of the Other, is quickly turned into a judgment on the relative intellectual powers of different cultures ... [I]t gives rise to the conclusion that the ethics of asymmetry in favor of the Other, is, when transferred to the cultural level, readily converted into an inequality in favor of the culture which produced that ethics of asymmetry. Levinas often expresses his enthusiasm for Western culture on precisely this point.[58]

Neo-primitivism's defence of the primitive's absolute alterity results in a similar, perhaps unintended, reversal of generosity into superiority for the Western theorist. Despite their differences, all the authors we will be discussing in the following chapters share the same thematic of Western anti-ethnocentrism and generosity to the Other. This anti-ethnocentric generosity, in turn, allows them to gain a position of knowledge not available to the Other to whom they address their generosity. They are able to decentre their own knowledge, critique their culture's ethnocentrism, and, in the process, become aware of their culture's limitation, an awareness they do not attribute to others. They achieve a critical reflexivity made possible but not necessarily shared by the Other.

Both Baudrillard and Lyotard, for example, see the primitive Other as that radical alterity which will deliver the West from universalizing metanarratives that would otherwise lead it into what Baudrillard calls 'the hell of the Same.'[59] However, for both Baudrillard and Lyotard, the Other's radical alterity means that there can be no knowledge of what the Other thinks or knows; hence, the Other functions merely as that incomprehensible, resistant alterity that nonetheless redeems the Western subject by delivering it from its will to universality. In Baudrillard's aphoristic remark: 'The Other is what allows *me* not to repeat *myself* for ever.'[60] Marianna Torgovnick too would like the primitive to be radically other, free from the ethnocentric grasp of the West. She wishes that Western primitivism 'had a different history – a history in which primitive societies were allowed to exist in their own times and spaces, within their own *conceptions of* time and space, not transposed and filtered into Western terms; ... a history in which primitive societies were acknowledged as full and valid alternatives to Western cultures.'[61] But even as she argues for the primitive's radical difference from the West, it becomes clear that the primitive's difference is acknowledged less for its own sake than for the 'full' and 'valid' alternative it provides to the West, hence making the West once again the centre of critical attention. The primitive's alterity is to be safeguarded because it offers a redemptive alternative to the West. Once again, what we see in Torgovnick's work is a narrative in which the primitive's otherness, presumably unknown because unassimilated by Western knowledges, nonetheless enables the Western subject to decentre itself and gain critical self-knowledge. The Other's significance seems to be ancillary and catalytic; it makes possible the development of the Western subject's critical, reflexive consciousness.

The same narrative is present in Marshall Sahlins's anthropological critique of Western ethnocentrism. According to Sahlins, cultural alterity or non-Western otherness is what allows anthropology to be anti-ethnocentric and relativist and, at the same time, achieve universal understanding. As we will see in Sahlins's work, anthropology's sensitivity to cultural alterity and diversity is in the service of a 'cosmopolitan anthropological consciousness of the species being,'[62] and anthropology's openness to all forms of *pensée sauvage* secures for itself, but not for the *sauvage,* access to a universal understanding of humanity.

Though Habermas would be critical of Sahlins's defence of cultural relativism, he would be sympathetic to the latter's anti-ethnocentric stance and sensitivity to otherness. Habermas in fact clearly acknowledges that the route to moral universalism requires the recognition of an unassimilated otherness. As he puts it: 'The equal respect for everyone else demanded by a moral universalism sensitive to difference thus takes the form of a *nonleveling* and *nonappropriating* inclusion of the other *in his otherness.*'[63] The inclusion of unassimilated or nonappropriated otherness is, however, a testimony to the West's ability to be anti-ethnocentric and self-reflexive: '[T]he West, molded by the Judaeo-Christian tradition, must reflect on one of its greatest cultural achievements: the capacity for decentering one's own perspectives, self-reflection, and a self-critical distancing from one's own traditions ... In a word: overcoming Eurocentrism demands that the West make *proper use* of its own cognitive resources.'[64] More directly and openly than the other critics of Eurocentrism we have mentioned, Habermas acknowledges that the West that is guilty of imposing its ethnocentric universalism on others is also the West that can atone for its guilt through a properly self-critical universalism that would include the other in its nonappropriated otherness. To be sure, Habermas admits that 'this is, God knows, easier said than done.'[65] What is clear, however, is that Habermas, like the other critics of ethnocentrism, shows a generosity to the premodern Other that is, in the final analysis, a redemption of the modern Western self. The Other has to remain as a nonappropriated, unassimilated otherness so that it can enable the West to achieve what it in itself is incapable of achieving – a critical self-distancing that confers greater theoretical insight.

In insisting on the unassimilability and, hence, unintelligibility of the primitive Other, anti-ethnocentric neo-primitivists find themselves confronting an aporia in which though the Other cannot be comprehended it can nonetheless be designated as different from their modern culture, even conceptualized as modern culture's symmetrical opposite. Criticizing Jacques Derrida's reduction of Chinese to a silent ideographic writing that is the very antithesis of Western phonetic languages, Rey Chow argues that the inscrutable alterity of Chinese is paradoxically converted into its scrutability as the Other that allows for certain theoretical insights. In her words: '[T]he silent graphicity of Chinese writing is both inscrutable and very scrutable: though Westerners such as Derrida may not be able to read it, they nonetheless proceed to do so by inscribing in it a new kind of theorizing; ... a new kind of intelligibility. The inscrutable Chinese ideogram has led to a new scrutability, a new insight that remains western and that becomes, thereafter, global.'[66] Similarly, in neo-primitivist discourses, the unintelligible primitive Other becomes intelligible as that which enables a critique of the modern West, its unrepresentability the very representation of the Other's power to mark the limits of Western knowledge. Thus, as our discussion so far has shown, the primitive Other's designated unassimilability and unintelligibility guarantee its exteriority to modern Western *epistemes*, its radical and incommensurable otherness. Ethnocentrism is, therefore, held in check and an external zone of authentic otherness is preserved, a utopian outside to remind us of our limitations. At the same time, however, the presence of an unintelligible, unrepresentable Other delivers the modern West from its ethnocentric imperiousness, making it more self-reflexive and self-critical, ensuring thereby that it is not duped by its own blind arrogance. The Other makes possible an awareness of limitation, but it is, nonetheless, an awareness that confers greater knowledge and enlightenment. Rey Chow again has astutely noted how the Western subject can use the Other for self-critique as well as for enhanced understanding and authority: 'Our fascination with the native, the oppressed, the savage and all such figures is therefore a desire to hold on to an unchanging certainty somewhere outside our own "fake" experience. It is a desire for being "non-duped," which is a not-too-innocent desire to seize control.'[67] Though Chow may overstate the subject's 'desire to seize control,' she is surely right to suggest that the subject's commitment to demystification, to being 'non-duped' (which should be supported) is enabled by its continuing mystification of an exterior, authentic Other (which poses a problem). Such an inseparability of demystification from mystification describes the powerful paralogic of neo-primitivism, which is anti-primitivist and primitivist at the same time. It may even be the case that our sharpest critiques of primitivist discourses still have to presuppose an Other whose primal, untouched authenticity provides the utopian exterior, the critical alternative to a globalizing Western modernity. Here a brief examination of Gayatri Spivak's recent writings will prove instructive.

Spivak is one of our most vigilant critics of primitivist forms of representation. Her devastating critique of Julia Kristeva's *About Chinese Women*, for example, concludes that the book's essentializing opposition of an archaic matrilineal Chinese society to Western patriarchy reflects 'a broader Western cultural practice, [in which] the "classical" East is studied with primitivistic reverence, even as the "contemporary" East is treated with realpolitikal contempt.'[68] In *A Critique of Postcolonial Reason*, Spivak is scrupulously alert to Kant's contemptuous primitivism, which is revealed in his dismissal of the New Hollander (or Australian Aborigine) and the Tierra del Fuegan as the not-fully-human, not-yet-subject whose lack can be made up by human (Western) culture.[69] In the same book, she also discusses how the primitivist appropriation of the native informant – the Western ventriloquizing of the primitive Other that Torgovnick warns us against – can be resisted by the strategic impenetrable silence of the Other. Reading J.M. Coetzee's *Foe*, Spivak argues that unlike Defoe's *Robinson Crusoe*, in which the savage Friday is converted into the obedient native informant, the Friday of *Foe* is

> the unemphatic agent of witholding in the text. For every territorial space that is value coded by colonialism *and* every command of metropolitan anticolonialism for the native to yield his 'voice,' there is a space of witholding, marked by a secret that may not be a secret but cannot be unlocked. 'The native,' whatever that might mean, is not only a victim, but also an agent. The curious guardian at the margin who will not inform.[70]

Critics like Benita Parry are therefore not quite correct when they accuse Spivak of silencing the subaltern or native Other. Spivak's notorious question, 'Can the subaltern speak?' is not just about whether the subaltern can speak without her voice being mediated or appropriated by the metropolitan well-wisher; it is also about the subaltern's strategic resistance to well-intentioned metropolitan efforts to make her yield her voice. Spivak pushes for a rigorous critique of ethnocentric benevolence, arguing that 'the sustained and developing work on the *mechanics* of the constitution of the Other' is more useful for the Western critic 'than invocations of the *authenticity* of the Other.'[71] Her work is in many ways admirable for setting the benchmark for critical vigilance against the ethnocentric appropriation of the Other to shore up the self or the equally problematic desire to constitute the Other as a romantic alternative to the self.

But Spivak's vigilance against the metropolitan constitution and invocation of the Other's 'authenticity' is curiously made possible by her belief in subaltern or aboriginal Otherness that cannot be recuperated. For example, the strength of subaltern resistance to the logic of modern capitalism lies, according to Spivak, in the fact that subalterns are 'non-narrativisable.'[72] They are like the Friday of *Foe*, uninformative guardians of an unassimilable margin. The subaltern maintains her difference refusing to become 'the object of emancipatory benevolence'; thus, 'the emancipatory project is more likely to succeed if one thinks of other people as being different; ultimately, perhaps absolutely different.'[73] The word 'subaltern,' we are told, 'is reserved for the sheer heterogeneity of decolonized space.'[74] In Spivak's work, therefore, the subaltern is conceived as an absolute alterity. In an astute analysis of Spivak's 'singularization' of the subaltern as an incommensurable Other, Peter Hallward writes: 'As if to conform to the familiar strictures of negative theology, the subaltern is defined as inaccessible to relations of nomination, situation and evaluation ... The subaltern, in other words, is the theoretically *untouchable*, the altogether-beyond-relation.'[75] But if the subaltern is radically heterogeneous, non-narrativizable, and theoretically unassimilable, the question becomes not so much whether the subaltern can speak but whether we can say anything about her. If '[k]nowledge of the other subject is theoretically impossible,'[76] how can the Other be described or represented? Can we in fact even name this unrepresentable Other 'the subaltern,' a term that becomes representative in Spivak's use, not only *referring* to those excluded or oppressed by modern nation states or neo-imperial global capitalism – that is, the tribal or aboriginal, the victims of internal colonization, the poor and exploited, and especially the doubly oppressed women of marginalized groups – but also *conferring* value on their resistance to and non-compliance with the powers that be? Can we define what not only is supposed to be undefinable, but should, ethically, remain undefinable? Can we explain what being subaltern means without doing violence to the subaltern's wish to be free from our explanations? Hasn't Spivak warned us that 'the desire to explain might be a symptom of the desire to have a self that can control knowledge and a world that can be known' and that '[e]xplaining, we exclude the possibility of the *radically* heterogeneous?'[77]

In her interview with Spivak, Jenny Sharpe addresses this problem directly when she asks: 'Does subalternity have to remain unnamable?' Spivak's reply is somewhat equivocal. She asserts that the problem is not that the subaltern is unnamable, but that it is all too nameable:

> When one thinks about subalternity in the sense of no lines of mobility into upward social movement, it's still not unnamable. We must, however, take a moratorium on naming too soon, if we manage to penetrate there ... There's nothing particularly good about penetrating into subalternity. I'm not in search of the primitive or anything. But if we are going to talk about it, then I will say that if one manages to penetrate in there, and it's not easy, then I think what we have to do is to take a moratorium on speaking too soon. I used to be against information retrieval years ago, but now I've thought it through in greater detail. We hear a lot of talk now – and I'm not particularly happy about it – about intellectual capital and cultural capital ...

> [I]f we are going to use that metaphorology, then I would say that this is like mercantile capitalism: buying cheap and selling dear because nobody can go there. So that's something one really must be careful about. It's not unnamable. In many ways, it's only too easily nameable![78]

Spivak appears to have softened her stance on the absolute inaccessibility of the subaltern and now admits that subalternity can be 'penetrated,' a word that a feminist like Spivak would surely recognize as equating knowing with a certain sexual violence. If the subaltern is no longer theoretically or discursively impenetrable, we must be even more careful not to do her violence by giving her a name or trading our knowledge of her in the academic marketplace. The subaltern or aboriginal Other may be namable; but, at the same time, we must guard against the subaltern being too easily named. What we have in this equivocation is Spivak's awareness that to assert the unnameability of the subaltern, to insist on the subaltern's radical alterity is to invite the criticism that she seeks to preserve some kind of untouched authenticity. Thus, she protests that she is 'not in search of the primitive or anything.' At the same time, however, she wants to retain the subaltern's resistant alterity, the radical difference that is not easily recuperable by the knowledge regimes of the hegemonic West. And so she uses the aggressive word 'penetrate' to refer to the act of knowing the Other and calls for a moratorium on naming the subaltern. Even if one gets to know the subaltern, that knowledge, Spivak argues, should remain heterogeneous and not be recoded as the dominant power's understanding of the subaltern. After all, the subaltern is who she is because her difference continues to resist the knowledge systems that seek to understand her, even those that try to do so responsibly.

Thus, in response to Sharpe's question, Spivak admits the possibility of an opening into subalternity only to close it again almost immediately. On the one hand, Spivak has to concede that the subaltern is accessible or nameable. How else can we name the subaltern as resistance, or, even more importantly, how else can we learn from the subaltern? Spivak states, for example, that she has 'no doubt that we must learn to learn from the original practical ecological philosophies of the world [that is, from aboriginal ecological practices].'[79] On the other hand, she remains suspicious of Western metropolitan attempts to retrieve information from subalterns, since she sees information retrieval as part of a strategy to recuperate resistant subaltern alterity. The word 'subaltern,' Spivak reminds us, 'is reserved for the sheer heterogeneity of decolonized space.'[80] The subaltern must remain resolutely other, elusive, ungraspable even to its metropolitan supporters. It is possible therefore to argue that when Spivak talks about learning from the subaltern, the learning in question can only be genuine if the subaltern remains heterogeneous to hegemonic *epistemes.* In other words, any form of accessibility to subalternity, if it is not to become another ethno- or Euro-centric act of violation and appropriation, has to acknowledge a subalternity that must, paradoxically, remain impenetrable and inaccessible. Spivak's admirable anti-ethnocentric vigilance against any act that ventriloquizes the subaltern depends, it seems, on the maintenance of a subaltern space radically heterogeneous to modern forms of knowledge-power. To be sure, Spivak denies that her view of subaltern alterity endorses a form of romantic primitivism. Nevertheless, it is hard not to see her work as an instance of what I have called anti-primitivist primitivism. Spivak's anti-primitivist gesture of uncovering Western metropolitan constructions and appropriations of the Other is enabled precisely by her insistence on the authenticity of an Other relatively untouched by and hence heterogeneous to the forces of the modern nation state and global capitalism.

Let us look at a number of other examples of Spivak's anti-primitivist primitivism. In the context of a discussion of 'the perhaps impossible vision of an ecologically just world,'[81] Spivak mentions a subaltern aboriginal group who may offer an alternative to modernity's instrumentalization of nature:

> Among Indian Aboriginals, I know a very small percentage of a small percentage that was 'denotified' in 1952. There forest-dwelling tribals, defined by the British as 'criminal tribes,' had been *left alone* not just by the British, but also by the Hindu and Muslim civilizations of India. They are not 'radicals.' But because they (unlike the larger ethnic groups) were *left alone,* they conform to certain cultural norms ... and instantiate certain attitudes that can be extremely useful for us, who have lost them, in our global predicament ... We are not proposing to catch their culture, but using some residues to fight the dominant, which have [*sic*] irreducibly changed us. They are themselves interested in changing their life pattern, and, as far as we can, we too should be interested in following into this desire ... But must that part of their cultural habit that internalizes the techniques of their pre-national ecological sanity be irretrievably lost to planetary justice in the urgently needed process of integration, as a minority, into the modern state?[82]

What makes this small group of Indian Aboriginals interesting to Spivak is the fact that they were *left alone* (a phrase she repeats twice) by all the dominant powers that have ruled India; untouched, the authenticity of their culture still uncompromised, these aboriginals can offer helpful alternatives to modernity's predicament. At the same time, however, Spivak does not wish to romanticize or primitivize them. She acknowledges their interest 'in changing their life pattern' and recognizes the political need to integrate them into the modern nation as full and equal citizens with all the rights and privileges that would otherwise be denied them. Unlike Kristeva, Spivak will not make the mistake of essentializing or primitivizing the Indian Aboriginals while ignoring their plight in the *realpolitik* of contemporary India. Nonetheless, there is a deep desire on Spivak's part not to see them lose that aspect of their culture that still retains a 'pre-national ecological sanity.'

A similar desire not to lose the subaltern's pre-national, premodern culture is expressed in a more mournful register in a passage in which Spivak recognizes both the practical, political need to integrate the subaltern as citizen and the resulting tragic loss of subaltern singularity through that integration:

> When a line of communication is established between a member of subaltern groups and the circuits of citizenship or institutionality, the subaltern has been inserted into the long road to hegemony. Unless we want to be romantic purists or primitivists about 'preserving subalternity' ... this is absolutely to be desired ... This trace-structure (effacement in disclosure) surfaces as the tragic emotions of the political activist, springing not out of superficial utopianism, but out of the depths of ... 'moral love.'[83]

We notice again the denial of any nostalgia for primitive authenticity. The subaltern needs to claim her right to full citizenship. But, at the same time, this political realism is a *tragic necessity* because it entails the effacement of the subaltern's singularity in her 'disclosure' to the nation, her accession to citizenship. As Spivak sees it, the tragedy is felt most deeply by the political activist, whose desire to gain political rights for the subaltern is balanced by the elegaic realization that an irreplaceable, singular way of life stands to be lost.

Since neither the (metropolitan?) political activist nor Spivak can or wish to 'penetrate' fully into the subaltern's singularity, there is no disclosure of what the subaltern feels about her integration as a citizen into the modern nation. But to a non-subaltern like Spivak, an *enthusiastic* integration of the subaltern, first, into the circuits of nationhood and, then, into the global circuits of international capital, seems like a betrayal of subalternity's oppositional otherness. The upwardly mobile, diasporic immigrant becomes a target of criticism for betraying her subaltern forbears' resistant alterity: 'Bhubaneswari [a young subaltern woman who killed herself in 1926 for failing to carry out a political assassination] had fought for national liberation. Her great-grandneice [a new U.S. immigrant with 'an executive position in a U.S. based transnational'] works for the New Empire. This too is a historical silencing of the subaltern.'[84] The subaltern, especially the unassimilated aboriginal subaltern who has been left alone,[85] is seen as the Other who poses a limit to triumphalist accounts of diaspora:

> The figure of the New Immigrant has a radical limit: those who have stayed in place for more than thirty thousand years. We need not value this limit for itself, but we must take it into account. Is there an alternative vision of the human here? The tempo of learning to learn from this immensely slow temporizing will not only take us clear out of diasporas, but will also yield no answers or conclusions readily. Let this stand as the name of the other of the question of diaspora. That question, so taken for granted these days as the historically necessary ground of resistance, marks the forgetting of this name. Friday?[86]

Opposing success stories of upwardly mobile immigrants and postmodern valorizations of mobility and migrancy (are writers like Salman Rushdie and Bharati Mukherjee indicted here?) is Friday, the mute and stubbornly uninformative guardian of the radically heterogeneous space of subalternity.

Spivak's work is dedicated to not forgetting Friday's name even as other nominations proliferate in our contemporary world. We must remember Friday's name for it enables us to discern the limits of those names that brook no alternatives, that seek to put an end to other names. Friday is the name of the primitive Other who resists assimilation into a triumphant Eurocentric modernity. Spivak's vigilance against the ethnocentric essentializing or primitivizing of the Other that is clearly present, for example, in her critique of Kristeva, depends paradoxically on the enduring presence of an unassimilated, uncompromised aboriginality. The aboriginal, Spivak argues, enables a 'traffic with the incalculable,' that is, with the sacred. The 'sacred,' Spivak cautions,

> need not have a religious sanction but simply a sanction that cannot be contained within the principle of reason alone. In this sense, nature is no

> longer sacred for civilizations based on the control of nature. The result is global devastation due to a failure of ecology. It is noticeable that less advanced groups in the fourth world still retain this sense as a matter of their cultural conformity. I am not exoticising or romanticizing the aboriginal, they are not all 'radicals' ... What we are dreaming of here is not how to keep the aboriginal in a state of excluded cultural conformity, but how to learn and construct a sense of sacred nature by attending to them ... We want to open our minds to being haunted by the aboriginal. We want the spectral to haunt the calculus. [87]

The 'less advanced groups in the fourth world' with their sense of the sacred are held up as salvific alternatives to modern civilization's devastation of the planet's ecology. Once again, despite Spivak's familiar denial of romanticizing the aboriginal, the primitive Other is valorized *in order to save us,* its radical heterogeneity *all too predictably serving our desire* for a way out of modern civilization. The aboriginal must remain untouched in all its inappropriable singularity, outside the teaching machine, so that, as a genuine alternative, it can deliver us from our ethnocentric arrogance. However, as Rey Chow has cautioned (a warning I have already cited earlier): 'Our fascination with the native, the oppressed, the savage and all such figures is ... a desire to hold on to an unchanging certainty somewhere outside our own "fake" experience.'[88] Spivak's injunction that we 'open our minds to being haunted by the aboriginal' is an example of our desire to have the radically heterogeneous Other save us from our illusions. The Other exists radically apart from us, but, curiously, its difference always refers to or is defined by *our* drama of guilt, remorse, and redemption. Whatever its difference, the subaltern Other is still made to underwrite our theoretical enterprise.

Like Spivak, the authors selected for study in this book are haunted by the figure of the aboriginal. Again, like Spivak, they are all, initially, sharply critical of the Eurocentric constitution of the primitive. Thus, to a person, they are all anti-primitivists. Baudrillard warns against an assimilative primitivism that would include the Other in the Western script of universalism. Similarly, upholding the idea of an incommensurable justice, Lyotard argues against the West's claim to know the Other and incorporate its difference into a metanarrative. Torgovnick, as we have already noted, is alert to the dangers she sees in Western primitivism's rhetorics of desire for and control of the Other. Sahlins criticizes primitivism's evolutionary narrative, which he detects in the benevolent Eurocentrism that would elevate the 'savage mind' by transforming it into a Western bourgeois intellect. Unlike the previous thinkers, whose anti-primitivism is directed at Western modernity's ethnocentric incorporation of the so-called primitive Other, Habermas's anti-primitivism is directed against their valorization of the Other as the other of (Western) reason; that is, Habermas's anti-primitivism warns us against the primitivism he detects in a theory of alterity that abandons modernity for the Dionysiac, the irrational, the archaic, and the primitive. To Habermas the anti-ethnocentrism of a Baudrillard or a Lyotard is a familiar version of counter-Enlightenment primitivism, and hence remains ethnocentric despite its dissent.

At the same time, however, the anti-primitivism of our authors is accompanied, as we have also noticed in Spivak's work, by a renewed reliance on the concept of the primitive. Thus, Baudrillard's and Lyotard's incisive questioning of the ethnocentric premises of earlier forms of primitivism ends up privileging the primitive as that radical, incommensurable Other who, by resisting universalizing Western metanarratives, delivers us from what Baudrillard calls 'the hell of the Same.'[89] The Other's radical incommensurability and unknowability, paradoxically, enables them to conduct a critical analysis of the West. Torgovnick's trenchant critique of the uses of primitivism in modern and postmodern Western culture is qualified by her openness to 'alternative lines of primitivism ... [that] should probe alternative versions of knowledge and social order, including many marginalized in the West.'[90] Her criticism of Eurocentric forms of primitivism provides the basis for her acceptance of a 'deep' primitivism in which is located a universal spiritual quest for ecstasy. Though Sahlins's 'native' is resolutely not the primitive of colonial and evolutionary anthropology, the 'native's' difference from Western modernity, a difference rooted in the primordial, cosmological origins of his indigenous culture, is essential for the anthropological project. Anthropology may long have given up believing in the primitives of an E.B. Tylor or a Sir James Frazer, but, according to Sahlins, it still has faith in a cultural relativism that challenges the ethnocentrism of Western reason with the *pensée sauvage* of other cultures. Habermas's defence of the progress of modern rationality requires him to reject the pre-rational, mythic, and ethnocentric collective thought of archaic or primitive societies. But a closer examination of his work reveals that Habermas's theory of rational communicative action remains linked to premodern, pre-rational forms of social solidarity and consensus and continues to draw on the semantic resources of the archaic and the sacred that modern rationalized societies lack. The premodern or primitive is thus at once superseded *and* needed as supplement in Habermas's theory of modern rationality.

Primitivism without Primitives, or Towards Alterity, Culture, and Modernity

In urging us to allow our minds to be 'haunted by the aboriginal' and to let the 'spectral' disrupt the calculus of global modernity, Gayatri Spivak relies on two assumptions: her references to haunting and the spectral assume, first, that the aboriginal or primitive has either disappeared or is in the process of vanishing, and, second, that in its vanishing the aboriginal has not been obliterated but has, in fact, paradoxically, gained the power to haunt us and our modern calculus. Spivak's first assumption is shared widely by theorists who write on postmodernism. For example, Gianni Vattimo and Fredric Jameson both see the disappearance of the primitive as signifying the exhaustion of alterity with the global spread of Western modernity. Vattimo contends that the purely primitive has disappeared as a result of the Westernization of the planet. According to his translator, Jon Snyder, Vattimo argues that it is impossible

> for philosophy to ignore the evidence of contemporary events, which reveals that cultural differences are being rapidly and definitively undermined by the spread of the electronic 'global village' described by McLuhan, and by the successes of imperalistic capitalism, which acts like an invisible solvent on local traditions and indigenous social formations. With this situation the authentic 'alterity' of primitive cultures becomes a less and less viable notion for postmodern thought.[91]

For Vattimo, instead of the pure, authentic alterity of the primitive, what we have today is 'an ensemble of contemporaneous swerves of the primitive, hybrid traces and residues contaminated by modernity.' Instead of 'encountering the other, with all its theoretical grandiosity,' we find ourselves 'faced with a mixed reality in which alterity is entirely exhausted.'[92] Alterity, in other words, vanishes into hybridity; the primitive no longer exists in its authentic, pure empirical form since it can only present itself, in our era of globalization, 'in the form of survival, marginality, and contamination.'[93] Thus, though the primitive has not vanished completely, in its present hybridized or contaminated form it can no longer be posed as a radical alterity or alternative to Western modernity.

The impossibility of heterological opposition to capitalist modernization is also emphatically noted in Fredric Jameson's periodization of postmodernism. Distinguishing between modernism and postmodernism, Jameson writes: 'In modernism, ... some residual zones of "nature" or "being," of the old, the older, the archaic, still subsist; culture can still do something to that nature and work at transforming that "referent." Postmodernism is what you have when the modernization process is complete and nature is gone for good.'[94] Our postmodern age, Jameson argues, is governed by the logic of what he calls 'late or multinational or consumer capitalism,' the 'purest' form of capital, which has expanded prodigiously 'into hitherto uncommodified areas,' even penetrating and colonizing 'Nature and the Unconscious.'[95] Moreover, the expansion of capital and the accompanying colonization or elimination of precapitalist enclaves (Nature and the Unconscious) have resulted in the loss of critical effectivity since there are no longer any more 'extraterritorial or Archimedean footholds' outside the global hegemony of multinational capital.[96] Going further than Vattimo, who at least acknowledges that the archaic and the primitive still survive even if only as traces in a mixed, hybridized postmodern world, Jameson characterizes the postmodern as

> a situation in which the survival, the residue, the holdover, the archaic, has finally been swept away without a trace ... Ours is a more homogeneously modernized condition; we no longer are encumbered with the embarrassment of non-simultaneities and non-synchronicities. Everything has reached the same hour on the great clock of development or rationalization (at least from the perspective of the 'West'). This is the sense in which we can affirm, either that modernism is characterized by a situation of incomplete *modernization*, or that postmodernism is more modern than modernism itself.[97]

While modernism was still able to oppose residual premodern alterities to the forces of capitalist modernization – hence its characterization by Jameson as 'incomplete modernization' – no such resistant or oppositional referents are available in postmodernism, which is 'more modern than modernism' because it is the completion of modernization.

To be sure, representations of the primitive or premodern seem ubiquitous in postmodern culture. We see them everywhere in advertisements and stores promoting New Age lifestyles, in the *faux* 'tribal' struggles of *Survivor*, in novels and films like *At Play in the Fields of the Lord*, *Dances with Wolves*, and *The Gods Must Be Crazy*, in the tattoos and piercings of 'urban primitives,' in the unending lament for vanishing peoples and cultures that issue from writers like Wade Davis in the pages of *National Geographic*, and in the romance of ecological indigenism or 'green orientalism.' But these representations are, for Jameson, postmodern simulacra of the premodern past, nostalgic responses that mark precisely the disappearance of the primitive and the completion of capitalist modernization.[98] Empirically speaking, then, Jameson may well be right; we no longer have premodern or archaic referents, we only have simulacra of these vanished entities. But, in a theoretical sense, both Jameson and Vattimo ignore Gayatri Spivak's second assumption (noted earlier) and overlook the fact, that even as the premodern or primitive referents disappear or are hybridized, or are turned into postmodern simulacra, a strengthened idea of the primitive returns to haunt us. Both Jameson and Vattimo are wrong to say that while modernism still relied on primitive Others to provide alternatives, postmodernism is left without any premodern alterities. In fact, it is the other way round. While modernism needed the vanishing referentiality of the primitive for its critical effectivity, in postmodernism the disappearance of the empirical primitive has led to its firmer entrenchment as a theoretical concept. The disappearance of the primitive and the archaic in our postmodern age has resulted in their greater power to haunt us as Spivak has noted, and as Jameson and Vattimo have not. The primitive's disappearance has meant the return of primitivism in its more powerful displaced, spectral form as neo-primitivism.

In a way, we should not be surprised by the paradoxical manner in which the primitive's disappearance enables its survival as a powerful critical concept in modern Western thought. In an article entitled 'Disappearing Savages? Thoughts on the Construction of an Anthropological Conundrum,' John W. Burton points out that 'for roughly 150 years ... one of the most consistent themes in anthropological discourse' has been the lament for the 'passing of the primitive.'[99] Burton compiles a record of anthropological disquisitions on the disappearance of primitives from Sir James Frazer's warning in 1927 that 'in another quarter of a century ... the savage ... will ... be as extinct as the dodo' to Lévi-Strauss's lament in 1966 that 'the various types of primitive life are on the point of disappearing,' from Malinowski's disappointment in 1922 that just 'when men fully trained for the work have begun to travel into savage countries and study their inhabitants – these die away under our eyes' to T.R. Trautmann's urgent plea seventy years later for ethnographers to record 'the facts of the fast-disappearing object of anthropological inquiry, primitive society.'[100] Why has this 'charter myth' of the perpetually disappearing primitive persisted over the years in anthropological discourse? Burton suggests that without the alarm over disappearing savages we would not have the discipline of anthropology or any 'basis upon which we could hang our assertion of modernity.'[101] In short, the narrative of vanishing primitives has to be repeated in order to validate the importance of anthropological work and to underwrite the constitution of modernity as that which has superseded primitive culture and society.

Modern Western thought thus appears to require the perpetual return of the savage for whose disappearance it is responsible, a paradoxical phenomenon clearly registered in the title of Leslie Fiedler's 1968 study of the Indian in American cultural and literary myths, *The Return of the Vanishing American.* Fiedler notes that 'an astonishing number of novelists have begun to write fiction in which the Indian character, whom only yesterday we were comfortably bidding farewell (with a kind of security and condescension we can no longer even imagine), has disconcertingly reappeared.'[102] He also points out that the American Indian, however vestigial a figure, remains the symbol of otherness aspired to by white Americans who wish to escape from their own society to 'a territory unconquered and uninhabited by pale faces, the bearers of "civilization," the cadres of imperialist reason.'[103] The Indian may have disappeared or may have been 'subdued, penned off, or costumed for the tourist trade,'[104] but his radical otherness survives in those white Americans who seek an 'alteration of consciousness' either through hallucinogenic drugs or through madness.[105] For Fiedler, then, the Indian vanishes only to be reincarnated in the hippy, the acid-head, the schizophrenic, or any other white American who seeks to be radically other. The Indian returns in Fiedler's work only to be incorporated or appropriated and transformed into the white neo-primitive; for Fiedler, Indians are us.

Though imbued with the psychedelic, counter-cultural romanticism of the sixties, Fiedler's book owes its inspiration to an earlier work published in 1924, D.H. Lawrence's *Studies in Classic American Literature,* a passage from which opens the introduction of Fiedler's own meditation on the vanishing Indian: 'The moment the last nuclei of Red life break up in America, then the white men will have to reckon with the full force of the demon of the continent ... [W]ithin the present generation the surviving Red Indians are due to merge in the great white swamp. Then the Daimon of America will work overtly, and we shall see real changes.'[106] Though the Red Indian will never again possess America, Lawrence asserts, 'his ghost will.'[107] Lawrence's prophecy may have overlooked the remarkable survival of Amerindian culture despite years of genocidal oppression and assimilationist policies, but in its insight into how the indigenous Daimon of America will work its force on the white men once the indigenous population has disappeared, Lawrence's pronouncement anticipates the spectral power celebrated by contemporary neo-primitivism, a conceptual or theoretical primitivism that no longer requires any 'real' primitives.

The paradox of the vanishing primitive who returns to haunt the modern Western mind can be explained as a safeguarding of the idea of the radically pure Other. In other words, the disappearance of primitives helps to preserve the concept of radical otherness, since surviving groups of 'actual' primitives, contaminated and hybridized by modernity as Vattimo has noted, may not adequately embody the idea of pure otherness they are supposed to represent. A primitivism without primitives thus acts as a counterfactual, regulative idea; it sets up a concept of the primitive so pure no empirical referent can contradict or refute it. A primitive-less primitivism resembles what Maurice Blanchot, in his review of Lévi-Strauss's *Tristes Tropiques,* calls the imaginary point zero or absolute beginning of humankind. It is an abstract, referentless primitivism (in fact, as we shall see later, the term 'primitive' itself will be displaced and erased) that Blanchot describes as the 'idea of a beginning or of a "theoretical model" of a society close to this force of beginning, *which we will certainly never encounter anywhere in realized form* ... [and which we must see] as a working hypothesis ... constructed fictitiously in order to help us see clearly into the complexities of existing societies.'[108] This point-zero primitivism emptied of empirical content, this idea of the primitive who will never be encountered anywhere in realized form, has the theoretical advantage of avoiding the problems of representation faced by older forms of primitivism. Since there is no pure primitive as such to represent, the pitfalls of ethnocentric appropriation or projection, as well as the 'orientalist' problem of speaking for or representing others, are avoided. The neo-primitivist thinker can deny accusations of ethnocentrism and admit to the fictitious nature of his representation of primitive culture and society in the same way that Roland Barthes, for example, can say that his book on Japan is not about the real Japan but an imagined system of signs he calls 'Japan':

> I can [Barthes writes] ... – though in no way claiming to represent or to analyze reality itself (these being the major gestures of Western discourse) –

> isolate somewhere in the world (*faraway*) a certain number of features ... and out of these features deliberately form a system ... which I shall call: Japan ... I am not lovingly gazing toward an Oriental essence – to me the Orient is a matter of indifference, merely providing a reserve of features whose manipulation – whose invented interplay – allows me to 'entertain' the idea of an unheard-of symbolic system, one altogether detached from our own.[109]

Like Barthes, neo-primitivism can claim to avoid the West's colonizing representations of others by admitting to the fiction of the primitive. Moreover, like Barthes, whose indifference to the real Orient nonetheless still relies on the Orient's 'reserve of features' in order to entertain the possibility of a symbolic system radically different from his own, neo-primitivism, though denying that it represents real primitives, must still depend on an existing repertoire of primitivist representations in order to pose a radical alternative to the modern West. In Barthes's book on Japan, as in neo-primitivism, the possibility of an alternative utopia involves a disavowal of referents that nonetheless still retains their representational, oppositional force.

In a provocative but illuminating critique of post-structuralist theory's interruption of referentiality, Rey Chow notes that 'when one is dealing with sexual, cultural, and ethnic others, it is always considered premature in poststructuralist theory to name and identify such references as such; instead, deconstruction's preferred benevolent gesture is to displace and postpone these others to a utopian, unrealizable realm, to a spectral dimension whose radicalness lies precisely in its spectrality, the fact that it cannot materialize *in the present.*'[110] The referentless, spectral utopia of the Other is premised, as Chow points out, on its absence from and its externality to the spatio-temporal present. As such, although post-structuralist theory can avoid ontologizing otherness, it still participates in what Carlos Alonzo, writing about the European figuration of the New World, calls 'a permanent exoticization ... the sort that cannot be undermined or dissolved by actual experience or objective analysis.'[111] A neo-primitivism that refuses to identify itself with primitive referents will be able, like post-structuralist theory, to circumvent problems associated with the representation of others, but, in doing so, it will not be able to avoid the further problem of exoticization that forms the very basis of the critical separation that enables its critique of the modern West. A referentless neo-primitivism, a primitivism without primitives, is a form of 'permanent exoticization' that safeguards primitivism from criticism since, without empirical content, it 'cannot be undermined or dissolved by actual experience or objective analysis.' In short, neo-primitivism is hard to refute empirically or to challenge theoretically because it is not directly referential or ontological, but spectral and 'hauntological' (to use Derrida's punning neologism).[112] Neo-primitivism's acknowledgment that the primitive cannot be represented, its questioning of Eurocentric representations of the primitive, even its admission that there are no authentic or pure primitives to represent paradoxically guarantee the power of the primitive as a counterfactual idea or spectral Other that both opposes and is complicit with contemporary Western thought.

Neo-primitivism's opposition to Western modernity should be clear from our discussion so far, but its complicity requires a further word of explanation. If neo-primitivism's critique of representations of primitives marks, on the one hand, the limits of Western knowledge, it also provides, on the other, a 'primitive sublime,' an unrepresentable ideal of the primitive, which Western thought can use to institute and regulate a politics of difference. To put it another way, if the referential absence of primitives absolves neo-primitivism of the 'Orientalist' sin of representing or speaking for concrete others, it also affords neo-primitivism the power to judge whether the speech or self-representation of others measures up to its non-referential, spectral ideal of the primitive. Neo-primitivism's safeguarding of the other from the power of representation is, at the same time, its power to police all representations of otherness by determining how far they fall short of the ideal Other.

What I have described as the 'primitive sublime,' in which the unrepresentability of the primitive is also a regulative ideal of what primitive alterity should be, is shown to pervade modern thought in Elizabeth Povinelli's *The Cunning of Recognition*, an insightful study of the ways in which indigenous alterities are both valorized and managed in multicultural Australia. Povinelli points out that in recent decades, many non-Aboriginal Australians and the Australian state itself have expressed both recognition and respect for Aboriginal traditional culture and law. She writes:

> When they think about it, many Australians are genuinely moved by the miraculous persistence of an Aboriginal law in the face of centuries of traumatic civil onslaught. There in the distance, although never wherever an actual Aboriginal subject stands and speaks, the public sense a miracle of modern times, a sublime material impossible to define but truly felt, an

> immutable and indestructible thing that predates and survives civil society's social and corporeal alterations. *The Last Wave*, *Picnic at Hanging Rock*, and numerous other popular films and books strive to evoke this affective state. The nation truly celebrates this actually good, whole, intact, and somewhat terrifying *something* lying just beyond the torn flesh of present national social life.[113]

While the national recognition, even admiration, accorded to Aboriginal alterity is an improvement over the forced assimilation policies of the past, Povinelli warns that its primitivist impulse, its fixation on the remote, archaic past leads it to reject or to question the complex, historically formed identity of present-day Aborigines. Contemporary white Australia's primitivist desire for an authentic or pure Aboriginal identity is thus similar to the Reverend Lorimer Fison's experience, expressed in the 1880 ethnology *Kamilaroi and Kunai*, of 'feeling "ancient rules" underlying the Kamilaroi and Kunai's sexual practices, catching fleeting glimpses of an ancient "strata" cropping up from the horrific given conditions of colonial settlement, sensing a "something else, ... something more" Kamilaroi and Kunai than even the Kamilaroi and Kunai themselves, a some *thing* that offered him and other ethnologists a glimpse of an ancient order puncturing the present, often hybrid and degenerate, indigenous social horizon.'[114] Both Fison and contemporary non-Aboriginal Australians desire a 'something else / something more,' a distant, authentic Aboriginality that present-day Aborigines can never measure up to. For non-Aboriginal Australians, then, the ideal Aboriginal subject is a forever receding subject of fantasy that actual Aborigines, more often than not, fail to live up to. The Aboriginal subject is an emptied alterity, a phantasm that enables, in Povinelli's words, the modelling of 'a national noumenal fantasy ... [in which] every determinate content of Aboriginal culture – every propositional content – forecloses the imaginary fullness of ancient law.'[115] Actual Aboriginal subjects not only fail to live up to their original, unrepresentable culture or tradition but they '*stand in the way of* this unrepresentable good object in the dual sense of being merely metonymic of it and a material barrier to it.'[116] Moreover, the contemporary Aboriginal subject is not only policed and judged by white Australia according to this fantastic, unrepresentable tradition, but is also made 'to identify with [this] lost indeterminable object' and to become 'the melancholic subject of traditions.'[117] Motivated by benevolent liberal intentions, the recognition of the indigenous subject by multicultural Australia is thus also a form of regulation and control carried out in the name of an impossible, imaginary ancient tradition against which the present-day indigene is compared, measured, and often judged inadequate. The cunning of this recognition, as Povinelli's book documents in convincing detail, becomes most evident when material stakes are involved. When Aboriginals bring forward claims to land rights and social entitlements, their claims are judged according to whether they can identify themselves with a 'maximally symbolic' but 'minimally determinate' ancient tradition on which white Australia's fantasy of the indigenous rests.[118] Aboriginal subjects are thus placed in an impossible situation: in order to gain cultural and legal recognition from the Australian state they find themselves forced to conform to a fantasized alterity emptied of historical meanings and quite often incongruent with their contemporary lives; but to refuse an identification with the fantasy of pure indigenous alterity is to lose white Australia's recognition along with the land rights and other material benefits that come with such recognition.

Povinelli's incisive critique of the modern Australian state's 'cunning' recognition of the Aboriginal subject clearly shows the former's adoption of what I have called neo-primitivism. This is a primitivism that values the primitive only in its spectral or phantasmatic form; a primitivism that imagines a primitive other so purely primitive and alterior it can have no referent; a primitivism without actual primitives. This is also a primitivism that appears to oppose Western modernity through its valorization of primitive alterity, only to reveal its complicity with modernity's nostalgic fantasy of recovering premodern losses. In her illuminating study of modern nostalgia in Japan, Marilyn Ivy has noted nostalgia's

> ambivalent longing to erase the temporal difference between subject and object of desire, shot through with not only the impossibility but also the ultimate unwillingness to reinstate what was lost. For the loss of nostalgia – that is, the loss of the desire to long for what is lost because one has *found* the lost object – can be more unwelcome than the original loss itself. Despite its labors to recover the past and deny the losses of 'tradition,' modernist nostalgia must preserve, in many senses, the sense of absence that motivates its desires.[119]

Modern nostalgia's paradoxical longing for a lost something that it must at the same time preserve as an absence suggests that neo-primitivism is not so much modernity's antithesis as its product. For neo-primitivism too longs for an impossible primitive alterity that it must continue to regard as not actually present. Ivy explains, for example, that Japanese modernity exhibits an intense nostalgia for vanishing, archaic forms of life, 'a longing for a premodernity, a time before the West, before the catastrophic imprint of westernization. Yet the very search to find authentic survivals of premodern, prewestern Japanese authenticity is inescapably a *modern* endeavor, essentially enfolded within the historical condition that it would seek to escape.'[120] What we find in Japanese modernity, then, is a complex, contradictory operation in which modernity seeks to disavow premodern losses through a phantasmatic recovery of primitive survivals; at the same time, however, this disavowal of loss through the phantasmatic recovery of the premodern is also a *modern* recognition of its nostalgia for what it knows is irrecoverable. Modernity, it seems, is constituted paradoxically (or spectrally) by premodern forms that are both present and absent, or better, present when absent and absent when present. In short, what Marilyn Ivy's study of contemporary Japanese cultural identity reveals is the complex entwinement, rather than opposition, between the desire for the archaic or primitive and its repudiation. Modernity *is* because it also longs for the premodern Other it knows it *is not.* The fetishistic logic that Ivy uncovers in Japanese modernity in which the loss of the premodern is at once recognized and disavowed is similar to the contradictory logic that we find in neo-primitivism's simultaneous recognition of the primitive as absent and its disavowal of that absence when the primitive is recovered in spectral form. Modernity is constituted as much by its supersession of the primitive as by its need for ghostly reminders of the premodern; similarly, neo-primitivism concedes the disappearance of the primitive only to assert its spectral persistence. Neo-primitivism and modernity are, therefore, not antithetical but complicitous; they are secret sharers, as the chapter on Jürgen Habermas will more clearly demonstrate.

Neo-primitivism as a primitivism without primitives will logically seek to dismiss or drop the term 'primitivism' altogether. It is, after all, a problematic term that some anthropologists as early as the 1940s sought to eliminate altogether from their vocabulary.[121] But though the term may be dropped, a primitivist deep structure that privileges the Other of modernity – an Other that critically interrogates the modern – is retained. The disappearance of the term 'primitivism,' like the vanished or vanishing primitive, is thus not so much a complete effacement as a displacement and transposition onto other terms or concepts that now occupy the oppositional role to modernity that primitivism once did. I will examine in the chapters that follow how primitivism has been displaced into three new terms: alterity, culture, and, paradoxically, modernity.

That alterity should be a form of neo-primitivism is perhaps not so surprising. A postmodern ethics of alterity has sensitized us to the dangers of ethnocentric claims to universal sameness. Particular, local forms of otherness have been mobilized in the struggle against the universalizing metanarratives of a Eurocentric modernity. These local others, often non-Western or seen as marginal to modernity, are not directly referenced as primitives or represented as such in order to avoid the evolutionary, hierarchical implications of the term. Nevertheless their alterity, symmetrically opposed to Western modernity, continues to exhibit characteristics present in earlier descriptions of primitive cultures and societies. The concept of alterity thus follows the fetishisitic logic of neo-primitivism in disavowing the primitive only to reinscribe its difference once again.[122]

As we will see, in the next chapter on alterity, Jean Baudrillard not only opposes the Eurocentric representation or incorporation of the primitive, he argues that there are no longer any primitives. He remarks that the death or disappearance of primitive others like the South American Indians is not only a sign of their uncompromised alterity but also of their return as 'viral spectral presence[s] ... [infecting] the synapses of our [Western] brains.'[123] According to Baudrillard, then, there are no longer any primitives and precisely for that reason they continue to haunt us powerfully. Another philosopher of alterity, Jean-François Lyotard, drawing loosely on the ethnographic work of André-Marcel d'Ans, mobilizes the cultural difference of the Cashinahua, a small South American Indian tribe, to interrogate Western universal or cosmopolitical thought. But, ever alert to the dangers of ethnocentric projection, he also admits that his description of Cashinahua difference may be 'simplistic' and part of a tradition of Western exoticism. This autocritique of his own primitivism does not, however, prevent him from regarding the Cashinahua example as being 'essential' to any theoretical investigation into processes of mythic or narrative legitimation that occur in modern forms of totalitarianism.[124] Again we see a disavowal of the primitive instance followed by its reinscription as an example of alterity essential to exposing the totalitarian terror present in the metanarratives of legitimation that constitute the modern West. Thus, in Baudrillard's and Lyotard's work we can trace a neo-primitivist logic in which the primitive disappears as a presence to serve as an irreducible idea.

Alterity is also the name that Marianna Torgovnick uses to question Western primitivism's ethnocentric projection of its fears and desires onto primitive others. To Torgovnick, primitivism reveals more about the West than about the primitive whose alterity continues to elude and challenge Western views of the self and the world. The primitive of Western primitivism therefore does not exist or, rather, exists only as the projection of Western fantasy. But if the fantasized, projected primitive does not exist, the argument for an authentic primitive alternative to modern Western thought is promoted in Torgovnick's work. She argues, for example, that in the oceanic experience, which Freud considered to be regressive and 'pre-Oedipal,' we have a primitive alternative to the modern Western separation of the self from the world. Our fascination with primitive life is thus an expression of the desire to undergo this oceanic experience in which the autonomous self is voided and merged with the entire sentient universe.[125] But, Torgovnick adds, this desire is to be found not only in primitive societies. It is a desire also present in certain religious forms and practices of the West. But this desire is more often repressed, 'hounded out of institutionalized religions,' and 'projected abroad in a complicated process by which an aspect of the self was displaced onto the Other.'[126] Even as Torgovnick incisively critiques Western primitivism's ethnocentric construction of an exotic Other, she also asserts that 'what has been sought elsewhere may yet be found in the folds and creases of the West's own neglected traditions.'[127] In short, the West's primitive Other disappears to become the Other *within* the Western self. Primitive alterity is to be sought *not outside* but *inside* the West itself. In Torgovnick's version of a primitivism without primitives, primitive others – geographically, temporally, or culturally separated from us – are no longer needed because the so-called primitive quest for oceanic ecstasy is to be found as much in the West as elsewhere. We no longer need to go in search of primitives because they have been generalized or universalized to the point where we can now say, 'primitives are us.'

In chapter 3, culture, a term closely related to alterity, is employed by Marshall Sahlins to replace the concept of the primitive. As with the term 'alterity,' culture does not have the evolutionary, colonial implications or the specific temporal limitation of 'primitive.' After all, doesn't culture define humanity? Don't we all have culture? But if the concept of culture is universally present, it is also the case that culture is expressed differently everywhere, as Sahlins argues, following the lead of Johann Gottfried von Herder and Franz Boas. For culturalists like Herder, Boas, and Sahlins, culture is synonymous with difference. When culture is conceptualized as a specific form of life, it becomes clear that since there are many forms of life there must also be many different cultures. As Sahlins reminds us, culture comes 'in kinds, not degrees; in the plural, not the singular.'[128] The culture concept's relativization of differences allows Sahlins to question the ethnocentrism of Western bourgeois-utilitarian reason and its claim to universality. Cultural difference is what indigenous movements all around the world claim when they resist 'the planetary juggernaut of Western capitalism.'[129] But even as the culture concept opposes domination by Western universalism, it also engages in the project of exoticism by emphasizing the otherness of societies that have not completely lost their cultural uniqueness or particularity in the face of historical changes and the global threat posed by the culture of modernity.[130] In resisting or opposing the powerful, homogenizing forces of modernity, particular, local, indigenous cultures have to draw on their past, on primordial cosmologies or archaic belief systems that have not yet been worked over completely or obliterated by modernity. Sahlins's celebration of indigenous cultures that have resisted assimilation into modern global monoculture is thus also a celebration of what can be called primitive cultural survivals. Though indigenous or native culture may no longer be the untouched and unchanging primitive culture of evolutionary anthropology, its role is still that of representing alterity, of being the Other of modernity. Like yesterday's primitive, today's indigene or native opposes modernity by drawing on the primordial or premodern origins of his culture. Like primitivism, the culture concept remains tied to the premodern and the exotic. Culture is seen as being synonymous with primordial difference. As Gayatri Spivak puts it, culture becomes 'a nice name for the exoticism of the outsiders.'[131] There may be no place for primitivism's evolutionary narrative or its romantic fantasies in Sahlins's concept of culture, but his natives assert their cultural difference from modernity in ways a primitivist would recognize.

If 'alterity' and 'culture' can be regarded as nice names for a neo-primitivism in which the term 'primitive' has been dropped though the primitivist opposition to modernity remains, the same, surprisingly, can be claimed for the term 'modernity' itself. But how can modernity be a version of neo-primitivism when it is precisely that which is opposed to primitivism? I will attempt to explain this paradox or conundrum in the chapter devoted to the work of one of modernity's greatest defenders, Jürgen Habermas. I will argue that though Habermas approvingly sees modernity as the necessary supersession of primitive or premodern mythic world views through the rationalization processes of communicative reason, he remains haunted by a subterannean desire for a premodern solidarity and consensus that has never completely disappeared. While, on the one hand, Habermas criticizes radical theories of alterity (such as those of Lyotard or Baudrillard) in the name of universal communicative reason, on the other, he remains sensitive to otherness and cultural particularity, seeing them as forces that may mitigate the harm done by the modern rationalization of lifeworlds. This tension in Habermas's work between the progress of modern rationalization and the persistence of archaic or premodern lifeworlds is an expression of what Giorgio Agamben, in a different context, has described as a logic of 'inclusive exclusion.'[132] Modernity is established through the exclusion of the premodern or primitive; at the same time, however, modernity discovers that the excluded premodern is a constituent part of itself, embodying certain intuitions that modernity will more clearly thematize or express. Modernity, in Habermas's work, is thus a form of neo-primitivism in so far as its exclusion of the premodern is, at the same time, the uncanny, ghostly return of the primitive Other who has supposedly been superseded by modernity.

2 Alterity: Jean Baudrillard, Jean-François Lyotard, Marianna Torgovnick

The Premodern Condition: Baudrillard, Lyotard, and Radical Otherness

The title of this section alludes to Jean-François Lyotard's *The Postmodern Condition* in order to make the point that the so-called postmodern critique of the modern relies heavily on the concept of the premodern or primitive. Tomoko Masuzawa, in her deconstructive reading of the quest for the origin of religion, uneasily observes: '[W]e wonder ... as to the meaning of the curious appendage *post-*. Is this an extension – some kind of an afterlife, perhaps, of what it qualifies (*structuralist, modern, industrial*)? Or does it indicate a reversal of some sort, an atavistic return of what once was ... a return of the *pre-*? These are nervous questions ...'[1] Masuzawa is understandably nervous because her questions raise the possibility that the postmodern is not only still attached to what it seeks to supersede but that it may in fact be strangely complicit with the premodern. As I hope to show, such a preposterous convolution of the *pre-* and the *post-* exists in the work of Jean Baudrillard and Jean-François Lyotard, both of whom, though usually described as postmodern theorists, may equally be seen as neo-primitivists.

Where primitivism attempted directly to know, appropriate, or incorporate the primitive Other to serve its own (Western) ends, Baudrillard's and Lyotard's neo-primitivism sees the primitive Other as that radical alterity which, by resisting universalizing Western metanarratives, allows us to escape from what Baudrillard calls 'the hell of the Same.'[2] But the primitive Other's resistance also functions as a redemptive power that delivers the modern West from its own will to universality. At once resistant alterity and redemptive force, the primitive Other has little choice or say in how it is positioned and used in neo-primitivist discourses. Though critical of primitivism, neo-primitivism is, therefore, in the final analysis, similar to its predecessor in that its anti-ethnocentric relativism reintroduces a subtler theoretical recuperation of the primitive. We see a clear example of this critical yet redemptive logic in Claude Lévi-Strauss's belief that in our encounter with primitive societies lies 'the possibility, vital for life, of *unhitching*' from our own.[3] Lévi-Strauss's assertion that 'we have a duty to free ourselves'[4] from our society in order to achieve self-renewal is echoed in the following statement by Lyotard: 'The real political task today, at least in so far as it is also concerned with the cultural ... is to carry forward the resistance ... to established thought, to what has already been done, to what everyone thinks, to what is well known, to what is widely recognized.'[5] The break with established thought advocated in Lyotard's avant-gardist declaration finds one of its exemplifications in the challenge posed to the modern West's grand narratives of legitimation by the narrative pragmatics of a 'savage' society such as that of Lyotard's favourite Cashinahua (who pop up in *The Postmodern Condition*, *Just Gaming*, 'Missive on Universal History,' and *The Differend*).[6] Similarly, Baudrillard's aphorism – 'The Other is what allows *me* not to repeat *myself* for ever'[7] – puts as much weight on the challenge posed by radical alterity (the primitive Other) as on its role in rescuing and renewing the creativity of the modern or postmodern subject.

Baudrillard has claimed that he has 'nothing to do with postmodernism.'[8] We should not take this statement as a flat denial or as self-mockery, but see in it an example of Baudrillardian reversibility in which to understand the postmodern is to re-address the premodern. Baudrillard's point, argued most clearly in *The Mirror of Production* and *Symbolic Exchange and Death*,[9] is that the West, since at least the Enlightenment, has instituted societies based on the twin myths of production and semiology – that is, respectively, a political economy that privileges an instrumental-rational view of labour, utility, and exchange value, and a political economy of the sign based on an abstract structural-linguistic code. The myth of production governed modern industrial society while the myth of semiology has given rise to our postmodern, post-industrial culture of signs and simulacra. But these societies or cultures are made possible, according to Baudrillard, only through the denial or repression of a radical and primordial principle he calls 'symbolic exchange,' a principle he finds at work in primitive societies.

Drawing on Marcel Mauss's work on the social relations of the gift,

Georges Bataille's writings on expenditure and *la part maudite*, and Marshall Sahlins's substantivist economic anthropology, which challenges the orthodox economic axioms of scarcity, need, and accumulation, Baudrillard argues that the symbolic exchange of primitive societies is opposed to the productivist myth in so far as it bypasses material wealth, economic calculation, and accumulation in favour of '*symbolic* wealth which, mocking natural necessity, comes conversely from destruction, the deconstruction of value, transgression, or discharge.'[10] Symbolic exchange is 'based on non-production, eventual destruction, and a process of continuous *unlimited* reciprocity between *persons*.'[11] In other words, in contrast to the productivist model, whose economic rationality presupposes the threat of scarcity and the necessity of material accumulation, the symbolic exchange of primitive societies, which privileges social reciprocity, obligation, and the ritual affirmation of community, requires 'the consumption of the "surplus" and deliberate anti-production whenever accumulation (the thing not exchanged, taken and not returned, earned and not wasted, produced and not destroyed) risks breaking the reciprocity and begins to generate power.'[12]

Foregrounding the reciprocal, even antagonistic, relationship between individuals in primitive symbolic exchange, Baudrillard pits its concrete, personal, and immediate qualities against that other myth of modern or postmodern society, namely, semiology or the political economy of the sign with its abstract structural code established on equivalence and substitutability. The gift that is central to symbolic exchange is totally opposed to the sign's decontextualized abstraction and reproductivity. As Charles Levin points out:

> The gift is, in its purest form ... something unique and irreplaceable, which cannot be substituted because it has no equivalent. It is something whose very existence symbolizes the interaction which it occasions, and which likewise could not have come into existence without the interaction ... The gift is not a sign because it cannot be separated from its context, and transferred to any other: it simply embodies its own meaning, which is nothing other than the way the bodies of the giver and receiver have come to exist in relation to each other.[13]

The concrete reciprocity embodied in the gift takes on greater importance for Baudrillard as the semiotic order becomes increasingly simulacral in contemporary Western society with signs breaking free from their referents and becoming free-standing and self-reproducing.

The centrality of symbolic exchange to Baudrillard's thought has been noted by commentators such as Gary Genosko, for example, who sees symbolic exchange as initiating a 'revolutionary anthropology' that seeks 'to destroy the prevailing semiocracy.'[14] Similarly, Douglas Kellner states that symbolic exchange 'emerges as Baudrillard's "revolutionary" alternative to the values and practices of capitalist society,'[15] and Julian Pefanis points out that it 'operates as [Baudrillard's] meta-position in the critique of political economy and its contemporary avatar, semiolinguistics.'[16] The critical standpoint provided by symbolic exchange can be subjected, however, to a certain ironic reversal that might amuse Baudrillard but blunts the force of his critique of Western thought. For while the principle of symbolic exchange allows Baudrillard to critique both bourgeois and Marxist theories of social and economic organization for their universalizing tendency, their 'retrospective finality'[17] that incorporates and assimilates the difference of earlier societies into their own ethnocentric and teleological paradigms, symbolic exchange, as a concept, can only function on the condition that it idealize primitive society as a positive antithesis to the West. Such a move replicates, albeit in a different register, the primitivism and ethnocentrism that Baudrillard accuses a Marxist anthropologist like Maurice Godelier of practising. Baudrillard charges Godelier with inscribing primitive society in 'the same discourse as ours: with the same code. It means looking at primitive society from the wrong end.'[18] But if Baudrillard's critique of Marxist anthropology is, on one level, anti-primitivist in that it seeks to correct a certain 'blindness about primitive societies,'[19] on another level it is neo-primitivist in that it reinscribes an all-too-familiar binary model of a debased modern West and an idealized primitive Other.

Among the first to point out the presence of this ironic reversal in Baudrillard's theory of symbolic exchange was Jean-François Lyotard. In *Libidinal Economy*, Lyotard argues that Baudrillard falls into the trap of primitivism by appropriating the primitive Other as a lost referent or elusive alibi for his own theoretical disillusionment with Western modernity. 'How is it,' Lyotard asks, 'that he [Baudrillard] does not see that the whole problematic of the gift, of symbolic exchange, such as he receives it from Mauss ... belongs in its entirety to Western racism and imperialism – that it is still ethnology's good savage, slightly libidinalized, which he inherits with the concept?'[20] Baudrillard's appropriation of the primitive Other as radical critique of and alternative to Western theory becomes for Lyotard merely the reintroduction of the Western primitivist fantasy of escaping to a 'non-alienated region.'[21] To Lyotard, Baudrillard's critique of Western modernity ends up confirming one of its long-standing desires – the desire to escape its own limits for a forgotten truth.

Baudrillard's primitive 'non-alienated region' belongs to a utopian genre of writing that is generally careless when it comes to verifying or documenting ethnographic details. This is a criticism that the anthropologist Robert Hefner has made of Baudrillard's *The Mirror of Production.* Hefner argues that although Baudrillard is quite right to insist that non-economic social relations based on reciprocity, kinship, and ritual are embedded in primitive exchange, he is wrong in ruling that the economic values of use and need are totally unheeded in primitive society. Thus, in response to Baudrillard's claim that to the primitives 'survival is not a principle' and that for them 'eating, drinking, and living are first of all acts that are exchanged, [and] if they are not exchanged do not occur,'[22] Hefner points out that not only is Baudrillard indulging in a 'rather cavalier generalization' that would 'leave most anthropologists perplexed if not dumbfounded,' but that survival is not a principle would come as a surprise to 'the starving Tikopia of Polynesia, who increasingly restricted the breadth of their social exchange outside minimal kin units in the face of an island-wide famine.'[23] In short, Hefner argues, not only is Baudrillard unconcerned about 'ethnographic particulars,' but his 'romanticized' image of symbolic exchange though presenting 'a perhaps admirable notion of reciprocity ... [is] one that never operated anywhere simply for the sake of its own poetry.'[24]

Though Hefner's criticisms of Baudrillard's romanticized anthropology and neglect of ethnographic particulars are cogent, they do not engage directly with the larger theoretical project of Baudrillard's work. Baudrillard is in fact not really interested in ethnographic details because for him ethnographic knowledge is part of the universalizing thrust of Western thought. As he puts it sarcastically in a critique of Lévi-Strauss's structuralist epistemology:

> This is the extreme of liberal thought and the most beautiful way of preserving the initiative and priority of Western thought within 'dialogue' and under the sign of universality of the human mind (as always for Enlightenment anthropology) ... This harmonious vision of two thought processes renders their *confrontation* perfectly inoffensive, by denying the difference of the primitives as an element of rupture with and subversion of (our) 'objectified thought and its mechanisms.'[25]

In later works such as *The Transparency of Evil* and *The Perfect Crime*, Baudrillard's view of primitive difference as a rupture with Western thought develops into a full-fledged valorization of a radical otherness that resolutely resists ethnographic comprehension.[26] An anti-cognitive and anti-representational stance is clearly evident in the distinction Baudrillard makes between *difference*, which is dialectical and hence intelligible and recuperable as part of a single, universal order, and *radical otherness*, which has to do with 'radical incomparability,' 'eternal incomprehensibility,' 'ultimate inscrutability,' 'unintelligibility,' and 'non-representability.'[27] 'Radical otherness,' Baudrillard tells us, 'is simultaneously impossible to find and irreducible ... The worst thing here is understanding, which is sentimental and useless. True knowledge is knowledge of exactly what we can never understand in the other.'[28] Advocating a form of anti-ethnography, Baudrillard recommends that one 'be ignorant of how one's subjects live' and respect 'non-representability, the otherness of that which is foreign to ... self-consciousness.'[29]

The problem with Baudrillard's valorization of radical alterity is that its incomprehensibility and incommensurability open up an absolute cognitive relativism that would not permit him to know or say anything about the Other, about whom he has in fact quite a lot to say. The Other may resist ethnographic understanding but Baudrillard not only knows about its resistance, he also confidently describes its feelings towards us. Thus, about other non-Western cultures he has this to say:

> Outward conversion to Western ways invariably conceals inward scoffing at Western hegemony. One is put in mind of those Dogons who made up dreams to humour their psychoanalysts and then offered these dreams to their analysts as gifts. Once we despised other cultures; now we respect them. They do not respect our culture, however; they feel nothing but an immense condescension for it. We may have won the right by conquest to exploit and subjugate these cultures, but they have offered themselves the luxury of mystifying us.[30]

But if the Other is unintelligible and inscrutable as Baudrillard constantly reminds us, then how does he know that it scoffs at us, that it shows an 'immense condescension' towards us, that it is deliberately engaged in 'mystifying' us? Baudrillard tells us that the otherness of primitive cultures is not recuperable and that they 'live on the basis of their own singularity, their own exceptionality, on the irreducibility of their own rites and values.'[31] But if these primitive cultures are absolutely singular, exceptional, and irreducible, then what Baudrillard says about them cannot be true since to be comprehended and described as such would be to have their singularity generalized, their exceptionality made into an example, and their irreducibility reduced to so many adjectives. Baudrillard's paradoxical knowledge of the radical incomprehensibility of the primitive Other reaches a dangerous point when he argues that South American Indians chose to die rather than surrender the secret of their otherness to the Spanish *conquistadores*:

> When they [the Indians] found themselves obliged to become part of an otherness no longer radical, but negotiable under the aegis of the universal concept, they preferred mass self-immolation – whence the fervour with which they, for their part, allowed themselves to die: a counterpart to the Spaniard's mad urge to kill. The Indians' strange collusion in their own extermination represented their only way of keeping the secret of otherness.[32]

Apart from the moral and factual dubiousness of Baudrillard's argument (it would be interesting to see what contemporary South American Indians make of Baudrillard's description of their ancestors' 'mass self-immolation'), there is the epistemological question of how Baudrillard can know the intention behind the Indians' actions when these actions were precisely designed to preserve the secret of their otherness. If the South American Indians were that radically Other, then how can Baudrillard so confidently know what they were up to?

The answer to this paradox lies in the realization that despite Baudrillard's critique of Western epistemology, he is not really concerned with epistemology at all. Though he may use historical and ethnographic accounts to illustrate his theory of radical otherness, his theory does not require the actual, living presence of the primitive Other since the Other is needed only as a *discursive* element of rupture, a *structural* antithesis to Western thought. This is why Baudrillard is not bothered by criticism, such as Hefner's, that his generalizations lack ethnographic evidence, or troubled by the aporia of describing an Other he is not supposed to know. The primitive Other functions primarily as a discursive proxy or theoretical place-holder and the secondary question of its phenomenological or material actuality may in fact interfere with or muddy its primary function. The real live 'primitive' can complicate matters with his behaviour, whereas the discursive proxy cannot. We can now see why to Baudrillard the extinction or imminent disappearance of the primitive Other can be turned into a theoretical advantage. The dead or disappearing Indian becomes a pure and perfect example of the Other; through his physical death, the Indian gains theoretical immortality. We have here an instance of a 'pataphysical' logic that Baudrillard elsewhere illustrates through the example of Alfred Jarry's dead cyclist who carries on cycling: '*Rigor mortis* is replaced by *mobilitas mortis*, and the dead rider pedals on indefinitely, even accelerating, as a function of inertia. The energy released is boosted by the inertia of the dead.'[33] Similarly, the primitive Other's death confers on it a greater power to 'destabilize Western rule.' The dead primitive returns powerfully as a 'phantom presence,' its 'viral, spectral presence ... [infecting] the synapses of our [Western] brains.'[34] Baudrillard's neo-primitivism thus exemplifies a bizarre logic in which the primitive dies as a presence to serve as an irreducible, internalized idea.

To be sure, Baudrillard is aware that in our time the primitive is allowed to exist only as a simulacrum, a model constructed by the human sciences precisely to replace the vanished or vanishing original. Baudrillard argues that such a simulation of the primitive occurred in 1971 when the government of the Philippines, on the advice of anthropologists, ordered that a few dozen Tasaday, a newly 'discovered' and allegedly 'stone age' tribe, be cordoned off in their remote jungle home and protected from further media and ethnological contact and attention.[35] The ethnologists were worried that the Tasaday would lose their primitive innocence and thus lobbied that they be sealed off from further exposure to a decomposing modernity. But this seemingly generous and self-denying gesture on the part of the scientists constitutes, for Baudrillard, a self-serving justification of their own discipline, allowing them to render the Tasaday into 'simulacra Indians who proclaim at last the universal truth of ethnology.'[36] Baudrillard's argument is worth quoting at length:

> Science loses a precious capital, but the object will be safe – lost to science, but intact in its 'virginity.' It isn't a question of sacrifice (science never sacrifices itself: it is always murderous), but of the simulated sacrifice of its object in order to save its reality principle. The Tasaday frozen in their natural element, provide a perfect alibi, an eternal guarantee ... The Indian thereby driven back into the ghetto, into the glass coffin of virgin forest, becomes the simulation model for all conceivable Indians *before ethnology*. The latter thus allows itself the luxury of being incarnate beyond itself, in

> the 'brute' reality of these Indians it has entirely reinvented – Savages who are indebted to ethnology for still being Savages: what a turn of events, what a triumph for this science which seemed dedicated to their destruction![37]

Simulation can thus be seen as the strategy adopted by the ethnologist, or *subject* of investigation, not only to gain control and mastery over the primitive, or *object* of investigation, but also to dispense with the primitive/object altogether. In the simulation model Baudrillard has sketched out, the Tasaday or primitive/object, once cordoned off and controlled, can be entirely dispensed with since it is only their theoretical or simulated presence that is required to prove ethnology's importance as a science of the primitive. But while this may appear to suggest that Baudrillard has deconstructed the concept of the primitive and shown it to be merely a discursive construct or simulation of Western theory, a closer examination of his work reveals that far from abandoning the concept of the primitive, he sees it as crucial and necessary to *his* theoretical enterprise.

In fact, what Baudrillard proposes is a simple binary reversal in which the power of the formerly privileged ethnologist or Western subject is questioned and replaced by the formerly disadvantaged primitive or non-Western object. What Baudrillard calls the principle of reversibility results in the fatal revenge of the object on the subject. As he describes it, 'The Object and the world let themselves be surprised for an instant (a brief instant in the general cosmology) by the subject and science, but today they are violently reasserting themselves and taking revenge ... Such is the figure of our fatality, that of an objective turnaround, of an objective reversal of the world.'[38] Though the object may appear passive, indifferent, and inert as opposed to the subject's active will to power and knowledge, Baudrillard points out that the object's very indifference and passivity make it an 'insoluble enigma,' 'an obstacle to all understanding,' 'ever more ungraspable,' and 'contemptuous of all attempts to manipulate it.'[39] The object is thus uncooperative and resistant to the subject's attempt to control and master it. Consequently, Baudrillard tells us,

> [s]cience has lost its interlocutor [the object], which, like the 'savage,' appears not to have responded with genuine dialogue. It seems that it is not a good object, ... that it secretly evades all attempts at scientific evangelization (rational objectification), and that it is taking its revenge for having been 'understood' by surreptitiously undermining the foundations of the edifice of science.[40]

Through an ironic reversal, the object, thought to be mastered by the subject, turns the table on the latter. Baudrillard shows how such a reversal is fatal to our usual ways of thinking, which assume the centrality of the subject:

> The main focus of interest has always been on the conditions in which the subject discovers the object, but those in which the object discovers the subject have not been explored at all. We flatter ourselves that we discover the object and conceive it as waiting there meekly to be discovered. But perhaps the cleverer party here is not the one we think. What if it were the object which discovered us in all this? This would give us not merely an uncertainty principle, which can be mastered by equations, but a principle of reversibility which is much more radical and more aggressive. (Similarly, didn't viruses discover us at least as much as we discovered them, with all the consequences that follow? And didn't the American Indians themselves discover us in the end?)[41]

According to Baudrillard's reversibility principle, the object, the virus, and the Indian have the last laugh over those who had thought to master them. Similarly, returning to Baudrillard's comments on the Tasaday, it turns out that the primitive ultimately escapes its role as ethnology's simulacrum, as the alibi and guarantee of Western science, by stubbornly refusing to come alive and thus validating its simulated role, choosing instead to remain inert and enigmatic like the dead. As Baudrillard remarks, at the very moment of its putative triumph, 'ethnology gives up its final and only lesson, the secret which kills it (and which the savages understood much better): the vengeance of the dead ... It is science which ostensibly masters the object, but it is the latter which deeply invests the former, following an unconscious reversion, giving only dead and circular replies to a dead and circular interrogation.'[42]

The primitive is thus both an ostensibly tamed or simulated object as well as a vengeful or fatal one. The simulated primitive is a product of the assumption that, in the act of simulation, ethnology possesses complete control and knowledge of its object. Baudrillard's argument, however, is that the primitive as object can never be completely knowable and, as such, can never be fully simulated. Like the object that wreaks vengeance on the subject, the primitive exceeds and subverts the simulated model produced by ethnology.

In Baudrillard's thought, then, the primitive as simulation is deconstructed only to be replaced by the primitive as pure or authentic object. The primitive is a pure object, however, only if it is unknowable.

As Baudrillard describes it, 'the Object is an insoluble enigma, because it is not itself and does not know itself. It resembles ... [a] savage, whom one could not understand for the same reason that he could not understand himself.'[43] It is precisely because the object is unknowable that it is able to master the knowing subject. There are a couple of problems, however, with Baudrillard's account of the triumph of the uncognizable object.

First, the object's (or primitive's) victory is surely pyrrhic; because it cannot know itself, it cannot know about its overcoming of the subject. The primitive as pure object may defeat ethnology's attempts to understand and manipulate it, but it has neither conscious agency nor comprehension of either its plight or its triumph.

Second, the pure primitive or object, described as being unlike the subject in that it is unknowing and unknowable, seems nonetheless to exhibit subject-like intentions, motives, and emotions such as vengeance, cunning, sly servility, and 'the *passion* of indifference.'[44] Supposed to be unknowable, the object appears amenable to all kinds of descriptions and imputations. Perhaps the object is not as purely objective as Baudrillard thinks it to be, and we may thus entertain the suspicion that the object may well be the most subtle theoretical trick yet employed by the subject, the most realistic simulation currently available and one that would offer an avant-garde edge to a theorist in the highly competitive Parisian academic scene. Douglas Kellner, for example, has described Baudrillard in such terms, calling him a double agent who while championing the object is really in fact speaking for the subject:

> [A]lthough Baudrillard wants to present himself as the voice and advocate of the object, he is really a double agent, secretly representing the subject as he anthropomorphizes the object world in an amazing creative display that out-Disneys Disney. For it is clear that, ultimately, he is projecting the categories of subjectivity, as well as his own subjective imagination, into the domain of objects (ascribing to them as objective features his subjective projections such as revenge, indifference and so on), thus secretly continuing in a different form the very philosophy of subjectivity that he pretends to combat.[45]

In the end, then, despite Baudrillard's valorization of the object, it is the subject that continues to run the theoretical show. Baudrillard's theory of the fatal object turns out to be a covert theory of the subject's fetishistic approach to the object in the same way that his critique of ethnology's simulation of the primitive merely reintroduces the primitive as a pure object simulated by the theorist's own subjective imagination.

Though in the past he declared, *contra* Baudrillard, that 'there are no primitive societies,'[46] in his later work Jean-François Lyotard seems to have forgotten his own criticism in opposing the self-legitimating narrative pragmatics of a 'savage' society such as that of the Cashinahua to the grand universalizing narratives of Western modernity.[47] Criticizing Baudrillard's appropriation of the primitive Other as a critical alternative to the West, Lyotard succumbs to the same temptation. Lyotard's interrogation of the universal history of the modern West is built on that same civilization's desire for an external, utopian space – a non-universal, particular, localized, self-enclosed, and unchanging primitive society.

In an essay entitled 'Tombeau de l'intellectuel' (published in 1983), Lyotard calls for an end to both the modern intellectual and the idea of universal value that gives the intellectual his raison d'être. Lyotard begins the essay by arguing that professionals who are often pressed by governments to provide expertise and leadership have to be distinguished from intellectuals because the intelligence of these professionals 'is not directed towards the fullest embodiment of the universal subject ..., but to the achievement of the best possible performance' in their domain of competence.[48] In contrast, intellectuals, according to Lyotard,

> are more like thinkers who situate themselves in the position of man, humanity, the nation, the people, the proletariat, the creature, or some such entity. That is to say, they are thinkers who identify themselves with a subject endowed with a universal value so as to describe and analyze a situation or condition from this point of view and to prescribe what ought to be done in order for this subject to realize itself, or at least in order for its realization to progress ... The responsibility of 'intellectuals' is inseparable from the (shared) idea of a universal subject. It alone can give Voltaire, Zola, Péguy, Sartre (to stay within the confines of France) the authority that has been accorded to them.[49]

Lyotard's description of intellectuals is, however, also an attack on them, as Bill Readings has pointed out. The intellectual separates himself from the particular and the local in order to instal himself in the position of the universal subject, described by Readings as 'a citizen of the universe, who speaks to everyone and to no one in particular.'[50] More importantly, in assuming the position of universal subject, the intellectual also legitimizes his authority to speak for all. It is the intellectual's recourse to universality that troubles Lyotard. For in claiming to speak for others because of his privileged access to the universal, the intellectual ends up effacing those for whom he claims to speak. Legitimating himself in relation to the universal and thereby incorporating his addressees into that same universal, the intellectual initiates what Readings describes as a 'domination effect' that is 'terroristic.'[51] Speaking for others, then, in the name of the universal, the intellectual determines a history, a politics, and an ethics that eradicate the possibility of history, politics, and ethics. In short, the modern intellectual may aim to be cosmopolitan in the Kantian sense, but his cosmopolitanism is achieved at the cost of a terroristic denial of particulars.

Moreover, Lyotard notes, what the modern intellectual refuses to accept is the fact that 'it is precisely this totalizing unity, this universality,' that has come into question as we gaze upon the historical ruins of the 'universal subject' of Marxism and the universal project of the Enlightenment. Lyotard therefore concludes that 'there ought no longer to be "intellectuals," and if there are any, it is because they are blind to this new fact in Western history since the eighteenth century.'[52] The death of the universal intellectual is thus, for Lyotard, an occasion for celebration rather than mourning. As he puts it: 'The decline, perhaps the ruin, of the universal idea can free life and thought from totalizing obsessions.'[53] And one of the ways of questioning and thus freeing oneself from these totalizing obsessions is to turn to the different and opposing example of the Cashinahua and their mode of discursive legitimation. Thus, at the tomb of the modern intellectual we come across the (resurrected) figure of the primitive storyteller. Or, to put it another way, what Lyotard approves of as postmodern incredulity towards universal narratives is accompanied by a kind of credulity towards premodern narrative pragmatics.

Whenever Lyotard needs a counter-example to challenge the Western idea of a universal history of humanity he turns to the Cashinahua, specifically to the pragmatics or mode of transmission of their cultural narratives as described by André-Marcel d'Ans in his ethnographic introduction to a translated collection of Cashinahua traditional tales entitled *Le Dit des Vrais Hommes* (published in 1978, a year before Lyotard's *The Postmodern Condition* appeared).[54] With a population numbering between 850 and 1200,[55] the Cashinahua are a small South American Indian tribe who live on the Peruvian-Brazilian border. But though their numbers are small, they play a large and important role in Lyotard's argument against the idea of a universal history. What especially interests him about the Cashinahua is the way in which they reproduce their cultural history through narratives that not only name the Cashinahua world but that are validated by Cashinahua proper names. Citing André-Marcel d'Ans, Lyotard provides the following description of the onomastic authorization of narrative practice in Cashinahua society:

> Among the Cashinahua, every interpretation of a *miyoi* (myth, tale, legend or traditional narrative) opens with a fixed formula: 'Here is the story of ... as I have always heard it told. It is now my turn to tell it to you. Listen!' And the recitation invariably closes with another formula which goes: 'Here ends the story of ... He who told it to you is ... (Cashinahua name), known to the whites as ... (Spanish or Portuguese name).'[56]

Cashinahua culture, in Lyotard's view, employs a ritual of 'strict denominations' to fasten narratives to a world of Cashinahua names, a world in which the narrative's referent, addressee, and addressor 'are all meticulously named.'[57] Generating a self-enclosed universe around Cashinahua names, these narratives procure 'an identity that is solely "Cashinahua."'[58] 'By inserting the names into stories,' Lyotard explains, 'narration shelters the rigid designations of common identity from the events of the "now." ... In repeating [the narratives] the community assures itself of the permanence and legitimacy of its world of names by way of the recurrence of this world in its stories.'[59] Cashinahua narratives are thus tautological in so far as the narrator gains the authority to tell his stories from his name, which is, in turn, authorized by the stories. We are presented, therefore, with discursive procedures that result in what Lyotard, using an English phrase, calls 'a very large scale integrated culture.'[60] Identification reigns supreme in Cashinahua culture and all unassimilable events are pushed aside or excommunicated. Self-legitimizing and self-enclosed, Cashinahua narratives construct 'an infrangible *we*, outside of which there is only they.'[61] As such, Cashinahua narratives are 'absolutely opposed to the organization of the grand narratives of legitimation that characterized modernity in the West.'[62] Cashinahua narratives are ethnocentric unlike those of the West, which Lyotard, following Kant, calls cosmopolitical in so far as they 'involve precisely an "overcoming" [*dépassement*] of the particular cultural identity in favour of a universal civic identity.'[63]

To Lyotard the cosmopolitical West overcomes ethnocentric particulars in order, however, to establish a universal history that is the West's own ethnocentrism writ large. In his view, the *petites histoires* or 'little stories' of primitive others like the Cashinahua are swallowed up by the single Western story of History: 'The little stories received and bestowed names. The great story of history has its end in the extinction of names (particularisms). At the end, of the great story, there will simply be humanity. The names humanity has taken will turn out to be superfluous.'[64] The importance of Cashinahua narrative organization with its insistence on local particularity thus becomes clear in Lyotard's work: Cashinahua narrative resists universal history by calling attention to 'the multiplicity of worlds of names, the insurmountable diversity of cultures.'[65] As the Other of Western universality, Cashinahua culture reminds us that 'traditions are mutually opaque' and that 'the universalization of narrative instances cannot be done without conflict.'[66] The Cashinahua, therefore, pose an instance of the differend (*différend*) to the Western idea of universal history. Lyotard defines a differend as 'a case of conflict, between (at least) two parties, that cannot be equitably resolved for lack of a rule of judgement applicable to both arguments ... [A]pplying a single rule of judgement to both in order to settle their differend as though it were merely litigation would wrong (at least) one of them.'[67] And yet applying a single rule is exactly what the West does by attempting to assimilate Cashinahua difference to a universal history of humanity. For to see Cashinahua narrative as part of a universal history is to see it not in its own light but from an already pre-established teleological perspective. In Lyotard's words, 'having assumed a universal history, the humanist inscribes the particular community into it as a moment in the universal becoming of human communities.'[68] As a result, the Cashinahua are done an injustice; the differend between 'savage' particularity and Western universality is either ignored or suppressed.

To observe the differend and to do justice to the Cashinahua will demand a complete epistemological break between Cashinahua culture and that of the West, a rupture not unlike that described by Baudrillard between primitive and modern society. To be sure, Lyotard admits that historical or anthropological attempts at understanding primitive cultures occur all the time. However, such cognitive genres of discourse are ultimately incommensurable with the narrative genre of primitive cultures. As Lyotard puts it:

> The heterogeneity between the cognitive genre and its referent, the 'savage' narrative genre, is not to be doubted ... There is an abyss between them. The savage thus suffers a wrong on account of the fact that he or she is 'cognized'

in this manner, that is, judged, both he or she and his or her norms, according to criteria and in an idiom which are neither those which he or she obeys nor their 'result.' What is at stake in savage narratives is not what is at stake in the description of those narratives.[69]

Lyotard's insistence on incommensurability, on the 'abyss' between cognitive descriptions of 'savage' narratives and the narratives themselves, leads, however, to a contradiction in his work. In his book on Lyotard, Bill Readings points out that Lyotard was concerned to show that we cannot derive a prescriptive judgment that refers to an indeterminate idea of justice from a descriptive statement that refers to a determinate object of cognition.[70] Political injustice occurs when this incommensurability or differend is ignored and the attempt is made 'to establish the justice of a prescriptive phrase by reference to a representable order of things (a descriptive statement).'[71] We will recall that Lyotard refers to the Cashinahua in order to establish a differend between their culture and the Western idea of a universal history. But such an incommensurable differend is made possible only through Lyotard's recourse to an ethnographic description of the Cashinahua provided in André-Marcel d'Ans's book. Lyotard is thus faced with a debilitating contradiction. To uphold the justice of his case against Western universality he has to commit the injustice of using descriptive statements about Cashinahua culture to support a prescriptive critique. But if he wishes to save the Cashinahua's differend by not subjecting them to a descriptive or cognitive genre of discourse, then he loses the use of an important counter-example in his criticism of the idea of universal history. In pursuing justice for the Cashinahua by observing their differend from the West, Lyotard commits an injustice against them by re-cognizing and describing their differend. As Allen Dunn has astutely remarked of this contradiction in Lyotard's thought, '[T]he terms in which the differend is described revive the very cognitive systems that the differend protests.'[72]

Lyotard's fidelity to the differend is also a refusal to engage in representation; for to honour the incommensurability of the Other is to abandon any attempt to represent or incorporate the Other. But Lyotard's anti-representationalist stance, which is intended to protect the Other, leads ironically to its silencing and to the verbal monopoly of the anti-representationalist. In his Lyotardian reading of Werner Herzog's *Where the Green Ants Dream*, a film about a conflict between Australian Aborigines and a mining company, Bill Readings calls on us to recognize that the encounter 'with the mute voice of the Aboriginal happens, although no translation is possible, although it cannot be spoken in any obvious sense, since language would only kill the silence in speaking (of) it. As Lyotard says, "Let us ... activate the differences."'[73] With all respect to their sense of justice, one is inclined to ask of Readings and Lyotard how they have access to the *knowledge* that the Other's silence is an untranslatable differend and not just indifference, tact, fear of punitive consequences, or a deficit caused by powerlessness? If we cannot know the Other, then surely we cannot also know what its silence represents. What is clear, however, is that for Readings and Lyotard the primitive Other in its silence becomes like the *in-fans*, the child without speech, a privileged antithetical figure to modernity's *Mündigkeit* (which in Jürgen Habermas's use retains both its sense of maturity and a self-reflexive interest in autonomy and responsibility).[74]

The primitive as child, the child as primitive. This equation has often been made in the history of primitivism. In evolutionary primitivism, the primitive/child is seen as undeveloped, not yet achieving the intellectual and moral maturity (*Mündigkeit*) of modern man. In a more romantic vein, Lyotard inverts this evolutionary ranking to make the primitive/child, if not the father, then certainly the conscience of our modern civilization, reminding it of its lack of humanity towards the 'in-human,' that is, the yet to be socialized, disciplined, or civilized being. In Lyotard's words:

> Shorn of speech, incapable of standing upright, hesitating over the objects of interest, not able to calculate its advantages, not sensitive to common reason, the child is eminently the human because its distress heralds and promises things possible. Its initial delay in humanity, which makes it the hostage of the adult community, is also what manifests to this community the lack of humanity it is suffering from, and which calls on it to become more human.[75]

For Lyotard, then, the child's undeveloped and indeterminate state, its in-humanity, is precisely what forces the adult to question the definition of his own humanity, to see his humanity as perhaps inhuman. But if the child, like the Aboriginal, is an *in-fans*, a mute, then it must remain not only indeterminate, but also, in its silence, inaccessible and incomprehensible. The 'debt to childhood' that Lyotard says we can 'never pay off' can only be a debt if we attribute a certain quality to the child, if we see the child as *representing* an alternative to our (in)humanity.[76] Children, like primitives, must remain indeterminate and silent so that the adult theorist can speak about the debt we owe to them for representing the role of the differend. As Tullio Maranhao observes of Lyotard's rethinking of the (in)human: 'Although Lyotard's "human" differs from that of empirical anthropology in most respects, there is at least this parallel: both seem to posit an inaccessible Other (the infant, the native), who cannot bridge the gap of representation or assert his identity in such a way as to pose a radical challenge to the constructions of the writing or describing subject (the philosopher, the anthropologist).'[77]

Lyotard's description of primitive society lands him in another problem. His defence and valorization of premodern particularity and the non-assimilability of difference can lead to an ironic transformation of the particular and the different into an undifferentiated cultural totality or uniformity. In opposition to the West's cosmopolitical narrative of a universal humanity, Cashinahua narratives are described as local, ethnocentric narratives of identity that result in a 'large scale integrated culture.'[78] But such a description is beholden to a notion of culture that is far too totalizing.[79] Cashinahua narrative practices are assumed to be evenly distributed and uniformly present throughout Cashinahua society and, consequently, Lyotard does not attend to the differences and tensions that he elsewhere scrupulously pays attention to in his work. A brief parenthetical mention in *The Differend* and 'Missive on Universal History' that only Cashinahua men are allowed to narrate bears out Seyla Benhabib's point that Lyotard's 'characterization of narrative knowledge as prereflexive, as a self-sustaining whole, flattens the internal contradictions and tensions which affect narrative no less than [modern] discursive practices.'[80] One of the tensions that is flattened by Lyotard's view of integrated primitive cultures is that of gender difference. In a recent study, the anthropologist Janet M. Chernela has argued that when attention is paid to the 'unofficial,' alternative narrative practices of women among Brazilian Indian tribes, we discover 'a wealth of intrasocietal diversity' that lays to rest the misconception that 'small-scale societies are ... homogeneous rather than diversified.'[81] In defending the integrity and particularity of the Cashinahua against Western universality, Lyotard ends up ignoring gender differences and downplaying the diversity of Cashinahua society. As John McGowan remarks, 'Lyotard's affirmation of Cashinahua cultural identity indicates that a holistic goal of communal integration conflicts in his thought with his more usual championing of pluralistic particularism.'[82]

Moreover, in emphasizing the tautological and self-sustaining character of Cashinahua culture, Lyotard finds himself representing the Cashinahua as a people without history, their mode of cultural and narrative transmission untouched by change or outside influence.[83] Such a primitivistic characterization is problematic not only because it equates Cashinahua authenticity with ahistoricity, thereby effectively writing off their capacity for cultural innovation and change, but also because it ignores the telling presence of colonial history in Cashinahua society, as evidenced by the Spanish or Portuguese names the narrators take on in addition to their own Cashinahua names. In *Just Gaming*, Lyotard tells us that 'the proper name, the Cashinahua one, is an esoteric one that allows the localization of the speaker in an extremely exact ... network of kinship relations.'[84] Similarly, in *The Differend*, he tells us that through the insertion of names into their stories, the Cashinahua shelter 'the rigid designators of common identity from the events of the "now."'[85] What Lyotard forgets to discuss, however, is that not only do the Cashinahua narrators acknowledge the adoption of foreign names, but they do not call themselves 'Cashinahua' in their own language; it is an exoteric appellation conferred on them from the outside world. André-Marcel d'Ans, in the introduction to his collection of Cashinahua tales, tells us that the Cashinahua call themselves in their own language, 'Honikoin,' or 'les vrais hommes' (true men). How, then, did they end up with the name 'Cashinahua'? D'Ans says that it was the name by which they were called when contact was first made with the Whites. In the Panoan language family, 'Cashinahua' means 'la gent chauve-souris' or 'the bat people.' D'Ans is not certain, however, as to how they got the name 'Cashinahua.' He says they didn't get it from a neighbouring tribe, the Yaminahua, who call them 'Saidawa' or 'the people who cry.' All d'Ans can be sure of is that the name 'Cashinahua' is a foreign term externally conferred on them: 'Il s'agit certes d'une appellation "de l'extérieur."'[86] The proper names that are supposed to act, according to Lyotard, as an affirmation of Cashinahua identity and shelter it from external events turn out to be more historically and culturally compromised in d'Ans's ethnographic account.

To be sure, in writing about the Cashinahua and in positioning their culture as an alternative to Western society, Lyotard is clearly aware that he runs the risk of inviting charges of Eurocentrism and primitivist exoticism. He admits that his description of Cashinahua narratives may be 'simplistic.' He also concedes:

> An ethnologist would have little trouble refuting my conclusions – by showing how my analysis flows from the ancient desire of the West to discover in

> the exotic the figure of what it has lost, as Plato did long ago in Egypt and Atlantis. I completely agree with this criticism. Our vision of myth is itself probably mythic; what we do with Cashinahua stories is evidently far less amusing than what the Cashinahua do themselves. Yet for the problematic that concerns us here, modern totalitarianism, this [Cashinahua] tendency to exaggerate the value of narrative as archaic legitimation is interesting in itself. It is even essential.[87]

Lyotard admits that his knowledge of the Cashinahua is limited and that it can be easily rejected as a form of Western exoticism or primitivism. But while conceding the weakness and possible ethnocentrism of his ethnographic example, he nonetheless affirms its theoretical necessity, its essential importance for explicating the problematic of political legitimation and authority in both despotic and republican forms of government.[88] Lyotard's work expresses, therefore, a certain tension between the impossibility of representing the Cashinahua Other and the necessity of representing it for theoretical purposes.

'Every man,' Clifford Geertz once wrote, 'has a right to create his own savage for his own purposes. Perhaps every man does. But to demonstrate that such a constructed savage corresponds to Australian Aborigines, African Tribesmen, or Brazilian Indians is another matter altogether.'[89] Geertz's attempt to separate the people from the construction that seeks to represent them reveals his desire to rescue the ethnographic subject from theory's nominalism. In the work of Baudrillard and Lyotard, however, what ultimately matters is not the actual existence of primitives but their *discursive* presence, their function as theoretical place-holders, as abstract differend in a conflict with Western universalism. Their description of the premodern condition is thus also a prescription for a primitive Otherness as necessary condition or pre-condition for interrogating the Western present. Their work reveals a postmodern primitivism in which, contrary to Geertz's project, theory comes before ethnography. As such, their primitives are, to borrow a phrase from Baudrillard, nothing but hyperreal effects or simulacra. The primitives merely represent, to use Mark Poster's felicitous phrase, an 'empty alterity'[90] and are made to fit what Michel-Rolph Trouillot has called 'the savage slot,' a pre-figured category awaiting occupation. As we have seen, to both Baudrillard and Lyotard ethnographic details remain secondary to the theoretical role played by 'the savage slot' in which, to quote Trouillot, 'the savage is only evidence within a debate the importance of which surpasses not only his understanding but his very existence.'[91] We end up, therefore, with a primitivism that does not really require the actual presence of the primitive, a primitivism without primitives. Arguing for an ethics of the Other, both Baudrillard and Lyotard rush to defend the singularity and incommensurability of the 'savage' from Western theoretical appropriation. But their valorization of the radical singularity of alterity ends up silencing the Other once more. For, as Rodolphe Gasché has astutely pointed out, an absolute, incommensurable singularity cannot exist for us because it would be completely unintelligible: '[S]ingularity, by refusing all translation and interpretation, becomes opaque, silent, or immediate in a non-dialectical sense. It becomes quite simply thoroughly unintelligible. Such a singular would be a failure in its own terms. No longer identifiable, it could not be recognized, let alone repeated as singular.'[92]

Baudrillard's and Lyotard's sharp criticism of Western primitivism's universalizing and colonizing aim comes to depend, as we have seen, on a reconceptualization and reinscription of the primitive as culturally and cognitively incommensurable and, hence, opposed to any assimilation or appropriation by the West. Their work can thus be regarded as a form of neo-primitivism, an anti-primitivist primitivism. As such, their project, for all its ostensible avant-gardism, rejoins that venerable European tradition, since Montaigne at least, that has imagined and relied on a valorized Other in its internal quarrel with its own culture. What Michel de Certeau has said about Montaigne's effort applies to Baudrillard and Lyotard as well: 'The finest gold tradition has to offer is used to forge a halo for the cannibals.'[93] Using the finest theoretical tools Western thought has to offer, Baudrillard and Lyotard likewise forge a halo for their primitives. But, as in all efforts at hagiography, it is the hagiographer who shows the most initiative and agency. The so-called cannibal or primitive may be given a halo, but the real distinction belongs to the person who forges it. What is not asked is what the primitive thinks of the halo placed on him. But he is not asked because while his discursive or theoretical presence is needed, his active response is not. He is, after all, only a hyperreal effect, only present, like Baudrillard's Tasaday, to guarantee the continued vitality of Western theory.

As we shall see, the hyperreal primitive does not provide a guarantee solely to postmodernists like Baudrillard and Lyotard. He seems to be a figure called upon even by those opposed to postmodernist theory. If Baudrillard and Lyotard depend on the concept of the premodern or primitive to launch their critiques of the project of modernity, then a staunch defender of that project such as Jürgen Habermas relies equally, as I will show in chapter 4, on the premodern. In Habermas's case, the premodern is read as a condition rightly surpassed by modernity's narrative of a progressive rationality. To demonstrate the progressive nature of modern social rationalization, Habermas contrasts it to the holistic and undifferentiated mode of mythic thought and action allegedly characteristic of primitive societies.[94] In making this distinction between the 'closed' world of primitive myth and the 'open' world of modern rationality, Habermas relies on the work of Claude Lévi-Strauss and Maurice Godelier, the very anthropologists critiqued by Baudrillard for displaying Western ethnocentrism. The so-called 'modern' versus 'postmodern' debate between the theorists of Frankfurt and Paris can thus be recast as a debate over the status of the premodern or primitive, a debate between opposing versions of philosophical anthropology. What is clear is that to both sides the primitive Other is a philosophical or theoretical necessity.

Primitives Are Us: Torgovnick, the Oceanic, and the Feminine

In *The Philosophical Discourse of Modernity*, Jürgen Habermas notes that it is fashionable to equate the other of reason with the feminine. He cites a passage from Hartmut and Gernot Böhme's *Das Andere der Vernunft* (*The Other of Reason*) that supports this identification of the feminine and the maternal with an archaic or primal otherness that reason has excluded:

> Separated from the body, whose libidinous potencies could have supplied images of happiness, separated from a maternal nature, which embraced the archaic *image* of symbiotic wholeness and nurturing protection, separated from the feminine, mingling with which belonged to the primal images of happiness – the philosophy of a reason robbed of all images generated only a grandiose consciousness of the superiority in principle of the intelligible over nature and over the lowliness of the body and the woman ... Philosophy attributed to reason an omnipotence, infinity, and future perfection, whereas the *lost childlike relationship to nature* did not appear.[95]

Habermas of course resists the Böhme brothers' contention that reason's separation from the primal, the bodily, and the feminine has proven to be disastrous for Western philosophy. As we shall see when we examine Habermas's work in a later chapter, he admits that while a subject-centred reason can be criticized for its instrumental approach to nature and for its will to mastery, reason in its communicative, intersubjective mode can be defended as one of modernity's greatest achievements. We need not, Habermas argues, renounce modern reason *tout court* for its primitive feminine other. The critique of a domineering subject-centred reason should not be generalized into an all-out attack on reason, or a complete rejection of rationality, but should present itself not as reason's Other but as reason's autocritique, its own diagnosis of a deficiency in itself. Such a critique, rather than overtrumping modernity, is in fact authorized by modern reason's own counterdiscourse. In Habermas's words: 'This critique renounces the high-flown originality of a return to archaic origins; it unleashes the subversive force of modern thought itself against the paradigm of the philosophy of consciousness [or subject-centred reason] that was installed in the period from Descartes to Kant.'[96]

In two acclaimed books, *Gone Primitive* and *Primitive Passions*, Marianna Torgovnick argues for a contemporary alternative to modern, male-centred primitivism. While critical of the ethnocentric uses to which the primitive has been put in Western culture, Torgovnick is attracted to an alternative feminine primitivism not unlike that sketched out by the Böhme brothers. Like Habermas, she conducts a perceptive critique of Eurocentric reason; but, unlike him, she does not make a distinction between different forms of rationality, adopting instead an ecstatic or 'oceanic' idea of 'Being-ness' that is opposed to the Western norm of a rational, autonomous self.[97] Habermas seeks an exit from a subject-centred reason, not through its dissolution but through the re-situation of the subject in an inter-subjective, communicative reason. In opposition to such a redefinition of the Western subject, Torgovnick proposes self-dissolution in an ecstatic, 'oceanic' experience. Criticizing a Western subjectivity that has adopted an aggressively masculine primitivism that seeks to master or control premodern others, she supports the desire for an alternative feminine primitivism that will heal the modern self's alienation from the sense of wholeness found in Nature. Her critique of the ethnocentric projections and constructions of Western primitivism seeks, finally, not to dispel primitivism but to question its restricted application in the name of a deeper, feminine primitivism that speaks to the universal desire for 'oceanic' unity with the cosmos. Torgovnick's work, as we shall see, is a good example of anti-primitivist primitivism, a disavowal that also acts as a profound restitution of primitivism.

Torgovnick's critique of Western primitivism is firmly established in *Gone Primitive* (1990) and further elaborated in *Primitive Passions* (1996). Primitivism, she argues, can be seen as the projection of the modern West's fears and desires onto an Other, to whom is attributed beliefs and forms of social organization and behaviour radically different from those of the West. These Eurocentric projections are therefore not so much accurate descriptions of primitives and primitive societies (whose existence, as we shall see, Torgovnick does not deny) as they are what she calls 'tropes,' 'sets of images and ideas' that control our perceptions of primitives. Primitives are seen negatively, as child-like, untamed, 'libidinous, irrational, violent, dangerous.' But they are also praised for being guileless, generous, unrepressed, and free, and admired as 'mystics, in tune with nature, part of its harmonies.' According to Torgovnick, '[t]he ensemble of these tropes – however miscellaneous and contradictory – forms the basic grammar and vocabulary of ... primitivist discourse, a discourse fundamental to the Western sense of self and Other.'[98] Primitivist discourse, Torgovnick notes, resembles the Orientalist discourse described by Edward Said insofar as the primitive, like the Oriental, is a fantasized figure of difference, a figure rendered silent and thus made to speak more to the needs of the West than to its own.[99] As Torgovnick puts it:

> [T]he needs of the present determine the value and nature of the primitive. The primitive does what we ask it to do. Voiceless, it lets us speak for it. It is our ventriloquist's dummy ... The real secret of the primitive in this century has often been the same secret as always: the primitive can be – has been, will be (?) – whatever Euro-Americans want it to be. It tells us what we want it to tell us.[100]

In a critical discussion of the Museum of Modern Art's spectacular but controversial 1984 exhibition '"Primitivism" in 20th Century Art: Affinity of the Tribal and the Modern,' Torgovnick acerbically notes that its Eurocentric, modernist outlook paid little or no attention to the primitive societies and artefacts it put on display:

> Only peripherally did the exhibition ask whether modernist conceptions of primitive societies matched available data ... All that mattered was the Western conception of the primitive. The exhibition freely confessed in its brochure that modernism contained many 'misreadings' of primitive societies or objects. But it passed lightly over those 'misreadings' since they were deemed necessary for the development of modern art.[101]

The exhibition is criticized for providing viewers with biased, ethnocentric representations of primitive art and life that speak more to the beliefs and values of Western curators than to those of primitive Others. Torgovnick can thus emphatically 'deny that [primitive] societies have been, or could be, represented and conceived with disinterested objectivity and accuracy.'[102] At the same time, however, she 'would not at all deny the reality and multiplicity of the societies we have tended to call primitive.'[103] In an instructive note, Torgovnick both doubts and affirms the possible existence of primitive societies. On the one hand, she firmly states that even the geographically isolated Asmat of New Guinea have come into contact with colonial and modern influences and hence cannot be regarded as truly primitive. On the other hand, she also singles out the Asmat as 'a good example of how rare an untouched example of a primitive society really is.'[104] There is an ambiguity in Torgovnick's last remark. Are the Asmat a rare example of a primitive society? Or are they an example of a primitive society already touched by modern civilization, hence proving the point about the near impossibility of finding an untouched primitive society? However one reads the sentence, what is clear is that Torgovnick only concedes to the rarity of primitive society not to its impossibility.

Torgovnick's book does not seek to deny the reality of primitive art and society or to abandon primitivism *tout court*; it seeks to rectify Western primitivism by leading us to a non-ethnocentric, power-free relationship with primitive Others. *Gone Primitive* attempts to find answers to the following two questions: 'Can we escape the implications of the Exposition Universelle, with its prurient interests and assumption of Western power? Can we forge new relations with the work of primitive Others?'[105] We are presented with a critique of primitivism that seeks not to displace it, but to establish a truer relationship with the primitive Other. Torgovnick's critique of primitivism is thus part of her neo-primitivism, an anti-primitivist primitivism that honours the alterity of the primitive by rejecting Eurocentric representations of it.

We see Torgovnick's anti-primitivist primitivism most clearly in her criticism of Western appropriations of primitive art. She argues that in 'asking Eurocentric questions about primitive masks and sculptures, we miss important opportunities: the opportunity to preserve alternative value systems, and the opportunity to reevaluate basic Western conceptions from the viewpoint of systems of thought outside of or aslant from those in the West.'[106] It is in the interest of preserving the 'alternative value systems' of primitive art that Torgovnick criticizes the Bloomsbury art historian Roger Fry for his ethnocentric writings on African art. Fry, according to Torgovnick, demonstrates an 'inability to understand African art on its own terms,' which results in 'partial, insensitive readings.'[107] But if Fry is criticized for his ethnocentric failure to recognize the alternative value system of African art, he is also accused of insisting on the radical difference between Western and African art, a difference Fry locates in the former's preference for representations of human nobility and the latter's indifference to representations of the human. Torgovnick chastises Fry for emphasizing this difference and argues that, like Western art, African art also represents human dignity, albeit in a different idiom, but 'not so dissimilar in intention and effect on the audience.'[108] She seems to want to preserve the difference of African art from Western appropriation, but, at the same time, she does not want it to be too different. In failing to understand the difference of African artefacts, Fry is guilty of ethnocentric incorporation; but in emphasizing the alterity of primitive representations, he is equally blamed for ethnocentric exclusion. What starts off as a critique of the imposition of Western aesthetic values on primitive artefacts ends as the reassertion of Western humanism in its generous universalist guise. As Walter Benn Michaels in a trenchant review of *Gone Primitive* points out, 'although the point of avoiding a Fry-like Eurocentrism is to "preserve alternative value systems," what's actually wrong with Fry is his failure to perceive that the value system in question is actually just a version of our own: Africans value nobility just like we do.'[109]

Torgovnick's critique of Fry's Eurocentric primitivism in the name of a primitive difference that truly represents an alternative to Western values is replicated in her analysis of William Rubin's 'Primitivism' exhibition at MOMA. She rebukes Rubin for omitting 'ethnographic concerns' in his desire to absorb primitive artefacts into a modernist aesthetic paradigm.[110] Her criticism of Rubin's modernist primitivism is, however, not a repudiation of primitivism as such, but an argument for a neoprimitivism that can do justice to the authentic difference of primitives and the alternative values they present to the West. Torgovnick's belief in primitive authenticity is clearly evident in her statement that 'primitive artifacts in a sense lost their authenticity as soon as the West got access to them.'[111] She argues that 'traditional African and other forms of what we call primitive art' have the potential to offer alternatives to Western aesthetic values; but in order to achieve this, 'Westerners need to allow what we call primitive art to interrogate the bases of our own art ... [while resisting] the persistent temptation to translate differences into similarities.'[112] Warning us further against the ethnocentric temptation to incorporate primitive alterity, Torgovnick states bluntly that 'African terms are *not fully translatable* into the Western'[113] and that 'the disjunctions between Western and traditional African aesthetics are strong and in some ways *absolute*.'[114]

There are two points to note with regard to Torgovnick's attempt to safeguard the alterity of primitive art. First, despite her assertion of the incommensurability and untranslatability of traditional African or primitive artefacts (primitive and African being interchangeable in Torgovnick's analysis), she is able to identify or 'translate' the artefacts as ritual items that reflect a collective sensibility. It would appear, therefore, that the difference or disjunction between Western and African understanding is neither absolute nor fully untranslatable. Torgovnick's declaration of cultural or aesthetic incommensurability in defence of primitive alterity is weakened by her own confident knowledge and description of the ritualistic function and collective values expressed by African art.

Second, the contradiction we have just noted in Torgovnick's writing can be resolved if we read her work not so much as an attempt to demonstrate the radical incommensurability and incomprehensibility of the Other, as Baudrillard and Lyotard have done for example, but as an effort at distinguishing between primitivisms. Faced with a 'bad' primitivism, that is, an appropriative, Eurocentric primitivism, the insistence on incommensurability or untranslatability becomes a way of defending the alterity of the primitive. At the same time, however, Torgovnick gives her approval to a 'good' primitivism that requires her to understand and translate the primitive as representing a set of beliefs or values that will challenge, interrogate, and offer an alternative to our own. Torgovnick's work thus outlines a way of discriminating between a 'bad' ethnocentric primitivism and a 'good' primitivism that provides an alternative to Western predicaments. We see this most clearly, for example, in her critical examination of the different versions of the Tarzan story and in her argument for 'alternative lines of primitivism'[115] that are more female-centred than male-centred, more receptive to the ecstatic, 'oceanic' experience of merging with other beings and with Nature, and more genuine in their pursuit of 'spirituality' and 'collectivity' than individualist, consumerist appropriations of the primitive can ever be.

In her discussion of the various versions of the Tarzan story, Torgovnick critically distinguishes the Tarzan whose utopian primitivism allows us to 'defamiliarize axiomatic Western norms and raise the possibility of their radical restructuring'[116] from the Tarzan who 'affirms existing hierarchies, including the hierarchy of male over female, white over black, West over rest.'[117] She prefers the youthful Tarzan, whose confusion and insecurity with regard to his identity confirm a 'sense of open possibilities,'[118] over the mature Tarzan, whose self-definition 'replicates the process of white male self-definition in our culture ... through establishing power hierarchies in which all others – and especially blacks and women – are subordinate to him.'[119] Criticizing the Tarzan stories that uphold an evolutionary, hierarchy-promoting primitivism, Torgovnick seeks examples of utopian primitivism in other stories that fleetingly reveal 'significantly altered relations between whites and blacks, men and women: Tarzan joining the Waziri *in their* dance and functioning within *their* societal norms, and Tarzan stroking Jane's hair and imitating the nurturing "maternal" role are two key examples.'[120] She confesses that the Tarzan she likes best is the 'doubt-filled Tarzan, willing to learn from blacks and women, willing to ask and examine the question What does a man do?'[121] Torgovnick's attempt to champion a non-Eurocentric, difference-respecting Tarzan merely reflects, however, the values of her own politically correct culture, not the values of the Other. Walter Benn Michaels acerbically notes: 'Far from representing a radical alternative to Western values, [Torgovnick's] Tarzan embodies a mainstream, middle-class, professorial version of them.'[122] While Torgovnick's liberal, feminist ideals should not be readily dismissed, it is important to point out that her valorization of 'rare, fugitive examples of more attractive forms of primitivism' (such as the 1984 film *Greystoke: The Story of Tarzan*, which depicts scenes in which Tarzan talks to animals, scenes that establish a 'harmony between humans and animals, humans and nature, without troubling relations of hierarchy and Otherness') is an example of anti-primitivist primitivism, a repudiation of 'bad' primitivism for an alternative 'good' version.[123]

While *Gone Primitive* devotes most of its pages to criticizing 'bad' primitivism, it also intermittently provides us with examples of the 'good' kind. 'Throughout this study,' Torgovnick admits,

> I have given hints of more positive forms of Western primitivism lurking behind the forms I have criticized: the potential to reject hierarchies in the original Tarzan story; the possibility of using African aesthetics to rethink the West's systems of art production and circulation; a desire to acknowledge and accept the full range of human sexual possibilities and variations in belief; the intuition that social classes or gender relations have doomed us to structures of mastery rather than mutuality; a reaching out to the natural world as our home and mother, not the exploitation of that world for profit.[124]

Most of these positive forms of primitivism are present in Torgovnick's description of a female-centred or feminine primitivism that, unlike male Western primitivism, is not hostile to the body and works to dissolve the boundaries of the self in order to achieve an ecstatic, 'oceanic' feeling of connection and oneness with other beings and Nature. In *Gone Primitive*, this feminine primitivism is mentioned in a number of places, most explicitly in the conclusion, where it is opposed to the 'male-centered, canonical line of Western primitivism' on which the book's attention is mainly focused. Such a feminine primitivism with its different selection of texts, Torgovnick speculates, 'would probe alternative versions of knowledge and social order, including many marginalized in the West.'[125] The exploration of an alternative, feminine primitivism becomes the explicit subject of *Gone Primitive*'s sequel, *Primitive Passions: Men, Women, and the Quest for Ecstasy*. Tracing the emergence of feminine primitivism from the first to the second book will allow us to see how Torgovnick's critique of primitivism is also the restitution of a primitivism more in line with her political and ideological views, a primitivism in which the primitive Other and a repressed version of the Western self resemble each other in their quest for ecstatic union with the cosmos.

A distinction gradually emerges in *Gone Primitive* between two gendered primitivisms: a masculine primitivism both fearful of and fascinated by the primitive that abjects the latter's alterity in the name of progress and civilization, and a feminine primitivism that embraces otherness and seeks a blissful 'oceanic' merger with the external world. To be sure, Torgovnick does not say that only men are capable of the first kind of primitivism and that only women respond to the second. Nonetheless the two kinds of primitivism remain gender-coded in her work. Thus Freud and Malinowski, for example, are reprimanded for adopting a male, civilizational attitude of self-superiority and mastery while rejecting a female-inflected, primitive openness to everything outside the self.

Freud raises the question of 'oceanic' feeling – 'a feeling as of something limitless, unbounded – as it were, "oceanic"'[126] – only to dismiss it as an infantile experience that must be left behind so that the self can reach maturity and enter civilized society. The 'oceanic,' Torgovnick argues, is identified by Freud with the primitive, the infantile, and the female, and as such is something to be feared and defended against. For Freud, she writes,

> [t]he 'oceanic,' with its absence of boundaries and divisions, is something we need to be protected *from* if we are to take our places in the 'mature'

> culture of the West: we must fear it as we fear the primitive and separate from it as we separate from 'primitive' sexual or aggressive urges and from the bodies of our mothers. That separation has fearful consequences Freud does not pause for long to examine: an alienation from one's past and from one's environment, the establishment and perpetuation of relations of mastery rather than reciprocity, the repudiation of the 'feminine' as a source of 'primary narcissism' and loss of self.[127]

Like Freud, Malinowski wishes to separate his Western self from the 'savages' whose society and 'sexual life' he studies. Attracted though he is to the bodies of native women, Malinowski resolutely continues to uphold, according to Torgovnick, a scientific detachment and objectivity. 'Theory' is invoked to resist 'foreign bodies.' Torgovnick argues that theory 'represents for Malinowski a high plateau, a place above lusts and temptations, a place of pure mind, above the body.'[128] There are times in his posthumously published diary when Malinowski confesses to enjoying the feeling of 'letting [himself] dissolve into the landscape' or the feeling of 'moments when [one] merge[s] with objective reality ... true nirvana.'[129] But such 'oceanic' impulses are immediately suppressed by the invocation of theory that is employed as 'a safeguard *against* feelings of Malinowski's merging with the physical world.'[130] Malinowski's repression of the body, fear of 'oceanic' merger, and use of theory as a means of safeguarding the rational self and allowing it to master and control unreflective, primitive instincts all reveal, Torgovnick argues, the characteristics of Western masculinity.

Freud and Malinowski's male-centred primitivism is unfavourably compared to Lévi-Strauss's and Margaret Mead's more open and feminine primitivism. Though Lévi-Strauss is, for Torgovnick, not 'an unqualified hero' (she mentions his elitism, sexism, and misanthropy), her account of his work is surprisingly sympathetic and infused with admiration. She points to his remark that the West 'lost the opportunity of remaining female'[131] to show how he came close to articulating a feminine, 'oceanic' primitivism. In the closing passages of *Tristes Tropiques*, Torgovnick argues, Lévi-Strauss admits that he is 'fundamentally attracted to the primitive as a site of alternative possibilities, including the possibility of a world blending male and female, inanimate, animal, and human – a world of oceanic oneness.'[132] Unlike Freud or Malinowski, Lévi-Strauss does not want civilization or 'theory' to act as a safeguard against the attraction of the primitive or the 'oceanic.' Torgovnick approves of what she calls Lévi-Strauss's 'organicist, Buddhist, oceanic aspirations.'[133] She can thus assert that Derrida's famous critique of Lévi-Strauss, though theoretically perceptive, remains blind to the latter's 'motivation,' which transcends logical contradiction and paradox in its search for an oceanic, cosmic harmony that can include a mineral, a lily, and a cat.[134] Just as Derrida's theoretical deconstruction of Lévi-Strauss is found wanting by Torgovnick because it scants the extra-logical essence of the 'oceanic' feeling, so too is Malinowski's recourse to abstract 'theory' to avoid the physicality of natives compared, unfavourably, to Mead's maternal, empathetic response to foreign bodies. 'Unlike Malinowski,' Torgovnick writes, 'Mead did not try to avoid the body; ... [she] believed that one of the foremost values of anthropology was to teach us about alternative relations that men and women can establish to their minds and bodies.'[135] But even Mead, who as a woman is seen to be more receptive to primitive Others, remains for Torgovnick 'a classic example of a woman who succeeded largely by virtue of having internalized her culture's dominant and therefore masculine values and attitudes.'[136] In other words, Mead is still too influenced by the dominant, male culture of her society to offer anything more than a compromised primitivism rather than a fully fledged feminine alternative.

While Torgovnick's discussion of Lévi-Strauss and Mead shows that she avoids biological essentialism by acknowledging that both men and women are equally capable of adopting each other's values and attitudes, she still remains beholden to a binary-structured gender essentialism. A masculine primitivism described as theoretically oriented, fearful of physicality, and hostile to 'oceanic' feelings is opposed to an alternative feminine primitivism based on empathy for the Other's body and a responsiveness to the 'oceanic' merger of the self and its world. Such an opposition of two gendered primitivisms, whose structure we have already seen emerging in *Gone Primitive*, becomes the explicit subject of Torgovnick's *Primitive Passions*, to which we turn next.

Primitive Passions explores what Torgovnick characterizes as 'the key element in the [West's] fascination with the primitive,' namely, the desire for the oceanic, for the dissolution of the self and its boundaries and a merging with the cosmos.[137] Parts One and Two of the book are respectively titled 'Men' and 'Women,' and together they 'demonstrate broad divergences in male and female ways of experiencing the primitive and the oceanic.'[138] Male writers and thinkers like Malinowski, Gide, Jung, and D.H. Lawrence are described as admitting to the desire for the oceanic only to back away in order to protect their 'mature European self.'[139] Western women, in contrast, are more willing to shed their normative selves and cultivate 'what men like Malinowski repressed: strong attachment to, even identification with, animal life or the land.'[140] Torgovnick examines feminine primitivism's embrace of the 'oceanic' in the work of women writers who travelled to or settled in Africa such as Isak Dinesen, Beryl Markham, and Kuki Gallmann, and in the art of Georgia O'Keeffe, who painted the stark landscapes of the American Southwest. But it is the primatologist Dian Fossey's work on gorillas that Torgovnick singles out as exemplifying 'an important pattern in female experiences' of the oceanic.[141]

In a sympathetic discussion of Fossey's life and career, Torgovnick argues that Fossey was less interested in primatology as the study of early human evolution than in understanding and protecting gorillas in their habitat. 'Fossey,' Torgovnick states, 'took the primitivist basis of primatology (the linking of apes and humans) and moved it in a different direction. She developed a radical identification with animals as profound symbols of Being-ness.'[142] But, as in the case of Lévi-Strauss, Torgovnick's admiration for Fossey is checked by an awareness of Fossey's many flaws, one of the most significant being her indifference to Africans, whose needs were made secondary to those of her beloved gorillas.[143] Still, while refusing to idealize the life and work of Dian Fossey, Torgovnick remarks that she feels compelled to tell with great sympathy 'the tale of her [Fossey's] love for the gorillas, stripping it down to what it was: a love of life-essence, as embodied in the gorillas, so intense that it did not, could not, hesitate to court isolation and even her own death.'[144] We are told that Fossey was overjoyed one morning when she woke up covered in the warm dung of a sick baby gorilla. The dung indicated that the baby was still alive and that it would survive its sickness. 'Fossey,' writes Torgovnick, 'gained access to the joy of life through the baby gorilla's diarrhetic dung.'[145] To be covered in ape-shit, it seems, is to be blessed with the oceanic experience of oneness with animal life.

According to Torgovnick, Sy Montgomery's study *Walking with the Great Apes: Jane Goodall, Dian Fossey, Birute Galdikas* claims that all three women 'chose to enter the animals' world with typically female generosity and to be receptive to it.' The three women, we are told, refused the scientific objectivity advocated by their predominantly male colleagues by caring passionately for their primate subjects. They therefore 'resemble not so much scientists as shamans, adopting animals as totems, at times *becoming* the animal.'[146] To be sure, Torgovnick questions the gender-based assertion of female generosity and receptiveness. 'Montgomery's view,' Torgovnick remarks, 'depends on an essentialist idea of female conduct that I must reject.'[147] Similarly, in an earlier passage, after describing how women writers and artists are more open to contact with the primitive and less defensive of their society's normative definitions of selfhood, Torgovnick warns against seeing such a gender-coded pattern of response as 'absolute.'[148] But if she rightly rejects both biological and gender essentialism, she equivocates over whether there is a gendered basis to an individual's approach to the primitive and the oceanic. Thus, after saying that she 'cannot *entirely* support' (my emphasis) Montgomery's gender essentialism, Torgovnick qualifies her remark and appears to accept that which she has rejected: 'Yet it remains true, at some inner level, that their dedication to animals depended upon their living apart from the modern human world, in quest of some essential primitive, defined as life force as embodied in apes.'[149] If, at one level, Montgomery's claim of a gendered pattern of response to animal life is rejected as essentialist by Torgovnick, 'at some inner level' a feminine primitivism as exemplified by Dian Fossey's passionate identification with her gorillas is reaffirmed.

A similar equivocation occurs in Torgovnick's discussion of Western women writers whose reflections on Africa are different from those of male writers. She argues that while gender may play a role in making female narratives attach a positive value to the oceanic, in contrast to their male counterparts' more negative valuation, it is more crucially the case that these women writers sought to go 'beyond gender.'[150] At the same time, however, even as the essentialization of gender and geography is resisted, Torgovnick still clings to a cultural essentialism that underwrites feminine primitivism when she says that rejecting essentialist explanations 'is not the same thing as saying that reasonable explanations cannot be found by thinking about "being female" and "being in Africa" as cultural realities.'[151] To argue that 'reasonable explanations' may be possible for the 'cultural realities' of 'being female' or 'being in Africa' is to continue to believe, despite the qualification of culture, that there is an essential difference, between 'being female' and 'being male,' or between 'being in Africa' and 'being in Europe.' Trying to go beyond the essentializations of gender and culture, Torgovnick finds herself returning to them again.

It is also interesting to note that there is an unresolved tension between Torgovnick's description of a distinctive feminine primitivism and that primitivism's ecstatic, oceanic quest to dissolve all boundaries and distinctions. Thus, while the oceanic experience transcends the differences of gender, gender in the form of a female primitivism opposed to a male primitivism is made to underwrite the quest for the oceanic. In writing about their experience in Africa, Torgovnick observes, European women writers describe 'the feeling of actually blending with the cosmic and ceasing at some level to be [themselves].'[152] But this oceanic dissolution of the self is at the same time the achievement of an individual vocation. For these women writers, Torgovnick argues, ignoring the contradiction she courts, 'the merging of the self with the landscape' is part of 'the process of becoming their writerly selves.'[153] Oceanic self-dissolution in these women writers, it seems, leads to vocational 'self-fulfillment.'[154] Similarly, the oceanic effacement of boundaries comes up against the insistence on the difference, the distinctiveness of Africa: 'For on this continent, so vast and so varied, it was possible for women to escape the nets of convention ... For only on their own would these women come fully into their own, test the limits of their being – in Africa, the place of possibility.'[155] However wary of essentialism Torgovnick may be, in statements like the above she seems to remain fixated on a gendered logic and to be attracted to what Valentin Mudimbe has called 'Africanism,' a cultural and geographical essentialism similar to 'Orientalism.'[156]

Torgovnick's feminine primitivism resembles in many ways the 'cosmic feminism' described in Kathy Ferguson's *The Man Question.* In cosmic feminism, Ferguson writes, 'the dominant notion of subjectivity ... is less one of a self than of a soul, a spiritual or natural dimension of a person that participates in some larger and higher scheme of things.'[157] Reacting against a self-centred male modernism, cosmic feminism longs for 'a consciousness that can participate in rather than dominate the world of trees and grass, ocean, mountain and sky.'[158] As in Torgovnick's description of feminine primitivism's longing for oceanic merger with the natural world, Ferguson's discussion of cosmic feminism sees 'bonding between women, other animals, and the earth' as a common theme.[159] Moreover, cosmic feminists look to premodern societies for inspiration and validation,[160] thereby linking cosmic feminism to a feminine primitivism.

Apart from its problematic essentialism, Ferguson notes, cosmic feminism is especially susceptible to appropriation and commodification by New Age kitsch. Warning that 'the appeal to a stable backdrop of cosmic connections' may degenerate into 'reassuring platitudes,' Ferguson mentions a list of New Age bestsellers, describing them as 'glib and superficial paeans to blissful merger with the cosmos [that] are often sold in upscale specialty stores along with overpriced crystals and other occult accessories.'[161] Like Ferguson, Torgovnick is clearly aware of the dangers of appropriation and commodification that await a feminine primitivism that adopts cosmic harmony as its goal. Part Three of *Primitive Passions*, titled 'Trends and Movements,' is devoted to an examination of certain New Age primitivisms as they manifest themselves in the idealization of Native Americans, the search for tribal solidarity through ritual in the mythopoetic men's movement, the longing for spirituality in New Age thinking, and the cultural phenomenon of piercing among those who are described as 'modern' or 'urban primitives.' Torgovnick is generally critical of these New Age primitivisms, taking them to task for their commercialism or for their contradictory attempt to achieve collective consciousness or oceanic impersonality while still attached to 'a thoroughly modern world view that takes the self as a thing to be owned, cultivated, and coddled – the veritable hub of the universe.'[162] But her criticism of New Age primitivism is in the service of what I have called an anti-primitivist primitivism that allows her to distinguish and judge between the false motivations driving our interest in the primitive and the authentic or genuine desire we express when we see the primitive as an alternative to our materialistic and destructive society.

Like the distinction between a masculine and a feminine primitivism, Torgovnick's distinction between a false and an authentic primitivism is designed to criticize and recuperate primitivism at the same time. Thus, in her analysis of the mythopoetic men's movement, Torgovnick distinguishes between authentic tribal rituals in which the male initiate loses his identity to become part of a community or the natural world and the transformation of these rituals by the men's movement into affirmations of Western, gender-based manhood. She quotes Malidoma Somé, a Dagara from Burkina Faso, as saying that in his traditional culture initiation is seen as 'the emergence of a mature male from a complex set of experiences consistent with (even dependent on) submission to the community, nature, and a sense of the sacred that is predicated on the interpenetration of the human and natural worlds.'[163] The Western men's movement does not wish to dissolve identity or gender categories. Thus, it adopts from tribal cultures those aspects of ritual 'it likes (for example, youth becoming manhood) and represses those it finds repugnant (for example, the feminine, the homosexual, and other confusions of boundaries).'[164] The distinction made here therefore marks the Western men's movement as embodying a false, appropriative, and ethnocentric primitivism in contrast to authentic primitive practices oriented towards boundary dissolution and a collective or cosmic unity.

A similar distinction between a false and a genuine approach to primitive experience is also present in Torgovnick's discussion of New Age spirituality and body-piercing. She confesses to a 'passionate ambivalence' towards New Age practices. She sees a similarity, for example, between her own concerns and those of New Age movements on questions of 'life and death, the self and the cosmos, harmonious relations between species and between the organic and the inorganic.' But, at the same time, she believes that many New Age beliefs are either mistaken or 'smug, superficial [and] ... silly.'[165] New Age practices fail most clearly for Torgovnick in their susceptibility to commercialization – 'The New Age's 'commercial base explains ... both its astonishing success and its greatest limitation'[166] – and the ease with which they can be 'domesticated'[167] and accommodated by contemporary Western societies. She argues that, unlike the disruptive, even pain-causing, spirituality of primitive rites, New Age beliefs are curiously anodyne and do not 'prevent anyone from enjoying a "normal" and comfortable existence.'[168] 'Indeed,' she adds, 'much that might ordinarily be jettisoned by the spiritual quester in other traditions – family, property, bodily health, good company, social acceptance, and comfort – can be preserved.'[169] The New Age's easy-going, middle-class appropriation of primitive spiritual traditions is thus a false primitivism, a Eurocentrism falsely claiming alterity. Authentic primitive spiritualism or mysticism, by contrast, cannot be accommodated so easily by our modern civilization and 'often attracts unfavourable attention from social institutions because it has a radical, disruptive edge.'[170] Similarly, the practice of body-piercing may either signify a trendy 'lifestyle' experiment or a search for spiritual ecstasy through the medium of the body. The former is clearly a *faux* primitivism, whereas the latter embodies a spiritual quest, a 'parable of transcendence' that Torgovnick can 'salute and even cherish.'[171] Thus, as in the distinction between a masculine and a feminine primitivism, or between a false, commercial primitivism and an authentic, radical primitivism, a distinction is drawn between piercing as primitivist play-acting and piercing as the serious pursuit of spiritual ecstasy. As Torgovnick puts it: '[T]he difference between committed piercers and casual, "Sunday" piercers epitomizes a fault line that runs throughout this book: between those who are open to transcendent experience ... and those who are just dabbling or playing around.'[172] In admiring the former and dismissing the latter, Torgovnick clearly demonstrates her anti-primitivist primitivism, a critical sorting out of the primitivism she favours over the primitivism she does not.

Torgovnick's recuperation of an authentic, feminine, spiritual primitivism is interestingly linked to an evacuation or omission of so-called primitive peoples and societies. This may not appear so surprising, however, if we recall that Torgovnick seeks to avoid projecting Western anxieties and desires onto primitive Others. An ethics of alterity compels her to reject the appropriation or representation of the Other. One of the greatest faults of the modern West is its presumption that it knows and that in knowing it has mastery over the rest of the world. 'Modernism,' Torgovnick observes, 'believed that it knew what *primitive* meant and had established the best possible relations with primitive societies; postmodernism sometimes makes the same mistake.'[173] We can, however, avoid these ethnocentric mistakes if we do not pretend that we have complete, objective knowledge of the primitive or treat it like a 'ventriloquist's dummy' who 'lets us speak for it.'[174] Walter Benn Michaels sees this refusal to engage in understanding or representing the primitive as a capitulation of truth to morality, of intellectual enquiry to 'what seems to us morally and politically good.'[175] Torgovnick's 'indifference to truth,' he states wittily, 'is the first sign of virtue.'[176] But though Benn Michael's criticism is generally sound, it is also a little hasty and fails to capture the complexity of Torgovnick's position on primitivism.

Torgovnick is not *completely indifferent* to the truth of the primitive, as Benn Michaels claims. Torgovnick never claims that primitives do not exist or that we should not try to understand them. She wants us to understand the alternative truths of primitives as they are *in themselves* before they are mediated by our Western tropes. As she puts it: 'In asking Eurocentric questions ..., we miss important opportunities: the opportunity to preserve alternative value systems, and the opportunity to reevaluate basic Western conceptions from the viewpoint of systems of thought outside of or aslant from those in the West.'[177] In this statement, Torgovnick, as I argued earlier, does not advocate treating the primitive Other as incommensurable and incomprehensible, as Baudrillard and Lyotard do. The primitive is not for her a radical, unknowable Other who we should simply let be. How then can we enter into a proper, non-ethnocentric relationship with the primitive Other without colonizing or appropriating it politically or epistemically?

For Torgovnick the answer lies in the movement away from *theory* with its detached objectivity and hierarchical subject-object dichotomy to an oceanic *feeling* that dissolves boundaries and merges subject with object. Pointing to Malinowski's work, Torgovnick argues that his recourse to theory, prompted by fear of being tempted by oceanic feelings, results in an ethnocentric separation of the knowing Western subject from the object of its knowledge, the primitive Other. She notes, for example, that '[w]hen these sensations [of merging with the Trobrianders' world] came over him, Malinowski gave himself a good shake, checked to make sure he was not developing fever, and plunged back with determination into his data and abstract theory. He wanted to get back to his intellectual work and shrugged off as a forbidden desire the impulse towards merging.'[178] Unlike Malinowski, Torgovnick wants Western theory to overcome its fear of merging with the Other and to accept instead the feeling or impulse towards such a merger. In short, rather than theoretical knowledge or understanding of primitive Others, Torgovnick seeks to rediscover the deep, oceanic feelings we share with them, feelings which we have repressed in our modern, individualistic culture. And in rediscovering and acknowledging *our* own oceanic feelings we no longer need to attribute the quest for spiritual ecstasy solely to primitive Others. The Western self, in relinquishing its will to know and master the Other, rediscovers the Other in its own self. The problem of ethnocentrism in Western primitivism is solved for Torgovnick when the so-called primitive turns out not to be an Other but an occluded or suppressed aspect of the Western self. The primitive as the constitutive outside or Other of the modern self becomes the suppressed inside of that same self.

Torgovnick can therefore propose a primitivism without primitives since they are no longer our Others but a suppressed part of ourselves. In the closing pages of *Gone Primitive,* the primitive no longer needs to be elsewhere because it has become ubiquitous, present everywhere in our modern, Western culture:

> The primitive is in our museums and homes, in our closets and jewelry boxes, in our hearts and minds. The primitive is everywhere present in modernity and postmodernity ... We have no need to 'go primitive' because we have already 'gone primitive' by the fact of being born into our culture. We are all like the writers and thinkers I have studied, imagining 'them' in order to imagine 'us' – savage intellects leading modern lives.[179]

To Torgovnick, primitives are us. Thus, the 'alternative conceptions of knowledge and social reality' held by primitive peoples can be found in 'our own traditions'; we need not invent 'a heightened (whether for better or worse) primitive as the screen upon which we project our deepest fears and strongest desires.'[180] The task before us, Torgovnick counsels, is 'to trace alternative patterns in western history that will do for us what we have wanted primitive societies to do – to do, even as we helped destroy them: to tell us how to live better, to tell us what it means to be human.'[181] Western primitivism need not seek elsewhere for a utopian alternative. It does not need destroyed or vanishing primitive societies to represent alternative values. What the primitive offers 'is also *native to the West*: more openness to the Other, more surrender to perceived divine forces, and most of all more willingness to suspend the normative conditions of the Western self.'[182] What Western primitivism has sought elsewhere, Torgovnick claims, 'may yet be found in the folds and creases of the West's own neglected traditions.'[183] In fact, in the concluding paragraph of *Primitive Passions*, Torgovnick states unequivocally that

> when all is said and done, texts or people that portray or embody the oceanic sensibility are as much a part of Western traditions as they are of any external primitive. The West has repeatedly tried to displace or dislodge the oceanic, severing it from the self and projecting it outward. But the projection has never really worked. The time for denial seems to be long past. The recognition is overdue that primitivism is much more about 'us' than about 'them.' In the same way, it is time to realize that the quest for ecstasy is as much a part of Western fears and desires as it is a part of the forest, the desert, or their people.[184]

Torgovnick's statement that primitivism is more about 'us' than about them, that the primitives with their openness to the oceanic are as much us as any geographically remote people, helps to explain what would otherwise seem to be a logical contradiction in her work. At several points in both *Gone Primitive* and *Primitive Passions*, Torgovnick chastises Western primitivists for scanting ethnographic or historical accuracy. Euro-Americans, she observes, approach 'the primitive as an inexact expressive whole – often with little correspondence to any specific or documented societies.'[185] A 'generalized notion of the primitive' is made to trump 'detailed ethnographic studies,' resulting inevitably in 'misconceptions' of actual primitive societies.[186] In his 'Primitivism' exhibition at MOMA, Torgovnick writes, William Rubin 'only peripherally ... [asked] whether modernist conceptions of primitive societies matched available data.'[187] Primitivist art historians, like Rubin, 'remain indifferent to ethnographic contexts or employ them superficially';[188] they even end up 'eliminating ethnographic concerns' altogether.[189] In *Primitive Passions*, Torgovnick continues her questioning of Western primitivism's neglect of ethnographic and historical accuracy. The New Age movement, for example, is accused of appropriating images and ideas from various exotic traditions without verifying them: 'What matters for the New Age is not the historical accuracy of its images so much as their conformity to and reinforcement of the movement's general principles.'[190]

At other moments in her writing, however, Torgovnick does not object to the scanting of ethnographic or historical truth. Thus, while admitting that Lévi-Strauss, for example, 'may scant the truth about individual peoples,' she also approves of the fact that 'he makes the scantiness of that local truth both a central topic and the essential condition of his work.'[191] In fact, Torgovnick argues, Lévi-Strauss's organicist yearning for oceanic holism deliberately and wilfully goes beyond Derrida's more logical, theoretical deconstruction of its contradictions; while Derrida looks only for 'logical flaws,' Lévi-Strauss's work is motivated by a deeper, 'lasting presence,' the oceanic moment in which 'meaning and non-meaning coalesce.'[192] 'Truth' in this instance is greater than logical or empirical verification. Similarly, in the work of Margaret Mead, what matters most is not accuracy so much as the more essential point about the primitive as a salvific, utopian alternative to the West. Thus, 'whether "Manu" or "Samoa" or "Bali" ever existed or existed any longer as she portrayed them mattered less, in a way, than the messages they conveyed to American society now.'[193]

The seeming contradiction in Torgovnick's call for ethnographic and historical accuracy and her assertion that accurate descriptions of primitive societies matter less than the idea of the primitive itself may be resolved if we accept that the first argument's insistence on an accurate account of primitives is not opposed to but, in fact, complementary to the second's understanding that accuracy finally does not matter because, at a more fundamental level, primitives are already us. In asking for ethnographic and historical accuracy, Torgovnick challenges Western culture's ethnocentric view of the generalized primitive. The demand for accuracy is, therefore, in a sense, a defence of the alterity of the primitive, a refusal to let the primitive be appropriated and turned into a cliché. Torgovnick rightly wants the primitive to be understood in its own context. Ethnocentric or 'bad' primitivism thus has to be corrected by approaching the primitive on its own terms. But once the primitive Other's authenticity is established, Torgovnick wants to lessen the distance between us and the primitive. Peter C. van Wyck notes that there are two ways of looking at the self–other relationship. The first can be phrased thus: 'By knowing you I seek to understand myself, but I realize that if I really know you I can never actually *be* myself again.' The second asserts: 'By knowing you I seek to recover myself, because I *was* you.'[194] Torgovnick's approach to the otherness of the primitive is closer to the second view than the first. In the first, the unknowability of the other also means the unknowability of the self. Torgovnick's view is like the second in that the alterity of the primitive is seen as an illusion in so far as the Western 'I' and the primitive 'you' are the same. If the alternative represented by an external primitive can be found in the 'folds and creases of the West's own neglected traditions,'[195] then we don't really need primitives since primitives are already us.

We can thus summarize Torgovnick's work as a demonstration of how Western primitivism has laboured under the illusion of the primitive's alterity. The separation between modern 'us' and primitive 'them,' she believes, is a historical creation caused by the need of the West to defend its beliefs and institutions:

> How did we arrive at the illusion of utter separation between a primitive 'them' and a civilized 'us'? I believe the answer to be this: Century by century, choice by choice, until by now the separation between 'them' and 'us,' like the separation between the physical world and ourselves, appears to be inevitable. Bit by bit, thread by thread, the West has woven a tapestry in which the primitive, the oceanic, and the feminine have been banished to the margins in order to protect ... the primacy of civilization, masculinity, and the autonomous self.[196]

To banish the illusion of the otherness of the primitive requires us therefore to rediscover *in* our own Western history and *in* our present society those alternative systems of value that we have so long mistakenly thought to belong exclusively to primitives or wrongly believed to be located elsewhere or in another time. Unlike Baudrillard and Lyotard, for whom primitive alterity remains irrecuperable, Torgovnick posits alterity only to remark that it is an illusion, since the primitive is ultimately no different from us. In fact we don't really even need the empirical primitive Other. As Torgovnick observes in her analysis of Lévi-Strauss: '[The primitive] may not exist and probably does not – but it is essential to act as though it does.'[197] We may need the idea of the primitive, but we do not require real, live primitives. We can have a primitivism without primitives since we already know what it is to have 'gone primitive.' Torgovnick's critique of Western primitivism ends up not dissolving primitivism but deepening and generalizing it, turning it into a universally present need.

3 Culture: Marshall Sahlins

Sahlins, Captain Cook, and the Apotheosis of Culture

This chapter will explore the ramifications of Gayatri Spivak's insightful remark that culture can be viewed in two ways: 'culture as a battle cry against one culture's claim to Reason as such ...; and culture as a nice name for the exoticism of the outsiders.'[1] In the first view, the relativization of culture combats ethnocentrism by questioning any one culture's claim to possess universal reason. In this sense, culture can be mobilized against evolutionary primitivism's ranking of peoples according to their achieved level of rationality. The concept of culture can thus be seen as anti-primitivist in spirit. In the second view, culture becomes an euphemism for the exoticist project of 'othering,' that is, of constructing difference as a way of affirming one's identity. According to this second conception, the modern culture of the West stands in contrast to indigenous or local cultures elsewhere that are still linked to their premodern traditions. Such a view returns us to a primitivist binary logic that opposes the modern, capitalist world-system to the particular, localized world views of cultures yet to be modern. The culture concept thus resembles an anti-primitivist primitivism in that its critique of primitivist ethnocentrism results in the renewal of primitivist othering. Culture becomes a neo-primitivism that supports the resistance of non-Western indigenous groups (the 'primitives' of old) against the cultural imperialism of the modern West. As Robert Borofsky explains, culture is seen

> as antagonistic to certain historical developments in Europe ...Culture (or cultures), in this sense, involves styles of life and learning that run counter to the negative effects of modernization. This perspective remains common

> among anthropologists: culture is often portrayed as the beliefs or behaviors people retain despite interaction with the 'West.' [Marshall] Sahlins, for example, refers to 'culturalism' as 'the claim to one's own mode of existence ... in opposition to a foreign-imperial presence.'[2]

To understand 'culturalism' as a neo-primitivist affirmation of primordial cultural survivals that resist a globalizing modernity, we will examine the work of the anthropologist singled out by Borofsky, Marshall Sahlins. Though the word 'culture' (rather than 'primitivism' or 'neo-primitivism') dominates this chapter's discussion of Sahlins's work, it should be kept in mind that it is a 'nice name' that nevertheless retains a deep primitivist logic. We will begin by describing the 'culture war' initiated by Sahlins's interpretation of the apotheosis and death of Captain James Cook in Hawaii.

When Captain Cook sailed into Kealakekua Bay on 17 January 1779, little did he know that he was sailing into a Hawaiian cosmological drama in which he would be the main protagonist. Cook was not aware that he was, in Sahlins's words, 'a tradition for Hawaiians before he was a fact.'[3] In several essays and book chapters published in the seventies and eighties, Sahlins, the anthropologist most cited in anthropology journals according to one source,[4] argued, in characteristically bold fashion, that Cook's alleged reception by the Hawaiians as a manifestation of Lono, their god of fertility and agriculture, can be verified by correlating Cook's arrival, sojourn, and death in Hawaii to indigenous cosmological or cultural categories.

Returning to the Hawaiian Islands after failing to find the North West passage, Cook and the crews of the *Resolution* and *Discovery* arrived off Maui on 26 November 1778, and then proceeded, in a slow and leisurely manner, to circumnavigate the island of Hawaii before anchoring at Kealakekua Bay on 17 January of the new year. Cook's arrival in November and his protracted clockwise circling of Hawaii island, with the coastline to his ship's right, appears to have matched in date and direction the annual Makahiki celebration honouring Lono's seasonal advent, an occasion during which an image of Lono – 'a cross-piece ensign, with white tapa cloth hanging from the horizontal bar'[5] – is carried in ceremonial procession in a 'right [hand] circuit' of the island. Sahlins argues that though the 'correlation between the ritual movements of the Makahiki image of Lono and the historical movements of Captain Cook in 1778–79 was not perfect, ... it was sufficiently remarkable'[6] that Hawaiians, already myth-minded and ritually primed, greeted and apotheosized

Cook as their god Lono. In short, the remarkable coincidence of dates and movements allowed Hawaiians to incorporate Cook's foreignness into their familiar ritual observances.

According to the Hawaiian ritual calendar, the popular Makahiki celebrations mark both the ascendancy of the peaceful and bountiful Lono and his eventual defeat and exile through the restitution of the king's war god, Ku. Arriving at Makahiki time, Cook, according to Sahlins, was received joyously by the Hawaiians as Lono and accorded more respect and honour than he had ever experienced on any other South Sea island he had visited. After a stay of some eighteen days, Cook and his ships left Hawaii island on 3 February 1779, right on ritual schedule. The Makahiki had ended and it was time for Lono to exit, ceding paramountcy once again to the war god Ku and his human representative, the king. Unfortunately, Cook's ships, soon after departure, ran into a storm that damaged the foremast of the *Resolution*, forcing Cook to sail back to Kealakekua Bay on 11 February. This time Cook-Lono's return was out of phase with the ritual cycle. He was, as Sahlins puts it, '*hors cadre*.'[7] Moreover, Cook-Lono's return precipitated a 'mythopolitical crisis,'[8] since it now evoked another cosmological myth that recounted how Hawaiian kingship or chieftainship was achieved through usurpation when a foreign chief with his patron god Kukailimoku (Ku-snatcher-of-the-island) came by sea from an invisible land (Kahiki) and conquered the local indigenous rulers.[9] The current king, Kalani'opu'u, and his chiefs, who traced their lineage to the usurping foreign chief, thus interpreted Cook-Lono's return as a sinister, cosmological reversal in which the indigenous god identified with the land's fertility, arriving by sea at an inappropriate time, now threatened to 'reopen the whole issue of sovereignty.'[10] Out of ritual cycle, the returned Lono-Cook must have appeared to the Hawaiian ruling class as a potential usurper, and when Cook took Kalani'opu'u hostage on 14 February 1779 in order to force the return of the *Discovery*'s cutter, which had been stolen by a native chief the previous day, the threat of usurpation became real. The crisis erupted into a violent scuffle that resulted in the deaths of Cook, four marines, and seventeen Hawaiians. The violence that led to Cook's death can be explained, according to Sahlins, as a ritual solution to the cosmological crisis occasioned by Cook-Lono's out-of-season return. Thus, Cook's death is described as 'the ritual sequel' to his earlier apotheosis; his fate becomes 'the historical metaphor of a mythical reality.'[11] A 'ritual inversion' occurs in which the ominous myth of the usurper chief, suggested by Lono-Cook's surprising return, is transformed to fit the mythic pattern in which Lono is defeated and turned into a sacrificial victim by his cosmic adversaries Ku and Ku's representative, the king. As Sahlins describes it, 'transformed from the divine beneficiary of the sacrifice to its victim, ... Cook's body would be offered in sacrifice by the Hawaiian King.'[12] Invoking Hawaiian cosmology, Sahlins is thus able to make sense of the confusion surrounding Cook's death on the morning of 14 February: 'For, in all the confused Tolstoian narratives of the affray ... the one recurrent certainty is a dramatic structure with the properties of a ritual transformation.'[13] To Sahlins, the different recorded accounts of Cook's arrival, reception, and eventual death can be shown to reflect a single meaningful structure when they are interpreted according to native cosmological and cultural schemes.

Though Sahlins's thesis of Cook's apotheosis and ritual death proved convincing to many anthropologists, it was not accepted by all. Jonathan Friedman, for example, in a review of Sahlins's *Islands of History*, which has a chapter on Cook as a Frazerian 'dying god,' criticized the book's structuralist methodology for promoting a form of cultural determinism that subordinates all historical and social practices to mythic or cosmological structures.[14] In another article, published in 1988, Friedman's students and colleagues at Copenhagen, Bergendorff, Hasager, and Henriques, questioned the historical evidence of Sahlins's thesis by arguing that the Makahiki festival in the form described by Sahlins appeared later in Hawaiian history, well after Cook's death.[15]

Sahlins responded rather testily at some length to both these critiques,[16] and there the matter would have rested, a heated scholarly exchange in the recondite pages of specialist journals. But in 1992, Gananath Obeyesekere, a senior and eminent anthropologist from Princeton, published *The Apotheosis of Captain Cook*, which, according to one critic, blew 'a post-colonial whistle' on Sahlins's theory.[17] Obeyesekere posed some of the same questions raised by Friedman and company, such as whether the Makahiki festival, during Cook's visit, occurred in the form described by Sahlins and whether Cook was recognized by Hawaiians as their god Lono or merely installed as a chief possessed of sacred powers. At the same time, however, Obeyesekere pursued his case against Sahlins, not just by questioning his methodology or his scholarship but also by accusing him of a Eurocentric view of Hawaiians in particular and non-Western natives in general that deprives them of reflexive agency, of the ability to think critically rather than just mythically. Hawaiians, Obeyesekere argued, were not so blinded by their myths that they could not distinguish a British naval captain and his crew from their own gods. The apotheosis of Cook was thus not a Hawaiian myth but a Western myth of the long run based on the idea of the redoubtable European who is a god to savage peoples.[18] In short, Obeyesekere positioned Sahlins as a primitivist who projected onto Hawaiians the Western myth of native irrationality, cognitive inflexibility, and cultural rigidity.

Published in a decade noted for its political-correctness debates, Obeyesekere's book with its polemical, post-colonial attack on one of the most distinguished members of the American anthropological establishment attracted many reviews, mostly favourable.[19] It was also awarded the Louis Gottschalk Prize by the American Society for Eighteenth Century Studies. Stung by the accusation of Eurocentrism and by the favourable reception of Obeyesekere's book, which he regarded as presenting 'a flimsy historical case,' Sahlins, in his own words, 'felt an obligation' to publish a response. Originally he had intended to write a pamphlet with a suitable eighteenth-century title: 'Natives versus Anthropologists; Or, How Gananath Obeyesekere Turned the Hawaiians into Bourgeois Realists on the Grounds They Were "Natives" Just Like Sri Lankans, in Opposition to Anthropologists and Other Prisoners of Western Mythical Thinking.'[20] But apparently the essay grew and Sahlins settled for a longer book with a shorter title: *How 'Natives' Think: About Captain Cook, for Example.* The book is an angry point-by-point rebuttal of Obeyesekere's case against the apotheosis thesis. In its impressive command of historical details, its remarkable erudition, its fierce wit and sharpness of argument, Sahlins's book constitutes both a formidable defence against and a ferocious counter-attack on Obeyesekere's criticisms. As his originally intended eighteenth-century title indicates, Sahlins deftly turns the charge of Eurocentrism back on Obeyesekere himself. Obeyesekere, in arguing that Hawaiians were not primitives deluded by their pre-logical myths into apotheosizing a white stranger, had endowed them with the instrumental, empiricist rationality of the West. In doing so, Sahlins notes, Obeyesekere ironically inverts his anti-ethnocentrism into a more encompassing and insidious ethnocentrism, with Hawaiians acting like European bourgeois rationalists and Western scholars 'slavishly repeat[ing] the irrational beliefs of their ancestors'[21] that 'natives' regard them as gods. Thus, Sahlins not only denies being an ethnocentric primitivist, he reverses and redirects the charge of primitivism back on Obeyesekere, accusing him of being covertly Eurocentric in assimilating Hawaiian difference into the likeness of the West. But, as we shall see, Sahlins's line of argument leads him to take a neo-primitivist turn.

Though he critiques the view that ranks European rationality above native culture, Sahlins nevertheless insists on the radical difference between the West and the rest, thereby reinforcing one of the main axioms of primitivism: the Other must always remain exotic. Moreover, as we will also see, Sahlins's neo-primitivism defends the difference of native cultures in order to affirm the universality of anthropological knowledge. As David Scott has observed: '[C]ulture, as ground and horizon of difference, is merely the most recent way of conceiving and explaining otherness, of putting otherness in its place.'[22]

With the publication of Sahlins's book it became clear not only to anthropologists but also to others in the scholarly community that an important debate was under way. Reviewed in influential non-specialist journals such as the *New York Review of Books* and the *London Review of Books* by intellectual heavyweights like Clifford Geertz and Ian Hacking, the Obeyesekere-Sahlins exchange gained a wide audience, partly no doubt because the spectacle of academic blood-letting can set some pulses racing.[23] But beyond the noise and fury, the Obeyesekere-Sahlins debate pushes into view, as Clifford Geertz astutely notes,

> some of the most central and most divisive issues in anthropological study. After one reads these two having at one another up, down, and sideways for five hundred lapel-grabbing pages or so, whatever happened to Cook, and why, seems a good deal less important, and probably less determinable, than the questions they raise about how it is we are to go about making sense of the acts and emotions of distant peoples in remote times. What does 'knowing' about 'others' properly consist in? Is it possible? Is it good?[24]

Despite the anger and pettiness that often threaten to overshadow their dispute, both Sahlins and Obeyesekere, to their credit, recognize that their work addresses larger issues of methodology, epistemology, and ethics and how these affect the discipline of anthropology. Thus, Sahlins states that the 'bygone events and remote practices at issue in Captain Cook's death assume a certain interest for an anthropology sensitive to the character and variety of forms of life.'[25] He also acknowledges that the 'debate over Cook ... can be situated in a larger historical context, an intellectual struggle [between cultural particularism and empiricist universalism] of some two centuries that probably has greater significance for most readers than the petty academic blood sports.'[26] Similarly, in an afterword wittily entitled 'On De-Sahlinization,' published in the second edition of *The Apotheosis of Captain Cook* as a response to Sahlins's counter-attack, Obeyesekere agrees that the debate is more than a dispute over Cook's death and that it touches on fundamental anthropological concepts. He points out that Sahlins addresses 'an important section of the discipline that has developed the ideal of cultural and ethical relativism as the charter myth for a special kind of ethnography that plays on difference and the uniqueness of cultures and is hostile to any form of [universalist] "essentialism."'[27] It is against Sahlins's 'doctrine of cultural relativism' that Obeyesekere's efforts are directed, since it is no paradox, to him, 'to make the claim that cultural differences can co-exist with family resemblances and structural similarities. It is cultural relativism that inhibits that recognition.'[28]

Despite their differences, Sahlins and Obeyesekere are thus agreed that the debate over Cook's death is centrally related to the issue most fundamental to the discipline of anthropology, namely, that of understanding culture, especially the culture of others. My discussion of the Obeyesekere-Sahlins debate will therefore focus primarily on the issue of culture. Let me state at the outset that it is not my intention to adjudicate between the combatants and declare a winner; in matters of intellectual debate, better understanding rather than choosing a winner should be our aim. Nor do I intend to scrutinize in detail all the points of contention between Obeyesekere and Sahlins; these can be followed in their respective books, and the task of ethnographic and historical verification is best left to specialists in Polynesian or Hawaiian studies. I will, however, examine closely a number of the disputed details, as these become relevant to our enquiry into the central role of culture in the debate.

Culture, in the classic anthropological sense, describes a specific form of life, that is, the distinctive set of shared beliefs and practices of a group of people. In this sense, as a description of a particular way of life in a world made up of many groups of people, culture becomes a statement about diversity, about distinct ways of life. In short, to talk about culture is always to talk in the plural about cultures and, thus, about cultural differences and cultural relativism. Culture can be seen, therefore, in Lila Abu-Lughod's words as 'the essential tool for making other' and, as such,

> culture is important to anthropology because the anthropological distinction between self and other rests on it ... As a professional discourse that elaborates on the meaning of culture in order to account for, explain, and understand cultural difference, anthropology also helps construct, pro-

> duce, and maintain it. Anthropological discourse gives cultural difference (and the separation between groups of people it implies) the air of the self-evident.[29]

In a more historical vein, George Stocking points to the shift from E.B. Tylor's nineteenth-century view of 'culture' as part of an evolutionary argument to modern anthropology's use of 'culture' to describe non-hierarchical and diverse ways of life: 'Tylor's actual usage of the term "culture" lacked a number of the features commonly associated with the modern anthropological concept: historicity, integration, behavioural determinism, relativity, and – most symptomatically – plurality. For though it is still spoken of as the "science of culture," modern anthropology might be more accurately characterized as the "science of cultures."'[30] Similarly, Bernard McGrane, in his survey of Western concepts of otherness, comes to the conclusion that only in the late nineteenth and early twentieth centuries does difference become synonymous with culture: '*Culture accounts for difference*, rather than "evolution," "progress," evolutionary development through fixed stages of progressive civilization, as in the nineteenth century; rather than the various possible modalities of "ignorance" and "superstition" as with the Enlightenment; and rather than the demonical and infernal as with the Renaissance.'[31]

It is important to note that the modern anthropological concept of culture as the non-hierarchical sign of the plurality and relativity of difference is an improvement over earlier binary or evolutionary schemes that ranked difference between groups according to innate characteristics or stages of development. Lila Abu-Lughod usefully reminds us that

> [u]nlike race, and unlike even the nineteenth-century sense of culture as a synonym for civilization (contrasted to barbarism), the current concept [of culture] allows for multiple rather than binary differences. This immediately checks the easy move to hierarchizing; the shift to 'culture' ... has a relativizing effect. The most important of culture's advantages, however, is that it removes difference from the realm of the natural and the innate.[32]

Inasmuch as culture is taken to be relative and arbitrary in diverse ways and not universal and naturally determined in a singular manner, its adoption allows anthropologists to avoid ethnocentrism and remain anti-essentialist. In North America, such a view of culture was promoted and institutionalized by Franz Boas and his students in the early years of the twentieth century. It is this influential Boasian concept of culture, anti-ethnocentric in its relativism and anti-essentialist in its non-naturalism, that is at stake in the Obeyesekere-Sahlins debate with the former questioning the relativism of the culture concept and the latter defending it.

In *How 'Natives' Think*, his reply to Obeyesekere, Sahlins acknowledges that the fate of culture is central to the debate on Cook's apotheosis and death. Sahlins astutely situates the debate in the context of a larger historical struggle between the Enlightenment principle of universal 'civilization' and 'the anthropological concept of culture as a specific form of life,'[33] which originated in German romantic thought. While McGrane sees the anthropological concept of culture as emerging in the late nineteenth or early twentieth century, Sahlins pushes it back to the eighteenth century and shows how German intellectuals used it to oppose the idea of 'civilization' propounded by the imperial powers of Western Europe, like England and France.

Singled out by Sahlins as the most notable of these counter-Enlightenment thinkers, Johann Gottfried von Herder, for example, 'opposed ways of life to stages of development and a social mind to natural reason. Unlike "civilization," which was transferable between peoples (as by a beneficent imperialism), culture was what truly identified and differentiated a people ... Culture came in kinds, not degrees; in the plural, not the singular.'[34] Since cultures are different in kind and not degree and each culture embodies a distinct way of life, it would be unjust to compare different national cultures with a view to ranking them. On the contrary, one can argue that their belief in what constitutes perfection or the good life or their idea of what is right or wrong can be judged only in accordance with their own unique standards or values. 'Each nation,' Herder writes, 'has its own centre of happiness within itself, just as every sphere has its own centre of gravity.'[35]

In approaching other cultures we must therefore adopt a relativistic stance lest we commit the error of assuming as universal reason what is merely local belief. According to Herder, we must guard against the Enlightenment *philosophes*' 'creation of an abstract cosmopolitanism, a "paper culture" predicated upon an idealized conception of eighteenth century European cultural life.'[36] The Enlightenment belief in progressive universalism turns out to be only the arrogant benevolence of European ethnocentrism. '[T]he general philosophical, philanthropic tone of our century,' Herder writes, 'wishes to extend our own ideal of virtue and happiness to each distant nation, to even the remotest age of history.'[37] Herder can thus assert (and Sahlins cites him approvingly) that '[o]nly a real misanthrope could regard European culture as the universal condition of our species.'[38] The exposure of the natural or the universal as merely the claim of a particular culture leads Herder to conclude that our knowledge of the world must invariably be mediated by our culture. Elaborating on Herder's concept of culture, Sahlins points out that we know what we know only through the categories afforded by our culture:

> [P]eople do not simply discover the world, they are taught it. They come to it not simply as cognitions but as values. To speak of reasoning correctly on objective properties known through unmediated sensory perceptions would be epistemologically out of the question. Seeing is also a function of hearing, a *judgement*, and in the economy of thought ... reason is invested with feeling and bound to imagination. It follows that the senses are culturally variable.[39]

Agreeing with Herder that our perceptions are culturally informed, Sahlins goes on to cite the German thinker's description of how cultural differences engender different sensory or perceptual sensitivities and accomplishments: 'The North American can trace his enemy by the smell ... the shy Arab hears far in his silent desert ... The shepherd beholds nature with different eyes from those of the fisherman.'[40]

Eighteenth-century *Kultur* theories of the uniqueness of the *Volk* or nation, Sahlins further contends, in a sharp reversal of the suspicion usually directed at such theories of cultural nationalism, can be regarded as precursors of contemporary 'culturalism,' which is described as 'a marked self-consciousness of "culture" [that] is reappearing all over the world among the victims and erstwhile victims of Western domination.'[41] The culture concept championed by counter-Enlightenment thinkers like Herder thus appears as a theory of postcolonial resistance *avant la lettre*. As Sahlins puts it:

> Ojibway Indians in Wisconsin, Kayapo in Brazil, Tibetans, New Zealand Maori, Kashmiris, New Guinea Highland peoples, Zulus, Eskimo, Mongols, Australian Aboriginals, and (yes) Hawaiians: all speak of their 'culture,' using that word or some close local equivalent, as a value worthy of respect, commitment and defense. A response to the planetary juggernaut of Western capitalism, their struggles recreate, if on a wider scale and in more critical form, the opposition to bourgeois-utilitarian reason that first gave rise to an understanding of cultures as distinct forms of life.[42]

Sahlins goes on to comment ironically on the spread of 'a postmodern panic' about the concept of culture precisely at a time when it is experiencing a renaissance among postcolonial populations: 'Just when so many people are announcing the existence of their culture, advanced anthropologists are denying it.'[43] This irony marks, for Sahlins, a crisis of confidence in the discipline of anthropology itself: '"Culture," it seems, is in the twilight of its career, and anthropology with it.'[44] But Sahlins believes that it is premature to mourn anthropology's end; he still wants to praise anthropology not bury it. 'May the owl of Minerva,' he hopes, 'take wing at dusk.' It is the 'afflictions of "culture" that he wishes to confront and overcome when he writes 'of our rationality and Hawaiian belief, and of the remote ideas entailed in the remote death of Captain Cook.'[45] Sahlins's debate with Obeyesekere over Cook's fate and his writings on Hawaiian history and culture thus serve primarily to defend the idea of anthropology as the study of cultural differences. What is crucially at stake is not just the question of historiographic or ethnographic accuracy, but also the very raison d'être of anthropology itself. Without a relativistic concept of cultural difference we would end up with an anti-anthropology, a 'common sense bourgeois realism ... [which] is a kind of symbolic violence done to other times and other customs.'[46] Anthropology must, therefore, always begin by considering 'ideas, actions, and ontologies that are not and never were our own'; guarding against ethnocentric incorporation, its slogan must always be: 'Different cultures, different rationalities.'[47]

The culture concept as formulated by Herder (and later, by Boas) has assumed theoretical centrality in Sahlins's work at least since the publication of *Culture and Practical Reason* in 1976. In that book Sahlins outlines what he sees as the two paradigms of anthropological theory as represented respectively in the work of Lewis Henry Morgan and Franz Boas. The paradigm represented by Morgan regards culture as the codification of human action guided by practical interest in its engagement with natural laws and forces independent of human will. Culture, in this view, is 'an instrumental system' determined by 'the "objective" logic of practical advantage.'[48] Culture is thus the institutional extension of utilitarian naturalism, that is, culture is organized practice based on fundamental human needs that observe the logic of nature. In short, culture in this anthropological paradigm is a form of practical reason in conformity with objective, natural laws.

The Boasian paradigm, by contrast, exalts cultural over practical reason. In the Boasian view, which Sahlins favours, culture is that *tertium quid*, that independent conceptual or symbolic scheme that intervenes and mediates between human action or behaviour and objective material circumstances. As such, culture is determining rather than determined; it is neither constrained by objective necessity nor dictated by natural needs. Opposing the culture concept to practical reason, Sahlins says that his work

> takes as the distinctive quality of man not that he must live in a material world, a circumstance he shares with all organisms, but that he does so according to a meaningful scheme of his own devising, in which capacity mankind is unique. It therefore takes as the decisive quality of culture – as giving each mode of life the properties that characterize it – not that this culture must conform to material constraints but that it does so according to a definite symbolic scheme which is never the only one possible. Hence it is culture which constitutes utility.[49]

Moreover, culture is not only a logic or system that determines and regulates human praxis (that is, the totality of our interactions) with the objective, material world, it is also 'an order that enjoys, by its own properties as a symbolic system, a fundamental autonomy.'[50] But since a culture or symbolic scheme 'is never the only one possible,' its autonomy also strongly suggests relativity and diversity. In *Culture and Practical Reason* we see not only how culture is installed as the central theoretical concept but also how it will be employed in Sahlins's subsequent work. Culture's autonomous and constitutive power will be used to question theories that accept the determinations of empirical and material realism, and its relativized plurality mobilized to challenge universalizing theories based on utilitarian or naturalist explanations.

In agreement with the Herderian/Boasian tradition's view of culture's autonomy and relativity, Sahlins would no doubt assign Obeyesekere to the 'naturalist' tradition represented by Morgan. While Obeyesekere may not approve of such a placement, it is interesting to note that he delivered the 1982 Lewis Henry Morgan lectures at the University of Rochester, subsequently published as *The Work of Culture* in 1990. In that book, Obeyesekere seeks a role for Freudian psychoanalysis in anthropology and in the process addresses the question of whether Freud's description of the Oedipus complex has universal application or whether it is culturally specific. While rejecting the universal status claimed by Freud's own description of the Oedipus complex, Obeyesekere wishes to retain the relevance of a generalized Oedipus complex for an ontology of human desire. He concludes that there is a general Oedipus complex which has a universal 'ontological anchorage'[51] in human nature, though only segments of it appear in different cultures, giving rise to different partial configurations or complexes. Thus, in addition to the Freudian (or Western) Oedipus complex, we may also have the Trobriand Oedipus complex, the Indian-Hindu Oedipus complex, and so on. The Freudian Oedipus is but one form of life, one cultural variant constructed out of the circle of desire that exists in 'the phylogenetically grounded human family.'[52] According to Obeyesekere, one can

> talk of different Oedipus complexes as 'fictions ['fictions' because they are only isolated segments of a more fundamental complex] existing in different cultures, though these fictions are probably limited and exhibit family resemblances to one another. Why so? Because of our common human nature or our basic human behaviours or existential universals or our species being or whatever – a muddy bottom that even Wittgenstein, for all his relativism, was forced to recognize. The ground of this universal human nature is psychobiological: man as a kind of species possessed of a complex brain, relatively freed from the instincts, with a capacity for complex symbolization, especially in language and fantasy.[53]

Obeyesekere attempts to do justice both to the observed differences between cultures as well as to the search for a necessary ontological foundation for the human sciences. He is aware, however, that any ontological foundation for the human sciences cannot be absolute or final in any sense 'since the very historicity of our being prevents that.'[54] At the same time, however, though wary of the 'naive universalism' of positivistic thought, he believes that cultural relativism is untenable, since if each culture can be known only according to its own conceptual scheme there can be no possibility of cross-cultural understanding and thus no point to the anthropological study of culture. Moreover, in seeing culture as a symbolic system rather than a natural phenomenon, relativists must posit a *human* capacity to create symbolic forms, and as a consequence must accept some kind of common human essence or nature.[55] Obeyesekere is therefore careful not to reject either naturalist ontology (Morgan) or culturalist relativity (Boas); while acknowledging difference and historicity, he also accepts the necessity of ontological anchorage in a heuristic assumption, not axiom, of a common human nature.[56]

Obeyesekere's *qualified assumption* of a common human nature informs his quarrel with Sahlins's cultural relativism. In opposition to Sahlins's view that different cultures possess different rationalities, Obeyesekere claims, in *The Apotheosis of Captain Cook*, that practical rationality, 'the process whereby human beings reflectively assess the implications of a problem in terms of practical criteria,'[57] is a pan-human capacity. As he puts it:

> The notion of practical rationality ... links us as human beings to our common biological nature and to perceptual and cognitive mechanisms that are products thereof. These perceptual and cognitive mechanisms are also not 'culture free'; but neither is culture free from them. The fact that my universe is a culturally constituted behavioral environment does not mean I am bound to it in a way that renders discrimination impossible.[58]

Adopting a model of checks and balances, Obeyesekere argues that, under certain circumstances, the determinations of culture have to yield to a pan-human capacity for critical reflexive thought just as common human neurobiology does not necessarily manifest itself in the same uniform way across cultures. In his response to Sahlins's criticism of practical rationality in *How 'Natives' Think*, Obeyesekere reminds us that his notion of a pan-human rationality 'must be emancipated from two erroneous assumptions: namely, that common biology must necessarily produce common culture and the reverse mythopraxical [that is, practices wholly determined by a cosmological or mythological script] assumption that culture is so supreme that it overrides common perceptual and cognitive mechanisms completely. In other words, practical rationality provides spaces for considering both cultural commonalities and differences.'[59]

Sahlins, of course, will have none of this. His strong culturalism will not countenance Obeyesekere's 'weak' or qualified ontology. While Obeyesekere believes that having a common practical rationality allows one to talk of other cultures in human terms, Sahlins says that such a belief results in an 'anti-anthropology': 'Since he [Obeyesekere] opposes this rationality to cultural particularity, the contention here is a pure negation of anthropological knowledge.'[60] Obeyesekere's attempt to balance common practical rationality with cultural differences is rejected by Sahlins, who interprets the former's 'somewhere-in-between'[61] position as dualistic, an opposition rather than balance. Where Obeyesekere sees the possibility of a dialectical relation between a common human nature and cultural variation, Sahlins can see Obeyesekere's pan-human rationality only as denying any role for culture, as being 'in principle independent of any specific cultural or historical knowledge.'[62] In short, Sahlins will have no truck with any theory of human nature no matter how qualified, because for him it is culture that selects and determines in the first place what counts as human nature. Referring to the work of Clifford Geertz, Sahlins reminds us how years ago Geertz had persuasively argued that 'human nature in and of itself is fundamentally indeterminate, that is, without its various cultural specifications.'[63] To Sahlins, therefore, there is no direct universal access to reality, no getting round culture's mediation in all its particularity and relativity. A 'biologically grounded cognitive realism'[64] such as that advocated by Obeyesekere on behalf of a common humanity ironically does a disservice insofar as direct unmediated access to reality disallows human creativity and flexibility by elevating physiological *sensations* over empirical *judgments*, *sense* over *meaning*. As Sahlins argues, 'The biological mechanisms of perception are not in question, nor is their universality. At issue, rather, is the organization of experience, including the training of the senses, according to social canons of relevance ... For things are not only perceived, they are thereby *known*, which is also to say that they are classified.'[65] Biological universality is accepted but seen as unexceptionable by Sahlins. What is more important and absolutely necessary is the work of culture, or, better, cultures, in organizing experience and in selecting, classifying, and constituting what counts as meaning in different human groups. To think otherwise and accept 'Obeyesekere's regressive opposition between a universal empirical reason and particular cultural constructions'[66] is to revert to the empirical position of a Bacon or a Locke and to believe in the possibility of an immediate sensory apprehension of reality, an ethnocentric belief relative to the European Enlightenment and everywhere contradicted by the diversity of human knowledge and practices. As Sahlins remarks with typical sarcastic wit, Obeyesekere's 'antithesis of reason and custom invites us to abandon the anthropology of the later twentieth century for certain philosophical advances of the seventeenth.'[67]

Sahlins's often brilliant exposition and defence of twentieth-century anthropology's culture concept depends largely on three assumptions that need to be examined carefully. These assumptions may be briefly characterized as *holism*, *continuity*, and *relativism*. In what follows, we will see how Sahlins deploys them in his account of Cook's Hawaiian apotheosis and in his subsequent debate with Obeyesekere, and how the elegant explanations they make possible nonetheless raise questions that threaten the very concept of culture Sahlins defends.

'Pensée Sauvage' and Cultural Holism

Cultural holism is implied in the standard anthropological definition of culture as a *whole way of life.* It is important to note, however, that holism is not just about wholeness as the sum of parts, a merely quantitative completion; it is about wholeness as an interconnected, integrated system, a structured unity. In his examination of the origins of the modern anthropological concept of culture, Christopher Herbert points out that

> [c]ulture as such is not ... society's beliefs, customs, moral values, and so forth, added together: it is the wholeness that their coexistence somehow creates or makes manifest ... For theorists of all persuasions, a cultural formation takes its meaning from its involvement in what Darwin, speaking not of culture but of nature, called an 'inextricable web of affinities ...,' and it is this presumption that renders the various elements of a way of life systematically *readable* just as the notion of organic unity in literary texts rendered them readable according to the norms of the discipline of 'new criticism.'[68]

The metaphor of culture as a complex, interconnected web and the notion that it is systematically readable are important characteristics of cultural holism and can be found in the work of influential anthropologists such as E.E. Evans-Pritchard and Clifford Geertz. Evans-Pritchard, for example, in his famous study of Zande witchcraft, furnished a classic statement of cultural integration in which the web metaphor appears: '[A]ll their beliefs hang together ... In this web of belief every strand depends upon every other strand, and a Zande cannot get out of its meshes because this is the only world he knows. The web is not an external structure in which he is enclosed. It is the texture of his thought and he cannot think that his thought is wrong.'[69] Similarly, Geertz, though acknowledging that 'coherence cannot be the major test of validity for a cultural description,'[70] employs the web metaphor in describing culture: 'Believing, with Max Weber, that man is an animal suspended in webs of significance he himself has spun, I take culture to be those webs, and the analysis of it to be therefore not an experimental science in search of law but an interpretive one in search of meaning.'[71] In his search for meaning, Geertz further transforms the culture-as-web metaphor into that of culture as 'an ensemble of texts ... which the anthropologist strains to read over the shoulders of those to whom they properly belong.'[72] If cultures are likened to texts, then, like texts, they must exhibit enough intelligibility, that is, have enough coherence of meaning, to be readable. Thus, though he does not underestimate the 'enormous difficulties'[73] of the interpretive process, his classic essay on the Balinese cockfight provides an example of cultural holism, showing how an aspect of Balinese life, the popular cockfight, draws together 'almost every level of Balinese experience ... – animal savagery, male narcissism, opponent gambling, status rivalry, mass excitement, blood sacrifice – ... [and binds] them into a set of rules, ... a symbolic structure in which ... the reality of their inner affiliation can be intelligibly felt.'[74]

The culture concept thus appears to depend on cultural holism; the presumption of cultural integration becomes the enabling condition for cultural intelligibility. Such an argument was explicitly advanced, for example, by one of Boas's students, Ruth Benedict, who stated that to deny cultural holism would be 'to renounce the possibility of intelligent interpretation.'[75] Similarly, Sahlins believes that culture must be studied in holistic terms. In *Culture and Practical Reason*, for example, he criticizes the differentiation of the cultural order into subsystems serving different purposes like the satisfaction of material needs or the maintenance of social relations between persons or groups. Such differentiations ignore 'the unity and distinctiveness of culture as a symbolic structure.'[76] In other words, for Sahlins, culture is not a thing of shreds and patches made up of different functions and needs, economic and practical here, social and religious there. Culture is a total symbolic structure or meaningful system that 'defines all functionality'[77] and constitutes all that we know of the world. Culture, defined in this way, becomes cosmology, a society's fundamental belief system. Such a view of culture as cosmology guides Sahlins's analysis of how Captain Cook became 'a tradition for Hawaiians before he was a fact.'[78]

Without such a cosmological or holistic concept of culture, we will understand neither the Hawaiians nor what they made of Cook. Or as Sahlins puts it in a somewhat abstract vein: 'Even to understand what did happen, it would be insufficient to note that certain people acted in certain ways, unless we also knew what that signified. The contingent becomes fully historical only as it is meaningful: only as the personal act or the ecological effect takes on a systematic or positional value in a cultural scheme. An historical presence is a cultural existence.'[79] In other words, culture is holistic precisely because it is that all-encompassing scheme which confers order and meaning to our life-world.

To be sure, Sahlins is aware that in any given culture we will find differences in ideas, interests, belief, and action. Thus, he concedes that 'it need not be supposed that all Hawaiians were equally convinced that Cook was Lono, or, more precisely, that his being "Lono" meant the same thing to everyone.'[80] Sahlins's concession to intracultural differences is, however, carefully qualified; the statement that not all Hawaiians thought Cook was Lono loses much of its constative force when we are told that it would be more precise to say that Cook *was accepted* as the god Lono even if that acceptance meant different things to different people. In other words, Sahlins prefers to think of differences as occurring within the framework of a collective whole, in the context of a holistic culture. Consider, for example, his explanation of how differences of opinion in Hawaiian society over what to make of Cook's visit were prevailed upon by the powers-that-be to conform to cosmological belief in Cook as the returned Lono. Sahlins points out that Hawaiian women who were physically intimate with the British sailors quickly realized the humanity of the visitors. The religious enthusiasm shown by those who welcomed Cook 'may not have been shared by the entire population, especially the people working priestly estates on the rich agricultural zones upland of Kealakekua.'[81] These differences of opinion and interpretation were, however, quickly normalized, brought into line with cultural cosmology by the Hawaiian authorities. As Sahlins explains:

> They could bring a whole set of schemes to bear in support of their cosmological opinions, including the controls on land and people that eventuated in a great flow of offerings – presented always in the appropriate ritual form – to Cook, as well as provisions to his company. Whatever the people in general were thinking, they were thus made practically and materially tributary to the religion of Lono of which the priests of Kealakekua were the legitimate prophets.[82]

One can argue, of course, that the authorities' pragmatic manipulation or management of the people's opinions and actions reflects not so much the strength of cultural holism as its insufficiency. I will return to this point later, but for now it should be noted that a certain uneasiness remains in Sahlins's attempt to minimize Hawaiian differences. For instance, though he stresses, in *Islands of History* and *How 'Natives' Think*, the critical role played by the authorities in normalizing interpretation, in 'Captain Cook at Hawaii,' an article Sahlins sees as his 'most extensive and best-documented argument,'[83] he appears to forward a contradictory explanation that rejects ruling-class manipulation in favour of a collective, popular response to Cook's appearance. The celebration attending Cook's arrival, according to Sahlins, 'was spontaneous and popular, not just something whipped up by the powers-that-were at Kealakekua ... Nor will we get historical information on the cheap from some *a priori* and tired ideas about how the ruling classes dupe the masses. On the contrary, the Hawaiian celebration of Cook as Lono was from the beginning a collective movement.'[84] Was the Hawaiian reception of Cook an imposed acceptance or a spontaneous collective celebration? The irresolution reflects, I think, a tension in Sahlins's thought between an uneasy acknowledgment of differences in Hawaiian culture and an anxious desire to defend the concept of cultural holism.

A similar tension surfaces in Sahlins's response to Obeyesekere's description of a Hawaiian chief who approached the British with ethnographic curiosity rather than the expected reverence. Obeyesekere produces this example to illustrate the point that Hawaiians were not unanimous in recognizing Cook as their god Lono, and therefore that one cannot assume cultural holism or uniformity among them.[85] While acknowledging that the chief's secular curiosity may be construed as a counter-example to cultural holism, Sahlins nonetheless asserts that the chief's desire to understand British lifeways and to see 'Brittanee' for himself can occur only in the larger context of Hawaiian cosmology in which the foreign is equated with the divine. Sahlins informs us that 'Insofar as "Brittanee" is encompassed in the Hawaiian conception of Kahiki, the overseas sources of the gods, the meaning of these inquiries is not self-evident.'[86] But if the meaning is not self-evident, this may be because the only meaning Sahlins will allow is one already determined in advance by the cosmological scheme. Conversely, it is not self-evident that the meaning of the chief's inquiries can be explained solely by native cosmology, since this would require us to believe that human action is totally predetermined or pre-programmed, a rigid determinism even Sahlins would repudiate.

Sahlins finds himself entangled in contradiction or pushed to equivocation because he chooses to defend a strong version of cultural holism. He adopts such a stance partly in reaction to a recent trend in anthropological studies, highly critical of the culture concept, that seeks, in Lila Abu-Lughod's words, to write against culture.[87] Of this postmodern or post-structuralist trend, Sahlins has this to say (and I quote him at some length in order to convey something of the sharp wit of his polemic):

> [W]e are not soon likely to hear an end to poststructuralist litanies about the contested and unstable character of cultural logics: about categories and perceptions that are different for women and men, chiefs and commoners, rich and poor, this village and that, yesterday and today. All the same, not everything in the contest is contested – which once more proves that we come here to paraphrase Durkheim, not to bury him. As polyphonic or heteroglossic as the monograph may be, one cannot legitimately insert a Japanese 'voice' in a Sioux Indian ethnography. In order for categories to be contested at all, there must be a common system of intelligibility, extending to the grounds, means, modes, and issues of disagreement. It would be difficult to understand how a society could function, let alone how any knowledge of it could be constituted, if there were not some meaningful order *in* the differences. If in regard to some given event or phenomenon the women of a community say one thing and the men another, is it not because men and women have different positions in, and experience of, the same social universe of discourse? ... If so, there is a noncontradictory way – dare one say, a totalizing way? – of describing the contradictions, a system of and in the differences.[88]

There are several things to be said about Sahlins's defence of cultural integrity or coherence. He is right to remind us that to recognize differences we need to have a common system of intelligibility. But what if that system or scheme of intelligibility is precisely what is in question? In other words, Sahlins assumes that for cultural differences or cultural contestation to exist there must be a coherent cultural system or scheme. What he does not consider, however, is how this cultural system came to be in the first place and how it has managed to structure differences so as to achieve coherence. To take Sahlins's example of Sioux Indian ethnography, while we may agree that no Japanese 'voice' is present in Sioux culture, this does not allow us to conclude that a bounded and coherent Sioux culture therefore exists unproblematically. We must not turn what is at issue – is there a Sioux culture and how is it coherent? – into a necessary presupposition – there is a Sioux culture that can comprehend Sioux differences but not Japanese ones. Similarly, to assert that different responses by men and women can occur only within a common social framework is to accept as given what may precisely be in dispute, namely, how this common framework came to be in place, how the term 'common' is defined and which party the definition favours.

The problem is that Sahlins believes that 'cultural life is both natural and presupposed,'[89] and this belief allows him to assume that system precedes difference, that Sioux culture exists prior to its being contested and that a common social universe is the enabling condition for differences between men and women. Such assumptions, however, can be seen as a case of putting the cart or the Hocart (to emulate a Sahlins witticism)[90] before the horse, that is, of putting the formed system ahead of its contested formation.

By affirming the priority of cultural system, Sahlins can de-emphasize, if not ignore, the specific political and material conditions that account for the system, especially since the system's priority allows it to account for those conditions as already culturally determined. What we have, therefore, is a questionable theory of culture as a self-determined system similar to that described by Talal Asad with reference to Edmund Leach's anthropological classic *Political Systems of Highland Burma*: 'the theory which gives logical priority to the system of authentic meaning supposedly shared by an ideologically-defined community and independent of the political activity and economic conditions of its members.'[91] Culture is supposedly a community's shared system of meaning; but since it also exists prior to and independent of the community, it can only be defined relative to itself: culture is what culture says it is. Such a concept of culture may be unassailable as tautology but its very unassailability makes it questionable as theory. Its presence in Sahlins's writings on Hawaiian culture is problematic. Sahlins gives logical priority, as we have seen, to a cosmological system that not only organizes the categories of Hawaiian culture and history but also sets the terms by which discussions about Hawaiians (or by Hawaiians) must proceed. To be sure, he acknowledges, as we have also seen, the persistence of social differences and political and ideological contestation in Hawaiian society. But these differences and conflicts are quickly shown to be contained in a pre-existing cosmological scheme that constitutes and confers significance on the differences in the first place. So again what we have is a tautological argument in which an a priori holistic cultural scheme lays the grounds for its own pervasive presence in Hawaiian life.

Sahlins's cultural holism poses other difficulties. A strong champion of intercultural differences, Sahlins minimizes differences intraculturally. A confirmed relativist when it comes to describing differences between cultures, he becomes an absolutist when it comes to affirming culture in the singular, for at this level differences are made to yield to a total cultural cosmology. We shall return to this contradiction when we examine Sahlins's cultural relativism later.

Another difficulty arises when we ask whether a holistic view of culture is held by everyone in a community and whose interests such a view would serve. Cultural holism supposes the possibility that all the different components, rules, and beliefs of a culture may be comprehended as an interrelated, coherent whole, that a culture's total pattern may be understood. But it is hard to believe that most people possess such a comprehensive understanding of their culture or go about their daily lives with a total cultural cosmology in the forefront of their consciousness. Ethnographic evidence certainly supports the view that the 'high' culture of cosmological or religious beliefs is often not a factor in people's everyday lives. Thus, among the Shilluck of the upper Nile, as Geoffrey Lienhardt has pointed out,

> cosmological ideas ... are not systematized by the people themselves, who reveal them only by their sayings and their behaviour. It is impossible to give an account of them without abstracting from the reality, formulating them as ideas with a certain degree of coherence between them, and thus constructing a system which has no exact counterpart in the thought of the Shilluck themselves.[92]

In another study which seeks to show that daily life is not ruled solely by cosmological or religious beliefs, W. van Beek points out that 'Dogon religion is not all-pervasive. Most of agriculture, most of daily interactions between people, be it at family level or elsewhere, is lived without any reference whatsoever to religious matters. There is a tendency to define religious issues as an occupation for old men.'[93] If a holistic view of culture is not central to the transactions of daily life, then who would advocate it and for what reason? It serves first of all to uphold the authority and power of the knowledge specialists and leaders of a community. Dogon religious issues, we are told, are the occupation of the elders. Similarly, we recall Sahlins's description of how the cosmological view of Lono's return was invoked by the priests and chiefs to interpret Cook's arrival and how they were able to impose this interpretation on the Hawaiian populace. A holistic view can therefore serve as an ideological justification for rule. A cosmological account of culture is a form of knowledge-power that confers authority on those who employ it.

As a discourse of authority, cultural holism may be invoked not only by 'insiders' – the knowledge specialists and the religious and political elite of a community – it may also be used to justify the ethnographic work of 'outsider' anthropologists. Sahlins states the importance of cultural holism for securing ethnographic authority in this way:

> [A]s an intersubjective field of which the people concerned have different social experiences and local perceptions, a cultural life in its complexity, let alone in its totality, involves reasons and relationships that no one who lives it can be expected to express. Significant differences (heteroglossia) there will always be ... But the important anthropological question is, *Are there any significant relationships in and of the differences?* Moreover, given that any such cultural life is both natural and presupposed, neither can those living it be expected to give an adequate account of why they say what they are saying or do what they are doing. One may relate why one fought in the Viet Nam war, but this is no explanation of why there was a war. One can give reasons for marrying this or that person, but such is no explanation of monogamy. All this is an argument *for* what postmodern anthropology has made us allergic to: ethnographic authority, the so-called construction of the other. A better phrasing would be *construing the other.*[94]

It is clear from what Sahlins says that ethnographic authority is achieved only by the anthropologist who trains his panoptic, structuralist gaze on the whole of cultural life and grasps how differences constitute a significant cultural order. But note that while authoritative knowledge of culture is not expected of those who live in it, possession of such holistic knowledge is what justifies anthropology as a discipline. While acknowledging the dangers of 'Orientalism or some such imperialist conceit,'[95] Sahlins's division of the field of knowledge into anthropologists who know and natives of whatever culture who live and act as through a glass darkly has not significantly advanced beyond Evans-Pritchard's claim, made freely in an era untroubled by post-colonial theory, that the social anthropologist 'discovers in a native society what no native can explain to him and what no layman, however conversant with the culture, can perceive – its basic structure.'[96] What is surprising is that Sahlins, one of the most scrupulously anti-ethnocentric and relativistic anthropologists around, should harbour a lingering positivism when it comes to achieving total ethnographic knowledge of another society. (I shall return to this paradox in Sahlins's thought in my concluding section on his cultural relativism.) Aiming for nothing less than an understanding of culture as a structured whole, Sahlins has little patience with what Malinowski famously called the 'imponderabilia of everyday life.'[97] He will have nothing to do with 'the currently fashionable idea that there is nothing usefully called "a culture."'[98]

Yet while Sahlins is right to worry about extreme postmodernist exaltations of the indeterminate and the fragmentary, his own position on cultural holism is equally immoderate. 'Either anthropology or the Tower of Babel,' he declares.[99] Surely this is a little too melodramatic. To express doubt as to whether a total cultural cosmology enters into every aspect of our lives or determines every action we take is not to abandon anthropology or the culture concept for some postmodern chaos. For Sahlins the only ethnography worth having is an ethnography of the whole. But an ethnography of the whole, however carefully qualified, as in Sahlins's account of eighteenth-century Hawaii, cannot but settle on the deep structures and cosmological schemes that help to define the unity of a culture. In the process, homogeneity, coherence, and the regularity of rule are privileged over the less systemic, less rule-bound particularities of everyday life and practice. Ethnographies of the particular are also necessary, Lila Abu-Lughod argues, to rectify the defects of generalization present in an ethnography of the whole. She points out that an ethnography that focuses closely 'on particular individuals and their changing relationships' allows us to understand human experiences that would otherwise be flattened or smoothed to fit the cultural paradigm. As she reminds us: 'Individuals are confronted with choices, struggle with others, make conflicting statements, argue about points of view on the same events, undergo ups and downs in various relationships and changes in their circumstances and desires, face new pressures, and fail to predict what will happen to them or those around them.'[100] Focusing on the life of an old Bedouin matriarch who is both pious and profane, observant of both tradition and custom yet sympathetic to the young who transgress social and religious codes, Abu-Lughod concludes that 'it becomes difficult to think that the term "Bedouin culture" makes sense when one tries to piece together and convey what life is like for [her].'[101] Similarly, in conducting fieldwork among the Karo Bataks of northern Sumatra, Mary Steedly discovered that despite all the usual anthropological markers of a culture – complex kinship system, distinctive language, historically marked territory, traditional crafts, myths and legends – she was still faced with the problem of radically different definitions of their own culture by Karo men and women, Christian converts and spirit mediums, highland and lowland villagers, and so on.

She also had trouble trying to determine when the Karo cultural 'standard' was set and was forced to conclude that '[a]ny definition, any fixing of the ethnographic object, generated its own set of claims to authority and its own exclusions. "Culture" in this sense has to be seen as a political category, and its definition a political act.'[102]

If defining culture involves political decisions on where to draw the cultural boundaries or set the cultural standard, what relations to valorize, what strategies of action to advance in response to changing material circumstances, and what aspects of everyday life to select and privilege as part of cultural knowledge and what to ignore and exclude, then the concept of cultural holism annuls the entire political process by subordinating it to a logically prior cultural cosmology. Thus Sahlins can say, for example, that Hawaiian politics 'appears as the continuation of cosmogonic war by other means.'[103] By assuming culture as a pre-given, fully formed ontological whole, cultural holism reduces or avoids, as we shall see, the ambiguities of interpretation for the coherence of a narrative system and the innovative, rule-transcending possibilities of agency for the assimilative and reintegrative powers of structure.

One of the strengths of Sahlins's holistic approach is its ability to turn the different, often incomplete and limited, observations supplied by the journalists of Cook's expedition into an elegant and coherently structured narrative of how Hawaiian culture accounted for the British strangers. But the insights generated by Sahlins's holistic interpretation are troubling because they match so precisely and tightly every available detail of the native cosmological scheme that little room is left for interpretative ambiguity or uncertainty. Even commentators sympathetic to Sahlins in his debate with Obeyesekere express their concern over the detailed fit between the descriptions of events that occurred during Cook's final days in Hawaii and the cosmological drama celebrated by the Makahiki festival. Geertz remarks, for example, that though Sahlins is right to insist on the particularities of Hawaiian culture, '[t]he enclosure of such particularities in such sharp-edged forms fitted tightly together like pieces in a picture puzzle risks the charge of ethnographical jiggery and excessive cleverness.'[104] Though generally supportive of Sahlins's interpretations and critical of Obeyesekere's, Robert Borofsky worries that Sahlins's 'powerful synthesis' of the diverse Cook materials 'sets off alarm bells for scores of postmodern scholars sensitive to the ambiguities of interpretation and the complexities of life.'[105] Hardly a postmodern scholar, the late Valerio Valeri, Sahlins's esteemed colleague and fellow Polynesianist at the University of Chicago, in a highly critical review of Obeyesekere's book saw fit nonetheless to bend the stick a little the other way by cautioning against Sahlins's desire to see everything 'in terms of ritual enactment of the god Lono's epiphany.' Such an approach, Valeri warns, is '[p]erhaps ... too reductive for the complexity of the events and for the multiplicity of possible readings inherent in the situation.'[106] In Sahlins's historical ethnography, every detail is made to illuminate a total cultural logic or scheme. But the intelligibility achieved may be reductive, providing too singular an account. Such a formulation of a single cultural narrative is precisely what Obeyesekere challenges.

Yet for Sahlins, no explanation other than that which has recourse to Hawaiian cosmology will do. All the details, all the descriptions of Cook's fate become meaningful only when they are interpreted according to a cultural or cosmological scheme. Sahlins informs us, for example, that 'in all the confused Tolstoian narratives of the affray ... the one recurrent certainty is a dramatic structure with the properties of a ritual transformation.'[107] Hence his conclusion that 'God is in such details.'[108] But God is in the details only because in Sahlins's work details come into view only as they can be shown to fit a total cultural logic or scheme; the details become meaningful only because they have been elevated into cultural significance – apotheosized, so to speak – in the first place. Thus, though empiricism plays an important role in Sahlins's approach, it is put in the service of an a priori cultural structure. Such a subordination of detail to cultural structure has been noted by Steven Webster in his incisive critique of the structuralist historicism employed by anthropologists like Sahlins:

> [T]he specific empirical particularity of any case in the data is irrelevant [or not meaningful, in Sahlins's terms] except insofar as it conforms to the structure ... The 'instantiations' which constitute members of a paradigm are defined by their common structure, not by the particular cases ... Structural form is entirely separated, conceptually, from any content, although the empirical methodology appears to maintain the connection. In this way, the combined methodology of positivist empiricism and idealism in structuralist historicism can appear both to have its cake and to eat it too.[109]

Sahlins's holistic view of culture not only enlists empirical details to support a pre-existing cultural scheme, but also requires the subordination of practice to structure. It is precisely such a reduction of Hawaiian practice or agency to myth-bound cultural rule that Obeyesekere accuses Sahlins of committing: 'Sahlins's concept of mythopraxis [that is, practice organized according to cosmological or mythic categories] is a continuation of a doxological belief, reified as theory, that non-Western people think "mythically" and that there is a kind of inflexibility to primitive mythic thought.'[110] Obeyesekere argues that Sahlins's Hawaiians are so inflexible, so incapable of independent and innovative thinking or acting that they can only follow a pre-given cultural script from which they cannot deviate. Boxed in by a pre-given structure or cosmological order, Sahlins's Hawaiians can only 'think of the melee in which Cook was killed as a ritual enactment ...; the death after a long illness of the ordinary English sailor Watman as a Hawaiian sacrifice; the events of two weeks following Cook's landing as an explication of the Makahiki calendar and so forth.'[111] Even though faced with a host of empirical discrepancies between Cook's appearance and actions and their cosmological or cultural beliefs, Hawaiians, nevertheless, apparently were not bothered, showed no puzzlement, and seemingly allowed their beliefs to override their perceptual and cognitive judgment. In Obeyesekere's view, by attributing 'an inflexible mode of thought' to Hawaiian natives, Sahlins also deprives them of rational agency and empirical judgment and turns them into total prisoners of their culture's pre-existing categories.[112]

To Sahlins, however, it is Obeyesekere who shows inflexibility in so far as he consistently misreads Hawaiian flexibility and improvisation as Hawaiian ignorance of empirical contradiction. In a skilful move, Sahlins turns Obeyesekere's accusation back on himself. Recall Obeyesekere's point that Sahlins's Hawaiians are so immured in pre-given cultural or cosmological categories that they are not bothered by any lack of fit or discordance between empirical fact and cultural belief. In response, Sahlins argues that Hawaiians are not troubled by the lack of fit between empirical fact and cultural script because they are relatively flexible and can improvise in such a way that an event or action need not match that cultural script to the letter. It is Obeyesekere, Sahlins points out, who insists that Hawaiians match exactly their actions to their rituals and their empirical observations to their cosmological beliefs lest they stand accused of intellectual inflexibility in their inability to discern empirical contradictions. Sahlins explains that eighteenth-century Hawaiians were able 'to flexibly and reflexively surmount ... empirical contradiction[s] in their own cultural terms – that is, without jettisoning their own concepts or constructions in favour of a universal perceptual realism (such as Obeyesekere recommends).'[113] Faced with an empirical discrepancy, Hawaiians improvised and creatively assimilated what was discrepant to their cosmological tradition. Take the death and burial of the old seaman Willie Watman, for example. Watman died on 1 February 1779, approximately the day on the Makahiki calendar in which 'the king's human god-image, Kahoali'i eats the eye of a sacrificial victim offered at the temple [Hikiau] used in the principal Makahiki ceremonies.'[114] Though the British sources differ on who wanted Watman to be buried at the same temple,[115] Sahlins believes that 'it was *at the request of the Hawaiian authorities* that Watman's body was brought to Hikiau.'[116] After Cook conducted the funeral service, the Lono priests performed 'their own ceremonies, expressing a wish to throw a dead pig, plantains, coconuts, and other offerings into the grave.'[117] Although they were 'in some measure stopped,' for three nights pigs were killed and prayers chanted at Watman's grave. Relying on these descriptions from the British journalists, Sahlins concludes: 'Everything thus suggests that the Hawaiians gave Watman's death a significance of their own, at a time and place that corresponded to the customary offering of a human sacrifice.'[118] Hawaiians, in this interpretation, are seen as flexible thinkers, capable of improvisation when the occasion demands, who creatively incorporate Watman's death into their ritual by converting the old sailor into a symbolic or metaphorical sacrifice.

Obeyesekere will have none of this. 'It is hard to believe,' he declares, 'that the Hawaiians, or anyone for that matter, could ever have made the connection between Watman, who died after a long illness, and a sacrificial victim killed and offered to the gods according to very specific cultural rules.'[119] One of these cultural rules involves, as we have noted, Kahoali'i, the king's human god-image, eating the sacrificial victim's eye. No such ceremonial consumption occurred in Watman's case. We need not be detained by the details of Obeyesekere's alternative interpretation of Watman's burial, which he sees as a 'deliberate violation of Hawaiian sacred values,' a pollution of temple taboos that the priests in attendance were compelled to cleanse ritually through the slaughter of pigs and the chanting of prayers.[120] Sahlins makes short work of Obeyesekere's interpretation and dismisses it not only as highly speculative and fictional. but also as a form of pidgin anthropology that invents 'a Hawaiian pollution-removal ritual' where none exists.[121] Moreover, the premise behind Obeyesekere's objection to Sahlins's interpretation of Watman's sacrificial role is that 'Hawaiians can only stereotypically reproduce their prescribed cultural schemes ... , or else all such cultural schemes are off.'[122] Obeyesekere, not Sahlins, thus appears to be the one who denies Hawaiians flexible thinking, creative agency, and the ability to improvise. As Samuel Parker, a student of Sahlins, points out in a hostile review of Obeyesekere's book, it is 'Obeyesekere's Hawaiians [who] are rigid ritualists incapable of departing from "very specific roles."'[123]

Sahlins's and Parker's criticism of Obeyesekere is certainly cogent. What Obeyesekere regards as empirical contradictions or discrepancies may not appear as such to Hawaiians. Neither does ignoring these discrepancies necessarily signal some kind of cognitive deficit on their part. Events or actions need not match the cultural or cosmological script to the letter; the gap between the two may be a sign of flexible interpretation and creative improvisation. But while we may agree with Sahlins on the irony of Obeyesekere's position, there is a predictability to Sahlins's description of Hawaiian improvisations that is troubling. The telos, so to speak, of all these improvisations seems to be to conform to and uphold the cultural script. Sahlins's Hawaiians appear relatively untroubled by contingency or novelty and seem to be able to assimilate or accommodate the discrepant rather easily to their own cosmological or cultural beliefs. They improvise creatively, but their improvisations always seem to be in the service of preserving, rather than questioning, their cultural tradition. Watman's death may be opportunistically fashioned into a metaphorical or symbolic sacrifice, but such an improvisation merely fulfils the ritual script. In Sahlins's work, terms like 'flexibility' and 'improvisation' seem curiously and inflexibly tied to a given cultural cosmology. Thus, it comes as no surprise to learn from Sahlins that 'flexibility' or 'improvisation' does not mean departing from or going beyond a given structure but rather an 'adjustment' that brings one closer to it: '[T]hat Cook's arrival did create discrepancies in the Hawaiians' ritual schedule to which they did *adjust* is a point I have made in detail.'[124] It appears, then, that Hawaiian puzzlement over Cook's arrival was momentary and that they were able to adjust to the strange and the unfamiliar by assimilating them to their own familiar cultural categories. Or, to be more precise, a pre-existing cosmology or culture allows Hawaiian agents to interpret and render the unfamiliar familiar, turning the stranger Cook into their god, Lono, for example. Sahlins can thus declare that Hawaiians, New Guineans, and others who practise a '*pensée sauvage*,'[125] are immersed in a cultural holism in which 'almost anything and its opposite could be the empirical induction of a cosmic conclusion.' A cultural cosmology or world view helps them to confer significance on what may be unfamiliar and to connect 'the meaning to the sensible sign (the strangers' behaviour).'[126] If, as Sahlins argues,

Obeyesekere's rejection of Cook's apotheosis 'on the a priori basis that ... [it] is a European myth' results in his making 'a conclusion out of a premise,'[127] then Sahlins is by that same measure guilty of turning empirical premises into part of a cosmic conclusion.

Teleological in orientation, Sahlins's work thus ultimately results in the reduction or subordination of agency to cultural system despite his assertion that he has always been alert to improvisation and innovation. For all his talk of Hawaiian flexibility and creativity and his repeated denial of cultural prescriptiveness, Sahlins's descriptions of Hawaiian agency always end up affirming the distinctiveness and systematicity of Hawaiian culture. There does not seem to be room for any sceptical questioning of custom or critical distancing from culture in his view of agency. Even political rivalry between the Lono priests and the King's Ku faction that resulted in very different attitudes to Cook is seen by Sahlins not as an example of Hawaiian *realpolitik* culminating in pragmatic manipulations of culture, but as the ritual expression of the 'cosmological antithesis of the Makahiki season.'[128] To Sahlins, therefore, all forms of practice and agency are, in the final analysis, subsumed by culture.

Historical Change and Structural Continuity

If, in a holistic view of culture, meanings and actions are dependent on, if not wholly determined by culture, we may wish to ask whether cultural change is possible. If culture is an all-encompassing system, does it not merely replicate itself? How does it deal with the contingency of events? Is historical change possible? Or does culture assimilate contingency and change into its structure? Sahlins is acutely aware of this perceived opposition of cultural change and cultural continuity that he characterizes, more concisely, as the opposition of history and structure. Sahlins recognizes the problem posed by such an opposition in his critique of a certain strain of structuralist anthropology that has uncritically adopted the Saussurean binary pair of *langue* (the language system) and *parole* (specific acts of speech), and has thus ended up with a similar unhelpful opposition of structure (the cultural system abstracted from time) and history (specific events and practices in time). He can, therefore, claim with some justification that Obeyesekere misrepresents him when he is criticized for regarding societies as replicating their structures in a process of 'stereotypic reproduction' (a phrase borrowed from the French anthropologist Maurice Godelier), which denies the possibility of historical change.[129] In Sahlins's words: 'Since 1977, I have repeatedly adopted the phrase "stereotypic reproduction" as a *negative characterization* of the ahistorical disposition of a certain structuralism ... "[S]tereotypic reproduction" has long been cited by me as a *defect* of classical structuralist theory – if only because such reproduction does not occur in historical practice.'[130]

Instead of 'stereotypic reproduction,' which first opposes and then collapses agency and historical change into the unchanging structural code of culture, Sahlins argues for an approach that rejects the distinction between structure and historical practice, system and event, and replaces it with a dialectics in which the opposing terms, no longer antithetical, come together to form a more comprehensive dialectical unity. As he points out, his writings on Polynesian histories insist 'that continuity and change are false alternatives, since they always go together in the dialectics of practice. In practice, there is cultural continuity even in novelty, inasmuch as the knowledge and communication of what is new has to be related to what people already know. But at the same time, what is known, the received understanding of things, has been risked.'[131] Cultural continuity persists because even the most radical change becomes intelligible or recognizable only when it has first been culturally comprehended. At the same time, however, the cultural schemes or categories that organize peoples' understanding and actions are not merely replicated; they are risked 'objectively' in a refractory world of people and things that does not always conform to them; and they are also risked 'subjectively' because 'nothing guarantees ... that intelligent and intentional subjects, with their several social interests and biographies, will use the existing categories in prescribed ways.'[132] 'Stereotypic reproduction' therefore does not occur because the cultural categories in encountering worldly circumstances and human interests that do not always conform to them are functionally revalued. As Sahlins puts it: 'Burdened with the world, the cultural meanings are thus altered. It follows that the relationship between categories change; the structure is transformed.'[133] Thus, what begins 'as reproduction ends as transformation.'[134]

Forcefully rejecting Obeyesekere's criticism that he can only envisage the 'stereotypic reproduction' of culture, Sahlins just as strongly denies the charge of cultural determinism levelled at him by Jonathan Friedman a few years before his more public and acrimonious debate with Obeyesekere. Friedman had argued that Sahlins's work can be seen as 'an application of cultural determinism to historical processes, an attempt to translate all forms of historical movement into an expression of culture as a "model for" the production of reality. There is, in other words, nothing that is not culturally generated!'[135] In reply, Sahlins points out that he is in fact explicitly opposed to cultural determinism and that Friedman has wrongly accused him of collapsing historical practice into cultural code, of subsuming the worldly 'interest' of pragmatic actors into the fixed 'sense' of a conventional sign system. What his work in fact shows 'is that in the capacity of interests, cultural categories [or the 'sense' of a sign system] are referred by people to the world, thus putting the categories at pragmatic risk and in the event changing their conventional sense.'[136] As such, the cultural code does not determine or generate anything. In fact, cultural categories are 'submitted to multiple risks.'[137] They can be affected by the properties and forces of things that do not conform to any conventional sense or received meaning; they are put at risk by the intentions and interests of agents who may improvise or otherwise depart from the known script; and they are further risked when different social groups with different interests and unequal powers compete to objectify their own cultural interpretations.

Sahlins calls this exposure of cultural categories to multiple risks 'the structure of the conjuncture,' by which he means 'the practical realization of the cultural categories in a specific historical context, as expressed in the interested action of the historic agents, including the microsociology of their interaction.'[138] The structure of the conjuncture is thus a concept that allows Sahlins to propose a structural theory of history that is able to relate dialectically, rather than oppose, structure to event, continuity to change, cultural code to pragmatic agency. However, critics like Obeyesekere and Friedman[139] may be forgiven for misreading Sahlins, especially since, on a number of occasions in his published work, he has made statements that seem to favour structure over conjuncture. What we often see in Sahlins's writings on culture is a two-part movement. First, we are told how structural categories are exposed to the risks of an unpredictable world of practice, to a conjuncture of contingent, refractory objects and pragmatic, intelligent subjects capable of unforseen improvisations and actions. But this concession to cultural risk and change is then qualified or reversed by the reassertion of structural order, the renewed encompassment by a cultural logic. In his debate with Friedman, for example, Sahlins admits that material realities like cyclones and the unforseen appearance of Captain Cook in Hawaii have compelling effects on people's lives and lead to changes in their culture. At the same time, however, these realities become meaningful only as they are culturally interpreted, achieving intelligibility only within a cultural scheme: 'According to their [that is, material realities'] specific capacities as culture, their general compulsions as force are variously realized. By these cultural mediations, the material realities become *historical* realities, the natural forces *historical* forces.'[140] What should be noted is the way in which Sahlins's argument shifts from a description of how cultural categories are risked objectively in a contingent and unpredictable world to a discussion of how unanticipated alien realities, such as the advent of Captain Cook in Kealakekua Bay, are 'comprehended, absorbed, amplified, impeded, diverted and otherwise orchestrated and transmitted along the lines of local cultural schemes.'[141] Cultural categories may be put at risk, but the overall cultural scheme remains to mitigate and manage the risks, turning the unfamiliar into the known and the new into the already familiar. As Sahlins puts it: 'The irruption of Captain Cook from beyond the horizon was a truly unprecedented event, never seen before. But by thus encompassing the existentially unique in the conceptually familiar [the stranger Cook is seen as the god Lono], the people embed their present in their past.'[142] Event is thus absorbed into structure, historical change into cultural tradition. It is not so much history as 'the historical work of the *cultural order*,'[143] that Sahlins seeks to highlight in his writings. Or, as he says, he wants 'simply to show some ways that history is organized by structures of significance.'[144]

We find the same two-part movement of risk and recuperation when Sahlins turns from discussing how cultural categories are objectively risked in events to how they are subjectively risked in practice. Again Sahlins begins by pointing out that people acting differently out of different interests and situations will produce new and different meanings rather than replicate received cultural categories. Thus, in the Hawaiian example, Captain Cook appears as a god, a divine warrior or something else to different segments of the population depending on their respective status, rank, or power. Cultural concepts are risked when these different perspectives and interpretations come into play. Yet out of such risks come innovations and new meanings. In short, rather than acting according to culturally prescribed rules, people 'cease to be slaves of their concepts and become their masters.'[145] This argument for innovation and autonomy from cultural prescriptiveness is, however, immediately qualified and reversed:

> Still, as in another famous dialogue about the relations of master and slave [Hegel's], this domination involves a certain servitude ... The improvisations (functional revaluations) depend on received possibilities of significance, if only because they are otherwise unintelligible and incommunicable. Hence the empirical is not known simply as such but as a culturally relevant significance, and the old system is projected forward in its novel forms.[146]

In *How 'Natives' Think*, Sahlins makes a similar point about the possibility of innovation and culturally unconstrained agency only to qualify it immediately in the next clause: 'The responses [to a practical situation] are not prescribed in content – however they may be limited by a system of intelligibility, to the logic of which all effective novelty must minimally conform.'[147] Sahlins argues that events and actions are not prescribed in advance and thus are not culturally determined. At the same time, however, he insists that 'they invariably do find a place in the ordering of history.'[148] Even though historic events and individual actions are not 'unreflexively determined or superorganically imposed,' they nevertheless 'entail specific understandings of the local cultural regime, predicable on its schemata and communicable in its terms ... [and can therefore be regarded as] culturally constructed, devised from a certain cultural logic and ontologic.'[149] This two-part movement, or what can be called the Sahlins shuffle (one step forward, one step back), in which the concession to innovative agency is immediately qualified by the recourse to cultural logic, is succinctly captured in Sahlins's remark that 'to say an event is culturally described is not to say it is culturally prescribed.'[150]

Sahlins's formulation is designed to facilitate a structural theory of history in which historical event or practice, if not culturally predetermined, is at least predictable and intelligible in cultural terms. We are presented with a dialectics of history in which 'the historical process unfolds as a continuous reciprocal movement between practice of the structure and structure of the practice.'[151] It is, however, a dialectics that seems to privilege structure more than practice. 'Practice of the structure' involves the instantiation or putting into play and into risk of cultural structures or concepts, while 'structure of the practice' requires that the unforseen and new elements ushered in by practice be reconceptualized as part of a cultural structure. In either case, however, practice though dialectically related, appears also to be subordinate to structure. First, practice is structure's unfolding in the world, structure's material or historical agent so to speak. But, then, practice as material or historical action in the world becomes meaningful and significant only when it is structurally ordered. To be sure, as Sahlins repeatedly informs us, structure is risked in practice; but, at the same time, the risks incurred by practice are mitigated by a cultural system that adjusts itself to accommodate the risks and changes brought about by practice. 'In any case,' we are told, 'action begins and ends in structure: begins in the projects of people as social beings, to end by absorption of the effects in a cultural practico-inert.'[152] Practice, the event it finds itself in, and the history it produces are all reabsorbed into structure. Or as Jonathan Friedman succinctly puts it: '[T]he effort to put structure into history is continuously inverted by the need to absorb history into structure.'[153]

What we see in Sahlins's dialectical approach to structure or culture, on the one hand, and event, history, and practice, on the other, is the subsumption of the latter into the former. We are presented with a dialectics, Hegelian in inspiration, in which a 'truer synthesis'[154] is aimed for. But it is a synthesis in which one of the elements – culture – is privileged as that encompassing concept which makes synthesis possible: 'Hawaiian history is surely not unique in the demonstration that culture functions as a *synthesis* of stability and change, past and present, diachrony and synchrony.'[155] But the synthesis is somewhat one-sided, since we notice, to begin with, how 'history' in the course of the sentence unproblematically becomes 'culture,' the master concept capable of synthesizing opposites.

When we start to examine some of Sahlins's other remarks, the one-sidedness becomes even more apparent. Hierarchical privileging within dialectic is evident in the following statement: 'Event is the empirical form of system. The converse proposition, that all events are culturally systematic, is more significant.'[156] In other words, though Sahlins admits that a cultural order is only realized empirically as an event, that is, an occurrence or action in the real world, it is the converse proposition to which he attributes greater importance or significance, namely, that occurrences or actions become meaningful only when they are culturally structured and interpreted. Similarly, in the dialectical synthesis of past and present it is the past that is privileged: 'structure is precisely the organization of the current situation in the terms of the past.'[157] Again in the dialectical synthesis of continuity and change it is the former that is more dominant: 'We know this anyhow, that things must preserve some identity through their changes, or else the world is a madhouse. Saussure articulated the principle: "What predominates in all change is the persistence of the old substance; disregard for the present is only relative. That is why the principle of change is based on the principle of continuity."'[158] Characteristically, Sahlins qualifies his admission of cultural change by asserting the principle of cultural continuity and identity. For Sahlins what *predominates* in change is the *persistence* of the old, allowing him to conclude, therefore, like Saussure, that the principle of change is *based* on the principle of continuity. There is clearly a hierarchical ordering, a privileging of one of the terms in Sahlins's dialectic. Cultural continuity encompasses change but not the other way round, lest the world become a 'madhouse.' Dismantling the sterile opposition of synchrony to diachrony, Sahlins's dialectic ends up encapsulating diachrony in synchrony, or as he puts it, 'The structure has an internal diachrony, consisting in the changing relations between general categories, or as I say, a "cultural life of the elementary forms."'[159] The 'burden of "reality,"' the empirical risks and contingencies of our world have 'real effects' only 'in the *terms* of some cultural scheme.'[160] If there is any doubt about this, we are told that 'in the final analysis' even 'the categories by which objectivity is defined are themselves cosmological.'[161] As in the Hegelian dialectic, there is a final synthesis in which culture is apotheosized, installed as the all-encompassing concept.[162]

Sahlins's insistence that 'things must preserve some identity through their changes' leads him to the view that cultural continuity means the survival of an original or authentic cultural identity. Such a view is evident in his critique of the 'invention of tradition' argument that has influenced many recent postcolonial historical and ethnographic studies. Sahlins is critical of the 'invention' argument because it undermines the cultural-continuity thesis by questioning the authenticity of the cultural identity that is supposed to have persisted through change. He argues that the 'invention' argument is especially insidious in the light of contemporary cultural revivals among third- and fourth-world peoples. Sahlins notes that the development of cultural self-consciousness

> among imperialism's erstwhile victims is one of the more remarkable phenomena of world history in the later twentieth century. 'Culture' – the word itself, or some local equivalent, is on everyone's lips. Tibetans and Hawaiians, Ojibway, Kwakiutl and Eskimo, Kazakhs and Mongols, native Australians, Balinese, Kashmiris and New Zealand Maori: all discover they have a 'culture.'[163]

But, according to Sahlins, this subaltern revival of culture is dismissed by Western anthropologists and historians as a form of inauthentic or false consciousness that invents a more or less counterfeit past.

> Western intellectuals have often been too disposed to write off the meanings [of this cultural turn] as trivial, on the grounds that the claims to cultural continuity are spurious. In the going academic view the so-called revival is a typical 'invention of tradition' – though no slight is intended to Maori or Hawaiian folks, since all traditions are 'invented' in and for the purposes of the present ... In any event, this Maori or Hawaiian 'culture' is not historically authentic because it is a reified and interested value, a self-conscious ideology rather than a way of life which, moreover, owes more in content to imperialist forces than to indigenous sources.[164]

Sahlins is concerned that the 'invention of tradition' argument might end up erasing culture's 'logical and ontological continuities' with the past,[165] thereby questioning its original and authentic identity while deeming it an ideological fabrication in response to imperialism rather than a revival of the primordial and the indigenous. Such a denial of an indigenous culture's authenticity results in a 'facile historiography' that, unintentionally perhaps, deprives natives of their agency by exemplifying the principle that 'there must be a white man behind every brown.'[166] Sahlins can therefore conclude that those intellectuals who invoke the 'invention of tradition' thesis ironically 'mimic on an academic plane the same imperialism they would despise ... As an attack on the cultural integrity and historical agency of the peripheral peoples, they do in theory just what imperialism attempts in practice.'[167] Hoping to avoid 'the mortal sin of essentialism,'[168] Western academics commit the even greater sin of denying indigenous peoples 'any cultural autonomy, coherence or authenticity.'[169] Sahlins regards this defence of the cultural continuity and authenticity of subaltern groups as more postcolonially correct than the view expressed by academics like Obeyesekere, who think that in opposing the attribution of essentialist traits (such as mythical thought or *pensée sauvage*) to indigenous cultures, they are challenging Western hegemony. In fact, argues Sahlins, they are themselves guilty of the same hegemony in arrogantly assuming that 'indigenous peoples could not have their own reasons for acting as they did.'[170] The anti-essentialist questioning of cultural identity by postcolonial and postmodern theorists is thus exposed as the erasure of indigenous cultural autonomy and agency.

But while Sahlins may be right about certain extreme and unnuanced uses of the 'invention of tradition' argument, he misreads its intention regarding indigenous cultural revivals. Rather than denying native cultural authenticity or agency, the 'invention' thesis may be interpreted more productively as seeking to direct analysis away from culture as the unfolding of an original cosmological or symbolic system to culture as a process of 'continuous production and construction' that cannot be predicated on any received or extant cultural order.[171] Consequently, the 'invention' argument is not interested in the authenticity or inauthenticity of a culture because it does not posit an original standard of authenticity against which inauthenticity may be judged. It is Sahlins in fact who projects the authenticity-inauthenticity opposition onto the 'invention' argument and then accuses it of questioning indigenous cultures and insulting them as 'inauthentic' or 'invented.' The 'invention' thesis has no use for the authenticity-inauthenticity opposition because the survival or the suppression of an original or primordial cultural identity is not at issue; on the contrary, culture is always in process, 'inventing' or 'constructing' itself in response to the situation or circumstance at hand and to the shifting field of forces present in any community. As such, 'invention' is not a denial of authenticity but an affirmation of human creativity and the belief that culture is best approached not as something already determined but as something in process, yet to be. 'Invention,' then, does not mean, as Sahlins thinks, that the counterfeit has replaced the genuine. The 'invention of tradition' argument neither signifies, as Sahlins fears, the onset of 'cultural decadence' nor implies 'a factitious recuperation, which can only bring forth the simulacra of a dead past.'[172] On the contrary, the 'invention' thesis asserts that the present is not weighed down by the dead hand of the past. Instead, the past is seen as a resource to be used for present and future purposes and not as an unchanging inheritance, failure to conform to which leads to inauthenticity and decadence. The 'invention' thesis believes that cultural traditions are always invented because they are not genetically programmed or naturally transmitted, that people are not wholly determined by their cultural traditions and that they have sufficient autonomy to reflect critically on their own culture and choose its present and future course. Thus, it is not the 'invention of tradition' theorists who deny indigenous people their autonomy and agency, it is Sahlins who denies them these values by subordinating them to pregiven cultural categories.

Opposing what he sees as the 'invention' argument's allegations about the 'inauthenticity' of recent cultural revivals, Sahlins strongly affirms the continuity and authenticity of local native cultures. To be sure, he is aware that global Western expansion since at least the sixteenth century has powerfully affected these local cultures. His discussion of how Cook's arrival in Hawaii and its aftermath changed Hawaiian culture is a case in point. At the same time, however, Sahlins insists that cultural continuity underlies cultural change and that 'innovations follow logically ... from the people's own principles of existence.'[173] The familiar argument propounded by capitalist world-system theories that Western modernization and cultural imperialism have led to global homogeneity is thus challenged by Sahlins, who points out that the 'first commercial impulse of [indigenous peoples] ... is not to become just like us but more like themselves. They turn foreign goods to the service of domestic ideas, to the objectification of their own relations and notions of the good life.'[174] As an example of indigenous appropriation of Western modernity, Sahlins describes a successful Paiwan artist and entrepreneur 'in the mountains of south-central Taiwan' who, while seriously committed to the project of restoring his traditional culture, enjoys, at the same time, driving around in a Jeep and dining in Western restaurants.[175] Then there is the other example of a 'mammoth old Tahitian' who, having successfully combined 'indigenous values with French influence,' is quoted as saying contentedly after a meal, '*le ma'a* [food] in the refrigerator – *voilà la vie tahitienne*!'[176] Both these men, in Sahlins's view, 'make an assimilation of the dominant [Western] culture the means of sustaining a difference.'[177] As a corrective to facile versions of the thesis that global cultural homogeneity is caused by capitalist modernization Sahlins's theory of 'the indigenization of modernity' is useful.[178] But it can also be argued that Sahlins is somewhat one-sided and deterministic in his view of the inevitability or predictability of modernity's indigenization.

The 'indigenization of modernity' examples provided by Sahlins are seen as 'expressions of a larger process of structural transformation: the formation of a World System of cultures, a Culture of cultures – with all the characteristics of a structure of differences.'[179] By emphasizing what appears to be a structurally inevitable process – 'the formation of a World System of cultures' – Sahlins turns our attention away from the contexts of political struggle, from the complex, uneven, and shifting array of possibilities and constraints that face people in their confrontation with the forces of modernity. What are political struggles with unpredictable outcomes, sometimes triumphant and at other times ending in defeat, become, in Sahlins's view, an inevitable 'process of structure.'[180] He is right to argue that Western capitalism, though 'planetary in its scope, ... is not a universal logic of cultural change.'[181] But he challenges one universalist teleology only to replace it with another: a global structural process in which indigenous cultures assimilate Western modernity as the means of sustaining their difference.

Sahlins would no doubt agree that a carefully nuanced and dialectical approach to global modernity and indigenous cultures is required. In practice, however, his work privileges local or indigenous cultural agency over the forces of modernity. As we have seen, by emphasizing the 'indigenization of modernity' to the relative neglect of the 'modernization of the indigenous,' Sahlins in fact abandons dialectics for binary contrasts. He plays down the importance of specific historical contexts, the circumstances surrounding practice, and the possibilities and limitations it has to face. Instead, seeking understandably to rectify universalizing theories of Western hegemony, he ends up assuming local cultural agency as an already secured outcome rather than as a politics without guarantees. Rather one-sided in its approach, Sahlins's theory of the 'indigenization of modernity' could have benefited from Nicholas Thomas's balanced critique of the tendency in colonial studies to operate in binary terms, with one of the terms often privileged at the expense of the other:

> Scholarship around colonialism tends to lapse ... into binary contrasts or reactive positions: it makes of *either* local continuity, culture, and agency *or* global intrusions, politics and dominance a sufficient and independent frame of analysis. Against the mutual exclusiveness of these frames of analysis, a zone of appropriations and cultural strategies can be imagined in which local and extralocal determinations are significant according to the nature of the encounter. It is not enlightening to argue that local agency and autonomy are significant *in principle*; what are important rather are the ways in which local efforts to encompass colonizers' activities and offerings may be efficacious in some circumstances and limited and unsuccessful in others. In *Black Harvest* [a film about the effects of modernization in the Papua New Guinean highlands], commercial modernization certainly takes a local form, and it is represented in various ways that are certainly distinctively indigenous; but this is not to say that the process has somehow been successfully accommodated.[182]

In a more direct exchange with Sahlins, Thomas points out that for Sahlins

> it appears to be a matter of theoretical principle that indigenous peoples possess autonomy and agency to such an extent that external offerings and impositions are incorporated into local practical and symbolic orders ... The effect or lack of effect of such a historically dispersed range of phenomena as colonial intrusions must be a matter of historical inquiry, not conceptual determination.[183]

Sahlins's work thus remains problematic insofar as it elevates cultural continuity, authenticity, and autonomy into theoretical postulates or axiomatic principles rather than subjecting them to context-specific analyses or approaching them as processes with uncertain outcomes.

How 'Natives' Think: Different Cultures, Different Rationalities

The first two of Sahlins's culturalist assumptions – namely, cultural holism, which regards culture as a total integrated system, and cultural continuity, which argues that a principle of structural stability underwrites change and innovation – make possible his third assumption: cultural relativism, or the view that not only is culture a whole way of life whose identity persists through change but that, as a consequence, each culture or way of life must be seen as distinctive, different from others and to be comprehended and evaluated only according to its own cosmology or deep belief-system. It is important to note that for Sahlins cultural relativism is not just about observable differences such as that some people eat with chopsticks while others eat with forks and knives, that some paint their lips while others paint their whole body, or that, in general, different groups of people do things differently. What these visible differences reveal is the presence of a more profound, systematic, and fundamental difference between cultures, a difference not only in some matters but that, so to speak, goes all the way down. Commenting on the Obeyesekere-Sahlins debate, Clifford Geertz has this to say about how the two anthropologists understand cultural difference and how 'deeply' it goes for them: 'For Sahlins, it is substance; for Obeyesekere, it is surface.'[184]

Affirming a substantive difference between cultures, Sahlins's relativism is totalizing and earnest, like the version described by Martin Hollis and Steven Lukes:

> That *some* concepts are relative ... to context is undeniable. That *all* are, and more particularly the basic categories of thought themselves, is the challenging thought. The thought is that each scheme, itself relative to context or culture, *organizes* or *fits* nature or the world or reality. In short, with the idea that neither reality itself, nor men's relation to it, nor the constraints of rational thinking set limits upon the content or form of such schemes, we reach relativism in earnest.[185]

What Sahlins proposes is nothing less than an ontological difference between cultures that leads to epistemological relativism or the claim that perception becomes meaningful only according to a particular cultural scheme or logic. In other words, since cultural concepts govern our perceptions, whatever we know of the world we know only relative to those concepts. This is how Sahlins describes epistemological relativism with reference to what he regards as the distinctive difference between Hawaiian and Western world views: '"[O]bjectivity" is culturally constituted. It is always a distinctive ontology ... It is not a simple sensory epistemology but a total cultural cosmology that is precipitated in Hawaiian empirical judgements of divinity [for example] ... Epistemologies vary in accord with world views (cultural ontologies).'[186] Or more succinctly: 'Different cultures, different rationalities.'[187]

The central premise of Sahlins's epistemological relativism is that there is no direct or unmediated sensory knowledge of reality; all empirical access to reality is determined or mediated by a priori cultural concepts. Or as Sahlins puts it: '[T]here is no such thing as an immaculate perception.'[188] Sahlins rules out the possibility of immaculate perception in order to assert the determining role of cultural categories in the constitution of what we regard as reality. Conversely, the belief in immaculate perception, in the possibility of a direct, transparent, and unmediated access to reality is shown to be an empiricist myth and not the achievement of universal objectivity. As Sahlins explains, every culture tends to believe in the objectivity of its perception of the world when in fact that perception is relative to received cultural concepts:

> People overestimate their objectivity because they are noticing only a fraction of the empirical characteristics of things, a selective attention and evaluation that corresponds to an act of categorization. Note that we are not dealing simply with physiological sensations but with empirical judgements ... At issue ... is the organization of experience, including the training of the senses, according to social canons of relevance. These canons, and therefore the distinctions people make among objects, vary [for different groups] ... For, things are not only perceived, they are thereby *known,* which is also to say that they are classified. Hence people who are perceiving the same objects are not necessarily perceiving the same *kinds* of things.[189]

In Sahlins's view, then, percepts are dependent on concepts. 'Human social experience,' he insists, 'is the appropriation of specific percepts by general concepts: an ordering of men and the objects of their existence according to a scheme of cultural categories.'[190] To argue that our perceptions are mediated by cultural categories is, as Obeyesekere notes, 'unexceptionable ... if it is not carried to an extreme, as Sahlins carries it.' Obeyesekere further argues that if 'immaculate perceptions' are impossible, 'to postulate "immaculate conceptions" (in the cultural sense) is equally naive, for this is to deny the physical and neurological bases of cognition and perception entirely.'[191] Although Obeyesekere's invocation of the centrality and universality of human neurology comes dangerously close to biological determinism, as Sahlins is quick to point out,[192] his remark about Sahlins's 'immaculate conceptions' as a form of cultural idealism is well taken. Despite Sahlins's assertion that his aim is to have a dialectic or even synthesis of 'the received categories and the perceived contexts,'[193] his writings give a very strong impression that cultural categories and structure are, in the final instance, both dominant and determining. Similarly, a dialectic in which percept and concept would be interdependent and mutually determining gives way in practice to the latter being privileged over the former. For example, Sahlins dismisses Obeyesekere's argument that the Hawaiians must have noticed an empirical discordance between percept (the English-speaking, un-Polynesian-looking British naval captain) and concept (the Hawaiian god Lono) as a version of the naive Western empiricist theory that seeks to tie sensory percept to ontological entity while bypassing the cultural scheme or logic that controls perception. As Sahlins points out, Obeyesekere's sensory or empirical realism that purports to defend Hawaiian practical rationality by showing that Hawaiians could never have mistaken Cook for Lono in fact does them a disservice by ignoring their concepts of divinity while turning them into European bourgeois empiricists. Hawaiian theology states that the gods are 'transcendent, invisible, and originate in places beyond the horizon [that is, they are foreign].'[194] As such, Hawaiian cosmology (which, according to Sahlins, Obeyesekere ignores) stipulates that gods have 'no recognizable form.'[195] One should not, therefore, compare Cook with Lono 'to see if the percept matches the concept' because it would make no cultural sense for the Hawaiians.[196] Nor should one rush to the conclusion that just because Cook does not look Hawaiian he cannot be taken for Lono. Percept, in this case Cook's appearance, is overruled by concept, that is, by the Hawaiian belief that gods are transcendent and have no recognizable form. The sensory, neurological basis of Obeyeskere's 'practical rationality' is, therefore, merely secondary, subject to an even more fundamental cultural cosmology. It is not sensory perception that constitutes objectivity because objectivity is culturally determined.[197] Thus, what may appear to be an empirical contradiction or disjunction according to our sensory perception may be perfectly intelligible to someone else with a different cultural or symbolic scheme. It is a symbolic operation that occurs rather than an empirical or literal identification when someone says, 'Cook is the god Lono.' As Sahlins explains: 'The issue is not sensory perception but meaningful predication.'[198] He approvingly cites Walker Percy, on the symbolic character of consciousness: 'Every conscious perception is of the nature of a recognition, a pairing, which is to say that the object is recognized as being what it is ... [I]t is not enough to say that one is conscious of something; one is conscious of something as *being something.*'[199] Consequently, if perception is always a form of recognition, then sensory percepts become meaningful only when they are paired to pre-existing concepts or cultural categories.

But sensory percepts are not that easily subordinated to cultural concepts. So even though Sahlins is right to accuse Obeyesekere of a certain literalism when he asserts that Hawaiians could not have mistaken a British naval captain for a Hawaiian god, we must not rush to the other extreme and embrace a cultural idealism that ignores or overrides sensory evidence. Though it is certainly true that cultural concepts help shape our perception, we must also observe dialectical parity and admit that concepts in turn are formed or built on perceptions that must at least have some material validity, some secure purchase on the world. Thus, in culturally meaningful statements like 'Cook is the god Lono,' 'This bread is the body of Christ,' 'The sweet potato is the body of Lono,' or 'I am descended from an eagle,'[200] the empirical referents though symbolically predicated must still undergo sensory or perceptual validation. For the preceding statements to be symbolically or culturally meaningful, there must first be empirical agreement and validation of the perceived entities such that Cook is Cook and not one of his lieutenants, that bread is not wine, that a sweet potato is unlike a rock, or that an eagle flies rather than swims. The point is not to elevate cultural predication over sensory perception or vice versa. The point, rather, is that cultural concept and sensory percept limit and qualify each other dialectically, thereby explaining why conceptual differences between cultures are nonetheless based on certain minimal, non-relative forms of perceptual accord. Different cultures, definitely; but not completely different rationalities as Sahlins presupposes.

The problem, therefore, with an absolute statement like 'There is no such thing as an immaculate perception' is that it abandons the dialectic of concept and percept for a cultural idealism in which, as Sahlins reminds us repeatedly, '"objectivity" is culturally constituted.'[201] But this comes dangerously close to Obeyesekere's charge of 'immaculate conception.' Where does the concept come from? Since Sahlins eschews biological or neurological universalism, does the concept emerge *sui generis*, immaculately on its own? Is there no initial sensory or perceptual input to the formation of the concept? Can sensory perception never question or contradict a concept since what 'might seem an empirical contradiction ... [can be] easily accommodated' in a cultural cosmology?[202] Are all percepts always already pre-programmed to fit cultural beliefs since, as Sahlins argues, 'almost anything and its opposite could be the empirical induction of a cosmic conclusion?'[203]

It appears that native cultural cosmology, or what, following Claude Lévi-Strauss, Sahlins calls *pensée sauvage*,[204] allows natives some empirical flexibility but only on the condition that it stay within the limits of a 'cosmic conclusion.' In other words, if sensory percepts are always destined to be accommodated by cultural concepts, there can be flexibility of cultural accommodation but no true learning, which involves a degree of critical distancing from one's inherited cultural categories. If there is no such thing as an immaculate perception, then it follows that perception is always conceptually determined. Thus, it would appear that people are immured in their own cultural concepts, which are so totalizing that nothing strange or puzzling can survive their assimilative and interpretive power. Armed with such a view of culture's power, Sahlins is able, for example, to rule out the possibility of Polynesian and Melanesian scepticism and thus the possibility that they might truly learn something new in their encounter with other cultures. According to Sahlins, what happens when they encounter something new and unfamiliar is not a cognitive crisis that may lead to an attempt to understand the new by reassessing their own world view. Instead, they interpret or adapt the new and the strange to fit their preconceived categories. Sahlins tells us that 'the Polynesian epistemological disposition when confronted with ... an extraordinary experience ... is ... not simply to revert to an unmediated sensory contemplation of the object, but to cover the gap between its unprecedented attributes and its evident significance by intimations of divinity [that is, by recourse to Polynesian cosmology].'[205] Melanesians acted similarly in first contact situations when they encountered strange new beings:

> In ways reminiscent of the story of Cook in the Mooolelo *Hawaii* [or Hawaiian history, collected and published by Rev. Sheldon Dibble in 1838],

> direct reports of Melanesians show them scanning their traditional knowledge, notably their so-called myths, to find whatever parallels they could to the observed behaviour of the White folks – and thus achieve a satisfactory interpretation. For the first 'reality' was embedded in myth and ritual practice: what they already knew about being and the world.[206]

There appears to be no attempt on the part of the Polynesians and Melanesians to revise, adjust, or even jettison their myths or culture concepts in the face of unfamiliar or extraordinary experiences; instead, they engage in a Procrustean project, working to fit these experiences into their cultural categories. It seems there is no possibility of cognitive growth or learning, only a reassuring cultural tautology in which percepts, however strange, are assimilated into pre-given concepts.

To be sure, Sahlins allows some room for epistemological scepticism. He gives the example of two New Guinea Highland warriors who closely observed the white strangers, discovered that they 'did not turn into skeletons at night, as myth had it,' and concluded that they should stop believing in the mythic concept that strangers were spirits of the dead. But, Sahlins notes,

> the suggestion did not get very far as collective representation or social memory. From the Asaro as far as Chimbu, people retained the notion that the White men turned into skeletons at night. Lacking a centralized or hierarchical order, it would be difficult to spread such skepticism, especially in the face of rapidly diffusing conceptions of a spiritual advent that could be accepted a priori.[207]

Epistemological scepticism is acknowledged but also very quickly contained by a cultural cosmology that is hard to overcome. But if two Asaro warriors can, through perceptual evidence, sceptically question their culture's belief in the White men as spirits, then there is no reason, social hierarchy or collective tradition notwithstanding, why other Asaro may not eventually arrive at a similar sceptical conclusion. As Margaret Archer argues, once the possibility of internal doubt or scepticism has been raised in a culture, there is no reason to assume that this doubt or scepticism can be unproblematically reintegrated or ignored. To think otherwise would be to believe in 'the primitive cultural dope, unable to exploit the intricacies of his own *Lebenswelt*.'[208] To put it another way, while Sahlins is right to insist that the innocent eye sees nothing, he fails to acknowledge that the culturally informed eye is also capable of broadening its sight by learning to doubt its own limited field of vision. In insisting on the primacy of local cultural concepts, Sahlins downplays the possibility of intercultural learning. As Nicholas Thomas points out, with Sahlins in mind,

> Structural history has generally proceeded by identifying an event in terms of precedents, novelties in terms of prior categories, and foreigners in terms of the local counterparts or types to whom the former are assimilated; this may be sound if a stranger actually is identified with some prior figure, but it neglects the learning process inherent in sustained contact: sooner or later an object such as a flag will not be treated as a special form of an indigenous feather girdle but will be given a distinct value that must draw upon both an indigenous perception and some understanding of how flags are used by the people who introduce them.[209]

As we have seen, in his discussion of the Polynesian and Melanesian examples, Sahlins subordinates sensory percepts to cultural concepts in order to defend cultural relativism against the universalism claimed by Western empiricism. In support of the primacy and relativity of culture, he also invokes the example of different taxonomies or empirical classifications of the world employed by different cultures. '[I]f the classifications of the same sets of organisms by different peoples so vary,' Sahlins argues, 'it must mean that objectivity itself is a variable social value.'[210]

That there are some conceptual and taxonomic differences between cultures is undeniable. The more challenging question is whether these differences suggest that cultures possess radically different and incommensurable rationalities. Sahlins believes they do. For example, he approves of Foucault's reaction to Borges's description of zoological classification in a Chinese encyclopedia, a taxonomy that would appear to Western eyes as irrational, bizarre, or maddeningly whimsical. Of this fantastic classificatory scheme Foucault says: 'In the wonderment of this taxonomy the thing we apprehend in one great leap, the thing that, by means of the fable, is demonstrated in the exotic charms of another system of thought, is the limitation of our own, the stark impossibility of thinking *that*.'[211] Sahlins agrees not only with Foucault's statement about how wonderment can produce an awareness of our limitation, but also with his conclusion on the impossibility of understanding the others' world view. The other not only shows up the limits of our epistemology but also demonstrates a belief in a radically different ontology. As Sahlins remarks: 'The evident difference between common average Western empirical judgements and Hawaiians' or New Guineans' is that ours suppose a world from which spirit and subjectivity were long ago evacuated.'[212] What is proposed here is nothing less than a great divide between the West and its others in which the West has disenchanted the world while other cultures still remain enchanted by spirits and the like. Though Sahlins draws a different conclusion from the dichotomy he has constructed, we should note that it divides the world up in exactly the same way as the Enlightenment thought he challenges.

According to Sahlins, the different rationalities and ontologies of the West and the rest can only lead to incommensurable taxonomies, with the former adopting an 'objective' and pragmatic approach to things and the latter favouring a 'subjective' and symbolic view. To be sure, he is aware that ethnographers who work on the so-called 'folk taxonomies' of non-Western others have pointed out that at an everyday, basic level all classification systems have to take empirical or pragmatic issues into consideration. 'It is commonly said of folk taxonomies,' Sahlins writes, 'that the higher, more inclusive classes tend to be constituted on "cultural" criteria ... , while the lower order, terminal taxa reflect "natural" and/or "utilitarian" contrasts.'[213] Nonetheless, he argues, the lower 'natural' or 'utilitarian' classifications are included or encompassed by the higher cultural forms as 'tokens of meaningful types.' Sahlins explains that 'the lower order, "natural specimens" must include in their own properties the cultural attributes that define the classes to which they belong – which also means that their "utilities," such as their edibility by certain categories of persons, are pragmatic aspects of their symbolic significance.'[214] There is a place for the empirical and the pragmatic in folk taxonomy, but it is a place strictly determined by cultural criteria.

But while culture's role is undeniable in folk and even scientific taxonomies, it can be argued that, in certain situations, cultural concepts may be suspended for purely pragmatic or utilitarian reasons such as the need for nourishment. One is reminded here of Robert Hefner's criticism of Jean Baudrillard's thesis that in primitive society survival is secondary to symbolic exchange. Hefner points out that such a view of absolute cultural primacy would come as a surprise to 'the starving Tikopia of Polynesia, who increasingly restricted the breadth of their social exchange outside minimal kin units in the face of an island-wide famine.'[215] Similarly, even Ralph Bulmer, whose extensive work on the zoological taxonomy of the Kalam of New Guinea is cited by Sahlins approvingly, has to admit that, at times, Kalam animal categories overlap and that pragmatic need is the reason behind this relaxation of classification boundaries. These overlaps, Sahlins explains, drawing on Bulmer's work, 'come about because, as a matter of practicality or convenience, the animals in question may be cooked or consumed in the ways appropriate to one category or the other – which would confirm, post factum, the prescriptive character of the cultural differentiations.'[216] In other words, though admitting that classification boundaries may be relaxed for reasons of 'practicality or convenience' (such as nutritional needs, for example), Sahlins nevertheless maintains that these exceptions prove the rule of cultural classification. But, equally, it can be argued that the exceptions disprove the rule and show that cultural classifications are not so rigid and unchanging that they cannot be modified or even overturned when seriously confronted by the hard lessons of biological necessity or the physical laws of nature. At a certain level, all cultures, however different their world views or classification systems, have to observe basic natural laws and meet certain practical challenges in order to survive. Cultural concepts cannot therefore completely override physical necessity or practical rationality; they have to interact dialectically with the latter. As Wittgenstein once remarked: 'The same savage who, apparently in order to kill his enemy, strikes his knife through a picture of him, really does build his hut of wood and cuts his arrow with skill and not in effigy.'[217]

What drives Sahlins to argue so passionately for cultural relativism? Is it his desire to avoid Eurocentric ideas of the universal that spurs him to champion cultural particularity and difference? Most of us can concur with Sahlins's anti-ethnocentric and anti-colonial sentiments. To avoid colonizing or assimilating the other into the order of the same, we must recognize and respect the other's particularity, the other's difference from us. Anthropologists like Sahlins who attempt to steer clear of epistemic colonization have argued strongly that we should not only 'give careful attention to the self-descriptions of the inhabitants of other times and places' but even concede priority and autonomy to these self-descriptions.[218] In their debate, for example, Sahlins accuses Obeyesekere of appealing 'to a Western sense of practicality and reality *at the expense of Hawaiian culture.*' It is important, Sahlins argues, not to substitute 'our rationality for their culture.' Instead, taking our lead from the work of Michel de Certeau, we should employ 'a true heterology or science of the other, which begins, as Certeau says, just where the specificity of another society "resists Occidental specifications." It begins with the apparent incongruities of the voyaging account, the shocks to our own categories, logic and common sense.'[219] By dismissing heterology, academics like Obeyesekere, though well intentioned in their desire to defend indigenous peoples, end up encompassing them in the West's own value system. We are thus presented with the paradox of a benevolent ethnocentrism in which the indigenous way of life is defended by 'endowing it with the highest cultural values of Western societies.'[220]

But while an awareness of difference may lead us away from ethnocentrism, a strong insistence on difference, as we shall see, leads us right back to it. Any recourse to heterology or the science of the other must confront two problems: the problem of exoticism and the problem of a renewed ethnocentrism.

The relationship between exoticism and Sahlins's view of what the anthropological attitude should be is clearly stated in the following rebuttal of Obeyesekere's recourse to common-sense explanations for Hawaiian behaviour: '"Strange" should be the beginning of anthropological wisdom rather than a way of putting an end to it.'[221] As a warning against the easy assimilation of other cultures' beliefs and a plea for a non-ethnocentric approach to understanding others, Sahlins's statement is salutary. Yet if it is followed axiomatically, we end up with the reification of cultural difference, a kind of automatic and essentialized exoticism. A 'true heterology' would demand that we seek the strange, the unfamiliar, the shocking even; we would be compelled to seek out otherness and even impose it on others. Thus, though heterology might prevent stereotypes produced by familiarity, it encourages what Jean-Pierre Olivier de Sardan calls stereotypes 'generated by unfamiliarity.'[222] What Sahlins regards as the Western sin of ethnocentric familiarity is replaced by the Western longing for exotic strangeness. Nicholas Thomas points out, for example, that the 'fabrication of alterity' is central to the discipline of anthropology:

> Without wishing to deprive the discipline of a thousand dissertation topics, it must be recognized that there is great scope for slippage from the appropriate recognition of difference, and the reasonable reaction against the imposition of European categories upon practices and ideas which, obviously, often are different, to an idea that other people *must* be different. Insofar as this is stipulated by this form of anthropological rhetoric, the discipline is a discourse of alterity that magnifies the distance between 'others' and 'ourselves.'[223]

The recognition of difference may safeguard anthropology from ethnocentrism, but the magnification of difference suggests anthropology's complicity with the West's long history of fascination with the exotic. Clifford Geertz has noted, for example, that anthropologists are 'merchants of astonishment' who 'hawk the anomalous [and] peddle the strange.'[224] In fact, an anthropology that did not have the strange or unfamiliar as its subject would not be the discipline it has popularly come to be identified as. In Geertz's concise formulation, 'If we wanted home truths, we should have stayed at home.'[225] Until recent years the canonical status of the exotic in anthropological circles crowded out other approaches that stressed similarities in the everyday practices of cultures. Commenting on his own discipline, the anthropologist Roger Keesing once remarked that 'our professional role as dealers in exotica impels us to seek deep and cosmologically salient meanings where native actors may find shallow, conventional and pragmatic ones.' Moreover, Keesing also observed, 'because of the reward structures, criteria of publishability, and theoretical premises of our discipline, papers that might show how un-exotic and un-alien other peoples' worlds are never get written or read.'[226] In declaring that 'strange' is the 'beginning of anthropological wisdom,' Sahlins is not only arguing against the ethnocentrism he discerns in Obeyesekere's privileging of a common 'practical rationality,' he is also supporting anthropology's disciplinary investment in the exotic.

We can best see the exoticizing tendency in Sahlins's work in the way contrasts are continually made between the West and other cultures. Thus, in *Islands of History*, he describes how 'the mytho-praxis of Polynesian peoples is contrasted with the disenchanted utilitarianism of our own historical consciousness.'[227] In *How 'Natives' Think*, he observes that '[t]he evident difference between common average Western empirical judgements and Hawaiians' or New Guineans is that ours suppose a world from which spirit and subjectivity were long ago evacuated.'[228] Such characterizations of a disenchanted, utilitarian West and of enchanted, spiritual natives are 'driven by an embedded rhetoric of comparison ... [and] written for some group of "us" about a "them" whose culture had, somehow, to be represented as a fundamentally different way of life.'[229] Sahlins's descriptions not only call on differences, they also utilize what Nicholas Thomas describes as 'contrast': '[T]he most persuasive and theoretically consequential ethnographic rhetoric represents the other essentially as an inversion of whatever Western institution, practice, or set of notions is the real object of interest.'[230]

A good example of how the anthropological rhetoric of contrast generates exoticism can be found in Sahlins's discussion of Western and

Hawaiian views of divinity. He notes that eighteenth-century Hawaiians believed in the doctrine of *kino lau* (or the gods' 'myriad bodies'), which saw no ontological division or distinction between divinity, humanity, and nature. The metaphysics of *kino lau*, as Sahlins points out, 'is just the opposite of Western distinctions of God, Man, and Nature, each occupying a separate kingdom of being. Empirically, then, never the three shall meet, or at least not until the last judgement; whereas, for Hawaiians, the appearance of Lonomakua at the Makahiki of 1778–79 could be substantiated by perceptual evidence.'[231] Now if it is indeed the case that eighteenth-century Hawaiians did not distinguish ontologically between man and god, then there is no need to talk about 'apotheosis,' which first requires the establishment of the ontological divide and then the crossing of the divide that results in the elevation of man into god. There is no need for Hawaiian natives to cross or to consider crossing the divide since for them there is no divide to begin with and thus no conceptual or lexical necessity for a term like 'apotheosis.' As Jonathan Friedman has remarked with reference to the Sahlins-Obeyesekere debate on Cook's apotheosis: 'The apotheosis of Captain Cook is ... not a Hawaiian phenomenon, because Hawaiians did not practice apotheosis. But their recognition of Cook's godly status might be argued to have been reinterpreted in later European and European-informed texts, where there is an absolute distinction between gods and humans.'[232] Sahlins thus appears to be caught in a contradiction of sorts. On the one hand, he assumes the native's point of view in which there is no ontological divide between god and man and hence no conceptual need for apotheosis. But on the other, he supports the thesis of Cook's apotheosis, which has been historically recorded mainly by and for Europeans, because it involves the exotic and shocking idea of crossing the ontological divide between god and man. The contradiction may, however, be a necessity of Sahlins's anthropological discourse. To avoid the charge of Eurocentrism, Sahlins foregrounds the distinctiveness of Hawaiian cosmology in which god, man, and native are not ontologically separated. At the same time, however, wishing to validate the Western anthropological principle that strangeness is required to shock us out of our complacent and ethnocentric world view, Sahlins retains the idea of the Hawaiian apotheosis of Cook, which requires the crossing of the ontological divide, the existence of which his description of Hawaiian cosmology had denied. Sahlins's apotheosis thesis is thus an example of the anthropological invention of the exotic where there is none.

Consider, for instance, an alternative approach. Instead of the apotheosis thesis, which requires the native other to behave in an exotic manner by crossing the divinity-humanity divide of our making, we can de-exoticize the native by adopting his or her perspective on Cook. When we do this from a perspective in which there is no difference in ontological kind between god and man, only a difference in degree of power and status, we discover that there is no apotheosis of Cook. Cook does not become a god in our sense; instead he is received as someone possessed of great power and extraordinary status, but ontologically no different from a high-ranking priest or chief. In other words, there are two ways in which we can translate the Hawaiian lack of distinction between the divine and the human. We can opt for the exotic translation and emphasize the gap or difference between us and them, between our ontological division and their cosmological holism, in the process validating the relativism of 'different cultures, different rationalities' as Sahlins does. In such a translation we can point to the remarkable apotheosis of Captain Cook by the Hawaiians. But we can also choose another translation that narrows the gap between Europeans and Hawaiians, without losing sight of the differences, to be sure, but without exaggerating them either. This would be a translation that would refrain from emphasizing what would appear, to Western eyes, as an exotic and strange form of worship, and attend, instead, to what Hawaiians would regard as a routine distinction of social rank, a process familiar no doubt even to Westerners.

Difference can be further de-exoticized if it is seen as politically or historically constituted rather than culturally pre-given. To do this would require a redirection of anthropological attention. Rather than focusing solely on other cultures' cosmologies or belief systems as given structural entities, anthropology should look into how these entities are discursively and institutionally produced and used. Moreover, the study of differences between cultures may be less about relativism than about what relativism masks: namely, that in our world, cultural relativism is not about equal and autonomous cultural units but about unequal relations and imbalances of power, about what David Scott calls 'the fundamentally areciprocal character of the ideological structure that makes anthropology possible.'[233] In recent years, anthropology has started to shift its attention from the study of cultural difference to the study of 'the processes of *production* of difference,'[234] of how cultures are formed and differentiated or contrasted by discourses of power. Nicholas Thomas, for example, has remarked that 'the challenge is not to do away with cultural difference, and with what is locally distinctive, but to integrate this more effectively with historical perception and a sense of the unstable and politically contested character of culture.'[235] Lila Abu-Lughod urges us 'to think about "culture" not so much as a system of meaning or even a way of life but as something whose elements are produced ... [and that this] should lead us to think about the ways that aspects of what we used to think of as local culture ... are themselves not neutral features to be interpreted but the sometimes contested result of other ... projects of power.'[236] In a similar vein, Verena Stolcke observes: 'It is not cultural diversity per se that should interest anthropologists but the political meanings with which political contexts and relationships endow cultural difference ... It is the configuration of sociopolitical structures and relationships both within and between groups that activates differences and shapes possibilities and impossibilities of communicating.'[237] We are also reminded by James Suzman that too much emphasis on 'cultural survival' may mask struggles over livelihood, social justice, and access to resources. 'Indeed,' Suzman observes, 'when and if culture enters into local narratives, it is usually as an adjunct to other concerns. Southern Africa's San people are frustrated not because they cannot pursue their "traditional culture" but because they are impoverished, marginalized, and exploited by the dominant population.'[238]

Resisting these recent calls from within the discipline for a reorientation of anthropological inquiry, Sahlins continues to believe in the existence of ontological differences between cultures, endorsing the slogan of 'different cultures, different rationalities,' while refusing the argument that cultural differences are produced within fields of power both discursive and material. It is noticeable, for example, that in Sahlins's work, Hawaiian politics is subordinated to Hawaiian cosmology. In his words: 'Politics appears as the continuation of cosmogonic war by other means.'[239] The exoticism necessary to anthropology is established when contests for power in Hawaiian society are seen as ritualized expressions of a pre-given cosmology rather than as the worldly and pragmatic political practices to which we are accustomed. The exoticism advanced by a cosmological reading of Hawaiian politics means that less attention is paid to the specific workings of power not only among the different strata of Hawaiian society or among the different interests represented in the Cook expedition, but also between these two parties. To be sure, Sahlins does not entirely ignore the various deployments of power; his aim, however, is not to argue that differences in power can result in the production and institution of social and cultural differences, but to demonstrate in particular the existence of a profound ontological difference between Hawaiian and European world views and to affirm in general the principle of cultural relativism. Cultural difference is assumed as a given fact and not something produced or activated in the exercise of power among and between Hawaiians and Europeans.

Sahlins's valorization of cultural difference and his disavowal of its relation to power are reflected clearly in what he takes and in what he dismisses from Foucault's work. Sahlins approves of the anti-ethnocentric and relativist aspects of Foucault's thought, as is evident in his citing favourably Foucault's description, borrowed from Borges, of the exotic Chinese encyclopedia. But he is extremely critical of Foucault's work on power, which he likens to a kind of functionalism in which 'specific cultural forms [are dissolved] into generic instrumental effects.' 'Power,' Sahlins adds scathingly, 'is the intellectual black hole into which all kinds of cultural contents get sucked.'[240] But, equally, it can be argued that we find in Sahlins's writings the dissolution of the specific workings of power into a generic heterology, a generalized cultural relativism as capable of sucking everything into it as Foucault's black hole of power.

Sahlins's criticism of what he describes as Foucault's neo-functionalist theory of power is similar to his earlier critique of Malinowski's functionalism for reducing the particularities of culture or what would appear to the Western eye as 'seemingly bizarre customs' to comprehensible 'practical values.'[241] As Sahlins explains in his critique of Malinowskian functionalism:

> There is more to this [functionalism] than the obvious implication that if the interpretation proves acceptable to the European, it suggests more about him than about the 'savages' – most generally that the anthropologist's 'etic' [or objective scientific description] is his own society's 'emic' [or culturally specific meaning system]. Something is to be said about the subject/object relation implied by the compulsion to make a practical 'sense' out of an exotic custom that is both intricate and not prima facie a matter of practical necessity. It raises the anthropologist to the divinity of a constituting subject, from whom emanates the design of the culture. Rather than submit himself to the comprehension of a structure with an independent and authentic existence, he understands that structure by his comprehension of its purpose – and so makes its existence depend on him.[242]

Similarly, Sahlins argues, the concept of power employed by Foucault and his followers results in a neo-functionalism in which the particularities or peculiarities of a culture are submitted to the totalizing explanatory framework provided by power. To anthropologists influenced by Foucault, interpreting another culture 'consists entirely of categorizing the cultural form at issue in terms of domination, as if that accounts for it.'[243] Power, the analytic concept used to uncover domination in social and cultural life, ironically becomes itself an instance of the very practice of domination. Malinowskian functionalists and Foucaultian neo-functionalists thus suffer alike from 'ethnographic hubris,'[244] an occupational hazard in which what begins as sympathy for the other turns into the ethnographer's own peremptory explication of the other. To guard against such ethnocentric dangers, Sahlins and other symbolically minded anthropologists therefore recommend a relativist approach that is concerned primarily 'with how people formulate their reality' and that directs attention to '*their* culture, not *our theories.*'[245]

But cultural relativists, like Sahlins, who argue that cultures are relative to their own cosmologies, and thus have different rationalities, find themselves in the awkward position of re-establishing the ethnocentrism they had hoped to avoid by adopting cultural relativism. For though cultural relativism prevents any culture from installing its own perspective as universal truth by insisting on profound ethical, epistemological, and ontological differences between cultures, it paradoxically ends up supporting a de facto ethnocentrism since in its view a culture can be understood and judged by others, or can understand and judge others, *only according to its own set of beliefs and practices.* In short, cultural relativism ushers ethnocentrism out the front door only to have it return through the back.

'Back-door' ethnocentrism is most clearly in evidence in Sahlins's argument that since native cultures view the world according to their own cosmologies, we can understand them only if we attend carefully to the particulars of their belief system, especially to those that appear most bizarre or strange to us. What this means in effect is that our avoidance of ethnocentrism depends paradoxically on the other (native) culture's resolute ethnocentrism, its assimilation of all events into its own pre-existing cosmology. Thus, in the controversy over Cook's apotheosis, Sahlins uncovers the Western ethnocentrism underlying Obeyesekere's argument for a universal 'practical rationality' by pointing out that the latter ignores Hawaiian cultural cosmology. In contrast, Sahlins painstakingly shows how eighteenth-century Hawaiians busily shored up their ethnocentric world view by assimilating the intrusion of the strange and the foreign into their own familiar cultural categories. Thus, Cook the stranger became a part of the Hawaiian belief that gods hailed from the distant land of Kahiki. As Sahlins puts it: 'The irruption of Captain Cook from beyond the horizon was a truly unprecedented event, never seen before. But by thus encompassing the existentially unique in the conceptually familiar [that is, by turning Cook into one of their gods], the people embed their present in the past.'[246] A similar ethnocentric cultural logic was deployed later by the Hawaiians to explain why the foreigners lost their divine status when Hawaiian women started to dine with them aboard their ships. In Sahlins's words, 'There is nothing in the act of eating with women that is inherently ungodly – except that in the Hawaiian system it is polluting of men and destroys their tabu. Events thus cannot be understood apart from the values attributed to them ... What is for some people a radical event may appear to others as a date for lunch.'[247] Sahlins's relativist conclusion, as we can see, is based on a mutual ethnocentrism: the Hawaiians followed their own cultural system of taboos and the disenchanted Europeans pursued their pragmatic interests and appetites.

Sahlins provides another example of native ethnocentrism in the encounter between white prospectors and the Huli in the Southern Highlands of New Guinea. In 1934, two gold prospectors named Jack and Tom Fox killed more than forty-five people as they traversed the Huli area. Fifty years later, when an anthropologist interviewed eight eyewitnesses of the terrible events, he discovered that for them the Fox brothers were not human but *dama* or spirits. So what may appear to us as 'a fateful world-historical irruption into their "traditional" existence is for many Melanesian peoples [like the Huli] not historically or socially remarked as such.' What for us is a historical first contact is for the Huli a familiar if devastating spiritual visitation, neither the first nor the last. Moreover, Sahlins warns us, European 'violence' was not seen as such by those on whom it was perpetrated :

> Huli history reminds us that such violence has neither self-evident meaning nor patent historical significance. The Huli did not lay their deaths on White men because the killers were not White men. So nothing can be taken for granted or deduced a priori, even from The Horror. Not without the indigenous understandings of what happened, why, and who was concerned – which may well turn out to be cosmic questions. Nothing here could have been deduced directly or transparently from our own moral sentiments.[248]

Again, Sahlins employs cultural relativism to combat ethnocentrism, only to end up with a renewed ethnocentrism. One man's violence, he argues, may be another's 'cosmic entropy.'[249] Apart from the problem that such a relativist argument may be used to excuse the perpetrators of violence – after all, their victims blame cosmic imbalance, not them – there is the additional paradox that in safeguarding Huli culture from our ethnocentric moral sentiments we end up exalting indigenous knowledge as self-enclosed and ethnocentric, impervious to any foreign intrusion, however devastating.

It appears then that Sahlins's anti-ethnocentric injunction that we respect the particularity of native cultures requires us to see these cultures as somehow confined in their own distinctiveness. As Arjun Appadurai argues, '[T]he critical part of the attribution of nativeness to groups in remote parts of the world is a sense that their incarceration has a moral and intellectual dimension. They are confined by what they know, feel, and believe. They are prisoners of their "mode of thought."'[250] To Sahlins's credit, however, he does not exempt European culture from the same ethnocentric incarceration he attributes to other cultures. To him, we are all natives. Here we have Sahlins's version of what we have called a 'primitivism without primitives.' In his view the 'native' as the West's inferior Other does not exist because the concept of 'native' encompasses the West itself. He thus re-signifies the term 'native' – a term that implies cultural primordialism – by extending it to include every culture, not just non-Western ones. Since we are now all natives, each with our own discrete and autochthonous cosmologies, the West can no longer claim the possession of a universal reason that allegedly distinguishes it from other native cultures. In fact, Sahlins's work is directed precisely against the arrogance that would turn native European cultural schemes into universal truths. In the Sidney Mintz lecture for 1994, entitled 'The Sadness of Sweetness: The Native Anthropology of Western Cosmology,' Sahlins has provided his most detailed exposition of the 'native cultural structures of the long term that still inhibit academic anthropology – as well as other Western social sciences – and bedevil our understandings of other peoples.'[251] The object of Sahlins's examination of native Western cosmology is to reveal 'the historical relativity of our native anthropology.'[252] It appears that to recognize the native, and hence relative, bases of Western culture, to acknowledge that we are prisoners of our own mode of thought is the first step towards combatting the ethnocentrism that bedevils our understanding of other cultures. We must admit to being imprisoned by our ethnocentrism in order to shed our ethnocentrism. But surely this is a paradox that needs to be explained.

A further difficulty arises, since to acknowledge the ethnocentrism of cultures is also to concede to the impossibility of inter-cultural understanding. Recall Sahlins's dictum that 'there is no such thing as an immaculate perception.'[253] In other words, there is for us no knowledge or understanding that has not already been informed or mediated by our own cultural concepts. But if this is true, if all cultures are locked up in their own ethnocentric categories, then there can be no inter-cultural understanding. Culture A cannot really be understood by culture B because culture B's 'understanding' of culture A will always be coloured or mediated by B's own cultural categories. Sahlins would end up safeguarding anthropology as the study of cultural particularity while questioning the possibility that another culture can ever be studied objectively. He would end up with an anthropology that would question the very possibility of anthropological knowledge, since any knowledge of another culture would be mediated by one's own cultural concepts and thus appear as a tautological confirmation of one's own culture rather than as knowledge of the other. What begins as cultural relativism would appear to end up as a limited and limiting ethnocentrism.

Sahlins cannot of course admit that anthropology is limited by ethnocentrism to the study of its own culture and not of others'. He therefore resolves the paradoxes and difficulties facing his account of cultural relativism by allowing the anthropologist the power to be culture-transcendent while all others, native others and native Westerners alike, remain culture-bound. 'Anthropology,' Sahlins declares firmly, 'is an attempt to transcend the customary parochial limits of ... discourse.'[254] But can Western anthropology transcend its own cosmology, the Judaeo-Christian traditions so carefully described in Sahlins's 1994 Mintz lecture? Is there 'the possibility of an alternative anthropology,' one no longer in the grip of its own native Western categories? Sahlins answers positively:

> I do tend to believe ... that the metadiscourse which is the Mintz lecture itself is already something of an alternative anthropology. There is some critical distance taken from the native folklore it describes. Analytic and at least crypto-sensitive to other possibilities, the perspective is not the same as the conceptions of humanity, divinity, society, and the universe it intends to understand. There is no need to suppose we are the prisoners of received categories.[255]

With that last statement Sahlins appears to have exempted anthropologists like himself from the condition that applies to all other natives, namely, that their understanding is culturally mediated and that 'in the final analysis the categories by which [their] objectivity is defined are themselves cosmological.'[256] Moreover, the alternative anthropology Sahlins envisages is cosmopolitan and not ethnocentric or culturally bound. As he remarks, '[I]t would be of no purpose to exchange our indigenous anthropology for another that is equally relative and particular.'[257] It is possible, Sahlins argues, to have an anthropological practice that not only transcends its own culture but is also at once comparative and objective. The analogy he uses to push for such an anthropological method is the model of the international phonetic alphabet:

> All etics or languages of objective scientific description (so-called) are based on a grid of meaningful or emic distinctions. Take the international phonetic alphabet ... The phonetic alphabet is made up of all known *phonemic* distinctions: of all differences in sound-segments known to signify differences in meaning in the natural languages of the world. So in principle the objective description of any language consists of its comparison with the meaningful order of all other languages.
>
> The same for ethnography. No good ethnography is self-contained. Implicitly or explicitly ethnography is an act of comparison. By virtue of comparison ethnographic description becomes objective ... [I]t becomes a universal understanding to the extent it brings to bear on the perception of any society the conceptions of all the others.[258]

What is interesting about Sahlins's use of the 'emic'/'etic' distinction is that it reveals how his strong belief in cultural relativism – the world of 'emic' differences – is based on a stronger faith in the universal understanding that can be achieved by anthropology – the world of objective 'etic' knowledge. As we have seen, Sahlins regards the existence of different cultures and the relativism they imply as of central importance to anthropology. But, as we have argued, if all cultures are relative to, and thus imprisoned in, their own conceptual schemes, then no culture can comment on another culture and the possibility of a cosmopolitan anthropology disappears. The problem arises because cultural relativism, against its own assumption, 'needs an external standpoint in order to declare objectively that one culture has one standard and another culture another.'[259] Sahlins's recourse to the 'emic'/'etic' model shows that he is aware of this relativist paradox or impasse. The solution is to subsume the 'emic' descriptions of different cultures under an external 'etic' scheme in which these different cultures can be meaningfully compared so as to achieve 'a cosmopolitan anthropological consciousness of the species being.'[260] Sahlins's solution to the relativist paradox thus involves a curious inversion in which cultural relativism flips over to reveal itself as anthropological universalism. Ironically, then, Sahlins's position comes to resemble that of his antagonist, Obeyesekere, whose heuristic assumption of certain pan-human capacities Sahlins has strenuously resisted.

The inversion of cultural relativism into anthropology's universal understanding raises the question of power in the study of other cultures. In a discussion that parallels his description of how 'emic' differences can be comparatively ordered into an objective 'etic' understanding, Sahlins talks about the necessity for 'the two moves of ethnography: submission to the understandings of the others and the integration of what is thus learned in a general anthropological understanding.'[261] Following Bakhtin, Sahlins calls the former 'endotopy' and the latter 'exotopy.' 'Endotopy' is described as 'the arduous, *einfühlen* [empathetic] aspect of the ethnographic encounter.'[262] But it is 'exotopy' that interests Sahlins more. He approvingly cites Todorov citing Bakhtin on the importance of 'exotopy' in the study of culture:

> To be sure, to enter into some measure into an alien culture [endotopy] ... is a necessary moment in the process of its understanding; but if understanding were exhausted at this moment, it would have been no more than a simple duplication ... The chief matter of understanding is the *exotopy* of the one who does the understanding ... in relation to that which he wants to understand creatively ... In the realm of culture, exotopy is the most powerful lever of understanding. It is only to the eyes of an *other* culture that the alien culture reveals itself more completely and more deeply.[263]

Combining endotopy and exotopy, anthropology aims for nothing less than 'the *identity* of another cultural logic and one's own thought.'[264] Referring to Lévi-Strauss, Sahlins declares that 'the distinctive project of anthropology consists in transforming the objectively remote into the subjectively familiar.' Anthropology attempts to achieve 'a substantial unity of the knowing subject with that which is known,' so that 'a Fijian logic by origin' becomes '*something going on inside us*.'[265] What began with endotopy or submission to the understandings of other cultures ends in an exotopic anthropology that not only transcends and supersedes other cultural understandings but also appears to have ingested or incorporated them into itself. An inversion, related to the one we discussed earlier, seems to have taken place. Where once we were told that '"strange" should be the beginning of anthropological wisdom,'[266] now we are reminded that it is anthropology's task to transform 'the objectively remote into the subjectively familiar.' Where once we were warned not to allow our categories of understanding to interfere with those of other cultures, now we are presented with an anthropology that anthropophagically incorporates other cultural logics as 'something going on inside us.' Where once heterology was recommended, now the aim is to achieve the 'substantial unity of the knowing subject with that which is known.' An ethics of alterity, the letting be of the other, is supplanted by the identity of the other with one's own thought.

What we see in this exotopic incorporation of the other into a general anthropological understanding is nothing less than the exercise of power by the anthropologist. It appears, at first, that dialogic understanding is the issue, not power. Thus, according to Sahlins,

> By virtue of the shared humanity of anthropologists and their interlocutors, which is also to say their common symbolic capacity, the former replicate in mind as the meaningful significance of custom, what the latter express and practice. By virtue of their common ability to grasp, analyze, and recombine meaning, the necessities of custom practiced by other peoples reappear as the logical sequiturs of an anthropological understanding. In a certain way, more or less imperfect of course, the anthropologist recapitulates as his or her own mind – as logical operations – the process by which the phenomena of custom were produced.[267]

A closer examination of Sahlins's account of 'the shared humanity of anthropologists and their interlocutors' reveals, however, a certain asymmetry and imbalance of power. The anthropologist can replicate *in mind* what the natives can only express *in practice*. The necessities of custom practised routinely by natives are transformed into the conscious, logical sequiturs of anthropological understanding. What this implies is that the native is neither fully conscious nor knowledgeable of his or her customary cultural practices, whereas the anthropologist can reconstitute these practices as meaningful logical operations. Thus, *contra* postmodernist suspicion, Sahlins recommends the turn to ethnographic authority because, in his view, people living in a culture cannot 'be expected to give an adequate account of why they say what they are saying or do what they are doing.'[268] Sahlins is essentially in agreement with Evans-Pritchard's contention that the anthropologist 'discovers in a native society what no native can explain to him and what no layman, however conversant with the culture, can perceive – its basic structure.'[269] What should arrest our attention in such claims is less their arrogance than their arrogation of great epistemic powers to anthropologists and their discipline. Recall Sahlins's description of the two moves of anthropology. If endotopy, the first move, is the moment of submission to the other's culture, it is also a submission that gains the anthropologist 'insider' knowledge. Exotopy, the second move, then allows the anthropologist to step outside and distance himself from the other culture, enabling him, at the same time, to position that culture objectively in a comparative field and thus understand it more deeply and completely than it could ever hope to understand itself. Able to move freely in and out of cultures, combining 'insider' knowledge with an external perspective that is comparative and cosmopolitan, anthropology's mobility and privileged access to many cultures reflect the power – material, political, and epistemic – it possesses over its native interlocutors. Though Sahlins concedes that anthropology's knowledge of other cultures is always 'more or less imperfect,' the qualification does not alter the argument that anthropology's cosmopolitan knowledge gives it a decided advantage over the relatively immobile and self-enclosed cultures it studies. Anthropology's superiority or advantage, though Sahlins does not quite put it that way, lies in its ability to see culture from both the inside and the outside, to understand the particularity of a culture as well as its particular place in a general anthropological comprehension of our species being. Native cultures lack such a double perspective and thus remain locked within their own categories or concepts. The difference between anthropologists and natives, a difference that also expresses the unequal power relation between them is well captured in Bernard McGrane's astute description:

> The Other [or native] becomes *an occasion for seeing the strength of custom.* He manifests, above all, his own imprisonment within culture. We see the logically necessary, relativity, whereas they are governed by the psychologically customary, absoluteness ... A principle [*sic*] characteristic of the Other, then, is that he is incapable of recognizing otherness ... The principle [*sic*] characteristic of different cultures, anthropologically conceived, is their inability to recognize difference, i.e., their inability to recognize, as we do, their own relativity. Our knowledge lies in the fact that we recognize, not, as in the Enlightenment, our ignorance, but rather our relativity: our relativity

and their relativity, whereas their ignorance lies now in their cultural absolutism.[270]

To put it another way, the anthropologist's awareness of cultural relativism puts him on the path of universal understanding, whereas the native's ignorance of the relativity of his own culture confirms his ethnocentrism.

Looking back at Sahlins's work, we can now see that his defence of the particularity of native cultures against the assimilative tendencies of Western ethnocentric thought is superseded by his proposal for a comparative anthropological method unrestricted by the limits of any one particular culture. At one level of Sahlins's thought, cultural particularity and cultural relativism are affirmed; but at another level, their parochial limits are noted and transcended by a 'cosmopolitan anthropological consciousness of the species being.'[271] What seems at first to be Sahlins's championing of a cultural relativism inspired by Herder turns out to be a more Hegelian desire for a 'self-consciousness of humanity,'[272] that is, for a universal anthropological understanding. To Sahlins, cultural relativism is a necessary stage for what is an even more central and urgent task: establishing anthropology as the *science* (or *universal understanding*) of cultural variation, especially at a time when '"culture" ... is in the twilight of its career, and anthropology with it.'[273] The reference to Hegel calls attention to an underacknowledged philosophical influence in Sahlins's work.[274] Like Hegel, Sahlins demands that we pay attention to the dimension of change in history, the phenomenal world of events, the existence of different cultures, and the relativism that follows in order to understand the totality they constitute together. In his discussion of the Hegelian concept of *Geist,* variously translated as cosmic spirit or infinite subject, Charles Taylor points out that in order for it to be known *Geist* requires an external embodiment, and since an external embodiment must be in space and time, that is, somewhere and sometime and in a particular being, *Geist* or the infinite subject 'can only be through a finite one.'[275] At the same time, however, though *Geist* requires a finite embodiment, it 'cannot be confined to the particular place and time of any one finite spirit. It has to compensate for its necessary localization, as it were, by living through many finite spirits.'[276] The fullness of the infinite subject requires that 'differences are maximally deployed.'[277] *Geist* as infinite subject can thus be seen as the unity or totality of its many different finite embodiments. Now Taylor reminds us that the Hegelian synthesis or unification of finite and infinite subject, of the phenomenal world and *Geist*, does not abolish the finite differences but retains them in a higher unity:

> Not only is the unity hard-won out of difference, as man struggles to rise to the level where the unity can be grasped; but the ultimate unity retains the difference within it. We remain finite subjects, ... men with all the particularities of their time, place and circumstances, even as we come to see this particular existence as part of a larger plan, as we come to be vehicles of a larger self-consciousness, that of *Geist*.[278]

But even though the differences of finite particulars are retained and not abolished in the larger synthesis, it is clear that Hegel's philosophy pushes for an understanding of the *totality* of these particulars, an understanding that leads to the larger self-consciousness of *Geist* and allows it to supersede the limitations of finite particulars. Similarly, though 'emic' cultural differences are valued in Sahlins's work, they are also subjected to an anthropological synthesis that leads to the totality of an 'etic' understanding. As Sahlins puts it, anthropology struggles 'to synthesize cultural and historical diversity in a unitary field of knowledge.'[279] But again, as in Hegel, though differences are acknowledged and allowed to retain their importance, they are also superseded by a higher consciousness that can grasp the totality they constitute. The anthropologist who is, according to Sahlins, 'already by training partly cosmopolitan' is best placed to compare and synthesize the cultural differences and variations of our world into a unitary field of knowledge, thus achieving a *Geist*-like 'self-consciousness of humanity.'[280] As in Hegel's philosophy, the ultimate aim of anthropology is to grasp the *totality* the different cultures constitute, or what Sahlins, in a decidedly Hegelian vein, calls 'a Culture of cultures.'[281]

For the past twenty or more years, Sahlins has conducted a scathing critique of ethnocentric Western theories that have tried to pass themselves off as universal. Thus, in a way, Sahlins's anti-ethnocentric, relativist approach resembles that of postmodern alterity theorists like Baudrillard and Lyotard; like them, he wishes to protect the difference of the Other from well-intentioned but ultimately colonizing forms of Western universalism (it is interesting to note that Sahlins and Baudrillard cite each other's work in the seventies). But Sahlins's position also diverges from postmodern theories in that he believes in cultural holism and identity, and seeks, through a comparative, cosmopolitan methodology, to instal the anthropologist in the seat of knowledge.

What we have noted as the Hegelian turn in Sahlins's thought is mirrored in the inversion that sees his cultural relativism flip over into anthropology's universal understanding and his defence of native cultural particularity turn into the greater need for a cosmopolitan transcendence of parochial limits. Here we have a version of neo-primitivism at work, a neo-primitivism Hegelian in inspiration. Though the native is no longer the 'primitive' of colonial and evolutionary anthropology, his difference, which remains linked to his primordial, holistic cultural origins, is essential for the anthropological project that studies the cultural differences and variations that make up our humanity or species being. In other words, the survival of native cultures, and hence of cultural differences and cultural relativism, guarantees the central epistemic role of the (Western) anthropologist who traverses these 'emic' differences in order to arrive at an 'etic' understanding of the totality the differences make.

Towards the end of his introduction to *How 'Natives' Think*, Sahlins sadly notes that anthropology and the 'culture' concept on which it depends have been subjected to so much criticism that they both appear to be in the twilight of their career. But, echoing Hegel, Sahlins sees in their threatened disappearance a portent of their revival: 'May the owl of Minerva take wing at dusk.'[282] The anthropological wisdom Sahlins would like to see take wing again requires the recognition of cultural particularity and relativity and endorses the slogan 'Different cultures, different rationalities.'[283] What Sahlins fails to mention, however, is that the wisdom anthropology imparts at the twilight of its career follows the same logic of subsumption that founded it as a discipline: a looking outward at the many that relativizes the discipline to be sure, but also gives it a panoptical, cosmopolitan perspective that allows it to subsume the many. Nicholas Dirks, for example, has alertly warned us of just such a problem: '[W]hile cultures were relative to one another, they could not be relative to anthropological knowledge.'[284] Anthropology's openness to all forms of otherness secures for it, but not for those others – call them 'primitives,' 'natives,' 'indigenous' peoples, or what you will – access to a universal understanding of humanity. Or, to put it concisely, anthropology's multiplication of cultural others results in a reduction to its singular, privileged knowledge. However circumspect and respectful of otherness, however insistent it is on jettisoning universalism for its own 'nativeness,' Sahlins's work still cannot do without the concept of the primitive in its claims for the importance of anthropological knowledge.

4 Modernity: Jürgen Habermas

'Followed as if by a shadow': Habermas's Other Discourse of Modernity

If 'culture' functions as a displaced form of neo-primitivism, as the previous chapter has shown, 'modernity' as a conceptual term can be shown to harbour a primitivist logic as well. To claim, as this chapter will, that 'modernity' is not opposed to, but in league with, neo-primitivism will come as a shock to most readers. And to argue further that Jürgen Habermas's committed and thoughtful defence of the project of modernity relies on the premodern or primitive Other, not only as its antithesis but also as its secret sharer, will seem an even more outlandish provocation. But a careful reading of his works, both with and against their grain, will yield some surprising conclusions and reveal a troubled complexity to his thought that more straightforward commentaries fail to uncover. We will therefore learn in this chapter that a critical examination of Habermas's theory of modernity also happens to be a discussion of neo-primitivism. If 'culture' is a 'nice name' that has replaced primitivism, in this chapter 'modernity' is the surprising new name primitivism has assumed.

The crisis of modernity is caused not by reason's repressive hold on society but by reason's distorted development. This, in brief, is the argument forwarded by Habermas in works of magisterial learning and synthesis, such as the massive two-volumed *The Theory of Communicative Action* and the twelve lectures published as *The Philosophical Discourse of Modernity*. In an interview in 1981, Habermas remarked that from the late fifties on, the principal problem that occupied him was 'a theory of modernity, a theory of the pathology of modernity, from the viewpoint of the realization – the deformed realization – of reason in history.'[1] Though phrased negatively, Habermas's statement signals its disagreement with Horkheimer and Adorno's bleak assessment of reason's complicity with domination in their *The Dialectic of Enlightenment.* In fact, by attributing modernity's pathology to the *deformed* realization of reason, Habermas questions Horkheimer and Adorno's totalized critique of reason and their 'lack of concern in dealing with the ... achievements of Occidental rationalism.'[2] Habermas contends that his predecessors at Frankfurt 'surrendered themselves to an uninhibited scepticism regarding reason, instead of weighing the grounds that cast doubt on this scepticism itself.'[3] In response, his work has been devoted precisely to a weighing of the grounds that can question scepticism while providing a defence of reason's achievements. The attempt to do justice to the rational content of modernity is thus the principal motivation behind his complex theoretical enterprise.

Habermas is without doubt one of the staunchest defenders of the Enlightenment idea of a modernity that 'understands itself in opposition to tradition ... [and] seeks a foothold for itself, so to speak, in reason.'[4] Habermas supports modernity's desire to 'create all its normativity from out of itself' and shares its belief that reason must be critical of all authority, save that claimed by reason itself.[5] To be sure, Habermas also agrees with the views of those who oppose modernity's subject-centred reason, 'which [has] objectified everything in its path, transforming all into possible objects of manipulation.'[6] But these critics of modernity, Habermas argues, erroneously go on to identify a part of reason with the whole, and are thus mistaken in totally rejecting reason for reason's *Other.* He is, therefore, critical not only of Horkheimer and Adorno, as we have noted, but also of all those like Heidegger, Bataille, Derrida, Foucault, Lyotard, and other 'postmodernists' who have followed Nietzsche in 'overtrumping modernity,'[7] on behalf of the Other of reason, which is prediscursive, premodern, archaic, 'resistant to any attempts at rational incorporation'[8] and answers to such names as the Dionysian, Being, sovereignty, the heterogeneous, and power.[9] The Other that threatens modernity's rationality is seen by Habermas not as a *diremption* of reason that can ultimately be reconciled, but as an *exclusion* from reason, not as 'a split-off and suppressed part of reason, but ... temporally related to something preceding it, something allegedly authentic and archaic.'[10] As Habermas explains, the experience of reason's Other 'is projected – by Nietzsche and his successors – backwards into archaic origins, onto the Dionysian, the pre-Socratic, the exotic and primitive.'[11] It is generally agreed, therefore, that Habermas's defence of modernity's rationally established normativity requires him to criticize severely discourses that pose alternatives to reason's hold on modernity. In one of the most astute critiques of Habermas's approach to the question of otherness, Diana Coole points out that his antipathy to the discourses of postmodernism and post-structuralism 'rests on his denial of any emancipatory role to alterity' and his conviction that the appeal to reason's Other is 'irrational, anachronistic and out of step with history's evolution.'[12]

We must, nevertheless, note that a persistent strand in Habermas's thought troubles his own project, namely, a muted acknowledgment that modern rationality needs the premodern Other not only as its antithesis, but also as its *supplément* in the Derridian sense, that is, as an inessential extra or 'add-on' that nevertheless fills a lack or absence in the original whole. On the one hand, Habermas's account of modern rationalization processes requires a narrative of reason's progress, an evolutionary account in which the premodern or primitive occupies the position of the Other that has been surpassed by a decentred, rationalized modernity. We have here modernity's 'othering' discourse in which the premodern is opposed to the modern, the archaic and the traditional to the rationalized and the post-conventional. On the other hand, Habermas acknowledges the continuing presence in modern life and society of pre-reflective, pre-discursive, premodern elements. Modernity's discursive need for a primitive Other against which the evolution or progress of reason can be measured is thus accompanied by a counter-discourse that conceives of premodern forms of solidarity as the hidden archaic core or prototype of modern communicative action and consensus. In other words, modernity not only requires the supersession and exclusion of the premodern or primitive in order to be modern, but also relies on the inclusion of primitivity as its own enabling presupposition. Habermas's theory of modernity is, paradoxically, a form of neo-primitivism; it has to presuppose and include the primitive Other even as it seeks to overcome and exclude it. The premodern Other superseded by modernity is folded back into Habermas's work to return as the other discourse that continues to inhabit and haunt modernity.

The other discourse of modernity is, as we shall see, already present in Habermas's attempt to establish the normative foundation of critical theory in language. Questioning Horkheimer and Adorno's pessimistic diagnosis of the one-sided development of instrumental reason in modern society, Habermas affirms reason's emancipatory potential by securing for it a universal ground in that most basic of human competences: our ability to communicate through language. Habermas strives to establish such a universal normative ground, according to Richard Bernstein, in order to show that 'emancipatory critique does not rest upon arbitrary norms which we "choose"; rather it is grounded in the very structures of intersubjective communicative competences.'[13]

Habermas's 'linguistic turn,' his thesis that an emancipatory reason can be grounded in human communication, was first tentatively broached in his Frankfurt inaugural address of June 1965 (published as an appendix to *Knowledge and Human Interests*):

> The human [emancipatory] interest in autonomy and responsibility [*Mündigkeit*] is not mere fancy, for it can be apprehended a priori. What raises us out of nature is the only thing whose nature we can know: *language*. Through its structure, autonomy and responsibility are posited for us. Our first sentence expresses unequivocally the intention of universal and unconstrained consensus.[14]

Since that promissory statement of 1965, Habermas has developed a theory of communicative action based on a philosophy of language or, more specifically, what he calls 'formal' or 'universal' pragmatics.

According to Habermas, 'The task of universal pragmatics is to identify and reconstruct universal conditions of possible understanding (*Verständigung*).'[15] These universal conditions are the general and unavoidable presuppositions of communicative action or action fundamentally 'oriented to reaching understanding (*verständigungsorientiert*).'[16] Any person acting communicatively, that is, any person participating in a speech act oriented to reaching understanding, cannot avoid raising universal validity claims that 'can be vindicated (or redeemed: *einlösen*).'[17] In any speech act oriented to understanding, the following rationality or validity claims (*Geltungsanspruche*) are unavoidably raised: the claim to comprehensibility, the claim to the truth of a proposition, the claim to the truthfulness or authenticity of the speaker's intentions, and the claim to normative legitimacy, or what is right according to social norms.[18] While the first validity claim of comprehensibility can be met by a grammatically well-formed sentence that is understood by all hearers, the other three validity claims reach beyond the sentence and are embedded in utterances or speech acts that have to be seen in relation to the *truth* of a proposition about a state of affairs, to the *truthfulness* of a speaker's intention, and to the *rightness* of the utterance of speech act in a normative context.[19] As Habermas describes it: 'Whereas a grammatical sentence fulfills the claim to comprehensibility, a successful utterance must satisfy three additional validity claims: it must count as true for the participants insofar as it represents something in the world; it must count as truthful insofar as it expresses something intended by the speaker; and it must count as right insofar as it conforms to socially recognized expectations.'[20]

Leaving aside the comprehensibility claim that is met by grammatical sentences, Habermas focuses on the other three validity claims of truth, truthfulness, and rightness and argues that these claims are met only when an understanding or agreement is reached between speaker and hearer. Each of the three validity claims refers to a particular world: truth to the objective world, truthfulness to the subjective world, and rightness to the social world. In communicative action, according to Habermas, speakers 'no longer relate *straightaway* to something in the objective, social, or subjective worlds; instead they relativize their utterances against the possibility that their validity will be contested by other actors ... The concept of communicative action presupposes language as the medium for a kind of reaching understanding, in the course of which participants, though relating to a world, reciprocally raise validity claims that can be accepted or contested.'[21] Thus, in all linguistically mediated communicative acts, participants reach understanding or agreement (*Verständigung*) by raising and judging, on a 'yes' or 'no' basis, validity claims about the truth of statements regarding an objective state of affairs, the rightness of statements in the context of existing social norms, and the truthfulness or sincerity of the person making those statements. Of importance to Habermas is the argument that understanding is not achieved monologically by the singular subject but by the intersubjective validation of claims, that is, through the necessary and unavoidable obligation of communicative partners to provide reasons for accepting or rejecting the claims that are raised. Habermas stresses the connection between understanding and mutually achieved agreement, or consensus that 'meets the conditions of rationally motivated assent (*Zustimmung*).'[22] As he puts it:

> Reaching understanding [*Verständigung*] is considered to be a process of reaching agreement [*Einigung*] among speaking and acting subjects ... Agreement rests on common *convictions.* The speech act of one person succeeds only if the other accepts the offer contained in it by taking (however implicitly) a 'yes' or 'no' position on a validity claim that is in principle

> criticizable. Both ego, who raises a validity claim with his utterance, and alter, who recognizes or rejects it, base their decisions on potential grounds or reasons.[23]

The universal validity claims necessarily present in any communicative act can be vindicated or redeemed only on the basis of intersubjective understanding or agreement arrived at rationally. Reason can thus no longer be conceived as the self-reflection of the monological subject; it must now be seen as communicative rationality based on intersubjective understanding or consensus. The theory of communicative action thus allows us, in Habermas's words, to give up the paradigm of the philosophy of consciousness – namely, a subject that represents objets and toils with them – in favour of the paradigm of linguistic philosophy. The focus of investigation thereby shifts from cognitive-instrumental rationality to communicative rationality. And what is paradigmatic for the latter is not the relation of a solitary subject to something in the objective world that can be represented and manipulated, but the intersubjective relation that speaking and acting subjects take up when they come to an understanding with one another about something.[24] Clearly, then, 'the central intuition informing [Habermas's] work,' as Arie Brand has noted, is the belief that 'the typically human element in language use is to be found in its communicative character ... [that is, in] a common endeavour to achieve consensus in a situation in which all participants are free to have their say and have equal chances to express their views.'[25]

Habermas's central intuition about the communicative character of language use assumes, in his words, that 'the idea of coming to a rationally motivated, mutual understanding is to be found in the very structure of language [and that] it is no mere demand of practical reason but is built into the reproduction of social life.'[26] In a related formulation we are told that 'reaching understanding is the inherent telos of human speech.'[27] In *The Philosophical Discourse of Modernity*, Habermas seeks to replace a Western logocentrism based on subject-centred reason with a theory of communicative rationality, 'always already operative in the communicative practice of everyday life,' which 'conceives of intersubjective understanding as the telos inscribed into communication in ordinary language.'[28] Elsewhere, linking moral consciousness to communicative action, he tells us that 'morality as grounded by discourse ethics is based on a pattern inherent in language from the beginning.'[29] These statements clearly underline Habermas's key assumption that an orientation to understanding or consensus (*verständigungorientiert*) is deeply ingrained in all human speech.

Though such a thesis may avoid the Kantian subject's transcendental apriorism by advancing an intersubjective view of reason, it does not escape a certain foundationalism insofar as its universal pragmatic approach presses empirical research into the service of a theoretical reconstruction of naturally given species competencies, a task that renders our pre-reflective, intuitive 'know-how' into explicit 'know-that' rules. Seyla Benhabib, one of Habermas's sharpest readers, has observed the strong tendency in his work 'to "naturalize" normative and evaluative comments by showing them to "have been always already made."'[30] Such a 'naturalization' resembles philosophical anthropology with its foundational assumption of 'the unchanging preconditions of human changeableness.'[31] Indeed, Habermas himself has argued that a reconstructive science has to 'ascertain the rational content of anthropologically deep-seated structures in a transcendentally orientated analysis which is initially unhistorical.'[32]

As the inherent telos of human speech, understanding or *Verständigung* is the anthropologically deep-seated structure that grounds Habermas's entire theoretical edifice; it is what guarantees the possibility of achieving rational consensus through the process of mutual validation. As such, the *Verständigung* thesis is a thesis about communicative rationality as a universal and unavoidable presupposition of human action. It allows Habermas to distinguish communicative rationality oriented to understanding from purposive rationality oriented to success, and thus enables him to propose a theory of modernity that is not darkened by Weber's *Zweckrationalität* (goal-rationality) or Horkheimer and Adorno's instrumental reason. But how convincing is the *Verständigung* thesis on which so much depends in Habermas's work?

An initial problem surfaces in the ambiguity of the term *Verständigung* itself. Habermas acknowledges that 'the word *understanding* [*Verständigung*] is ambiguous.' In a minimal sense, 'it indicates that two subjects understand a linguistic expression in the same way.' In a maximal sense, it signifies 'an agreement [*Einverständnis*] that terminates in the intersubjective mutuality of reciprocal understanding.'[33] But while Habermas sees no problem in the double meaning of *Verständigung*, his colleague Karl-Otto Apel worries that the word's ambiguity (which is available in German, but not in English or French) allows Habermas to conflate both meanings, thereby permitting the strong conclusion that to understand is to arrive at a rational agreement. According to Apel, such a view is based on 'a terminological *petitio principii*' since it assumes or anticipates in advance that to understand linguistic communication is already to have reached consensus. In Apel's words: 'From the standpoint of an analytical semantics and pragmatics of language, Habermas has *already loaded the concept of understanding normatively*, so that a consensual-communicative solution to the problem of rational communication, and thus to the problem of linguistic understanding in the broadest sense, tends to be *anticipated*. Indeed, the whole point of discourse ethics [that is, achieving universal norms through consensual discourse] is *already anticipated*.'[34]

To Apel's penetrating criticism of the terminological *petitio principii* committed in exploiting *Verständigung*'s ambiguity can be added another logical problem in Habermas's *Verständigung* thesis. The problem in question is that of circularity or tautology. Doesn't the *Verständigung* thesis which asserts that reaching consensual understanding is the inherent telos of human speech presuppose, in an a priori and anthropologically naturalized fashion, the very goal of consensual understanding it is supposed to reach? Isn't there a self-cancelling circularity or self-referentiality at work in the *Verständigung* thesis? Reaching a rationally motivated agreement or the ideal speech situation, as Habermas also deems it, requires a discursive procedure that involves the mutual raising and redemption of validity claims within a set of conditions or rules that stipulate universal inclusion, the right to freely express and introduce any topic, and non-coercive equal participation for all competent communicative agents.[35] In short, participants engaged in a discursive process have to work towards achieving consensual understanding. At the same time, however, *verständigung* is regarded as a pre-given axiom, an intuitive competence inherent in the very structure of language, an originary deep-seated anthropological trait. The following question thus arises: How can a consensual understanding that is already *given* or *presupposed* be squared with an understanding that has to be *achieved* consensually through a discursive or argumentative process? If a rational consensus is achieved only through a discursive process of reciprocal validation, then how can it also be regarded as preceding such an intersubjective process? We seem to be in the presence of a problematic circular logic, a self-cancelling self-referentiality in which the understanding or agreement reached through rational argument is already anticipated by the deeply ingrained presupposition of consensual understanding that requires no rational argument because as presupposition it is what makes argument possible. Seyla Benhabib thus concludes that 'the ideal speech situation is a circular construction; it presupposes those very norms whose validity it was supposed to establish.'[36]

Habermas accepts the argument that a tautological or circular logic informs *Verständigung* and its orientation to an ideal consensus. He acknowledges that the presupposition of speech as teleologically oriented towards understanding is inescapably self-referential. Anyone who speaks and wants to be understood must presuppose that speech is oriented towards understanding (*Verständigung*). Consequently, the speaker cannot but be aware of the self-referentiality of his or her speech. But if the inescapability of self-referentiality prevents us from providing an external justification for presupposing *Verständigung*, this inability to provide deductive justification need not be a theoretical disadvantage. In fact, Habermas's justification for the *Verständigung* presupposition is not deductive. Instead, he justifies its self-referentiality by arguing that the sceptic who wishes to deny or refute the *Verständigung* presupposition is involved in a performative self-contradiction. Drawing on the work of Karl-Otto Apel, Habermas argues that 'any subject capable of speech and action necessarily makes substantive normative presuppositions as soon as the subject engages in any discourse [or argumentation] with the intention of critically examining a hypothetical claim to validity.' The sceptic who wants to argue against such presuppositions finds that 'no sooner does he object (and defend his objection) than he commits himself to an 'argumentation game' and thus to propositions that entangle him in a performative contradiction.'[37] Thus, the *Verständigung* presupposition, which insists that consensual understanding is based on the giving of reasons (that is, through argumentation), cannot be denied without the sceptic or denier, who seeks to convince us of his objection through the force of the better argument, becoming caught in a performative contradiction. The *Verständigung* thesis is a necessary and unavoidable presupposition because any attempt at refuting it cannot but presuppose it to avoid performative self-contradiction.

It is interesting to note, however, that the performative-contradiction weapon Habermas so skilfully wields against his opponents can be turned on him as well.[38] The performative-contradiction argument used to defend the *Verständigung* presupposition may itself be subject to a performative contradiction. Recall that the presupposition that speech is oriented towards a rational consensus or ideal speech situation requires procedural conditions or rules that allow for non-coercive, universal, free, and open debate. As such, the *Verständigung* presupposition must itself be open to challenge and debate on pain of performative contradiction. On the one hand, we cannot refute the *Verständigung* presupposition without becoming entangled in performative contradiction. But equally, on the other hand, the *Verständigung* presupposition must allow itself to be questioned and even refuted if it is not itself to fall into performative contradiction by disallowing challenges to its own status as an unavoidable presupposition.[39] Though he does not turn the charge of performative contradiction on Habermas himself, Michael Kelly astutely observes that 'Habermas' own notion of the ideal speech situation, in which all participants are free to introduce whatever topic they want, must allow the conditions of rational speech themselves to be subject to dialogue; they can only be the result of consensus, not the presuppositions thereof.'[40] In short, the presupposition that consensus is the *outcome* of free and rational argument is a performative contradiction since the presupposition of consensus cannot be accepted without violating its propositional content, which claims that it is the result, not the premise, of intersubjective validation. To presuppose consensual understanding is, thus, by its very own definition, to revoke it.

Apart from the theoretical or logical difficulties that beset it, the *Verständigung* thesis is also dogged by the suspicion that its claim to be a deep-seated, universally inherent, communicative competence may merely be the reflection of a modern, Western, liberal-democratic ethos. Rolf Zimmerman, for example, argues that Habermas has attempted to convert an earlier socio-political interest in an emancipatory bourgeois public sphere that promotes discussion and will-formation free from domination into the more secure and unavoidable presupposition of consensual understanding inherent in human speech. Zimmerman asks somewhat ironically:

> For would it not in fact be a fascinating prospect, if we could show that the basic rules of language leave us no other choice, as it were, but to orientate ourselves in consensual terms and if this fact, together with our insights into the fundamental importance of an interactive schema of mediation, could demonstrate the consensual norm of emancipation to be indispensable? Or to put it more simply: what if we could show that we require nothing more than a consideration of our 'communicative competence' to support the interest in emancipation as a discursive-communicative schema? We should witness the birth of emancipation from the spirit of language.[41]

But, in fact, as Zimmerman implies, we should approach the birth the other way round. It is not language that gives birth to emancipation (that is, to a domination-free communicative consensus), it is the Enlightenment principle of emancipation that engenders the theory of communicative rationality. As Zimmerman puts it: 'Habermas attempts to provide a potentially transcendental kind of foundation for the idea of the positive elimination of domination – *an idea which originally entered the scene as a purely political concept.*'[42] Adopting Zimmerman's line of critique, we can argue that Habermas's unavoidable and hence universal presupposition of language as oriented towards communicative interaction and uncoerced consensus is in fact an assumption derived from his preference for a historically formed, liberal-democratic political culture. What is presupposed as universal and unavoidable may in fact be culturally specific and historically contingent. Consequently, if that which is presupposed is in fact what is valued in modern participatory democracies, then what we learn from the supposedly necessary and universal presupposition is what we as good modern democrats have projected into it in the first place. For example, in the *Verständigung* presupposition, one of the conditions for arriving at consensual understanding, namely, that all who speak must be included in the communication community, reflects the beliefs of a modern culture that prizes egalitarian universalism. As Seyla Benhabib reminds us:

> For the ancient Greeks the barbarians were those whose language they did not understand, and who, from their point of view, did not speak, but merely babbled. Our assumption that all speakers of any natural language speak and do not merely babble is the product of moral *Bildung* of the Enlightenment and secularization which destroyed the ontological bases of human inequality. To say that this assumption is a product of such a process is not to say that it is therefore less defensible; my intention is simply to point out that even the so-called 'universal' pragmatic presuppositions of human discourse have a cultural-historical content built into them.[43]

In fact, one can discern a tension in Habermas's thought between his desire to establish a communicative rationality on deep-seated universal grounds and his awareness that such an idea of discursive consensus 'arose under specific historical conditions, together with the idea of bourgeois democracy.'[44] Thus, for example, Habermas has to admit that 'moral universalism [based on discursive consensus] is a *historical result.* It arose, with Rousseau and Kant, in the midst of a specific society that possessed corresponding features.'[45] To be sure, Habermas's admission of universalism's historical provenance leads him to draw a conclusion different from that which I have offered above. For him the historical rise of secularism and democracy reflects the uneven and not always predictable realization of the universal presupposition of communicative reason, and is *not* a confirmation of the opposing contention that communicative reason's universalism may only reflect the particular values of a historically contingent modern society such as ours. Though he concedes that universalism is a historical manifestation, Habermas remains cautiously confident that history is merely the space in which the inherent universality of communicative reason gradually displays itself:

> The last two or three centuries have witnessed the emergence, after a long seesawing struggle, of a *directed* trend toward the realization of basic rights. This process has led to, shall we cautiously say, a less and less selective reading and utilization of the universalistic meaning that fundamental-rights norms have; it testifies to the 'existence of reason,' if only in bits and pieces. Without these fragmentary realizations, the moral intuitions that discourse ethics conceptualizes would never have proliferated the way they did. To be sure, the gradual embodiment of moral principles in concrete forms of life is not something that can be safely left to Hegel's absolute spirit. Rather, it is chiefly a function of collective efforts and sacrifices made by socio-political movements. Philosophy would do well to avoid haughtily dismissing these movements and the larger historical dimension from which they spring.[46]

This is a remarkable passage not least for the many qualifications surrounding its central argument about the intuitive presence of universal moral principles (moral principles that are intuitive and universal because grounded in the unavoidable presupposition of communicative consensus). Habermas first asserts that there is a *directed* trend towards the realization of moral universalism, thus appearing to support a teleological historicism. But this *directedness* is somewhat mitigated by the insertion of a qualification like 'shall we cautiously say,' or by remarks about universalistic reason existing 'only in bits and pieces' and as 'fragmentary realizations.' Moreover, Habermas is especially anxious that his argument not be mistaken as a version of Hegel's philosophy of history with its providential entelechy. Sociopolitical agency shaped by a 'larger historical dimension' is seen as helping reason to establish itself in the world, however fragmentarily or fitfully. There is no guarantee that universal reason will unfold smoothly guided solely by providential design, as in Hegel's philosophy of history. Inasmuch as reason requires non-providential historical agency for its realization, it seems that history, far from being determined by reason, may in fact condition the latter's appearance. Yet the ahistorical presupposition of 'the universals of language use'[47] that undergird moral universalism remains in place and the directionality of reason's progress is unquestioned. The ambivalence we have just noted does not, therefore, provide a clear answer to the question of whether Habermas's presupposition of moral universalism based on universal pragmatics is in fact nothing more than a historically contingent belief. What is clear, however, is that Habermas's attempt to salvage a formal Kantian universalism by articulating it to a less providential Hegelian historicism raises as many problems as it had hoped to have avoided, as we shall see in greater detail when we turn later to his theory of social evolution and modernity.

Astute readers of Habermas like David Rasmussen and Maeve Cooke have pointed out that the *Verständigung* thesis, which asserts that the original mode of language use is oriented towards consensual understanding, is 'central not only to [Habermas's] theory of language but to his entire theory of communicative action.'[48] Thus, despite all the difficulties that attend it, the *Verständigung* thesis remains the keystone of Habermas's later work. It is the foundational claim on which his master narrative is based: a quasi-Hegelian narrative of how communicative reason, an intuitive competence inherent in humanity from the beginning, persists and develops in history despite the distortions that often seem to overwhelm it. This metanarrative, in Habermas's words, traces 'the historical fate of a reason that has been arrested again and again, ideologically misused and distorted, but that also stubbornly raises its voice in every inconspicuous act of successful communication.'[49] In another similar description, he says that he is concerned

> with the analysis of power constellations that suppress an intention intrinsic to the rationality of purposive action and linguistic understanding – the claim to reason announced in the teleological and intersubjective structures of social reproduction themselves – and that allow it to take effect only in a distorted manner. Again and again this claim is silenced; and yet in fantasies and deeds it develops a stubbornly transcending power, because it is renewed with each act of unconstrained understanding, with each moment of living together in solidarity.[50]

What emerges from these statements is Habermas's belief in a universal and primordial core of communicative rationality that may not unfold providentially according to a Hegelian logic of history, but that cannot, nonetheless, be neglected by any human society, avoided in any act of communication, or destroyed by any strategic or instrumental action. In a powerful passage that is worth citing in full, Habermas makes it absolutely clear that as social beings we have no choice but to opt for communicative action oriented to reaching understanding, since to do otherwise is to court the destructive causality of fate that attends all ruptures of the social bond:

> Participants in discourse do not have to come first to an agreement about this [communicative] foundation; indeed a decision for the rationality inherent in linguistic understanding is not even possible. In communicative rationality we are always already orientated to those validity-claims, on the intersubjective recognition of which possible consensus depends ... Thus for individuals who cannot acquire and maintain their identities otherwise than through carrying on traditions, belonging to social groups, participating in socializing interactions, the choice between communicative and strategic action is open only in an abstract sense. Opting for a long-run withdrawal from contexts of action orientated to reaching understanding and thus from communicatively structured spheres of life, means retreating into the monadic isolation of strategic action; in the long run this is self-destructive. That communicative rationality, precisely as suppressed, is already embodied in the existing forms of interaction and does not first have to be postulated as something that ought to be is shown by the causality of fate which Hegel and Marx, each in his own way, illustrated in connection with phenomena of ruptured morality – the reactions of those who are put to flight or roused to resistance by fateful conflicts, who are driven to sickness, to suicide, crime, or to rebellion and revolutionary struggle. Communicative reason operates in history as an avenging force.[51]

Communicative reason functions as an avenging force in history in so far as its primordial and unavoidable presence in humanity acts as a deep moral norm whose betrayal or distortion can only lead to a violation or destruction of human community. On the unavoidable supposition of communicative rationality, Habermas concludes, 'rests the humanity of relations among men who are still men.'[52] Of this strong supposition of communicative rationality, Martin Jay has warned that there is a danger that history would be replaced by 'abstract philosophical anthropology.'[53]

What I have described as Habermas's metanarrative of the fate of communicative reason in history resembles in a way the narrative myth of the Fall. Like the Christian myth, there is a prelapsarian communicative condition – in this case, the original mode of language oriented to consensual understanding – from which we have fallen into a world of speech rife with dissensus and distorted by strategic, instrumental forms of power. At the same time, however, even in our postlapsarian world, communicative reason, like Christian grace, remains a saving force 'gentle but obstinate, ... never silent although seldom redeemed.'[54] As Romand Coles acutely observes, for Habermas 'agonism is a privative "fallen" condition in light of communicative suppositions, one that calls for the rehabilitating effects of consensual striving.'[55]

In the unavoidable presupposition of *Verständigung* as the original, prelapsarian mode of communication, we have an *arché* or primordial point of departure, an inherent potential of reason that will make its risky way through the contingencies and difficulties posed by history. At the same time, however, the *arché* of communicative reason already harbours the *telos* of the ideal speech situation, in which the original intuition of *Verständigung* is raised to the conceptual level of rational discourse or argumentation. We will trace, in greater detail, this movement, this evolution or development from *arché* to *telos* when we examine Habermas's theory of social evolution and modernity in the next section of this chapter. But for now it will be enough to note that the *telos* of rational discourse folds back into its *arché* or origin in the pre-theoretical, communicative orientation to *Verständigung*; enlightened, modern rationality makes explicit, through reconstruction, the consensual understanding present in the first primordial instance of speech. Thus, we find in Habermas's thought a double narrative: a prominent narrative of development or rationalization in which the instinctive primitivity of *Verständigung* is surpassed or transcended by theoretically conscious and reflective forms of modern argumentation; and another less noticeable narrative in which the instinctive primitivity of consensual understanding, far from being surpassed by modern rationalization processes, accompanies them, anticipates and guarantees their possibility, and acts as an avenging force that troubles them when they fail to live up to their instinctive origin. Though adamantly opposed to any nostalgic yearning for the premodern, the archaic, or the traditional, Habermas, nonetheless, has to concede that

> [m]odernization processes have been followed, as if by a shadow, by what might be called an instinct formed by reason: the awareness that, with the one-sided canalization and destruction of possibilities for expression and communication in private and in public spheres, chances are fading that we

> can bring together again, in a post-traditional everyday practice, those moments that, in traditional forms of life, once composed a unity – a diffuse one surely, and one whose religious and metaphysical interpretations were certainly illusory.[56]

The caveat at the end notwithstanding, we see in this statement an admission that the project of modernity, which Habermas seeks to defend from its neo-conservative detractors, still remains beholden to a primordial or primitive condition, to a prelapsarian, communicative 'instinct formed by reason.' No wonder then that Dieter Henrich has astutely pointed out the 'Rousseauistic origins' of Habermas's thought 'concealed behind a theoretical orientation towards Peirce and Anglo-Saxon theory of language.'[57] Henrich argues that Habermas's presupposition of an original, deeply ingrained intersubjective rationality 'nourished the conviction that a human life can only reach peace and completion when *it finds its way back* through praxis to the human community which precedes it.'[58] The path of progress to modernity thus cannot resist looking or circling back to the premodern condition it has supposedly transcended. 'Progress,' as Gianni Vattimo has noted ironically, 'is in a sense nostalgic by nature.'[59]

The Linguistification of the Premodern: From Myth to Modernity

The deep structures of human rationality, the pre-reflective and implicit communicative 'know-how' of our species explicitly reconstructed by universal pragmatics, constitute what Richard Bernstein has called 'the synchronic dimension of [Habermas's] theory of communicative action and rationality.'[60] Complementing and completing this synchronic reconstruction of the rules and structures underlying communicative rationality is its diachronic counterpart, a theory of social evolution that seeks to analyse the universal and logical 'stage-like development' of communicative deep structures 'in the phylogenetic dimension of the history of the species.'[61] Habermas stresses the importance of the historical development or evolution of structures of rationality because he wants to avoid being accused of reinstating metaphysics by establishing these structures on transcendental, a priori foundations. Thus, as Seyla Benhabib has observed, 'unlike transcendental philosophy, reconstructive theorems do not assume that such deep structures [of rationality] are ahistorical, non-evolving frameworks. To the contrary, Habermas views such deep structures as patterns of rule competencies which evolve in the history of the individual and the species ... [Reconstructive sciences] produce an "empirical phenomenology of mind" tracing the development of ontogenetic and phylogenetic competencies.'[62]

Since he does not want to rely on Kantian apriorism to validate the universality of communicative rationality, Habermas has to turn to sociological and historical evidence to support his claim that communicative rationality is a universal human attribute. But this is a difficult task since, as Thomas McCarthy points out,

> the claimed universality of the structures Habermas singles out cannot be established inductively, for it is quite clear that they are not characteristic of communication in all cultures and in all historical epochs, nor even of all communication in advanced industrial societies. The abilities to differentiate the 'worlds' of external nature, internal nature, and society, to distinguish the 'validity claims' of propositional truth, moral-practical rightness and sincerity/authenticity, to deploy these distinctions in communicative action and, at a reflective level, in argumentative discourse are not, as a matter of empirical fact, to be met with universally.[63]

From McCarthy's description it appears as though the universal-pragmatic characteristics of communication are to be found mainly in modern, liberal Western cultures, a coincidence we noted earlier in discussing Rolf Zimmerman's critique of Habermas's linguistic turn. Do Habermas's universal and unavoidable presuppositions of communicative rationality, therefore, reflect nothing more than a covert Western ethnocentrism? Habermas seeks to avoid such allegations by adopting a Hegelian strategy without the providential guarantee provided by Hegel's philosophy of history. Communicative rationality is not universal in the sense that it appears fully all at once everywhere; rather it is a potential, universally inherent in humanity, and, though it is not always actualized or manifested evenly, it follows a developmental logic that can be reconstructed through empirical research programs such as Jean Piaget's and Lawrence Kohlberg's that investigate ontogenetic learning processes and cognitive-moral development. That there is a logic of development to reason is a non-defeasible principle of paramount importance to Habermas's work. As he declares:

> The release of a potential for reason embedded in communicative action is a world-historical process; in the modern period it leads to a rationalization of life-worlds, to the differentiation of their symbolic structures, which is

> expressed above all in the increasing reflexivity of cultural traditions, in processes of individuation, in the generalization of values, in the increasing prevalence of more abstract and more universal norms, and so on. These are trends which do not imply something good in themselves, but which nevertheless indicate that the prejudiced background consensus of the life-world is crumbling, that the number of cases is increasing in which interaction must be co-ordinated through a consensus reached by the participants themselves ... I would not speak of 'communicative rationalization' if, in the last two hundred years of European and American history, in the last forty years of the national liberation movements [Habermas is speaking in 1984], and despite all the catastrophes, a piece of 'existing reason,' as Hegel would have put it, were not nevertheless also recognizable.[64]

It is clear from Habermas's account of the historical development of reason's potential that he sees modern Euro-American culture with its differentiation of symbolic domains and validity claims, its capacity for self-reflection and abstraction from local contexts, and its orientation to achieving consensus through reasoned discourse and argumentation as 'a developmental-logically advanced stage of specieswide competences.'[65] To the criticism that his universalizing claims conceal a Eurocentric bias, Habermas can thus respond by arguing that his theory can simultaneously affirm that reason's potential is universally present in humankind and that this potential is so far most fully developed in *modern* Western societies. The problem of Eurocentrism is thus circumvented, in Habermas's view, by a theory of social evolution that is also a defence and validation of a theory of modernity as the end point of reason's development. In the rest of this section, we will examine the difficulties that attend Habermas's theory of the sociocultural evolution of modernity.

The theoretical interest in periodization, that is, in demarcating history into significant epochs labelled 'premodern' or 'traditional,' 'modern,' and 'postmodern,' is not without its problems. The term 'modern' or 'modernity,' for example, foregrounds what Jean Baudrillard has described as a 'morale canonique du changement,'[66] which entails the dismantling of traditional beliefs and moralities. Moreover, modernity's imperative to change also harbours what I want to call a 'canonic belief in progress or development.' For advocates of modernization, change is always change for the better; for less sanguine defenders of modernity, change always involves a learning process, an advancement of universal rationality. Once 'modernity' is seen not merely as a chronological but also as a qualitative category, then its availability for comparative cultural and geopolitical uses becomes evident. As Naoki Sakai has incisively remarked, though the series 'premodern-modern-postmodern may suggest an order of chronology ... it must be remembered that this order has never been dissociated from the geopolitical configuration of the world.'[67]

Charles Taylor has argued that the dominant theories of modernity have been of the sort he calls 'acultural.' An 'acultural' theory of modernity characterizes social or cultural transformations as arising not from a specific constellation of values and understandings belonging to a particular culture at a particular historical moment, but from 'a rational or social operation which is culture-neutral ... [that is to say], the operation is not seen as supposing or reflecting an option for one specific set of human values or understandings among others; rather it is seen as the exercise of a general capacity, which was awaiting its proper conditions to unfold.'[68] Thus, in Taylor's view, an 'acultural' description of modernity promotes a narrative that stresses a universal capacity for change and, more importantly, that portrays modernity as a single-track development or growth of human understanding and reason. But, as Taylor goes on to note, 'the belief that modernity comes from one single universally applicable operation ... unfits us for what is perhaps the most important task of social sciences in our day: understanding the full gamut of alternative modernities that are in the making in different parts of the world. It locks us into an ethnocentric prison, condemned to project our own forms onto everyone else.'[69] Though Taylor never really specifies what these 'alternative modernities' are, his argument allows him to retain 'modernity' as a chronological concept that can still mark, compare, and even, in certain limited ways, evaluate social, cultural, and technological changes within and between particular societies without buying into 'modernity' as a strongly qualitative or evaluative category that presents a single, universal model of progress and development for all societies.

One especially influential 'acultural' theory of modernity can be found in Habermas's work. His theory of modernity can be described, without simplifying greatly, as a narrative of the progress of rationality. At the heart of this narrative is the notion of modernity as a self-conscious break or diremption from past epochs and beliefs. As Habermas puts it: 'Modernity can and will no longer borrow the criteria by which it takes its orientation from the models supplied by another epoch; *it has to create its normativity out of itself.*'[70] Modernity's historical self-consciousness, its attempt at normative self-grounding without the help of any previous customary models, is thus linked, in Habermas's work, to the development of autonomous human reason, the progressive actualization of rationality in society. But Habermas is also aware that this confident Enlightenment narrative of reason's progress has been severely criticized as masking the progressive domination of both external and internal worlds by an instrumental rationality interested only in the technical control and mastery of nature and in orienting social life to calculating, goal-directed forms of action. One can in fact argue that the whole thrust of Habermas's theory of modernity is directed towards avoiding the bleak Weberian conclusion that rationality has led modern society into an 'iron cage' and refuting Theodor Adorno's pessimistic diagnosis of historical progress: 'No universal history leads from savagery to humanitarianism, but there is one leading from the sling shot to the megaton bomb.'[71]

Defending modernity, Habermas argues that its achievements are not merely material or technological but also cognitive and moral. As we shall see, this argument relies heavily, first, on the distinction between the 'closed' mythic world of archaic societies and the 'open' rational world of modern occidental society and, second, on a theory of social evolution that enables Habermas to rank modern rationality above mythic or traditional thought. In arguing for the achievements of modern rationality, Habermas hopes to show us how far we have progressed, while warning us at the same time that to abandon achieved levels of rationality is to court the danger of a regression to mythic thought. But, as we shall see, Habermas's warning about cognitive recidivism, about relapsing into myth, leads him, ironically, to reconstitute the very danger he seeks to avert. Habermas's defence of modernity is not without its vicissitudes.

Following Max Weber, Habermas sees modernity as the transition from undifferentiated archaic societies to a society in which the lifeworld has been rationalized or differentiated into separate value spheres, each with its own validity claims. By 'lifeworld' (or *Lebenswelt*), Habermas means that 'prereflective web of background assumptions, expectations and life relations that serve as a source of what goes into explicit communication while always itself remaining implicit.'[72] '[The] lifeworld,' Habermas explains, 'is formed from more or less diffuse, always unproblematic, background convictions. This lifeworld background serves as a source of situation definitions that are presupposed by participants as unproblematic.'[73] We will be examining the concept of the lifeworld and its rationalization in greater detail later in this chapter, but for now it is enough to know that the modern rationalization of the lifeworld involves the process of problematizing and separating out the diffuse and implicit elements of the lifeworld and subjecting them to critical reflection through institutionalized forms of validity-testing and argumentation. According to Habermas, modernity's rationalization of the lifeworld results in the differentiated spheres of objective, social, and subjective reality, each with its own proper validity claim – truth, rightness, authenticity – and each forming a separate domain of knowledge – science, morality, and art.[74]

It is important to Habermas that modernity, with its clearly differentiated rational structures, be seen not just as a manifestation of recent European culture but as a universal development of species-wide competencies. As Stephen K. White points out, Habermas wants to show that 'modernity represents a universally significant achievement in human learning, rather than a way of organizing social and cultural life which is *simply* different from or incommensurable with premodernity.'[75] In other words, Habermas argues for a universal, 'acultural' theory of modernity because he wants to avoid describing modernity either relativistically or ethnocentrically as simply the recent culture of the West. The latter 'culturalist' and 'ethnocentric' definition of modernity is one that an anti-foundational, communitarian pragmatist like Richard Rorty has advocated.[76] Distancing himself from Rorty's frank avowal of a liberal, ironic ethnocentrism, Habermas argues that the discourse of modernity is not ethnocentric precisely because it has achieved a level of rationality that allows for context-transcendent judgments, for post-conventional critical reflexivity and an openness to learning processes.[77] But, as we shall see, Habermas's defence of modernity's anti-ethnocentric openness owes its cogency to two fundamental yet problematic assumptions: first, Habermas's theory of modernity presupposes and constructs a complementary opposite, an Other, namely the premodern or traditional closed society; and second, while seeking to avoid ethnocentrism, Habermas's theory reinstates an even more powerful version of it in the form of a universal narrative that deploys a normative developmental or evolutionary logic, a narrative of cognitive development and moral maturation best illustrated, it seems, by the history of Western Enlightenment.

In elucidating the structures of communicative rationality, Habermas admits to relying on a definition of rationality based on 'a *preunderstanding* anchored in modern orientations.' He concedes that '[h]itherto we have naively presupposed that, in this modern understanding of the world, structures of consciousness are expressed that belong to a rationalized lifeworld and make possible in principle a rational conduct of life. We are implicitly connecting a claim to *universality* with our *Occidental understanding of the world*.'[78] Therefore, in order to show that the synchronic model of rationality he has constructed is universal and not merely an expression of Occidental modernity, Habermas turns to a diachronic narrative that has to demonstrate that modern rationality is the logical end point of a universal developmental process. Such a narrative of development requires a starting point or origin from which progress or development can be tracked or measured. To understand the universality of modern rationality, we must, therefore, seek to understand its origin; and since modernity results from change and development, its origin can only be characterized as different from and antithetical to what it is now. Moreover, the presuppositions of modern rationality, the end-point of development, become clearer when they are contrasted to the characteristics of their premodern origin. As Habermas argues, to understand the significance of modern Occidental rationality

> it would be well to draw a comparison with the mythical understanding of the world. In archaic societies myths fulfil the unifying function of worldviews in an exemplary way – they permeate life-practice. At the same time, within the cultural traditions accessible to us, they present the sharpest contrast to the understanding of the world dominant in modern societies. Mythical worldviews are far from making possible rational orientations of action in our sense. With respect to the conditions for a rational conduct of life in this sense, they present an antithesis to the modern understanding of the world. Thus the heretofore unthematized presuppositions of modern thought should become visible in the mirror of mythical thinking.[79]

As his statement clearly indicates, Habermas offers a definition (and valorization) of modern rationality that depends on its being contrasted to its premodern antithesis, myth. Modern rationality is clarified and made visible through its Other, premodern myth. Habermas's theory of modernity is thus also a theory of 'othering,' the construction of the premodern as everything that the modern is not. Habermas's contrastive definition is not dissimilar to those ethnographic accounts that 'have typically been driven by an embedded rhetoric of comparison, ... written for some group of "us" about a "them" whose culture had, somehow, to be represented as a fundamentally different way of life.'[80] In fact, ethnographic comparison is often a deliberate exercise in contrast, as Nicholas Thomas points out: '[T]he most persuasive and theoretically consequential ethnographic rhetoric represents the other essentially as an inversion of whatever Western institution, practice, or set of notions is the real object of interest.'[81] Like ethnographies that seek to maximize cultural difference, Habermas's distinction between modern rationality and premodern myth-mindedness activates a rhetoric of contrast. However, unlike a cultural anthropologist like Marshall Sahlins, who emphasizes difference and otherness in order to combat Western ethnocentrism and arrogance, Habermas describes and defends the cognitive and moral achievements of Occidental modernity by sharply contrasting them to primitive world views. If certain forms of anthropological practice utilize a discourse of alterity, exaggerating the distance between 'us' and 'them,' in order to guard otherness from the threat of an assimilative Western universalism, then Habermas, employing a similar discourse of alterity, invokes otherness in order to show its cognitive and moral limitations in comparison to Occidental rationality. Clearly, alterity can be used to achieve different ends.

According to Habermas, the premodern, mythic mode of understanding approaches the world as an undifferentiated, seamless totality in which nature and culture, objectivity and subjectivity, dream and reality, word and thing are indistinguishably lumped together on the same cognitive or experiential plane.[82] He sums up the deficiencies of what he calls the 'closedness' of mythical world views as 'the insufficient differentiation among fundamental attitudes to the objective, social, and subjective worlds; and the lack of reflexivity in worldviews that cannot be identified as worldviews, as cultural traditions.'[83] The inability of mythical thought to distinguish between different domains of reality (the objective, the social, and the subjective), with their different validity claims (propositional truth, normative rightness, and expressive sincerity), results in a lack of critical reflexivity and an incarceration in a closed, total system that is unable to recognize itself as a particular world view or cultural tradition, and hence is impervious to alternative interpretations of reality or to other approaches to problem solving. Mythical world views are thus ethnocentric enclosures, not open to learning processes or critical revision; they remain enchanted like some spellbound character in a fairytale. To continue the conceit, modernity's rationalization processes can be seen as lifting the spell and leading us out of the enchanted realm of myth. As Habermas, in his best Enlightenment voice, puts it: 'Only demythologization dispels this enchantment which appears to *us* to be a confusion between nature and culture. The process of enlightenment leads to the desocialization of nature and the denaturalization of the human world; we can conceive of this with Piaget as a *decentering of world view.*'[84]

As an example of a yet to be decentred premodern world view, Habermas refers us to Evans-Pritchard's classic account of Azande beliefs in his 1937 study *Witchcraft, Oracles, and Magic among the Azande.* According to Evans-Pritchard, the Azande offered coherent and logical explanations when questioned about their belief in the malevolence of witchcraft and the predictive power of oracles. Their mentality is thus not 'pre-logical' as Lévy-Bruhl had believed the primitive mind to be.[85] However, the coherence of the Zande world view is based on the inability of their culture to differentiate between objective reality and other domains of reality; in other words, the Zande are not critically reflexive or cognitively open to alternative explanations or world views. As Evans-Pritchard describes it:

> All their beliefs hang together and were a Zande to give up faith in witch-doctorhood he would have to surrender equally his belief in witchcraft and oracles ... In this web of belief every strand depends upon every other strand, and a Zande cannot get out of its meshes because this is the only world he knows. The web is not an external structure in which he is enclosed. It is the texture of his thought and he cannot think that his thought is wrong.[86]

To Habermas, this example of an undifferentiated, holistic world view in which the individual is inescapably enmeshed, and thus unable to think his thought wrong, points to a higher tolerance for contradictions than rationality can accommodate. Referring to Evans-Pritchard's observation that the Azande cannot consistently explain contradictions, and that, consequently, they seek to evade the outsider anthropologist's demands for a non-contradictory explanation, Habermas asks: '[I]sn't this refusal, this higher tolerance for contradiction, a sign of a more irrational conduct of life? Must we not call action orientations that can be stabilized only at the cost of suppressing contradictions irrational?'[87] Habermas is aware of Peter Winch's argument that it is illegitimate on the part of the European outsider 'to press the demand for consistency further than the Azande of *themselves* do.'[88] He cites Winch's conclusion that 'it is the European, obsessed with pressing Zande thought where it would not naturally go – to a contradiction – who is guilty of misunderstanding, not the Azande. The European is in fact committing a category mistake.'[89] But while Habermas can agree with Winch that the European anthropologist 'should not impute to the natives his own interest in resolving inconsistencies,' he thinks that the lack of theoretical interest shown by the Azande can be 'traced back to the fact that the Zande worldview imposes less exacting standards of rationality and is in this sense less rational than the modern understanding of the world.'[90]

Acknowledging Winch's warning about the dangers of ethnocentric 'category mistakes,' Habermas nonetheless takes the side of Robin Horton and Ernest Gellner in the so-called rationality debate against Winch's relativist account of incommensurable world views.[91] Like Horton and Gellner, Habermas insists that world views can be evaluated in a way that is both context-independent and non-ethnocentric. While he cautions that Horton's rationality criteria may be based on a too narrow and selective focus on scientific or cognitive-instrumental reason, he nonetheless sees Horton's distinction between a 'closed' and 'open' world view as compatible with his own distinction between the mythic and the modern understanding of the world. Both Horton and Gellner, according to Habermas, characterize the modern, 'open' worldview as manifesting an awareness not only of the differences between the objective, social, and subjective worlds, but also of the differentiation of validity claims related to the cognitive-instrumental, the moral-practical, and the expressive domains that form those worlds. Moreover, the modern 'open' world view, unlike its 'closed' mythic opposite, allows for a differentiation between language and reality. It is also reflective, unlike its unreflective premodern counterpart, and thus permits greater individual autonomy and less dependence on the inherited, traditional forms of thought, or what Gellner calls the 'sacred and entrenched convictions' found in 'savage thought-systems.'[92] In short, agreeing with Horton and Gellner, Habermas sees Western modern societies as differentiated, reflective, critical of tradition or established conventions, and oriented to individual, autonomous thought. Premodern or primitive societies, however, are seen as holistic, unreflective, completely enmeshed in traditional beliefs, and protective of an integrated, collective world view.

In reading Habermas's distinction between the modern 'open' world view and the premodern 'closed' world of myth, one recalls Marshall Sahlins's account, in the previous chapter, of myth-minded Hawaiians with their entrenched cosmological beliefs encountering the disenchanted rational world view of British seamen in the eighteenth century. Like Winch, however, Sahlins sees myth-minded societies as providing evidence of cultural and epistemological relativism, whereas Habermas sees them as societies that have not yet undergone the process of rationalization and thus have not yet transcended their particularity for a universal rationality. For Habermas, 'the modern understanding of the world is indeed based on general [*allegemein*, which can also be translated as *universal*] structures of rationality.'[93] To be sure, Habermas is aware that modern Western societies have helped cognitive-instrumental or scientific rationality achieve a one-sided dominance at the expense of moral-practical and expressive rationality. As a result, it can be argued that Western modernity exhibits a certain particularistic world view. But understood properly, modernity leads to universal rationality and away from all provincialisms, especially premodern world views in which traditions and conventions are not only uncritically accepted but also protected from alternative interpretations. Thus, however guarded and qualified Habermas's description of the modern Western world view may be, it is clear that contrast and antithesis guide his distinction between premodern, myth-minded 'closed' societies and modern, rationalized 'open' societies. As Robert Wuthnow has astutely remarked:

> The main problem with Habermas's conception of the past and of the cultural material left over from the past is that he views it only as a point of comparison with the present ... [Myth] is relegated to the distant past; [modern rationality] is made to characterize the entire present. In short, myth and tradition become stylized elements of Habermas's dialectical form of argumentation. They present an extreme contrast against which to compare rationality; therefore, those features of myth that differ most distinctly from rationality are emphasized at the exclusion of other elements.[94]

Habermas's distinction between myth and modernity is too sharply, one might even say too mythically, drawn. If myth, by Habermas's definition, is a 'totalizing power'[95] that analogically 'weaves all appearances into a single network of correspondence,'[96] and that refuses to distinguish conceptually between the different domains of reality, levelling, in the process, the distinctions between nature and culture, language and world, and the objective, the social, and the subjective,[97] then his own account of the myth-modernity antithesis is mythical insofar as both myth and modernity are described in a totalizing and undifferentiated manner. Myth is given a single, essentialized description, but so is modernity. Mythic modes of thought and action in being described as 'closed' have closure imposed on them. Similarly, modern rationality in being characterized as 'open' is, by that characterization, no longer open to alternative interpretations such as those found in religious or mythic discourses. Part of the problem with Habermas's account of the myth-modernity opposition lies in the cultural holism of the anthropological sources he uses, such as Evans-Pritchard's description of the Azande's 'web of belief' or Claude Lévi-Strauss's and Maurice Godelier's tightly organized, structuralist studies of myth. There is no mention in his work of any detailed ethnographic study of tribal society that may have yielded a less holistic, more differentiated or nuanced, account of mythic thought. The totalizing assumption behind Habermas's myth-modernity divide thus needs to be questioned.[98]

A careful reading of Evans-Pritchard's account of the Azande's belief in witchcraft and oracles ironically reveals a tolerance for contradiction and an evasiveness regarding the question of contradiction similar to those attributed to the African natives. Evans-Pritchard's belief in Azande cultural holism prevented him from acknowledging fully the presence of internal scepticism within that culture. When scepticism towards witchcraft was clearly shown by some segment of the Zande population, he dismissed it as exceptional, not part of the general or common belief. Of Evans-Pritchard's evasive dismissal of internal doubt and contradiction among the Azande, Michele Moody-Adams astutely observes:

> He frequently complains about Zande royalty, for instance, whom he found distant and unforthcoming, and thus 'with rare exceptions ... useless as informants' (Evans-Pritchard 1937, 13–14) ... The ethnographer's apparent disdain, and even personal dislike, for the 'detached attitude' of the uncooperative royal class – whose attitudes seemed to pose a problem for his web-of-belief account – is an important and disturbing element in explaining his curious readiness virtually to dismiss a 'considerable body' of skeptical opinion.[99]

Noting that Habermas 'reifies the importance of myths in native life,' Raul Pertierra, in examining the philosopher's reading of Evans-Pritchard, offers a helpful explanation that allows us to look at myth not as the expression of cultural holism but as a discursive political strategy:

> The Azande may well typify mythical world-views in their belief in witches, but their aristocratic overlords present a different picture. A re-reading of Evans-Pritchard is more likely to present witchcraft not so much as a belief-system, but as a form of political domination. The question that one would

> then ask is why is it that this form of domination requires this set of beliefs? The answer shifts the attention from the solidary effects of beliefs to the ideological consequences of political structures.[100]

We have seen a similar refusal to accord significance to political or social differences in a so-called mythic, premodern society in Marshall Sahlins's work on eighteenth-century Hawaiians. The natives, according to the cultural holism argument, live in a fully integrated society and their behaviour is determined by their mythic or cosmological belief-system. But to hold such a holistic doctrine, in the face of counter-examples of internal doubt and differences of opinion, is to subscribe to a mythic mode of thought that is totalizing, highly tolerant of contradiction, and 'closed' to alternative, sceptical interpretations, precisely the *pensée sauvage* that Habermas thinks we have surpassed as moderns.

There are numerous other ethnographic examples that clearly reveal the myth-mindedness of premodern societies to be the projection of a *modern myth* of the Other. Ethnographic fieldwork in a relatively remote area like Tinombo in northern Sulawesi, Indonesia, would have allowed Habermas to understand that although the Lauje people of the region, a large number of whom are animists, see a continuity between dream and reality – a lack of differentiation Habermas would characterize as mythic – they also employ interpretations that enable them to negotiate quite pragmatically with the world around them. Thus a Lauje farmer, for example, may interpret a dream as an injunction from the spirits not to plant his crops in a certain field. But that interpretation may in turn be interpreted as having a temporal clause attached to it that will allow the farmer to plant in that forbidden field after a suitable lapse of time. What this example shows is that good animists are not necessarily bad agriculturalists and that mythic thought need not be so totalizing that it cannot find ways of interpreting reality differently and pragmatically.[101] Stanley Tambiah has reported a similar ability on the part of farmers in northeast Thailand to shift in and out of 'different orderings of reality'; the Thai farmers are able to hold together 'at least two modalities of thought and action – participation and causality.' The farmers propitiate the goddess or female spirit of rice, Maephosob, during the growing season for a good harvest; but they equally acknowledge that 'good agricultural techniques enable a good harvest.'[102] Tambiah gives a further example of the way in which mythic ritual and modern technological rationality are intertwined in practice, thereby questioning the myth-modernity divide. 'In Kathmandu in 1981,' Tambiah writes, he 'witnessed during the Dassein festival several bus drivers, taxi drivers and garage mechanics sacrificing to their machines, daubing blood on them and decorating them with flowers. Thus Western technology and Western technological knowledge ... does not necessarily drive out or displace ritual and magical acts which combine the purposive aims of better mechanical performance, or larger yields of rice, with the aims of a moral and prosperous social and religious life.'[103]

Let us turn to one more example that questions Habermas's mythic essentialization of the myth-modernity divide. What I want to emphasize in this example is not so much the West's totalizing and essentializing view of other societies (a process studied brilliantly by Johannes Fabian and Edward Said, among others) as its totalizing and essentializing view of its own modernity. Of course the process of essentializing the Other is always dialectically related to the essentializing of the Self. Orientalists, for example, are able to essentialize the Orient so confidently because they feel secure that their own society is uniformly the same and thus uniformly different from the Eastern societies they study. Orientalists are therefore also occidentalists. Similarly, modernists who see premodern mythic societies as enclosed in 'a gigantic mirror-effect'[104] are themselves caught in a mirror-effect, the premodern totality they see made possible only by their belief in the unity and totality of their own point of view. An example of modern occidentalism, of identifying the West *tout court* with rationality, occurs in the anthropological literature on the gift. In a perceptive discussion, James Carrier reminds us that Marcel Mauss's classic study *The Gift* (1925) bases its arguments on a distinction between archaic societies of the gift and modern societies of rational economic exchange. In transactions in archaic societies, 'objects are inalienably associated with the giver, the recipient and the relationship that defines and binds them.'[105] Moreover, in gift transactions, according to Mauss, 'all kinds of institutions are given expression at one and the same time – religious, judicial, ... moral ... [and] economic.'[106] Transactions in modern Western societies, by contrast, do not confuse economic exchange with kinship, religious, judicial, or moral obligations. Modern societies are societies 'of purely individual contract, of the market where money circulates, of sale proper, of the notion of price reckoned in coinage, ... [of the strict distinction between] things and persons.'[107] In short, as Carrier points out, we have two essentialisms at work in Mauss's discussion of the gift: 'At the most obvious level, they define the two ends of the evolutionary continuum. Equally, they define each other dialectically, in that they are generated as opposites of each other. Archaic societies show the embeddedness of economic activities in a web of social relations that is significant precisely because in the modern West the economy is no longer embedded. Each pole, then, defines what is significant about the other dialectically.'[108] As we have seen, Habermas too works with a polarizing essentialist model, opposing premodern mythical societies to modern rational societies. Moreover, referring to Mauss's study of the gift and Malinowski's work on symbolic exchange, Habermas also opposes modern economy to archaic or primitive exchange with its lack of differentiation between economy, kinship, religion and social norms:

> [E]conomic transactions in the narrower sense have no structure-forming effects in tribal societies ... Thus, an important part of the circulation of economic goods is dependent on kinship relations ... [T]he ritual exchange of valuable objects serves the purpose of social integration. In the non-monetarized economic activities of archaic societies, the mechanism of exchange has so little detached itself from normative contexts that a clear separation between economic and noneconomic values is hardly possible.[109]

One consequence, however, of this essentializing division into archaic gift societies and modern economic societies is not just the denial of economic rationality to archaic societies, but also the refusal to acknowledge that gift-like forms of transaction occur in modern exchange systems of the West. Carrier points to a number of studies that show that gift-like transactions occur among small retail trade and manufacturing firms and their suppliers, and even among employees in factories. Carrier is of course careful to argue that these studies do not assert an identity between premodern gift transactions and modern economic exchanges; but they show that there is enough resemblance to warrant our suspicion that a powerful and levelling essentialism is at work when modern Western societies are declared to have impersonal commodity relations totally different from relations in gift societies. As Carrier remarks:

> Even if Western societies are commodity systems in the last analysis, elevating that last analysis to an analytical first principle will needlessly and wrongly simplify a complex social form. Saying that commodity relations are important or even primary in the West does not warrant essentializing the West as a system in which commodity relations are of such overwhelming importance that we can ignore the existence of other sorts of relations.[110]

Habermas's essentialization of both premodern and modern forms of life is caused by an exaggerated polarization of the two, a polarization prompted, in turn, by a speculative view of premodern or primitive society as undifferentiated, holistic, and totally integrated (thereby generating its modern antithesis, which is seen as differentiated, pluralistic, and separated into different domains of value). We can characterize Habermas's description of a totally integrated premodern society as speculative because he provides little or no ethnographic evidence to support his description, with the exception of the problematic example of Azande society. In fact, Habermas has described his view of premodern society as the construction of 'a hypothetical initial state,' the taking up of a 'thought experiment.' As he puts it:

> The construction I am proposing is based, on the one hand, on the limit state that Durkheim assumes for a totally integrated society, and on the other hand, on the disintegrating effects that speech acts ... give rise to when the symbolic reproduction of the lifeworld gets tied to communicative action. This thought experiment requires that we think of the Durkheimian zero point of society as composed of a sacred domain that does not yet *need* a linguistic mediation of ritual practice, and a profane domain that does not yet *permit* a linguistic mediation of cooperation with its own dynamics. Particularly, this last assumption is artificial, but it is not completely inappropriate.[111]

Habermas's 'thought experiment,' his conceptual fiction of primitive society, places him directly in a long line of European thinkers from Hobbes and Rousseau to Bachofen, Maine, Fustel de Coulanges, Morgan, Tylor, Spencer, Marx, Freud, Weber, and Durkheim who speculated on our primordial origins and, in Adam Kuper's phrase, 'invented primitive society.' The idea of primitive society, Kuper notes,

> provided an idiom which was ideally suited for debate about modern society... It could be used equally by right or left, reactionary or progressive, poet and politician. The most powerful images of primitive society were produced by very disparate political thinkers – Maine, Engels, Durkheim and Freud. Yet all were transformations of a single basic model. What each did, in effect, was to use it as a foil. They had particular ideas about modern society and constructed a directly contrary account of primitive society. Primitive society was the mirror image of modern society – or, rather, primitive society as they imagined it inverted the characteristics of modern society as they saw it.[112]

Kuper's description applies equally to Habermas, who, drawing directly on the work of Durkheim, propounds a view of modern society by constructing a 'contrary account of primitive society.' As we have noted earlier, Habermas believes that the 'unthematized presuppositions of modern thought ... become visible in the mirror of mythical thinking.'[113] Modern society based on communicative or intersubjective consensus achieved through rational argumentation and agreement over differentiated validity claims is thus contrasted to primitive or archaic society in which social integration is achieved through unquestioned adherence to ritual and the powers of the sacred.

Following Durkheim's theory of the evolution of law and of changing forms of social integration, Habermas explains that his view of sociocultural evolution or development is

> guided by the hypothesis that the socially integrative and expressive functions that were at first fulfilled by ritual practice pass over to communicative action; the authority of the holy is gradually replaced by the authority of an achieved consensus. This means a freeing of communicative action from sacrally protected normative contexts. The disenchantment and disempowering of the domain of the sacred takes place by way of a linguistification of the ritually secured, basic normative agreement; going along with this is a release of the rationality potential in communicative action. The aura of rapture and terror that emanates from the sacred, the *spellbinding* power of the holy, is sublimated into the *binding/ bonding* force of criticizable validity claims.[114]

Habermas's Durkheimian hypothesis of the evolution of modern social consensus out of premodern ritual practice requires us to assume that an initial, primitive state existed in which the power of the sacred seamlessly integrated the whole of society and that it is only through 'the linguistification of the sacred' (*die Versprachlichung des Sakralen*) – that is, the dissolution of social unity secured by the sacred into the differentiated validity claims raised by linguistic communication – that archaic society can develop into a modern society based on argumentation and communicative consensus. In proposing the 'linguistification' thesis, Habermas has to resort to a fiction about primitive society as holistic and as lacking in the linguistic forms that allow modern societies to achieve discursive consensus rather than obey prescribed rituals. 'Let us *imagine*, for the moment,' Habermas writes,

> the limit case of a totally integrated society. Religion serves only to interpret existing ritual practices in concepts of the holy ... It secures, in the sense of cultural determinism, the unity of the collectivity and largely represses conflicts that might arise from power relations and economic interests. These counterfactual assumptions signify a state of social integration in which language has only minimal significance ... In a somewhat different context, Wittgenstein spoke of language 'going on holiday'; when it is released from the discipline of everyday practice, disengaged from its social functions, it luxuriates, kicks over the traces. We are trying to *imagine* a state in which language is on holiday, or at any rate, one in which language's proper weight has not yet made itself felt in social reproduction.[115]

Habermas has to 'imagine' the premodern limit case of a totally integrated society because such a society probably never existed.[116] Habermas's primitivism is thus a primitivism without primitives or, better, a primitivism with imaginary primitives. Actual primitives (if there be any) may, in fact, be more of a theoretical liability than an asset. Zande society, for instance, which is supposedly premodern because it is held together by a seamless web of belief turns out in actuality to be differentiated by rank and social class, as we have seen. Moreover, not only is the premodern case imagined, but it is imagined as the structural inversion or negation of the modern exemplar. Thus, if modern society is complex, heterogeneous, and differentiated into separate value spheres, then premodern society must be simple, homogeneous, and totally integrated. If modern society relies on language to achieve communicative consensus based on the raising and redemption of validity claims, then in premodern society language is seen to be 'on holiday.'

We have in Habermas's imagined primitive society an example of what Peter Fitzpatrick calls the modern myth of origins. Fitzpatrick argues that modernity's devaluation of myth as belonging to our primitive past is itself a myth of an aberrant origin from which we have progressed:

> The mythology of European identity is founded in an opposition to certain myth-ridden 'others.' These are constructed not as the exemplary affirmations of classic mythology but in terms of a negative teleology ... Occidental being is impelled in a progression away from aberrant origins ... which it sets beyond itself, beyond its exemplary models, as its opposition and difference. But this is also its own pre-creation, and Enlightenment finds there its mythic origins. In the taking of identity from these origins, they become

> something to be departed from and negated rather than something to be positively emulated. They form negative exemplars. Hence, modern myth is the ascent from savagery instead of the descent from gods.[117]

Seeking to oppose premodern myth to modern rationality, Habermas finds himself compelled to imagine a totally integrated primitive society, to create a mythic primal scene. His theory of modern communicative rationality thus depends on an origin myth, a myth that, like all myths, goes beyond fact, beyond memory, beyond reason to 'a time of beginnings ... whose empirical authenticities cannot be tested.'[118] Moreover, like other modern myths of origin that Fitzpatrick has examined, Habermas's primal scene is peopled by primitives who do not seem to need language to communicate beliefs or coordinate actions because they unreflectively accept collective values and tacitly share the same world views. Language is 'on holiday' in this totally integrated premodern society and its inhabitants are 'conveniently inarticulate';[119] they cannot speak, and thus must be spoken for by the modern philosopher. Like all myths, then, Habermas's myth of primitive society requires neither empirical evidence nor historical testimony. His thesis about the development of modernity as the 'linguistification of the sacred' depends on the delinguistification of the primitive. The primitive Other owes its existence to what Habermas imagines it to be.

Modernity's origin myth, the myth of the primitive Other, is accompanied, as we have seen, by the myth of evolutionary progress. We are modern, the story goes, because we have progressed from a simple, undifferentiated, unreflective primitive state towards a complex, differentiated, reflective form of life. As Peter Fitzpatrick observes:

> The very progression from the primitive to the modern, from the simple to the complex, from the homogeneous to heterogeneous and so on, fundamentally involves an increasing differentiation in form and function. The story of progression comes in retrospect to be the story of a constant, enduring entity, developing in the negation of its origins and prior manifestations, always moving towards greater differentiation and autonomy.[120]

Though he does not subscribe to Herbert Spencer's naive positivism, Habermas shares the Victorian thinker's idea of evolution as 'the development from the simple to complex' and the 'identification of social evolution with progress.'[121] Habermas writes, for example: 'When we speak of evolution, we do in fact mean cumulative processes that exhibit a direction. Neoevolutionism regards *increasing complexity* as an acceptable directional criterion.'[122] To be sure, Habermas also admits that the concept of 'complexity' is too unspecific and vague and wishes to replace it with the 'development of productive forces' (the 'progress of empirical knowledge') and 'the maturity of forms of social intercourse' (the progress of 'moral-practical insight') as the criteria of social progress.[123] Both these criteria, however, embody a process of learning that takes us from simple to complex forms of life. For Habermas the evolution from mythic consciousness to modern rationality involves a learning process that passes through different cognitive and interactive stages and that progressively decentres and renders more reflexive a relatively simple, self-enclosed, and unreflexive world view. He clearly states: 'Viewed in terms of a *progressively decentered understanding of the world*, the stages of interaction [from pre-conventional to post-conventional] express a development that is directed and cumulative.'[124]

In Habermas's narrative of progress, modern societies, with their increased capacity for reflexive criticism and validity-testing, manifest a certain cognitive and cultural maturity no longer dependent on the unexamined authority of mythic, sacred, or traditional beliefs. In turn, this developmental narrative is seen to be homologous to and dependent on the universal learning processes that we find in the development of the individual. The ontogenetic development that all individuals go through thus becomes the basis for the phylogenetic development of human societies. As Habermas points out:

> [I]ndividuals can develop structures of consciousness which belong to a higher stage than those which are already embodied in the institutions of their society. It is primarily subjects who learn, while societies can take a step forward in the evolutionary learning-process only in a metaphorical sense. New forms of social integration, and new productive forces, are due to the institutionalization and exploitation of forms of knowledge which are individually acquired ... Thus I start from the trivial assumption that subjects capable of speech and action cannot help but learn, and use this to support the assumption that ontogenetic learning processes acquire pacemaker functions.[125]

For evidence of ontogenetic learning processes, Habermas relies on Jean Piaget's studies of cognitive development in children and Lawrence Kohlberg's investigations into the development of moral understanding, empirical studies in which certain universal competencies are shown to develop cumulatively through learning processes. But the attempt to link a phylogenetic account of social development with the ontogenetic studies of Piaget and Kohlberg is problematic not only because of a questionable isomorphism between society and the individual but also because of a Eurocentric bias present in these studies.

In 'projecting the developmental logical structure of the ontogenetic learning process onto culture and society' Habermas commits what has been called the 'ontogenetic fallacy.'[126] The ontogenetic model cannot be mapped onto social or cultural change without incurring serious problems. An explanation of sociocultural evolution that strictly follows the pattern of individual problem-solving and learning must necessarily ignore both the complexity of historical events and the uniqueness of historical experiences in order to concentrate on identifying the developmental logic of cognitive or moral stages found in ontogenetic schemes. Axel Honneth and Hans Joas have argued that Habermas's evolutionary theory uses historical material only with the aim of proving that sociocultural change can be patterned like the sequenced stages of ontogenetic developmental logic. In his work, they write, 'the historical process, in its experiential breadth and its ... density, is examined with a view solely to finding the historical evidence that scientifically substantiates the hypothesis of developmental logic regarding the sequence of stages of communicative and instrumental rationalization.'[127]

A related problem surfaces when the ontogenetic stage-model is projected onto historical societies. Günter Frankenberg and Ulrich Rödel point out that the application of the ontogenetic model to sociocultural history presupposes 'that societies, social groups or classes in a particular historical period – comparable to children at a particular stage of their cognitive development – are not yet able to understand and to produce arguments and justifications with reference to moral and legal norms.'[128] A similar criticism is made by Michael Schmid, who argues that Habermas, in linking ontogenetic problem-solving and learning stages to similar pre-conventional, conventional, and post-conventional stages of sociocultural development, is in danger of claiming 'that the people of earlier social formations did not pass through all the stages of their possible ontogenetic development ... [and that their] maturity [is] restricted ... to preconventional or conventional stages of development.'[129] Unless Habermas is willing to admit that adults in earlier historical societies never passed through full ontogenetic development and thus remained arrested at a child-like cognitive and moral stage, he must refuse any strict homology between individual ontogenesis and social phylogenesis.

The link between ontogenetic development and social evolution also breaks down when we consider how the former has an end, whereas the latter has no comparable end point, and is unrelated to any teleological philosophy of history. As Seyla Benhabib has acutely observed:

> [W]hereas in the case of ontogenesis, concrete life histories of individuals have an end, and every human child that is born recapitulates a given course of development to become an adult, at the level of phylogenesis this is hardly the case. Neither are we at the end of history, nor can we point to a 'normal' course of development in light of which we can judge 'regressions' and 'deviations.' The history of the species is so far unique, *sui generis*; we have no established model of development to compare it with.[130]

Unless we know what the end of history will be, unless we are able to look back as it were from the end point of human history, we cannot pass any definitive judgment on what constitutes 'normal' development or rank the stages of development according to some measure or scale of progress.

In formulating his theory of social evolution, Habermas takes great pains to avoid just such a teleological model; he wishes to keep his distance from the Hegelian and Marxist philosophies of history in which the pattern and goal of progress are theorized in advance. In seeking to avoid the problem of teleology, Habermas makes a careful distinction between the *logic* and the *dynamics* of social evolution, between a reconstruction of how species-wide competencies develop through a series of logically connected learning stages and the actual historical development of a society. He explains: 'If we separate the logic from the dynamics of development – that is, the rationally reconstructible *pattern* of a hierarchy of more and more comprehensive structures from the *processes* through which the empirical substrates develop – then we need require of history neither unilinearity nor necessity, neither continuity nor irreversibility.'[131] Through the logic-dynamics distinction, Habermas hopes to avoid not only the objectivism of a teleological philosophy of history but also the criticism that modern forms of rationality are ethnocentric insofar as they appear to manifest themselves only in Western societies. For by invoking the *logic* of social evolution as the elucidation of how species-wide competencies develop over time, Habermas can assert that rationality is not just a Western trait but is available to all. At the same time, he can argue that complex material and socio-historical circumstances affect the *dynamics* of evolution and are responsible for preventing the appearance of modern forms of rationality in non-Western societies or for causing the stagnation or regression of reason in modern Western societies. Finally, Habermas thinks that the distinction allows him to avoid a Kantian transcendental argument, since his reconstructive logic cannot rely on strong a priori claims, but must be linked to empirical studies of ontogenetic development and checked against data gathered a posteriori from actual historical societies.

A closer examination of Habermas's logic-dynamics distinction shows, however, that it is as much a form of ranking as it is a separation of analytical domains; the *logic* of development appears to override or subsume the *dynamics* of development. This is especially the case since at the heart of Habermas's enormous theoretical enterprise, as we have seen, is the strong presupposition of universal communicative rationality, that is, of language as oriented towards mutual understanding rather than strategic manipulation or control. This presupposition of communicative rationality becomes both the normative guide as well as the normative goal of Habermas's ontogenetically modelled, stage-based logic of development. Following Piaget and Kohlberg, Habermas's developmental logic dictates a progression through three ontogenetic stages (the pre-conventional, the conventional, and the post-conventional) in the fields of human interaction, socio-cognitive structures and perspectives, and moral judgment.[132] Progression through the three stages reflects 'the ontogenesis of a decentered understanding of the world that is structurally rooted in action oriented toward reaching understanding.'[133] Habermas sees the final post-conventional stage, in Piet Strydom's words, as 'essentially an anticipation or projection of fully developed cognitive [and moral] structures. These structures represent the principle of mutual understanding, agreement and cooperation, or practical reason for short' – in the German philosophical tradition, practical reason is another name for morality – 'which is absolutely crucial for the humane and rational organization of society.'[134] Moreover, Habermas argues that the development of these anticipated or projected normative structures is 'the pacemaker of social evolution.'[135] In short, Habermas's logic of development has a normative goal – the post-conventional stage with its fully rational, decentred, reflexive, and autonomous socio-cognitive structures that permit principled moral judgments – and a normative standard – the progressive realization in society of these rational moral structures that are already presupposed, already present *in potentia* in all human communicative actions oriented towards understanding. Noting these normativistic implications, Klaus Eder, Habermas's one-time research collaborator, has argued that 'Habermas is engaged in the construction of ideal stages of social evolution or, rather, the mere postulation of social evolutionary potentialities to the exclusion of all attempts to identify real processes of social evolution and their peculiar structural elements. His theory of social evolution is not a theory of historical evolutionary processes but a normative theory about counterfactually conceived possible evolutionary processes.'[136] In short, not only does Habermas appear to be more interested in the logic of development than in its dynamics, but he makes the former the counterfactual normative standard against which the latter is measured and often found wanting. It is certainly the case that while great attention is paid to describing the ontogenetic stages of development, concrete historical processes and actual histories of individuals and societies are either neglected in Habermas's work or, when they are remarked on, appear merely as overdetermined empirical data that accelerate or retard the logic of development.[137]

The normativistic orientation of Habermas's theory of social evolution, with its logical end point of development located in modern post-conventional society, raises again the two problems that its logic-dynamics distinction had hoped to have circumvented: Kantian apriorism and Hegelian philosophy of history. In emphatically identifying the *logic* of social evolution with the counterfactual but universal development of communicative rationality, Habermas is in danger of contradicting his attempt to reconstruct universal competencies through empirical studies of cognitive-moral and socio-historical development because these studies of empirical *dynamics* find themselves subsumed under the presupposed universal development of communicative reason. In other words, the logic of evolution is supposed to be derived from the empirical and the actual, but they, in turn, find themselves ceding priority to the logic. This contradiction worries even a critic as sympathetic to Habermas as Thomas McCarthy, who anxiously notes that questions might arise concerning 'Habermas's rather a priori arguments in support of what are intended to be judgements a posteriori.'[138] Drawing on Klaus Eder's critique, Piet Strydom observes that the normativistic implications of Habermas's theory of social evolution result in what he calls 'neo-Kantian apriorism,' that is, Habermas's 'commitment to something objective outside society, a so-called "metasocial guarantee," "metadiscourse," or "grand narrative," as the secure foundation of practical reason' or universal morality. Like Eder, Strydom is

> convinced that Habermas's ontogenetically informed and cognitivistically grounded concept of developmental logic represents nothing less than a

> contemporary variant ... of apriorism. This theoretical basis allows him to devise an aprioristic and thus pre-sociological concept of practical reason beyond society. It is given the form of the standard and goal of social evolution ... [S]ocial evolution is reduced to being nothing more and nothing less than the realization of this objective standard beyond society.[139]

Strydom's discussion points to a certain circularity in Habermas's developmental logic in so far as its end point or telos of a universal, communicatively based practical reason or morality is already aprioristically presupposed as that which has to be attained. This circularity has devastating consequences for Habermas's theoretical reliance on the empirically based 'reconstructive sciences' as a way of avoiding transcendental apriorism. For it appears that the rational reconstruction of sociocultural and historical developments has already been anticipated and presupposed in the aprioristically given logic of the universal development of communicative rationality. Habermas cannot escape the critical thrust of Georgia Warnke's question aimed at the tautology unavoidably present in his attempt to square rational reconstruction with a presupposed developmental logic: 'How can we prove our communicative competence to reflect a higher stage in a species-wide development process if all the research that we undertake in order to show it is a higher stage assumes what is to be proven?'[140] Warnke's question clearly suggests that a serious problem dogs Habermas's theory of the universal development of communicative reason in so far as the criteria for development have already been presupposed, already assumed in advance. The apriorism of the criteria for rationality's development has prompted Seyla Benhabib to observe that 'Habermas's analysis of modernity as rationalization *begs the question* concerning the validity of these criteria. Since these criteria constitute features of *our* rationalized lifeworld, we first presuppose their validity and subsequently reconstruct all previous development as leading to their emergence. What we extract from this account is what we have already put into it.'[141]

Benhabib's critique not only accounts for the circularity that emerges out of the apriorism of Habermas's developmental logic, it also points to the logic's teleological orientation that makes it resemble the Hegelian philosophy of history it wants to avoid. Our suspicions are raised when we notice that the end point or telos of Habermas's developmental logic – namely, a rationalized, post-conventional, modern lifeworld and society – provides the criteria for development. In other words, Habermas's criteria for distinguishing between developmental stages and assessing the level of rationality attained do not appear sufficiently independent 'from a restatement of the salient features of modern Western culture: a potential for cognitive learning, an unlimited criticizability and the differentiation of *praxis* and discourse into a cognitive, moral, and expressive point of view.'[142] Once the concepts and values of modern Western culture begin to determine research into ontogenetic processes or the investigation of historical societies and other cultures, concerns over unilinear development and teleological determinism will correspondingly arise. The resemblance between Habermas's logic of development and Hegelian philosophy of history, the former's denial notwithstanding, is further emphasized both by the argumentative structure and the language Habermas employs in his description of cognitive and moral development. He agrees with 'the assumption that higher-level cognitive structures replace the lower ones while preserving them in reorganized form.' He says that while it is difficult to analyse 'this *dialectical sublation of structures that have been superseded*,'[143] a few developmental trends can nevertheless be identified:

> For instance, it is possible to derive the more complex structures ... from the relatively simple ones ... What happens in each of these cases is that the central semantic component of the more elementary concept is decontextualized and thus thrown into sharper relief, which allows the higher-level concept to stylize the superseded concept as a *counterconcept*. From the perspective of the next-higher stage, for instance, the exercise of authority by reference persons becomes *mere* arbitrary will, which is then explicitly contrasted with legitimate expressions of will. To cite another example, personal loyalties or pleasure-pain orientations become *mere* inclinations sharply set off from duties. Correspondingly, the legitimacy of action norms is viewed at the next stage as their *mere* social acceptance, which is contrasted with ideal validity, while action based on concrete duties is now contrasted with autonomy as something *merely* heteronomous.[144]

What we see in this remarkably Hegelian passage is a description of socio-cognitive and moral development as a dialectical progression involving at once a process of ranking and devaluation. Such a dialectic of development thus clearly affirms a hierarchy of communicative rationality and morality, with the modern culture of the West occupying the latest and highest post-conventional stage.

Indeed, in choosing to support this theory of sociocultural evolution by drawing on the ontogenetic studies of Piaget and Kohlberg, Habermas finds that he has to adopt a teleological perspective on development and, consequently, accept a modern Western bias as well. In his criticism of the Piagetian model, Thomas McCarthy points out convincingly that 'the end-state toward which the developmental process is construed as heading is clearly Western in conception. Indeed it has been characterized as "the development of a Western scientist."'[145] To regard sociocultural and moral evolution as heading towards and culminating in Western modernity is to believe in what Eder has called an 'evolution theoretic myth.'[146] Focusing on Habermas's discussion of moral evolution, Eder expresses his concern over its ideological claim that modern society is the telos of moral development and thus the standard against which other societies are to be judged. The key question for Eder 'is whether a society when it claims to possess a higher form of morality than another, does not in effect advance a power claim. Or more precisely: When a society tries to monopolize universalistic morality, claiming that it and it alone has achieved such a morality, is it not then engaging in an attempt to obtain a better position for itself in relation to other societies?'[147] In short, doesn't Habermas's theory of sociocultural and moral evolution lead to a Eurocentric valorization of modernity, to the claim that the 'West is best'?[148]

But doesn't Habermas himself say that his theory is based on 'a universalism that is highly sensitive to differences'?[149] What about his insistence that the cognitive and moral universalism advocated by his theory, far from proclaiming Western superiority, allows the possibility of dialogue and mutual understanding between the West and the rest, between modern "us" and premodern "them"? Contesting Richard Rorty's contextualist ethnocentrism and in agreement with Hilary Putnam and Thomas McCarthy, Habermas argues that there is 'a *symmetrical* relationship between "us" and "them" in the exemplary cases of intercultural or historical understanding, in which rival conceptions collide not only with each other but with conflicting standards of rationality as well.'[150] He points out that Rorty fails 'to capture the symmetry among the claims and perspectives of *all* participants in a dialogue' because he sees understanding as an 'assimilative incorporation of what is alien into our (expanded) interpretive horizon.'[151] Habermas, by contrast, asserts that in a symmetrical process of understanding, 'we' learn from 'them' as much as 'they' learn from 'us.' There is no assimilation of one by the other; rather there is a mutual attempt not only to grasp each other's perspective but also to recognize each other's limitations. As a result, instead of assimilation, we have a 'convergence' brought about by a symmetrical learning process. 'For learning itself,' Habermas proclaims, 'belongs neither to us nor to them; both sides are caught up in it in this same way.'[152]

So far, so reasonable. But then Habermas goes on to say: 'Certainly, some cultures have had more practice than others at distancing themselves from themselves. But all languages offer the possibility of distinguishing between what is true and what we hold to be true. The *supposition* of a common objective world is built into the pragmatics of every single linguistic usage.'[153] Surely this poses a problem. The concession that some cultures may be more reflexive, more able to relativize themselves, than others leads to the conclusion that they are also more open to learning processes than those cultures that are less reflexive, less capable of self-distancing. What is interesting here is that the symmetrical learning processes that are allegedly present in intercultural or historical understanding become somewhat asymmetrical when we are also told that some cultures are less context-bound and thus better at learning about themselves and others than are other cultures. Not surprisingly, cultures that are better at distancing themselves from themselves are modern cultures; by implication, primitive or traditional cultures are more context-dependent and ethnocentric. The relationship between modern 'us' and premodern 'them' cannot, therefore, be symmetrical since, being reflexive, we clearly learn better and, consequently, understand more than they do.

Habermas could of course argue that despite modern Western culture's greater capacity for learning, its espousal of moral universalism demands 'equal respect for everyone,' sensitivity to difference, and 'a *nonleveling* and *nonappropriating* inclusion of the other *in his otherness*.'[154] Another problem emerges at this point, however, to trouble Habermas's generous call for an inclusive yet symmetrical and egalitarian relationship with the Other. Difference is recognized, but Habermas's universalism and strong objection to relativism compel him to place an equal emphasis on 'the supposition of a common objective world.'[155] But, given the acknowledged differences, how can we understand an alien culture, let alone arrive at a common understanding of an objective world?

Let us begin by examining how Habermas deals with the question of interpreting another culture. In trying to understand another culture, Habermas argues, an interpreter must give up the objectivating attitude of a third-person observer and adopt the performative attitude of an interlocutor or participant.[156] The interpreter understands the Other's meaning only if he/she also understands the reasons given by the Other for the truth, rightness, or authenticity of the stated meaning. In other words, 'the assertion of meaning has been transformed into the making of validity claims.'[157] The interpreter has to treat what the Other says as a validity claim; that is, instead of merely accepting the reasons given by the Other, the interpreter has to judge these reasons as reasons by taking a 'yes' or 'no' position on them. For 'reasons can be *understood* only insofar as they are taken seriously as reasons and *evaluated*.'[158] To understand the Other therefore requires the interpreter to evaluate the rationality of the Other's meaning according to 'standards of rationality ... that he himself considers binding on all parties,' including the Other.[159] The interpreter, Habermas writes, 'can descriptively grasp the meaning of the actual course of a process of reaching understanding only under the presupposition that he judges the agreement and disagreement, the validity claims and potential reasons with which he is confronted, on a common basis *shared* in principle by him and those immediately involved.'[160]

What then would be the 'common basis' shared in principle between, say, Professor Habermas and a myth-minded Azande or Cashinahua?[161] The common basis is the objective world that both presuppose when they enter into the pragmatics of communication. Of course both will presuppose this objective world from their own particular, sociocultural perspective. But there is a difference between how Habermas conceives of the objective world and how the myth-minded Azande or Cashinahua would. To begin with, for Habermas, there is the acknowledgment of a distinction between the objective world and the world as it appears to him. He affirms the universal 'possibility of distinguishing between what is true and what we hold to be true.'[162] He argues that we can 'distinguish between "the" world and the world as it appears from the agent's standpoint. We can descriptively ascertain what the actor *takes* to be true in contradistinction to what *is* (in our opinion) true.'[163] But is this critical reflexivity, this ability to distinguish between what is subjectively believed and what is objectively true, or between context-dependent conventions and counterfactual, discursively achieved universals, available to the premodern agent as well? Clearly the answer is no; after all, the premodern agent, as Habermas has argued, lacks critical reflexivity, does not differentiate the world into separate domains of reality, and thus confuses nature and culture.

It appears, therefore, that as moderns we have a better understanding of the objective world and of the universality of truth than do unreflexive premoderns whose closed, ethnocentric consciousness knows neither objective world nor universal truth. To be sure, in line with his assertion that a symmetrical learning relationship obtains between 'us' and 'them,' Habermas can argue that the modern world view can equally be criticized by the premodern agent. However, for the latter to do this he must first surmount his closed world view and learn to become more open and reflexively critical like us. Symmetry or equality between us and the premodern agent can occur 'only if we were to equip him with competences other than those permitted by the teleological model of action' – that is, action predetermined by his closed worldview. '*Mutual* critique would be possible only if the agent could for his part take up interpersonal relations, act communicatively, and even participate in the special form of communication (loaded with presuppositions) that we have called "discourse."'[164] It can be pointed out, however, that such a form of symmetry or equality favours our world view over theirs. Bernard Flynn perceptively notes, for instance, that

> [t]he condition for this equality is that *we* do a good deal of equipping. Since Habermas knows, and even says so ... that the concept of an 'objective world' – a world investigated by critizable claims to knowledge – is not a part of a 'mythical' worldview, it would appear that he is claiming that the condition of our equality is that you give up your culture and let me *equip* you for ours. For example, when an anthropologist is told by an informant that it is the belief of his tribe that this sacred tree is the center of the universe, if the anthropologist wants to 'take this belief seriously,' he would have to say, 'No it is not the center of the universe, but if you come with me to the Max Planck Institute and study for a couple of decades, then we can have a *discourse* about it.[165]

Thus, however sensitive to cultural difference Habermas's moral universalism may be, it is difficult to see how its regulative criteria can, in practice, not be critical of myth-minded or even teleologically centred cultures. As Brian Shaw observes: 'One does not respectfully welcome into public debates persons offering what are in principle suspect arguments.'[166] It can in fact be argued that the principle of symmetry that Habermas sees in intercultural and historical understanding is introduced only *after* an asymmetry or hierarchy has been established through his distinction between myth-minded primitive society and reflexive modern society, a distinction that clearly favours the latter as the end stage of a theory of sociocultural evolution. Habermas himself, despite his assertions about symmetry, has admitted that 'we must take account of an *asymmetry* that arises between the interpretive capacities of different cultures in virtue of the fact that some have introduced "second-order concepts" whereas others have not. These second-order concepts fulfill necessary cognitive conditions for a culture's becoming self-reflective ... This kind of decentered understanding of the world is characteristic of modern societies.'[167] The epistemological and political consequences of such an asymmetry – an asymmetry expressive of geopolitical power – between the modern and the premodern has been lucidly outlined by the subaltern studies historian Dipesh Chakrabarty:

> [D]ialogue can be genuinely open only on one condition: that no party puts itself in a position where it can unilaterally decide the final outcomes of the conversation. This never happens between the 'modern' and the 'non-modern.' Because, however non-coercive the conversation between the Kantian [or Enlightenment] subject (i.e. the transcendent academic observer, the knowing, judging and willing subject of modernity) and the subaltern who enters into a historical dialogue with the former from a non-Enlightenment position, this dialogue takes place within a field of possibilities that is already structured from the very beginning in favour of certain outcomes.[168]

Though Habermas claims that the moral universalism advocated by the modern world view insists on the inclusion of the Other, the Other is included, as we have seen, only according to the terms or outcomes determined by modern rationality. The premodern other has to rationalize or question its own sociocultural context and local attachments and adopt a post-conventional, hypothetical attitude – in short, become modern – in order to be included fully as a communicative partner. Habermas's theory of sociocultural evolution with modernity as its telos results in a developmental logic that shows how premodern mythic consciousness is superseded by modernity's communicative rationality. In addition, as Diana Coole points out, '[t]here is no place, and certainly no radical role, for disruption and transgression in this process. For Habermas, failings in communication can only signify a distortion to be overcome, never a salutary challenge to the hubris of reason.'[169] What we have, then, is an unfailing logic of development that can turn 'present inadequacies ... [into] portents of their supersession.'[170] But such a totalizing logic, with its counterfactual yet determined outcome, and its ability to reconcile opposites and redeem present inadequacies, appears to possess both the features as well as the powers of myth. Habermas's theory of the development of universal modern rationality can thus be seen as a Western myth itself.

It is this Western myth of universal rationality that Frantz Fanon questioned when, in the context of decolonization, he remarked: 'The colonialist bourgeoisie, in its narcissistic dialogue, expounded by the members of its universities, had in fact deeply implanted in the minds of the colonized intellectual that the essential qualities remain eternal in spite of all the blunders men may make: the essential qualities of the West, of course.'[171] But it is not enough just to identify and expose examples of Western myth; it is also important to understand that the modern, Enlightenment critique of myth forgets its own mythical origins, forgets that the disenchantment of myth is itself *the myth of disenchantment.* One of the conditions of myth is that it does not see itself as a particular world view but as the natural order of things. Bernard Flynn points out that

> if savage societies are defined as societies that cannot perceive their world view as a world view ... then there is a sense in which Habermas is himself a savage, since according to him, insofar as our world view has universal validity, it is not viewed as an interpretive system that is attached to a cultural tradition, or if attached only circumstantially so. If primitives regard their world view not as a world view but as natural, so, in a sense, does Habermas.[172]

Thus, a naturalized or 'white' mythology comes into being precisely at the very moment when its own mythic conception is forgotten, denied, or erased. As Jacques Derrida, to whom we owe the term 'white' mythology, observes: 'White mythology – metaphysics has erased within itself the fabulous scene that has produced it, the same that nevertheless remains active and stirring, inscribed in white ink, an invisible design covered over in the palimpsest.'[173] One of the most incisive critiques of modernity's project of disenchantment comes from Sister Hermann Marie, a character in Don DeLillo's novel *White Noise*:

> As belief shrinks from the world, people find it more necessary than ever that *someone* believe. Wild-eyed men in caves. Nuns in black. Monks who do not speak. We are left to believe. Fools, children. Those who have abandoned belief must still believe in us. They are sure that they are right not to believe but they know belief must not fade completely. Hell is when no one believes. There must always be believers. Fools, idiots, those who hear voices, those who speak in tongues. We are your lunatics. We surrender our

> lives to make your nonbelief possible. You are sure that you are right but you don't want everyone to think as you do. There is no truth without fools.[174]

There are some sharp critiques of Habermas's work, but none as sharp as Sister Hermann Marie's. For she shrewdly shows us that it is Enlightenment philosophers like Habermas who need the primitive, the premodern, the mythical. It is the enlightened and the rational who require their mythical, irrational Other. Sister Hermann Marie reveals the truth about modernity's project of disenchantment: it is a white myth, a myth that in demythologizing myths forgets its own fabulous origin, its own mythical need.

So far we have been examining Habermas's narrative of development, which regards the rationalization of premodern mythic consciousness (in Habermas's Durkheimian idiom, a 'linguistification of the sacred') as an enlargement of reason. But, as I noted in the previous section, there is another less visible narrative in Habermas's work, a narrative that reveals a more ambivalent attitude to the premodern and the sacred. It is this ambivalence that the next section will explore.

Rationality, Loss, and the Recovery of the Premodern Other

Even as he argues for the greater cognitive adequacy, reflexivity, and learning capacity of modern forms of 'open' understanding over 'closed' mythical world views, Habermas nonetheless sees fit to remind us that we should not ignore the 'pathos' that attends Peter Winch's defence of premodern, mythic thought. Habermas asks: 'Can't we who belong to modern societies learn something from understanding alternative, particularly premodern forms of life? Shouldn't we, beyond all romanticizing of superseded stages of development, beyond exotic stimulation from the contents of alien cultures, recall the losses required by our own path to the modern world?'[175] Even a defender of scientific rationality like Robin Horton, Habermas remarks, admits to a sense of loss in the transition to modern society. He quotes Horton's confession, which I will reproduce in full both for its interesting ambivalence and for its eloquence:

> As a scientist it is perhaps inevitable that I should at certain points give the impression that traditional African thought is a poor shackled thing when compared with the thought of the sciences. Yet as a man, here I am living by choice in a still-heavily-traditional Africa rather than in the scientifically oriented Western subculture I was brought up in. Why? Well, there may be lots of queer, sinister, unacknowledged reasons. But one certain reason is

> the discovery of *things lost* at home. An intensely poetic quality in everyday life and thought, and a vivid enjoyment of the passing moment – both driven out of sophisticated Western life by the quest for purity of motive and the faith in progress.[176]

Horton's statement is not free of nostalgia and may even be guilty of perpetuating the myth of the sensuous, carefree native; but it is also honest in its self-critical admission that modern Western rationality is not achieved without loss and that the advancement of reason does not necessarily bring with it happiness.

Habermas expresses a similar recognition of loss in the midst of rationality's triumph when he says that we must 'not only comprehend the learning processes that separate "us" from "them," but also become aware of what we have *unlearned* in the course of this learning.'[177] He is especially concerned over the 'unlearning' that occurs when rationalization proceeds in a one-sided manner, resulting in the dominance of cognitive-instrumental rationality over the other two modes of moral-practical and aesthetic-expressive rationality. He can thus see in Horton's ambivalence a 'self-critical emphasis'[178] aimed at modern Western society's fixation on scientific or purposive-instrumental rationality at the expense of rationality's other non-objectivating, communicative role. In Habermas's words: 'What seems to belong to the idiosyncratic traits of Western culture is not scientific rationality as such, but its hypostatization. This suggests a pattern of cultural and societal rationalization that helps cognitive-instrumental rationality to achieve a one-sided dominance not only in our dealings with external nature, but also in our understanding of the world and in the communicative practice of everyday life.'[179] Thus, unlike Weber or Horkheimer and Adorno, Habermas does not equate Western modernity with a totalizing purposive-instrumental rationality; instead, arguing that reason also has a communicative dimension and not just an objectifying, instrumental drive, Habermas holds out the possibility of criticizing, and thus of avoiding, Western modernity's 'selective process of rationalization – where purposive-rational rationalization prevails, encroaches upon, and deforms the life-world of everyday life.'[180] But while devoting greater attention to the lifeworld would help correct the selective emphasis on purposive rationality and functional integration that has resulted in what Habermas calls 'the colonization of the lifeworld' by system imperatives, the lifeworld's own rationalization is not without its problems, as we shall see.

The lifeworld (*Lebenswelt*) forms an invariant horizon or context within which processes of reaching understanding occur. It functions as a common background for participants – 'an intuitively known, unproblematic, and unanalyzable, holistic background.'[181] Like language and culture, to which it is internally connected, the lifeworld is unproblematically present, familiar, assumed without reflection, taken for granted like the very air we breathe.[182] In addition to its horizon-forming *context*, the lifeworld also provides the cultural resources and assumptions necessary for forming group solidarity.[183]

Though aided by the lifeworld's intuitively known and unquestioned background convictions, communicative participants nonetheless still have to work to achieve mutual understanding or agreement when they are faced with an action situation or interpretive problem that emerges in the everyday world. They can reach agreement only through a conscious yes or no position they take on three differentiated validity claims that are raised respectively in the objective, social, and subjective domains of their world: the claims to truth, rightness or justice, and expressive truthfulness or sincerity.[184] Up to this point, the lifeworld has been described as a stabilizing and conservative factor in the process of reaching understanding. Habermas in fact sees the lifeworld in its intuitively pre-understood, holistic background role as 'the conservative counterweight to the risk of disagreement that arises with every actual process of reaching understanding; for communicative actors can achieve an understanding only by way of taking yes/no positions on criticizable validity claims.'[185] However, as Habermas points out, italicizing his statement for emphasis, '*The relation between these weights changes with the decentration of worldviews.*'[186] The decentration of world views becomes possible through the growing reflexivity achieved in ontogenetic learning processes that act as pacemakers for the sociocultural development of modernity. Thus, as we become more and more reflexively modern, our world view also becomes increasingly decentred. Correspondingly,

> the more the worldview that furnishes the cultural stock of knowledge is decentered, the less the need for understanding is covered in advance by an interpreted lifeworld immune from critique, and the more this need has to be met by the interpretive accomplishments of the participants themselves, that is, by way of risky (because rationally motivated) agreement, the more frequently we can expect rational action orientations.[187]

Habermas characterizes this transition as 'the rationalization of the lifeworld' and sees it as a switch from 'normatively ascribed agreement' to 'communicatively achieved understanding.'[188]

The rationalization of the lifeworld thus appears to follow a developmental trajectory much like that of the sociocultural evolution from premodern mythic to modern decentred world views. Habermas puts it this way: 'A directional dynamics is built into the communicatively structured lifeworld in the form of the polarity between a state of pre-established pre-understanding and a consensus to be achieved: in the course of time, the reproductive achievements switch from one pole to the other.'[189] This 'directional dynamics' shown in the rationalization of the lifeworld resembles the larger-scale rationalization of society that Habermas, following thinkers like Durkheim and Weber, describes as the transition from primitive tribal groups with their pre-reflective, 'collectively shared, homogeneous lifeworld'[190] to the reflexive, differentiated, and communicatively achieved lifeworld of modern politics. Recognizing the similarity between premodern societies and the lifeworld in its original, concrete, pre-rationalized state, Habermas writes: 'The lifeworld concept of society finds its strongest empirical footing in archaic societies,' which in their ideal state are 'almost homogeneous, and nearly ultrastable.'[191] Just as the 'nearly ultrastable,' normative authority of the sacred and the mythic in premodern societies is 'linguistified,' that is, dissolved by reflexive communicative action oriented to understanding, so too the rationalization of the lifeworld involves a process in which the pre-established agreements and prelinguistically guaranteed norms of the everyday concrete lifeworld are opened up to reflexive forms of discourse or argumentation with their yes/no stance on validity claims raised in the course of communicative interactions. 'By the rationalization of the lifeworld,' Seyla Benhabib notes, 'is meant nothing other than the increase in argumentative practices within the everyday world.'[192] Once rationalization is seen as an 'increase in argumentative practices,' the lifeworld turns critical and reflexive and can no longer rely on pre-established normative contexts secured by the authority of the sacred or the unquestioned holism of mythic world views. Modern societies thus undergo a process of rationalization that Habermas also calls 'the linguistification of the sacred.' The modern *rationalized* lifeworld is no longer beholden to the authority of the sacred, but depends solely on rationally motivated forms of understanding that lead to a consensus based on the authority of the better argument.[193] In the idealized or fully rationalized lifeworld, we can see its differentiated components – culture, society, and personality – renewing themselves autonomously, unconstrained by any pre-given tradition, norm, or convention: in the case of culture we would see 'a state of the constant revision of fluidized traditions, i.e. traditions which have become reflexive; ... a state in which legitimate orders depend on discursive procedures for positing and justifying norms.'[194]

It should be noted, however, that the critical reflexivity, the constant sceptical revision of all pre-established traditions and norms we find in the rationalization process lands the lifeworld in an aporetic situation. On the one hand, the lifeworld is the ever-present, intuitively understood background within which all communicative action and forms of understanding occur; it also provides a store of pre-interpreted knowledge that enables cultural understanding, forms group solidarity, and shapes the competences of socialized individuals.[195] On the other hand, the lifeworld's rationalization gains it the critical reflexivity and autonomy that threaten to devalue, if not destroy, the very context in which it stands and the resources on which it draws. To his credit, Habermas recognizes this problem, although, as we shall see, his attempts at resolving it result in what Stephen Crook has described as an example of his 'having the honesty to make his own problem worse.'[196]

The rationalization of the lifeworld thus involves a rather destructive hermeneutics of suspicion that calls into question customary forms of life. As Habermas puts it:

> [T]he transition to argumentation has something unnatural about it: it marks a break with the ingenuous straightforwardness with which people have raised the claims to validity on whose intersubjective recognition the communicative practice of everyday life depends. This unnaturalness is like an echo of the developmental catastrophe that historically once devalued the world of traditions and thereby provoked efforts to rebuild it at a higher level.[197]

Words like 'unnatural' and 'catastrophe' attest to the radical change visited on all past claims and traditions by modern rationalization processes. J.M. Bernstein argues that the distrust shown to all conventions established by tradition should cause alarm, since it appears to suggest that 'up to the moment of modernity the forms of recognition that traditional practices permitted were illusory through and through.'[198] Such a sweeping scepticism is, however, central to Habermas's view of rationalization as the progress towards a post-conventional modernity: 'No normative validity claim raised in the lifeworld is immune to challenge; *everything* counts as a hypothesis until it has regained its validity through the authority of good reasons.'[199]

If nothing in the lifeworld is immune to challenge and everything in it counts as a hypothesis, and if the lifeworld's background knowledge 'is submitted to an ongoing test across its entire breadth,'[200] then a difficult question arises for Habermas: can the lifeworld still be an inescapable horizon or context of understanding and the source of cultural knowledge and normative values, if, at the same time, it is constantly challenged or tested across its entire breadth? Even though Habermas might respond that the lifeworld's rationalization through moral argumentation (or discourse ethics) can be seen as a correction and transcendence of the lifeworld's conventional limits, doesn't the unmerciful gaze of rationalization threaten, at least in theory, to dissolve the very ground of the lifeworld from which the corrective gaze emanates? And wouldn't such a rational dissolution of 'normatively ascribed agreement' for a risk-laden, counterfactual 'communicatively achieved understanding' place us 'within the impossible space of an unlivable scepticism and undischargeable rationalism'?[201] In her perceptive study of Habermas's work, Maeve Cooke worries, for example, that the lifeworld's 'fabric could be worn away through constant critical examination and rejection of its traditions, practices, and fixed patterns of personality development.'[202]

The 'precarious status' of the lifeworld concept is underscored by the ambiguous, if not contradictory, descriptions Habermas gives to it. On the one hand, as we have seen, the lifeworld is subjected in its entire breadth to an ongoing test; nothing in it is immune to challenge and its entire store of cultural givens and established norms is opened up to an unmerciful, critical gaze and submitted to the unrelenting pressure of argumentation. On the other hand, the lifeworld that is not immune to challenge is also said not to be completely thematizable or susceptible to objectification, and hence not completely knowable or challengeable. Thus, though 'the general structures of the lifeworld [are] capable of being rationalized,' particular 'lifeworlds in their specific, concrete historical totalities ... form a context that remains in the background and is experienced by us only as an horizon; this context cannot be objectivated in toto.'[203] The aim of the distinction is clear: it is to set a limit on rationalization processes and to illustrate that the lifeworld 'can never be made fully conscious or be fully rationalized.'[204] Perhaps the clearest example of Habermas's ambivalent view of the lifeworld's rationalization occurs a few pages before the end of his two-volume magnum opus *The Theory of Communicative Action.* The limitation of a naive, pre-reflective lifeworld is duly noted: 'The horizontal knowledge that communicative everyday practice *tacitly* carries with it is paradigmatic for the *certainty* with which the lifeworld background is present; yet it does not satisfy the criterion of knowledge that stands in internal relation to validity claims and can therefore be criticized.'[205] At the same time, however, despite the increasing reflexivity demanded by modernity, the lifeworld can only be rationalized a little at a time; much of it remains ungraspable, beyond anyone's disposition. As Habermas observes:

> It is only under the pressure of approaching problems that relevant components of such background knowledge are torn out of their unquestioned familiarity and brought to consciousness as something in need of being ascertained. It takes an earthquake to make us aware that we had regarded the ground on which we stand everyday as unshakable. Even in situations of this sort, *only a small segment of our background knowledge becomes uncertain* and is set loose after having been enclosed in complex traditions, in solidaric relations, in competences. If the objective occasion arises for us to arrive at some understanding about a situation that has become problematic, background knowledge is transformed into explicit knowledge *only in a piecemeal manner.*[206]

There is a peculiar honesty in Habermas's work; the monumental labour expended on the construction of an elaborate theory of rationalization and argumentation ends up yielding a disarmingly modest and almost self-cancelling admission that the rationalization of the lifeworld is not only piecemeal but can never achieve full realization. Thus, as Fred Dallmayr pointedly notes, to assert that the lifeworld is never fully knowable or assessible 'seems odd or out of place in a study [*The Theory of Communicative Action*] whose centerpiece is discursive rationality and a theory of communication anchored in reviewable validity claims.'[207]

Habermas also recognizes that rationalization requires decentration and abstraction from the concrete, pre-reflective totality of the lifeworld and that such an abstraction from the lifeworld's substantive aspects can lead to an empty formalism. Ethical formalism, according to Habermas, can be one-sided in its neglect of concrete aspects of ethical life (*Sittlichkeit*). In his words:

> *The critique of ethical formalism* takes exception, first of all, to the fact that preoccupation with questions of the validity of moral norms misleads us into ignoring the intrinsic value of cultural life-forms and life-styles. From the perspective of Durkheimian analysis, there is the question of what remains from the collective consciousness constitutive of the identity of

> tribal societies when the ritually secured, basic normative consensus about concrete values and contents evaporates into a merely procedurally secured consensus about the foundations of communicative ethics. The content has been filtered out of this procedural consensus.[208]

What is interesting about this critique of formalism is that it suggests that the lifeworld's content (including its premodern, ritually secured consensus) continues to haunt the procedural or formal rationality that had sought, in the first place, to abstract itself from the concrete lifeworld. It appears that rationalization and the deontological formalism it entails can never be completely detached or abstracted from the prereflective, substantive totality of the lifeworld.

The limits of rationalization, indicated by the need to redress formalism by instituting compensatory measures, become most visible in Habermas's discussion of discourse ethics. Discourse ethics concerns itself with the process of moral argumentation or rationalization that transforms ethical life (*Sittlichkeit*), with its unproblematically accepted, tradition-based, context-bound norms, into morality (*Moralität*), with its unrelenting norm-testing, context-transcending approach to securing consensus through argumentation. As we have seen, such a process of moral argumentation or rationalization can lead, at least in theory, to a full-scale emptying or uprooting of the normative certainties of tradition-based lifeworlds or ethical life. Since argumentation relies on decontextualized, universal rules, the dense particularities, the historical and cultural thickness of our ethical life not only count for little or nought, they are dismissed as provincial limitations, ethnocentric barriers to the achievement of a universalistic morality. A rationalized, universal morality must, therefore, be rigorously decontex-tualized, abstracted from all traces of the ethical life. Yet, as Habermas recognizes, Hegel was right to critique Kant's moral formalism for neglecting 'the substantive ethics (*Sittlichkeit*) of ... lived contexts, subjecting them to hypothetical reasoning without regard to existing motives and institutions. This causes norms to become removed from the world (*entweltlicht*) – an unavoidable step in the process of justification but also one for which discourse ethics might consider *making amends*.'[209] He concedes that only those life forms that 'meet universalist moralities halfway' can reverse the demotivation caused by moral decontextualization.[210]

Habermas's idea of compensation is, however, another example of his honesty making matters worse for himself. As J.M. Bernstein critically observes:

> [I]f universalist morality requires a form of life to meet it 'halfway,' which is to say, to contextualize it and thereby give its norms and requirements a motivational anchoring in everyday practices, then communicative reason is not self-sufficient ... Or, we could say, by inference that although communicative reason is self-sufficient *as reason*, modern rationality is not self-sufficient but requires the cooperation of the nonrational for its effectiveness. Rationalized reason and enlightened moral universalism are *dependent upon* what is extrinsic to them.[211]

To be sure, Habermas could respond to Bernstein's argument by saying that it is not any non-rational form of life that he sees as providing motivational anchorage for universalist morality. The form of life required to meet morality 'halfway' is a rationalized form of life already decontextualized from ethical life and attuned to universalist principles. But, by Habermas's own argument, it is precisely because a rationalized life is one that is already decontextualized, and hence demotivated, that it needs to be remotivated through recontextualization. So to avoid Bernstein's point about rationality's dependence on the non-rational by arguing that universalist moral rationality is motivationally anchored in an already universalized or rationalized life form is to engage in a self-defeating tautology.

A similar problem occurs in a related discussion about how 'justice conceived deontologically' – that is, as a desubstantivated, decontextualized, universal moral procedure – 'requires solidarity as its reverse side.'[212] Habermas insists that 'universalization must remain powerless unless there also arises ... a consciousness of irrevocable solidarity, the certainty of intimate relatedness in a shared life context.'[213] We are reminded, however, that for Habermas solidarity does not mean the sort of collective, ritually constituted binding force that Durkheim, for example, saw in premodern tribes. As Habermas explains:

> As a component of a universalistic morality, of course, solidarity loses its merely particular meaning, in which it is limited to the internal relationships of a collectivity that is ethnocentrically isolated from other groups – that character of forced willingness to sacrifice oneself for a collective system of self-assertion that is always present in premodern forms of solidarity. The formula 'Command us, Führer, we will follow you' goes perfectly with the formula 'All for one and one for all' – as we saw in the posters of Nazi Germany in my youth – because fellowship is entwined with followership in every traditionalist sense of solidarity. Justice conceived in postconventional

> terms can converge with solidarity as its reverse side only when solidarity has been transformed in the light of the idea of a general discursive will formation.[214]

Solidarity is required in the first place to compensate for what justice deontologically conceived lacks in affect, feeling, and 'intimate relatedness'; without the motivational, affective force of solidarity, justice would remain an abstract, demotivated idea. But if solidarity has to lose its particular meaning, undergo decontextualization, and be transformed into a consensus achieved discursively and universally, then solidarity would become as abstracted, deontologized, and universalized as justice, in which case it would also, like justice, require compensation for being emptied of 'intimate relatedness.' To escape its premodern, traditional, and ethnocentric limitations (limitations Habermas sees as dangerous insomuch as they recall the Nazi Germany of his youth), solidarity has to be lifted out of particular lifeworlds such as that of family, tribe, or nation, and extended universally to include all humanity. But in its decontextualization and universal extension, solidarity becomes much like justice; and, consequently, the argument that justice requires solidarity turns into a tautology. Habermas observes that even 'in the cosmopolitan ideas of the close of the eighteenth century, the archaic bonding energies of kinship were not extinguished but only refined into solidarity with everything wearing a human face.'[215] This is a noble but question-begging sentiment. Can there be an unproblematic refinement, a Hegelian sublation of archaic kinship solidarity into a solidarity with humanity at large, when it is precisely the abstraction of the latter that has called forth the need for the concreteness of the former? It is hard to imagine that one can find the same degree of 'intimate relatedness' in the idea of universal solidarity that one finds, for better or worse, in the 'bonding energies of kinship.'

Habermas finds himself either embracing a tautology or courting a contradiction because of the rather stark binaries with which he structures his thought. Distinctions are drawn between premodern myth and modern rationality, *Sittlichkeit* and *Moralität,* decontextualized justice and context-bound solidarity. But these distinctions soon generate problems that require Habermas to relax the distinctions, hence raising the possibility of contradiction (one part of the distinction denies the other) or tautology (one part of the distinction becomes like the other). We can thus discern a certain tension, even anxiety, running through Habermas's otherwise confident architectonic order. As we have seen, every *push* forward towards rationalization or modernization seems to necessitate a *pull* back to the lifeworld as conservative counterweight; every step in the direction of a deontologized morality (*Moralität*) starts off a compensatory movement in the direction of a concrete ethical life (*Sittlichkeit*); the linguistification of the sacred and the mythic is accompanied by a renewed call to conserve something of the binding energy and pre-reflexive meaningfulness made available in sacred ritual.

It is important to note that whatever problems Habermas may face in his attempts to mitigate the radical differentiation of reason, the compensatory attempts indicate his unflinching awareness of the ambivalence of rationalization; he understands that learning processes are accompanied by evidence of unlearning, and that the cognitive and morally reflexive powers gained through the rationalization of the lifeworld also put the lifeworld at risk along with its solidaristic energies and its meaningful unity. Though he warns us of the dangerous nostalgia for the premodern mythic and the pre-reflective, Habermas also recognizes the need to regain 'the lost unity of reason.'[216] Stephen White, for example, sees Habermas's attempt at restoring balance between the dirempted cultural spheres as a way of addressing 'the sense of loss of wholeness or unity which haunts modernity.'[217] We may also recall, in this context, Habermas's approving citation of Robin Horton's lament for '*things lost* at home.'[218] Thus, even though he is a great defender of the project of modernity and the progress of rationalization, Habermas is also acutely aware of the losses incurred by the lifeworld and peculiarly attached to the notion of instinct or intuition, which is surely primordial and pre-reflective. He talks, for example, about 'a fundamental intuition' behind his work, an intuition about 'undisturbed intersubjectivity' that informs his theory of communicative action.[219] Elsewhere, he writes:

> We learn what moral, and in particular immoral, action involves *prior* [his emphasis] to all philosophizing; it impresses itself upon us no less insistently in feelings of sympathy with the violated integrity of others than in the experience of violation or fear of violation of our own integrity. The *inarticulate, socially integrating experiences* of considerateness, solidarity and fairness shape our intuitions and provide us with better instruction about morality than *arguments* ever could.[220]

What is curious about this passage is that the elaborate theory of moral rationalization or argumentation Habermas has constructed is made secondary to inarticulate, pre-reflective intuitions. Similarly, in a long essay devoted to a discussion of moral rationalization we are told that 'morality as grounded by discourse ethics is based on a pattern inherent in mutual understanding in language *from the beginning*.'[221] Modernity as the *telos* of rationalization or argumentation only makes explicit what it already includes within itself from the beginning, namely, the *arché*, the primordial instinct or intuition of mutual, consensual understanding present in our first words. Thus, however far modernization or rationalization may have progressed, a primordial or premodern intuition of 'undisturbed intersubjectivity' will always accompany it, sometimes even acting as 'an avenging force'[222] when rationalization becomes selective and allows instrumental-purposive reason to colonize the lifeworld.

At this point, let us recall our earlier remark about the two narratives that structure Habermas's work. There is of course the prominent evolutionary narrative of rationalization and modernization. But there is also a less noticeable narrative that regards rationalization ambivalently and that focuses on the unlearning process, on what may have been left out or what may continue to trouble rationalization processes. It is this narrative that we have been tracking in our discussion of the lifeworld as conservative counterweight and in our examination of the compensatory and reconciliatory measures taken to mitigate the rationalization of the lifeworld. This narrative acts to remind Habermas that the pathologies of modernity cannot be corrected merely by a less selective, more balanced development of reason. This narrative argues that unless there is a renewal of the substance of the lifeworld, rationalization's constant questioning of the lifeworld's semantic resources will lead us to face 'the counter-intuitive prospect of a fully rationalized but barren lifeworld.'[223] This counter-narrative therefore acts, if you will, as a Benjaminian conscience in Habermas's affirmative story of reason's progress.

In an essay on Benjamin, Habermas has expressed just such a conscience:

> Could an emancipated humanity one day confront itself in the expanded scope of discursive will-formation and nevertheless still be deprived of the terms in which it is able to interpret life as good life? A culture which, for thousands of years, was exploited for the purpose of legitimating domination would take its revenge, just at the moment when age-old repressions could be overcome: not only would it be free of violence, it would no longer have any content. Without the store of those semantic energies with which Benjamin's redemptive criticism was concerned, there would necessarily be a stagnation of the structures of practical discourse [or discourse ethics] that had finally prevailed.[224]

Habermas's Benjaminian doubt cuts right into the heart of rationalization, posing the question of whether a fully rationalized world, emancipated from prejudice, domination, and the dead hand of tradition, can also be happy: 'Now it is true that the liberation of culture is not possible without overcoming the repression anchored in institutions. Yet, for a moment, one is beset by suspicion: wouldn't it be just as possible to have an emancipation without happiness and fulfillment as it is to have a relatively high standard of living without the abolition (*Aufhebung*) of repression?'[225] Rationalization's constant critical questioning erodes the lifeworld's primal stock of meaning, resulting in what David Ingram has eloquently described as 'the enervating limpidity of reflection.'[226] To avoid a rationalized lifeworld that can only yield an enervating reflective limpidity would require a renewal of the semantic energies Habermas refers to in his essay on Benjamin.

In his recent work, Habermas has grudgingly conceded that the premodern, pre-rationalized world views of religion and myth may serve as sources of these semantic energies. This concession weakens, though it does not cancel, his earlier account, in volume 2 of *The Theory of Communicative Action*, of the necessary 'linguistification of the sacred' (*die Versprachlichung des Sakralen*), a process in which the unquestioned, ritually secured authority of the sacred is replaced by the rational authority of a consensus achieved communicatively through argumentation:

> The disenchantment and disempowering of the domain of the sacred takes place by way of a linguistification of the ritually secured, basic normative agreement; going along with this is a release of the rationality potential in communicative action. The aura of rapture and terror that emanates from the sacred, the *spellbinding* power of the holy, is sublimated into the *binding/bonding* force of criticizable validity claims and at the same time turned into an everyday occurrence.[227]

Such a view of 'linguistification' or rationalization, as Donald Jay Rothberg points out, assumes 'a fundamental kind of zero-sum game in which as rationality develops, the "sacred" is "linguistified" and eliminated.'[228] Peter Dews has discerned, however, a softening of Habermas's adamant defence of secular rationality against religious or mythic authority and, thus, the emergence of 'significant tensions ... in his recent thought.' 'For in a number of recent essays,' Dews writes, 'Habermas has emphasized that religious discourse – and also, in a different way, the language of art – may continue to convey an existentially orientating and inspirational semantic charge, a sense of contact with the "extraordinary" or the "unconditioned," which cannot be entirely appropriated and discursively redeemed by philosophy.'[229] Dews draws this insight from the extraordinary closing paragraph of Habermas's essay 'Themes in Postmetaphysical Thinking,' in which he admits that the immanent transcendence of formal, rational argumentation is not enough to satisfy the human desire for contact with an external transcendence that is more substantial and existentially inspiring:

> In the wake of metaphysics, philosophy surrenders its extraordinary status. Explosive experiences of the extraordinary have migrated into an art that has become autonomous. Of course, even after this deflation, ordinary life, now fully profane, by no means becomes immune to the shattering and subversive intrusion of extraordinary events. Viewed from without, religion, which has largely been deprived of its world-view functions, is still indispensable in ordinary life for normalizing intercourse with the extraordinary. For this reason, even postmetaphysical thinking continues to coexist with religious practice – and not merely in the sense of the contemporaneity of the noncontemporaneous. This ongoing coexistence even throws light on a curious dependence of a philosophy that has forfeited its contact with the extraordinary. Philosophy, even in its postmetaphysical form, will be able neither to replace nor to repress religion as long as religious language is the bearer of a semantic content that is inspiring and even indispensable, for this content eludes (for the time being?) the explanatory force of philosophical language and continues to resist translation into reasoning discourses.[230]

A similar admission of the need to revitalize rationalized, modern political life by drawing on the pre-rational, pre-discursive semantic potentials present in religion or art appears in an appendix to *Between Facts and Norms*:

> The fact that everyday affairs are necessarily banalized in political communication also poses a danger for the semantic potentials from which this communication must still draw its nourishment ... Even the moment of unconditionality insistently voiced in the context-transcending validity claims of everyday life [i.e., the immanent transcendence of rational argumentation] does not suffice. *Another* kind of transcendence is preserved in the unfulfilled promise disclosed by the critical appropriation of identity-forming religious traditions, and *still another* in the negativity of modern art.

> The trivial and everyday [i.e., the lifeworld] must be open to the shock of what is absolutely strange, cryptic, or uncanny.[231]

What is interesting about these two rather lengthy passages that I have cited is that they indicate a shift in Habermas's thought from the 'zero-sum game' in which rationality's progress causes the complete eclipse and supersession of premodern mythic and sacred forms to the more conciliatory view that the pre-rational semantic potentials provided by art and religion should be seen as existentially revitalizing supplements to the banal and empty limpidity of a rationalized world. The Habermas who once criticized Nietzsche and his French successors for valorizing 'archaic origins, ... the Dionysian, the pre-Socratic, the exotic and primitive'[232] now sees the need for exposure to the explosive powers of the extraordinary, the strange, the cryptic, and the uncanny. To be sure, Habermas still strongly distances himself from the archaic or primitivistic turn; he does not advocate a Nietzschean or postmodern capitulation to the Other of reason. Moreover, his concessions notwithstanding, Habermas continues to refuse to give to the religious or artistic discourses of the extraordinary the same cognitive or moral status as rational argumentation, since to do so would be to de-differentiate or collapse together the cultural value spheres that have been so carefully differentiated by modern rationality, to level the genre distinctions generated by different validity claims, and to regress behind the emancipatory achievements of modernity.[233] Nonetheless, despite the grudging and conditional nature in which they are phrased, the concessions are still significant in that they signal what Dews has called Habermas's 'subterranean preoccupation' with the meaning 'once conserved by myth and religion.'[234] We can see in the return of the pre-discursive, the pre-reflexive, and the premodern to Habermas's thought a sign of the continuing tension between what I have described as his more prominent narrative of modernity as progressive rationalization and his less visible narrative of the persistence of those archaic, premodern forms that rationalization was supposed to have superseded or obliterated.

In his discussion of Adorno and Horkheimer's *The Dialectic of Enlightenment*, Habermas accuses his Frankfurt predecessors of being covert undialectical ontologists who thought they could escape an ideologically compromised reason through its totalized critique. However, Adorno and Horkheimer's ideology critique turns into a metaphysical idea of purity: 'The intention of a "final unmasking," which was supposed to draw away with one fell swoop the veil covering the confusion between power and reason, reveals a purist intent – similar to the intent of ontology to separate being and illusion categorically (that is, with one stroke).'[235] Leaving aside the question of whether this is a fair criticism of Adorno and Horkheimer, what is of interest is Habermas's assertion that communicative rationality, in contrast to the 'purism' of ideology critique, operates in an impure medium. Unlike Adorno and Horkheimer, whose totalized critique would purge the lifeworld of all forms of ideology, prejudice, and myth, Habermas believes that reason is situated in a world in which being and illusion, myth as meaning and myth as enchantment, are intertwined. Thus: 'Only a discourse that admits this [i.e., lack of purity] might break the spell of mythic thinking without incurring a loss of the light radiating from the semantic potentials also preserved in myth.'[236] Turning the tables on theorists who are suspicious of modernity's metanarrative of reason by characterizing them as ontological purists, Habermas can claim to have reinstated an impure, situated reason that can still hold faith with balanced forms of rationalization while remaining open to the semantic energies of the pre-discursive, the pre-reflective, and the premodern.

Many problems beset Habermas's attempt to hold on simultaneously to the two narratives that structure his work. More often than not the narrative of rationalization either trumps the narrative of semantic renewal or so constrains the latter that it is assimilated as an image of the former. Nonetheless, what is of interest to us is the way in which the two narratives appear to be entwined in a logic of inclusive exclusion. The logic of inclusive exclusion is explored brilliantly by Giorgio Agamben in his book *Homo Sacer*. Referring to the Aristotelian categories of *zoé* (bare or natural life) and *bios* (politically qualified life), Agamben observes that the inaugural constitution of Western politics involves the inclusive exclusion of *zoé* from the *polis* or city in which we find *bios*: 'The opposition [of *zoé* to *bios*] is, in fact, at the same time an implication of the first in the second, of bare life in politically qualified life ... Western politics first constitutes itself through an exclusion (which is simultaneously an inclusion) of bare life.'[237] Translating Agamben's Aristotelian language into Habermasian terminology, we can say that 'bare life' represents the pre-discursive, pre-reflective lifeworld and 'politically qualified life' represents the lifeworld that has undergone rationalization or modernization. What Agamben calls the 'inclusive exclusion' of *zoé* is thus equivalent to Habermas's initial construction and exclusion of modernity's Other, that is, of the sacred and the mythic, *and* his subsequent supplementary inclusion of the premodern Other and its semantic energies in modernity. What we have called Habermas's prominent narrative is concerned, as we have seen, with a process of rationalization that not only defines modernity's other as everything that modernity is not – the modern is differentiated, reflexive, and universal, whereas the premodern is holistic, pre-reflexive, and ethnocentric – but that also progressively excludes the premodern from the rationalized, modern domain. At the same time, however, having established his narrative of rationalization, Habermas acknowledges the need to redress the problems of imbalance and impoverishment inflicted on the lifeworld by rationalization. A process of controlled inclusion thus begins as the excluded premodern elements begin to reappear in his work.

But although the logic of inclusive exclusion may appear to achieve some kind of balanced resolution between two antithetical forces, Agamben clearly sees it as a discourse of power. In the final analysis, the resolution it achieves favours *bios* over *zoé* even if the inclusion of *zoé* continues to trouble *bios*. This exertion of discursive power is most clearly described in Peter Fitzpatrick's astute deployment of a similar logic of inclusive exclusion to expose modernity's invention and containment of its savage Other:

> Because a universalist encompassing modernity cannot allow of an engendering position apart from itself, its own 'self' creates the other against which it is constituted. Not only that, not only must the other be absolutely excluded from an encompassing modernity, this very quality of encompassment means that the other must also be included. Freud's savagery, to take a convenient example, externally opposes civilization yet is also within it. Modernity, then, is split between the constituent exclusion of what is other, what is ever apart from it, and the inclusion with-in itself of that same other.[238]

Fitzpatrick's description of modernity's logic of inclusive exclusion is especially insightful in that it portrays both modernity's power to represent and contain its premodern Other and the aporetic nature of that power. Modernity establishes itself forcefully; but in its establishment it has to acknowledge its split position. Modernity establishes itself by excluding what is other to it, and yet finds that it has to include again what it has excluded. This aporetic logic, in which the premodern Other is first excluded or superseded by rationality's progress, only to be included again because it is a constituent part of modernity and rationality, defines what can be called Habermas's neo-primitivism. In his work, the premodern or primitive condition, though surpassed by modernity, not only returns to supplement the latter with its semantic content, it also embodies the implicit presupposition or intuition of undisturbed intersubjectivity and consensual understanding that modernity subsequently thematizes more explicitly. Habermas's neo-primitivism, therefore, reveals itself as a complex theoretical operation in which the disavowal of the primitive or premodern is, at the same time, a recovery of the prototype of normative consensus and communicative intersubjectivity present in the premodern condition that has been disavowed. No wonder, then, that J.M. Bernstein has heard in 'Habermas's call for solidarity "a longing for the life that has been lost," a plea for forgiveness from the lifeworld that has been dirempted into the moral and the solidaristic.'[239]

What Habermas has called 'the unfinished project of modernity' can therefore be more accurately re-titled 'the aporetic dilemma of modernity.' For, try as it may, modernity's rationalization of the world can never fully dismiss the pre-rationalized, premodern lifeworld's attachment to archaic or primal images of 'symbiotic wholeness and nurturing protection.'[240] In rationalizing away the premodern Other, modernity finds that it has to accommodate it once again. That such an aporia continues to haunt Habermas's thinking is evident in his remarks on modern secularization and religious fundamentalism in the aftermath of September 11, 2001. In an interview that took place three months after the catastrophe, in the very same city in which terror struck, Habermas, responding to a question about fundamentalism, criticized it as an atavistic regression that suppresses the reality of modern pluralism.[241] At the same time, however, Habermas understands the temptation to regress to premodern beliefs as a defensive reaction against the progress of a secular, Western modernity that has destroyed, without the promise of compensation, other lifeworlds, other customary ways of life, and the traditional sources on which they draw for sustenance.[242] Habermas insists, of course, that we must not abandon the hard-won secularism and pluralism of modern society for the premodern and the mythic. At the same time, however, modern rationality is still in need of the semantic resources that were lost when premodern religious beliefs were secularized. As Habermas observes: '[T]he unbelieving sons and daughters of modernity seem to believe that they owe more to one another, and need more for themselves, than what is accessible to them, in [secular] translation, of religious tradition – *as if the semantic potential of the latter was still not exhausted.*'[243] It appears, therefore, that modernity's self-definition still requires its premodern Other.

Conclusion: 'Theorizing always needs a Savage'[1]

There is an excellent illustration of neo-primitivism as an anti-primitivist primitivism in a short story by the British writer Will Self. 'Understanding the Ur-Bororo' is a comic send-up of Western primitivist longings. The point of Self's satirical story is that there is no primitive that we can turn to for an exotic alternative to the banality of everyday modern life. The primitive is neither a romantic 'noble savage' nor the source of ancient wisdom that can redeem us from our modern malaise. To the surprise of the Western ethnographic gaze, the Ur-Bororo are a rather dull tribe showing indifference to the threat modernity poses to their society. The Ur-Bororo do not resist Western cultural imperialism. There is nothing about them to interest those on the lookout for the exotic, the redemptive, or the resistant.

The Ur-Bororo, as the anthropologist Janner reports to the story's first-person narrator,

> are a boring tribe ... The Ur-Bororo are objectively boring. They also view themselves as boring ... [T]he more time I spent with the Ur-Bororo, the more relentlessly banal they became ... Unlike a great number of isolated tribal groups, the Ur-Bororo do not view themselves as being in any way the 'typical' or 'essential' human beings. Many such tribes refer to themselves as 'The People' or 'The Human Beings' and to all others as barbarians, half-animals and so forth. 'Ur-Bororo' is a convenient translation of the name neighboring tribes use for them, which simply means 'here before the Bororo.' The Ur-Bororo actually refer to themselves with typically irritating self-deprecation as 'The People Who You Wouldn't Like to be Cornered by at a Party.'[2]

We are told that the Ur-Bororo are singularly lacking in those semiotic markers that we have long attached to primitives: they are not 'tattooed or cicatrized';[3] they are not naked, but go about dressed in 'the traditional Ur-Bororo garment – a long shapeless grey shift';[4] they are racially and physiognomically unremarkable and 'don't really have any defining characteristics as a people.'[5] Their language is equally unremarkable and literal-minded in its simplicity, their rituals mere small-talk that go unperformed, and their *pensée sauvage* excruciatingly banal and repetitive.[6] Unlike Malinowski's *The Sexual Life of Savages,* Janner's description of the Ur-Bororo's sexual life focuses on its enervation and indifference: 'in practice the Ur-Bororo's sexual drive is so circumscribed that no one really minds what anyone else gets up to. The general reaction is simply mild amazement that you have the energy for it.'[7] The Ur-Bororo's surroundings are neither Edenic nor a frightening heart of darkness; rather, they are described as 'a scene of unrivalled monotony – the Amazonian equivalent of an enormous municipal park.'[8] Instead of a Lévi-Straussian lament for the sad tropics threatened by the juggernaut of Western civilization, the story shows how the Ur-Bororo, in the form of Janner's wife and brother-in-law, readily embrace the routines of British middle-class life in Purley. In his 1983 'Distinguished Lecture' to the American Anthropological Association, Clifford Geertz had this piece of advice for his fellow anthropologists: 'If we wanted home truths, we should have stayed at home.'[9] Self reverses Geertz's dictum by showing satirically that the anthropologist's professional home does not necessarily have to be where the hut is, since the hut's 'truths' are not so remarkable and can also be found at home. As Janner puts it in his undistinguished lecture to the narrator: 'Despite the singular character of the Ur-Bororo I felt that on balance I might as well have never left Reigate.'[10]

But even though 'Understanding the Ur-Bororo' dispels the myth of primitivism, comically demonstrating that primitives are not that different from the inhabitants of Purley or Reigate, the reader still takes away from the story a sense of longing for the horizon of difference represented by the primitive. This longing can be located in the narrator's reaction to Janner's tale of disillusionment. The narrator tells us that during their student days, Janner's anthropological research opened him to 'the idea of mystery.' Janner was, for him, a 'Prospero' who could conjure up an island on which 'lurked the beautiful, the tantalizing, the Ur-Bororo.'[11] Drifting apart from Janner, the narrator recounts how he had settled into a life of middle-class tedium, a life both 'modest and unturbulent.' He confesses, however, to a dissatisfaction with his life: 'The reality was that I felt padded, as if all the gaps in my view of the world had been neatly filled with some kind of cavity life insulation. I felt ludicrously contained and static ... I felt, I emoted, but the volume control was always on. Somewhere along the line someone had clapped a mute on my head and I hadn't any idea who, or why.'[12] In the midst of this existential crisis, the narrator accidently meets Janner again and immediately pins his hopes on the anthropologist as a representative of the wonderful and the mysterious, a 'merchant of astonishment' (to borrow Geertz's phrase). 'Janner had represented for me,' he tells us, 'a set of possibilities that were unfulfilled. Even after twelve years these wider horizons continued to advance beyond my measured tread.'[13] But Janner's tale disappoints the narrator's primitivist longings and leaves him disillusioned and forlorn, stuck once more in a disenchanted, mundane existence, insulated from the wonder of the exotic: 'As for me, I went on teaching, playing volleyball and asking recalcitrant pupils the names of power stations. The lagging which had for a brief period been removed from my mind came back – together with new, improved, cavity-wall insulation.'[14] Janner's account of the boring and bland Ur-Bororo demystifies the myth of the primitive and strips the narrator of his romantic fantasies. But it also leaves the narrator with a more complex yearning for what he has lost; disillusionment wins him an awareness of his reality, but the circumscribed and impoverished nature of that reality leads to a renewed longing for that which has now been demystified and disenchanted. As he puts it: 'Not everyone has the opportunity to experience a real mystery in their lives. I at least did, even if the disillusionment that has followed the resolution of my mystery sometimes seems worse than the shuttered ignorance I might otherwise have enjoyed.'[15] The romantic fantasy of primitive life may be deflated, but the price for this disenchantment is that you are left only with Purley or Reigate. Little wonder, then, that the disillusioned narrator, stripped of his faith in actual primitives, continues to mourn and yearn for the *idea* of the primitive as exotic alternative to the neatly insulated modern mind. The satirical anti-primitivism of 'Understanding the Ur-Bororo' results in a neo-primitivism in which primitivism is evacuated of 'real' primitives so that it can remain a counterfactual idea, an intimation of a something that can deliver the narrator from the all-too-familiar world he inhabits. The story's humorous demystification of primitivism's exotic fantasies cannot finally escape the lure of the primitive as alternative to modernity's 'hell of the Same' (to borrow Baudrillard's phrase).

Like the work of the theorists and critics we have examined, 'Understanding the Ur-Bororo' demonstrates that the primitive Other, even if it does not exist, has to be imagined in order for us to entertain not only the utopian hope for something different from our present, but also the possibility of critical reflexivity in general. In other words, to be critical means to be able to recognize our own conceptual limits, the ethnocentric boundaries of our world view. This requires us to challenge those limits through the postulation of an outside, an alternative to them. Such an alternative is readily supplied by the idea of the primitive. As we have seen, Baudrillard, Lyotard, Torgovnick, Sahlins, and Habermas all turn to the concept of the premodern to test the limits of the modern world-picture. The primitive is thus what enables them to ward off ethnocentrism and to be critical of their own Western world. Moreover, as we have noted, it is the idea or concept of the primitive that is important for these theorists, not the primitive's actual presence, which may in fact contradict or question its conceptualization or idealization. What Dipesh Chakrabarty has said of the utopian role of the subaltern applies equally to the primitive in the work of the theorists we have studied: 'The subaltern here is the *ideal* figure ... No actual member of the subaltern classes would resemble what I imagine here.' The subaltern embodies 'a utopian line that may well designate the limit of how we are trained to think.'[16]

The idealization of the primitive Other, however, leads to a number of problematic, if unintended consequences, as we have seen in the preceding chapters. While the primitive Other enables our theorists to expose the limits of Western thought, it also gains them a renewed epistemic advantage that once again opens up a gap between the West and the rest. From Baudrillard to Habermas, what we have observed is a troubling movement in which the West's self-critical generosity to the primitive Other returns as a greater form of Western awareness not necessarily shared by the Other. Generosity to the Other wins for the Western thinker, but not for the incommensurable Other, theoretical insight. Thus for Baudrillard, Lyotard, and Torgovnick the resistant Other who cannot be known is nonetheless also that which redeems them from the Western will to universality. Conversely, for Sahlins, sensitivity to the difference of non-Western cultures enables the Western anthropologist to escape his ethnocentrism and gain a truly universal understanding of humanity. Habermas too urges respect for alterity, but, more openly than the others, he admits that this respect is one of the West's greatest achievements and sets it apart from others. In short, for all our theorists the primitive Other who cannot be known fully and whose alterity demands respect is nonetheless also the Other who enables the West to know its own limits, a knowledge we cannot be sure the Other possesses. The West *knows* it does not know and therein lies its epistemic advantage over other cultures that lack that reflexive knowledge. Their role appears simply to be that of embodying a resistant alterity that makes possible Western critical reflexivity. What appears to be an ethics of alterity that asymmetrically favours the Other turns out, on the epistemic and cultural levels, to asymmetrically privilege the culture that produced that ethics.[17]

Our discussion has also shown, however, that a critique of neo-primitivism must acknowledge neo-primitivism's entwinement with some of the most fiercely anti-Eurocentric theories of the present. It is not enough merely to deconstruct neo-primitivism by uncovering its primitivist tropes of othering; we must also recognize that these very forms of primitivist othering underpin Western self-criticism and its ethics of generosity to the Other. To be sure, this ethical awareness and generosity may serve only to affirm the West's cognitive and ethical superiority. In any case, the deconstruction of neo-primitivism should not result simply in its dismissal; there should also be an understanding of neo-primitivism's continuing theoretical, ethical, and political usefulness. My criticisms, sometimes severe, of the theorists in this book should not therefore be seen as a rejection of their valuable contributions to the critical questioning of the West. They offer considerable insights into the problems generated by modern Western thought, and what I have attempted to do is to develop these insights by turning them back on their sources. The book's critique of neo-primitivism is thus not about scoring critical points, but about drawing attention to a problematic we all share. The problematic can be posed in the following manner: Can we avoid the figure of the Other when we engage in theorizing? Can we have a critical theory of modernity without first presupposing the idea of the premodern? Can there be theory without the savage?

In a brilliant exposé of Western philosophy's self-constituting division between intellectual reflection and manual labour, Jacques Rancière writes: 'In the beginning, there was the following: philosophy defined itself in defining its other. The order of discourse delimited itself by tracing a circle that excluded from the right to think those who earned their living by the labor of their hands.'[18] Just as philosophy's first act of self-definition required the unthinking poor, so theory's understanding of itself as critically reflexive and self-questioning needs, as its constitutive opposite and outside, the unreflective and instinctive savage.

Theory's need for a savage Other is dramatically expressed in an interview in which Emmanuel Levinas rather casually makes the following pronouncement: 'I often say, though it's a dangerous thing to say publicly, that humanity consists of the Bible and the Greeks. All the rest can be translated: all the rest – all the exotic – is dance.'[19] Similar sentiments are expressed in another interview where Levinas, referring to television images of South African Blacks dancing at the funeral of a murdered victim, says that while he can, as a *philosopher*, try to *understand* (or *theorize*) their way of life, he is nevertheless surprised by an event that 'gives the impression of a dancing civilization in which they cry in another way.'[20] While Levinas's philosophical writings on alterity provide some of the most useful tools for deconstructing the Western ontological tradition, his observations on 'dancing' cultures show that he has not completely extricated his own thought from that tradition. Be that as it may, what is of interest for our purposes is the suggestion that in order for the West to reflect, the savage must dance. It is as though the identity of Western *theoria* can be confirmed and validated only through a contrast with the primitivist trope of dance – a trope we find everywhere in Western writing from Conrad's *Heart of Darkness* to the *Globe and Mail*'s foregrounding of dancing Aborigines in its review of *Living Tribes*. What Levinas's pronouncement clearly demonstrates is that theory's distinctive claim to critical knowledge comes into full focus only when it is contrasted to the visceral spontaneity of savage dance. While theory allows the West, in Levinas's words, 'to understand the particular cultures which never understood themselves,'[21] dance traps those particular cultures in unreflective self-ignorance. Nevertheless, Western theory does not appear to be able to define itself or stand on its own without the ignorance of the savage Other to prove its superior knowledge. The savage may be theoretically or cognitively deficient, but his presence, it seems, is indispensable for Western theory's very identity.

If theory requires primitivism, then neo-primitivism questions theory only to renew it. Unlike Levinas, neo-primitivists see the dancing savage in a positive light as that being that resists assimilation into Western theory. The difference of the primitive marks the limits of theorizing and rescues us from a monotonous universalism that Baudrillard calls 'the hell of the Same.' From the differend of Cashinahua narrative in Lyotard's work to Sahlins's remark that '"Strange" should be the beginning of anthropological wisdom rather than a way of putting an end to it,'[22] the primitive has no other role than that of challenging the ethnocentric universalism of Western theory. Even the empirical primitive's disappearance, as we have seen, does not affect its oppositional role to theory. In fact, its disappearance further empowers its opposition. For the primitive's disappearance does not mean the triumph of capitalist modernity or the Westernization of the world; it means just the opposite. It means that the vanished primitive has become a counterfactual, spectral ideal. Loosened from its empirical and historical complexities, the spectral or virtual primitive becomes a powerful presence that returns to haunt our troubled modernity. As Adam Kuper observes, the discredited primitive has resurfaced even more powerfully in our imagination as the noble Green indigene who resists globalization and represents 'a world to which we should, apparently, wish to be returned, a world in which culture does not challenge nature.' 'As always,' Kuper further reminds us, 'our conceptions of the primitive are best understood as counters in our own current ideological debates.'[23]

But if neo-primitivism uses the primitive to deconstruct Western theory, it is also the case that the primitive is used to redeem theory. In primitivism, theory needs the savage to affirm its epistemic distinctiveness and superiority; in neo-primitivism, the savage is needed to deconstruct theory so that it can be saved from itself. This is captured perceptively in Baudrillard's aphorism: 'The Other is what allows *me* not to repeat *myself* forever.'[24] What the Other is or wants is less important than its role in delivering the Western theorist from himself, thereby also renewing theory by preventing it from repeating itself. The savage Other plays a similar role in the work of Lyotard, Torgovnick, and Sahlins. Challenging the ethnocentric universalism of Western theory, the Other forces it to engage in self-criticism and to rethink its premises, hence helping it to renew itself. The Other's ancillary role in the drama of Western theory's renewal is most clearly articulated by Habermas, for whom the Other that challenges Eurocentrism is also the Other that makes possible the self-reflection and self-critical distancing that distinguish modern Western thought from premodern myth.

If, as our discussion has shown, even the most advanced and powerful critiques of Western theory end up strengthening it, what can we do to escape this impasse? What if the attempt to 'provincialize' European theory (to paraphrase the title of Dipesh Chakrabarty's book) only leads to its further empowerment? My sense is that there is no straightforward deliverence from this dilemma; one can only hope to understand it better so that one can avoid its more egregious aspects. I allude to Chakrabarty's book because it brilliantly engages with just such a dilemma. Chakrabarty acknowledges at once that to 'provincialize Europe' by opposing it to its Other is not to shun European thought or theory; in fact, it is to admit Europe's inescapable hold on modern critical thought. At the same time, however, to render justice to Europe's Other requires us to undertake a questioning of the modern critical or theoretical attitude that we, Chakrabarty included, cannot but assume. Staying within his discipline of history, Chakrabarty describes the dilemma in the following way:

> To provincialize Europe in historical thought is to struggle to hold in a state of permanent tension a dialogue between two contradictory points of view. On one side is the indispensable and universal narrative of capital [or modernity] – History 1, as I have called it. This narrative both gives us a critique of capitalist imperialism and affords elusive but necessarily energizing glimpses of the Enlightenment promise of an abstract, universal but never-to-be-realized humanity. Without such elusive glimpses ... there is no political modernity [that is, the possibility of critique]. On the other side is thought about diverse ways of being human, the infinite incommensurabilities through which we struggle ... to 'world the earth' in order to live within our different senses of ontic belonging. These are the struggles that become ... the History 2s that in practice always modify and interrupt the totalizing thrusts of History 1.[25]

In his analysis of Ranajit Guha's account of the Santal rebellion of 1855 in Bengal and Bihar provinces, Chakrabarty presents a concrete historical example of this unresolvable tension between the History 1 of modern Western thought and the History 2s that represent incommensurable non-Western lifeworlds. Guha, Chakrabarty explains, listened sympathetically to the subaltern rebels' voices without immediately translating them into the modern, secular categories of History 1. But even Guha's hermeneutic generosity cannot finally accommodate the rebels' belief that their deity Thakur made them rebel. Avoiding an instrumentalist reading of the Santal rebellion as more conventionally minded historians might have done, Guha nonetheless feels compelled finally to adopt History 1's analytical distance to explain (away) the Santals' belief system as 'a massive demonstration of self-estrangement ... which made the rebels look upon their project as predicated on a will other than their own.'[26] As Chakrabarty puts it:

> [I]n spite of Guha's desire to listen to the rebel voice seriously, his analysis cannot offer the Thakur the same place of agency in the story of the

> rebellion that the Santals' statements had given him. A narrative strategy that is rationally defensible in the modern understanding of what constitutes public life – and the historians speak in the public sphere – cannot be based on a relationship that allows the divine or supernatural a direct hand in the affairs of the world. The Santal leaders' own understanding of the rebellion ... needs to be reinterpreted [as self-estrangement or false consciousness]. Historians will grant the supernatural a place in somebody's belief system or ritual practices, but to ascribe to it any real agency in historical events will be to go against the rules of evidence that give historical discourse procedures for settling disputes about the past.[27]

In his own work, Chakrabarty tries to resist the conversion of History 2s into History 1 even as he recognizes that he cannot simply reject the secular, modern values, the analytical techniques, and the knowledge protocols represented by History 1. The two Histories, Chakrabarty notes, are 'contradictory but profoundly connected.'[28] Oscillating continuously between History 1's unavoidable modern rationality and the equally unavoidable alterity of History 2s, Chakrabarty seeks to remain within the tension rather than resolve it by moving in one or the other direction.

Neo-primitivism inhabits an in-between space similar to the one described by Chakrabarty. It too oscillates between the universalizing thrust of the modern West and the resistant, incommensurable alterity of the primitive. Just as History 1 cannot be uncoupled from History 2s, so too the modern West and its premodern Others are inseparably joined. Just as History 1 defines its rationality against History 2s' belief in supernatural agency, so too Western theory affirms its identity by contrasting it to the spontaneous physicality of savage dance. Europe needs its Others to prove itself even as these Others provincialize it. Similarly, Western theory needs the savage even as the savage questions its universalism. In the examples of neo-primitivism we have examined the ethnocentric appropriation of the primitive by Western theory is criticized, but the criticism is made possible only by theory's recourse once again to the resistant figure of the primitive, even if, these days, the primitive goes under other names like alterity, culture, or (in Habermas) the prerationalized lifeworld.

In the course of our study of neo-primitivism, we have come to understand that theorizing needs the savage especially when it critically examines or theorizes itself. To dismiss the primitive Other is thus to dismiss theory itself, a price we may be unwilling to pay. Can we then avoid primitivism if to avoid it is to stop theorizing? Our answer must necessarily be faithful to the aporia we find ourselves in. We will, like Chakrabarty, have to acknowledge the inescapability of the predicament we face when we theorize. We need the incommensurable primitive Other to mark the limits of theory, but we must also admit to the impossibility of our task since we can never be sure who or what this *incommensurable* Other is. Rodolphe Gasché has perceptively noted that '[a]n Other must always be invented for something to be, but by the same token, such inevitable invention also means that no being can ever be taken for granted, for being what it is.'[29] Our examination of neo-primitivist discourses bears out Gasché's observation about the necessary invention of the Other, while also revealing that the caveat in the second half of his statement ('no being can ever be taken for granted, for being what it is') often goes unheeded. A critically reflexive theory requires an Other to question its universalizing thrust; at the same time, however, since the Other's opposition is based on its incommensurability or unknowability, theory can never be sure that the Other is or will be what theory wants it to be. It appears, therefore, that we can neither theorize without the savage nor theorize with it. If we want to remain within theory, then it is incumbent on us to keep this aporia in mind.

But, it will be asked, doesn't such a conclusion about neo-primitivism as an unavoidable and insuperable dilemma for contemporary theorists weaken the preceding pages' critique of it? On the contrary, what may appear as an undermining or self-deconstructing claim about neo-primitivism's inescapability, paradoxically, supports the book's thesis about neo-primitivism's persistence even in works that are critical of it, that seek to go beyond it. What some readers may regard as the conclusion's performative contradiction can therefore be seen as the conclusion's performative reinforcement of the book's central argument that even anti-primitivist discourses find themselves relying on primitivism, caught in an aporetic logic that I have described in chapter 1 as an anti-primitivist primitivism. To admit to neo-primitivism's unavoidability is thus also to testify to its adaptable and persistent constitutive force. The neo-primitivism present in certain forms of contemporary thought cannot simply be deconstructed or dismissed. We need of course to be constantly vigilant in our examination of neo-primitivism's shifting traces, but this vigilance must also be accompanied by the recognition that neo-primitivism's theoretical power and productivity are not unrelated to that same vigilance at the heart of our critical enterprise. Thus, it would be a failure of critical vigilance on my part were I to refuse to admit that my own book contains the trace structure, the spectral presence of neo-primitivism itself. I cannot escape from this aporia of at once criticizing neo-primitivism and of relying on certain of its theoretical assumptions. I can only acknowledge my dilemma. For who would want to be a neo-primitivist uncritically, when one can at least know critically the aporia in which one finds oneself?

Notes

Preface

1 'Culture Shock,' *Globe and Mail,* 2 August 2003, D12. Also see Colin Prior, *Living Tribes* (Toronto: Firefly Books, 2003). Carolyn Fry, in her introduction to *Living Tribes,* warns that '[f]or the estimated 70 uncontacted tribes that remain in the world, the chances of keeping their unique lifestyles intact are fragile' (17). In using words like 'uncontacted,' 'unique lifestyles,' and 'fragile,' she subscribes both to the myth of pure primordiality and to the fear that the uniqueness or difference of these 'uncontacted' tribes will vanish into a homogeneous Western modernity.

2 See Michel-Rolph Trouillot, 'Anthropology and the Savage Slot: The Poetics and Politics of Otherness,' in *Recapturing Anthropology: Working in the Present,* ed. Richard G. Fox (Santa Fe: School of American Research Press, 1991).

3 Elazar Barkan and Ronald Bush, eds., *Prehistories of the Future: The Primitivist Project and the Culture of Modernism* (Stanford: Stanford University Press, 1995), Helen Carr, *Inventing the American Primitive: Politics, Gender, and the Representation of Native American Literary Traditions, 1789–1936* (New York: New York University Press, 1996), Micaela di Leonardo, *Exotics at Home: Anthropologies, Others, American Modernity* (Chicago: University of Chicago Press, 1998), Shelly Errington, *The Death of Authentic Primitive Art and Other Tales of Progress* (Berkeley: University of California Press, 1998), Johannes Fabian, *Time and the Other: How Anthropology Makes Its Objects* (New York: Columbia University Press, 1983), Peter Fitzpatrick, *The Mythology of Modern Law* (London: Routledge, 1992), Adam Kuper, *The Invention of Primitive Society: Transformations of an Illusion* (London: Routledge, 1988), Sieglinde Lemke, *Primitivist Modernism: Black Culture and the Origins of Transatlantic Modernism* (Oxford: Oxford University Press, 1998), Bernard McGrane,

Beyond Anthropology: Society and the Other (New York: Columbia University Press, 1989), Nicholas Thomas, *Colonialism's Culture: Anthropology, Travel and Government* (Cambridge: Polity, 1994), Marianna Torgovnick, *Gone Primitive: Savage Intellects, Modern Lives* (Chicago: University of Chicago Press, 1990).

4 I owe the term chronopolitics to Fabian, *Time*, 144.

1. The Neo-primitivist Turn

1 McGrane, *Beyond Anthropology*, 93.

2 Ibid., 77.

3 Thomas, *Colonialism*, 173.

4 See Fabian, *Time*, 11–18.

5 Cited in J.W. Burrow, *Evolution and Society: A Study in Victorian Social Theory* (Cambridge: Cambridge University Press, 1966), 272. Popular versions of evolutionism, especially when they turned their attention to social forms, departed from the Darwinian theory of biological evolution in so far as they adopted the Spencerian belief in a teleology of progress and accepted the Lamarckian ideas of inherited traits rather than Darwin's more ambivalent account of the unpredictable course of evolution and the more random processes of natural selection. See Kuper, *Invention*, 2–3, and Henrika Kuklick, *The Savage Within: The Social History of British Anthropology, 1885–1945* (Cambridge: Cambridge University Press, 1991), 81.

6 Fabian, *Time*, 17.

7 McGrane, *Beyond Anthropology*, 94.

8 Kuklick, *The Savage Within*, 84.

9 Burrow, *Evolution*, 236.

10 Cited in George W. Stocking Jr, *Race, Culture, and Evolution: Essays in the History of Anthropology* (New York: Free Press, 1968), 81.

11 For useful discussions of Tylor's views, see Burrow, *Evolution*, McGrane, *Beyond Anthropology*, Stocking, *Race*, and George W. Stocking Jr, *Victorian Anthropology* (New York: Free Press, 1987).

12 Cited in Stocking, *Race*, 81–2.

13 Henrika Kuklick has warned against a hasty identification between evolutionary anthropology and British colonialism. She is right to argue that evolutionary anthropologists were often political radicals who disagreed with their government's colonial policies and use of force. Nonetheless, I think it is plausible to say that their evolutionary ranking schemes must have given ideological support to the view that the West in being better than the Rest should also govern the latter. See Kuklick, *The Savage Within*, 255.

14 Cited in Burrow, *Evolution*, 254.

15 Errington, *The Death,* 14.
16 McGrane, *Beyond Anthropology,* 98–9.
17 Ashley Montagu, 'The Concept of "Primitive" and Related Anthropological Terms: A Study in the Systematics of Confusion,' in *The Concept of the Primitive,* ed. Ashley Montagu (New York: The Free Press, 1968), 152.
18 Cited in Stocking, *Victorian,* 153.
19 Cited in Edward P. Dozier, 'The Concepts of "Primitive" and "Native" in Anthropology,' in *The Concept of the Primitive,* ed. Ashley Montagu (New York: Free Press, 1968), 233.
20 Stocking, *Race,* 122.
21 Cited in Montagu, 'Concept,' 155.
22 George W. Stocking Jr, 'The Ethnographic Sensibility of the 1920s and the Dualism of the Anthropological Tradition,' in *Romantic Motives: Essays on Anthropological Sensibility,* ed. George W. Stocking Jr. (Madison: University of Wisconsin Press, 1989), 214.
23 Kuklick, *The Savage Within,* 265.
24 Ibid., 266.
25 Cited ibid., 265.
26 Carr, *Inventing,* 200.
27 Cited ibid., 207.
28 Edward Sapir, 'Culture, Genuine and Spurious,' in *Culture, Language and Personality: Selected Essays,* ed. David G. Mandelbaum (Berkeley: University of California Press, 1966), 92–3.
29 Michèle H. Richman, *Sacred Revolutions: Durkheim and the Collège de Sociologie* (Minneapolis: University of Minnesota Press, 2002), 11.
30 Ibid., 133.
31 Ibid., 188.
32 Ibid., 14.
33 Maurice Blanchot, *Friendship,* trans. Elizabeth Rottenberg (Stanford: Stanford University Press, 1997), 78.
34 Claude Lévi-Strauss, *Tristes Tropiques,* trans. John Weightman and Doreen Weightman (Harmondsworth: Penguin, 1976 [1955]), 513–14.
35 Ibid., 514–15.
36 Ibid., 509.
37 Stanley Diamond, *In Search of the Primitive: A Critique of Civilization* (New Brunswick, NJ: Transaction Publishers, 1974), 98–9.
38 Eric R. Wolf, 'Foreword' to Diamond, *In Search,* xiii.
39 Diamond, *In Search,* 174–5, 226.
40 Ibid., 159–60; emphasis mine.
41 Ibid., 100.

42 Marcel Hénaff, *Claude Lévi-Strauss and the Making of Structural Anthropology*, trans. Mary Barker (Minneapolis: University of Minnesota Press, 1998), 158.
43 George E. Marcus and Michael M.J. Fischer, *Anthropology as Critique: An Experimental Moment in the Human Sciences* (Chicago: University of Chicago Press, 1986), x.
44 Ibid., 1.
45 Ibid., 134.
46 See di Leonardo, *Exotics.*
47 Marcus and Fischer, *Anthropology*, 135.
48 Ibid., x.
49 Ibid., 3; emphasis mine.
50 Torgovnick, *Gone Primitive*, 9.
51 Hal Foster, *Recodings: Art, Spectacle, Cultural Politics*, ed. Hal Foster (Port Townsend, Wash.: Bay Press, 1985), 188–9.
52 Ibid., 196.
53 Ibid., 200.
54 Ibid., 204.
55 Jean Baudrillard, *The Mirror of Production*, trans. Mark Poster (St Louis: Telos Press, 1975), 90n. Cited in Foster, *Recodings*, 198.
56 Foster, *Recodings*, 208.
57 Cited in Robert Bernasconi, 'One-Way Traffic: The Ontology of Decolonization and Its Ethics,' in *Ontology and Alterity in Merleau-Ponty*, ed. Galen A. Johnson and Michael B. Smith (Evanston, Ill.: Northwestern University Press, 1990), 78.
58 Ibid., 78–9.
59 Jean Baudrillard, *The Transparency of Evil: Essays on Extreme Phenomena*, trans. James Benedict (London: Verso, 1993), 122.
60 Ibid.; emphasis mine.
61 Torgovnick, *Gone Primitive*, 247.
62 Marshall Sahlins, 'Reply to Borofsky,' *Current Anthropology* 38, no. 2 (1997): 276.
63 Jürgen Habermas, *The Inclusion of the Other: Studies in Political Theory*, ed. Ciaran Cronin and Pablo De Greiff (Cambridge, Mass.: MIT Press, 1998), 40.
64 Jürgen Habermas, *Religion and Rationality: Essays on Reason, God, and Modernity*, ed. Eduardo Mendieta (Cambridge: Polity Press, 2002), 154; emphasis mine.
65 Ibid.
66 Rey Chow, 'How (the) Inscrutable Chinese Led to Globalized Theory,' *PMLA* 116, no. 1 (2001): 72.

67 Rey Chow, *Writing Diaspora: Tactics of Intervention in Contemporary Cultural Studies* (Bloomington: Indiana University Press, 1993), 53.

68 Gayatri Chakravorty Spivak, *In Other Worlds: Essays in Cultural Politics* (London: Methuen, 1987), 138.

69 See Gayatri Chakravorty Spivak, *A Critique of Postcolonial Reason: Toward a History of the Vanishing Present* (Cambridge, Mass.: Harvard University Press, 1999), 9–37.

70 Ibid., 190.

71 Gayatri Chakravorty Spivak, 'Can the Subaltern Speak?' in *Colonial Discourse and Post-Colonial Theory: A Reader*, ed. Patrick Williams and Laura Chrisman (New York: Columbia University Press, 1994), 90.

72 Gayatri Chakravorty Spivak, *The Post-Colonial Critic: Interviews, Strategies, Dialogues*, ed. Sarah Harasym (New York: Routledge, 1990), 144.

73 Ibid., 136.

74 Spivak, *Critique*, 310.

75 Peter Hallward, *Absolutely Postcolonial: Writing between the Singular and the Specific* (Manchester: Manchester University Press, 2001), 30.

76 Spivak, *Critique*, 283.

77 Spivak, *Other Worlds*, 104–5.

78 Jenny Sharpe and Gayatri Chakravorty Spivak, 'A Conversation with Gayatri Chakravorty Spivak: Politics and the Imagination,' *Signs* 28, no. 2 (2002): 619–20.

79 Spivak, *Critique*, 383.

80 Ibid., 310.

81 Ibid., 382.

82 Ibid., 384–5; emphasis mine.

83 Ibid., 310.

84 Ibid., 311.

85 In a footnote in *A Critique of Postcolonial Reason*, Spivak explains how subaltern singularity or authenticity may be indexed to its being left alone: 'It is again instructive that, mining "indigenous knowledge" or the DNA of "the subaltern body," transnational organizations are aware that *the real source is the smaller and remoter* groups, historically distanced from the cultures of domination, for whatever reason.' Ibid., 403n119.

86 Ibid., 402.

87 Gayatri Chakravorty Spivak, 'Supplementing Marxism,' in *Whither Marxism?: Global Crises in International Perspective*, ed. Bernd Magnus and Stephen Cullenberg (New York: Routledge, 1995), 115–16.

88 Chow, *Writing*, 53.

89 Baudrillard, *Transparency*, 122.

90 Torgovnick, *Gone Primitive,* 248.
91 Jon R. Snyder, 'Translator's Introduction,' in Gianni Vattimo, *The End of Modernity: Nihilism and Hermeneutics in Postmodern Culture* (Baltimore: Johns Hopkins University Press, 1988), xlv.
92 Vattimo, *The End of Modernity,* 158–9.
93 Ibid., 162.
94 Fredric Jameson, *Postmodernism, or, the Cultural Logic of Late Capitalism* (Durham: Duke University Press, 1991), ix.
95 Ibid., 36.
96 Ibid., 49.
97 Ibid., 309–10.
98 Ibid., 309.
99 John W. Burton, 'Disappearing Savages? Thoughts on the Construction of an Anthropological Conundrum,' *Journal of Asian and African Studies* 34, no. 2 (1999): 205.
100 Cited ibid., 204–5.
101 Ibid., 199.
102 Leslie A. Fiedler, *The Return of the Vanishing American* (London: Jonathan Cape, 1968), 11.
103 Ibid., 185.
104 Ibid., 186.
105 Ibid., 174–87.
106 D.H. Lawrence, *Studies in Classic American Literature* (Harmondsworth: Penguin, 1971 [1924]), 41. Cited in Fiedler, *The Return,* 9.
107 Lawrence, *Studies,* 40.
108 Blanchot, *Friendship,* 78; emphases mine.
109 Roland Barthes, *Empire of Signs,* trans. Richard Howard (New York: Hill and Wang, 1982), 3.
110 Rey Chow, 'The Interruption of Referentiality: Poststructuralism and the Conundrum of Critical Multiculturalism,' *South Atlantic Quarterly* 101, no. 1 (2002): 182–3.
111 Carlos J. Alonzo, *The Burden of Modernity: The Rhetoric of Cultural Discourse in Spanish America* (New York: Oxford University Press, 1998), 8. Cited in Chow, 'Interruption,' 183.
112 See Jacques Derrida, *Specters of Marx: The State of the Debt, the Work of Mourning, and the New International,* trans. Peggy Kamuf (New York: Routledge, 1994).
113 Elizabeth A. Povinelli, *The Cunning of Recognition: Indigenous Alterities and the Making of Australian Multiculturalism* (Durham: Duke University Press, 2002), 52.
114 Ibid., 35.

115 Ibid., 55.
116 Ibid., 59.
117 Ibid., 39.
118 Ibid., 58.
119 Marilyn Ivy, *Discourses of the Vanishing: Modernity, Phantasm, Japan* (Chicago: University of Chicago Press, 1995), 10. See also Susan Stewart, *On Longing: Narratives of the Miniature, the Gigantic, the Souvenir, the Collection* (Durham: Duke University Press, 1993), 23.
120 Ivy, *Discourses*, 241.
121 See Ashley Montagu's 1945 article 'The Concept of "Primitive" and Related Anthropological Terms: A Study in the Systematics of Confusion,' reprinted in Montagu, *Concept*, 148–68.
122 A word or two about my equation of alterity to neo-primitivism is in order. It is true of course that an ethics of alterity as described by Levinas or Derrida would oppose the naming or categorizing of the Other as 'primitive.' In fact, all instances of naming the Other would be regarded as an act of violence, a violation of its otherness. But while post-structuralist or postmodernist thought may theoretically advocate such an ethics of alterity, in practice there is often a slippage resulting in an identification of alterity with a group or groups of people whose social and cultural characteristics, often described as premodern, are opposed to those of the modern West. Thus, the radical or absolute alterity valorized by Baudrillard, Lyotard, and Spivak, for example, is identified by them respectively with the Tasaday in the Philippines, the Cashinahua in South America, and the 'denotified' Aboriginal tribes of India.
123 Baudrillard, *Transparency*, 137.
124 Jean-François Lyotard, *The Postmodern Explained: Correspondence 1982–1985*, ed. Julian Pefanis and Morgan Thomas, trans. Don Barry et al. (Minneapolis: University of Minnesota Press, 1993), 46–7.
125 Marianna Torgovnick, *Primitive Passions: Men, Women, and the Quest for Ecstasy* (New York: Knopf, 1997), 15.
126 Ibid., 14.
127 Ibid., 19.
128 Marshall Sahlins, *How 'Natives' Think: About Captain Cook, for Example* (Chicago: University of Chicago Press, 1995), 11–12.
129 Ibid., 13.
130 While the culture concept opposes Western universalism, the valorization of culture may pose the danger of a cultural fundamentalism in which culture stands in for a racialized identity. For excellent discussions of how the emphasis on cultural difference can lead to racialization and neo-

racism, see Paul Gilroy, *Against Race: Imagining Political Culture Beyond the Color Line* (Cambridge, Mass.: Harvard University Press, 2000), Verena Stolcke, 'Talking Culture: New Boundaries, New Rhetorics of Exclusion in Europe,' *Current Anthropology* 36, no. 1 (1995), and Pierre-André Taguieff, *The Force of Prejudice* (Minneapolis: University of Minnesota Press, 2001).

131 Spivak, *Critique*, 355.

132 See Giorgio Agamben, *Homo Sacer: Sovereign Power and Bare Life*, trans. Daniel Heller-Roazen (Stanford: Stanford University Press, 1998), 7.

2. Alterity

1 Tomoko Masuzawa, *In Search of Dreamtime: The Quest for the Origin of Religion* (Chicago: University of Chicago Press, 1993), 13.

2 Baudrillard, *Transparency*, 122.

3 Lévi-Strauss, *Tristes Tropiques*, 544.

4 Ibid., 514.

5 Jean-François Lyotard, 'An Interview with Jean-François Lyotard,' *Theory, Culture and Society* 5, nos. 2–3 (1988): 302.

6 Jean-François Lyotard, *The Differend: Phrases in Dispute*, trans. Georges van den Abbeele (Minneapolis: University of Minnesota Press, 1988), Jean-François Lyotard, *The Postmodern Condition: A Report on Knowledge*, trans. Geoffrey Bennington and Brian Massumi (Minneapolis: University of Minnesota Press, 1984), Jean-François Lyotard and Jean-Loup Thébaud, *Just Gaming*, trans. Wlad Godzich (Minneapolis: University of Minnesota Press, 1985).

7 Baudrillard, *Transparency*, 174; emphasis mine.

8 Mike Gane, *Baudrillard: Critical and Fatal Theory* (London: Routledge, 1991), 47.

9 Jean Baudrillard, *Symbolic Exchange and Death*, trans. Iain Hamilton Grant (London: Sage Publications, 1993).

10 Baudrillard, *Mirror*, 43.

11 Ibid., 70.

12 Ibid., 143.

13 Charles Levin, *Jean Baudrillard: A Study in Cultural Metaphysics* (Hemel Hempstead: Prentice Hall, 1996), 85.

14 Gary Genosko, *Baudrillard and Signs: Signification Ablaze* (London: Routledge, 1994), xx.

15 Douglas Kellner, *Jean Baudrillard: From Marxism to Postmodernism and Beyond* (Cambridge: Polity Press, 1989), 44.

16 Julian Pefanis, *Heterology and the Postmodern: Bataille, Baudrillard, and Lyotard* (Durham: Duke University Press, 1991), 61.

17 Baudrillard, *Mirror*, 66.
18 Ibid., 75.
19 Ibid., 90.
20 Jean-François Lyotard, *Libidinal Economy*, trans. Iain Hamilton Grant (Bloomington: Indiana University Press, 1993), 106.
21 Ibid., 107.
22 Baudrillard, *Mirror*, 79.
23 Robert Hefner, 'Baudrillard's Noble Anthropology: The Image of Symbolic Exchange in Political Economy,' *Sub-Stance* 17 (1977): 110.
24 Ibid., 113.
25 Baudrillard, *Mirror*, 90n34.
26 Jean Baudrillard, *The Perfect Crime*, trans. Chris Turner (London: Verso, 1996).
27 See Baudrillard, *Transparency*, 128, 132, 146, 147, and 152.
28 Ibid., 148.
29 Ibid., 152.
30 Ibid., 136.
31 Ibid., 132.
32 Ibid., 133.
33 Ibid., 102. See also Jean Baudrillard, *America*, trans. Chris Turner (London: Verso, 1988), 115.
34 Baudrillard, *Transparency*, 137.
35 Jean Baudrillard, *Simulations*, trans. Paul Foss et al. (New York: Semiotext(e), 1983), 13. Baudrillard's date for the cordoning off of the Tasaday is incorrect. Ferdinand Marcos, then president of the Philippines, issued a presidential decree in 1972 (not 1971) that made 'the Tasaday territory a reservation on which no one could enter without prior permission' (Jean-Paul Dumont, 'The Tasaday, Which and Whose?: Toward the Political Economy of an Ethnographic Sign,' *Cultural Anthropology* 3, no. 3 [1988]: 263). What Baudrillard didn't know, in the late seventies or early eighties when he wrote about the Tasaday as an example of a primitive tribe turned into a simulated ethnological example, was that the Tasaday were not as pristinely neolithic as the ethnologists had thought. Officially 'discovered' in 1971 by Panamin, the Philippine bureau of ethnic minority protection, the Tasaday's genuineness as an untouched 'stone age' tribe was questioned in 1986 by a Swiss journalist, Oswald Iten. In an article published in a Zurich newspaper in April 1986, Iten claimed that the Tasaday were a hoax. Jean-Paul Dumont summarizes Iten's arguments thus: 'Someone – not to say Elizalde [Manuel Elizalde Jr, then director of Panamin and close friend of Marcos] – had forced them [the Tasaday], by resorting in a grand way to false promises, to pose, half-naked, clustered at the entrance to a cave in which they had never lived but

which had been for them a holy place where they had regularly brought offerings' (Dumont, 'The Tasaday,' 263). The controversy that followed the publication of Iten's article pitted anthropologists against each other; some continued to believe that the Tasaday were a genuine primitive tribe, even though they agreed that some of the earlier claims made about them were exaggerated, while others supported the hoax theory. For a lively account of the controversy see Bettina Lerner, 'The Lost Tribe,' *Nova/Horizon*, 1989. Whatever the complex truth of the Tasaday – whether they were *already* simulated primitives *even before* Baudrillard criticized ethnology for simulating them or whether they are indeed real primitives – what is most instructive about their rise to *National Geographic* fame and subsequent fall into suspicion and disfavour is the fascination and meaning they hold for us in the modern or postmodern world. In the words of Jean-Paul Dumont, who has examined how the Tasaday have functioned as an ethnographic sign in a contested political and historico-cultural field, '[I]t is the extrinsic importance of the Tasaday, that is to say the meaning that they, in spite of themselves, have acquired for us as a sign which is what holds ... [our] interest. From this standpoint, there are no Tasaday *per se*, but only a social and symbolic relationship, and it is the only analyzable reality here' (Dumont, 'The Tasaday,' 263).

36 Baudrillard, *Simulations*, 16.

37 Ibid., 14–15.

38 Jean Baudrillard, *The Ecstasy of Communication*, trans. Sheila Faria Fraser, ed. Sylvère Lotringer (New York: Semiotext(e), 1988), 87.

39 Baudrillard, *Transparency*, 172.

40 Ibid., 173.

41 Baudrillard, *Perfect Crime*, 55.

42 Baudrillard, *Simulations*, 17.

43 Baudrillard, *Transparency*, 172.

44 Baudrillard, *Ecstasy*, 93; my emphasis.

45 Kellner, *Jean Baudrillard*, 180–1.

46 Lyotard, *Libidinal Economy*, 106.

47 Jean-François Lyotard, 'Missive on Universal History,' in *The Postmodern Explained*, 31. Lyotard has reservations over the term 'savage,' but nonetheless uses it 'for convenience' (ibid.).

48 Jean-François Lyotard, *Political Writings*, ed. Bill Readings and Kevin Paul Geiman (Minneapolis: University of Minnesota Press, 1993), 4.

49 Ibid., 3.

50 Bill Readings, 'Foreword: The End of the Political,' in Lyotard, *Political Writings*, xxi–xxii.

51 Ibid., xxiii.
52 Lyotard, *Political Writings*, 6.
53 Ibid., 7.
54 André-Marcel d'Ans, *Le Dit des Vrais Hommes: Myths, Contes, Legendes et Traditions des Indiens Cashinahua* (Paris: Union Générale d'Éditions, 1978).
55 Phillip Wearne, *Return of the Indian: Conquest and Revival in the Americas* (London: Cassell, 1996), 212.
56 Lyotard, 'Missive,' 31–2. See also Lyotard, *Differend*, 152; Lyotard, *Postmodern Condition*, 20; and Lyotard and Thébaud, *Just Gaming*, 32.
57 Lyotard, 'Missive,' 32.
58 Lyotard, *Differend*, 155.
59 Ibid., 153.
60 Lyotard, 'Missive,' 33.
61 Ibid.
62 Ibid.
63 Ibid., 33–4.
64 Lyotard, *Differend*, 155.
65 Lyotard, 'Missive,' 30–1.
66 Lyotard, *Differend*, 157.
67 Ibid., xi.
68 Lyotard, 'Missive,' 34.
69 Lyotard, *Differend*, 156.
70 Bill Readings, *Introducing Lyotard: Art and Politics* (London: Routledge, 1991), 108.
71 Ibid., 110.
72 Allen Dunn, 'A Tyranny of Justice: The Ethics of Lyotard's Differend,' *boundary 2* 20, no. 1 (1993): 197.
73 Bill Readings, 'Pagans, Perverts or Primitives? Experimental Justice in the Empire of Capital,' in *Judging Lyotard*, ed. Andrew Benjamin (London: Routledge, 1992), 185.
74 Jürgen Habermas, *Appendix to Knowledge and Human Interests*, trans. Jeremy J. Shapiro, 2nd ed. (London: Heinemann, 1978), 310–11.
75 Jean-François Lyotard, *The Inhuman: Reflections on Time*, trans. Geoffrey Bennington and Rachel Bowlby (Stanford: Standford University Press, 1991), 3–4.
76 Ibid., 7.
77 Tullio Maranhao, 'Invitation to an Anthropology Party,' *L'Esprit Créateur* 31, no. 1 (1991): 142.
78 Lyotard, 'Missive,' 33.
79 Lyotard advocated a totalizing notion of culture early in his career. In 1962,

he wrote: 'Inhabiting all the relations of a people to the world and to itself, all of its understanding and all of its work, culture is simply existence accepted as meaningful ... This weight of meaning in activity is present in *L'île nue*, in *Come Back, Africa*, in the tattered rags of living culture dispersed around the Mediterranean basin and elsewhere, in black music ... We are essentially cut off from it. In our society sign and signification, activity and culture, living and understanding, are dissociated' (Lyotard, *Political Writings*, 34). We find in this passage a holistic definition of culture coexisting with a longing for premodern or primitive cultures in which such cultural holism is thought to be found.

80 Seyla Benhabib, 'Epistemologies of Postmodernism: A Rejoinder to Jean-François Lyotard,' in *Feminism/Postmodernism*, ed. Linda J. Nicholson (New York: Routledge, 1990), 119.

81 Janet M. Chernela, 'The "Ideal Speech Moment": Women and Narrative Performance in the Brazilian Amazon,' *Feminist Studies* 23, no. 1 (1997): 73.

82 John McGowan, *Postmodernism and Its Critics* (Ithaca: Cornell University Press, 1991), 190.

83 For a compelling critique of how some recent thinkers, including Lyotard, still use the antinomy of people with and without history, see Kerwin Lee Klein, 'In Search of Narrative Mastery: Postmodernism and the People without History,' *History and Theory* 34, no. 4 (1995).

84 Lyotard and Thébaud, *Just Gaming*, 32.

85 Lyotard, *Differend*, 153.

86 d'Ans, *Le Dit*, 13.

87 Lyotard, *Postmodern Explained*, 46.

88 Ibid., 46–7.

89 Clifford Geertz, *The Interpretation of Cultures* (New York: Basic Books, 1973), 347.

90 Mark Poster, 'Postmodernism and the Politics of Multiculturalism: The Lyotard-Habermas Debate over Social Theory,' *Modern Fiction Studies* 38, no. 3 (1992): 578.

91 Trouillot, 'Anthropology and the Savage Slot,' 33.

92 Rodolphe Gasché, *Inventions of Difference: On Jacques Derrida* (Cambridge, Mass.: Harvard University Press, 1994), 14.

93 Michel de Certeau, *Heterologies: Discourse on the Other*, trans. Brian Massumi (Minneapolis: University of Minnesota Press, 1986), 76.

94 See Jürgen Habermas, *The Theory of Communicative Action: Reason and the Rationalization of Society*, trans. Thomas McCarthy, vol. 1 (Boston: Beacon, 1984), 43–74, and Habermas, *The Philosophical Discourse of Modernity: Twelve Lectures*, trans. Frederick Lawrence (Cambridge, Mass.: MIT Press, 1987), 114–15.

95 Cited in Habermas, *Philosophical Discourse*, 307.
96 Ibid., 310.
97 Torgovnick, *Primitive Passions*, 15.
98 Torgovnick, *Gone Primitive*, 8.
99 Ibid., 252–3n17.
100 Ibid., 9.
101 Ibid., 12.
102 Ibid., 20.
103 Ibid.
104 Ibid., 280n3.
105 Ibid., 84.
106 Ibid., 83.
107 Ibid., 92.
108 Ibid.
109 Walter Benn Michaels, 'The New Modernism,' *ELH* 59, no. 1 (1992): 261.
110 Torgovnick, *Gone Primitive*, 124–5.
111 Ibid., 125.
112 Ibid., 130.
113 Ibid., 132.
114 Ibid., 136; my emphasis.
115 Ibid., 248.
116 Ibid., 48.
117 Ibid., 46.
118 Ibid., 47.
119 Ibid., 55.
120 Ibid., 69.
121 Ibid., 70.
122 Benn Michaels, 'The New Modernism,' 262.
123 Torgovnick, *Gone Primitive*, 71.
124 Ibid., 246–7.
125 Ibid., 248.
126 Ibid., 205.
127 Ibid., 207–8.
128 Ibid., 230.
129 Cited ibid., 231.
130 Ibid.
131 Ibid., 216.
132 Ibid., 217.
133 Ibid., 220.
134 Ibid., 220–1.
135 Ibid., 237.

136 Ibid., 242.
137 Torgovnick, *Primitive Passions,* 16.
138 Ibid.
139 Ibid.
140 Ibid.
141 Ibid.
142 Ibid., 93.
143 Ibid., 94.
144 Ibid., 110.
145 Ibid.
146 Ibid., 108.
147 Ibid.
148 Ibid., 17.
149 Ibid., 108–9.
150 Ibid., 85.
151 Ibid.; my emphasis
152 Ibid., 83.
153 Ibid., 87.
154 Ibid., 62.
155 Ibid., 86.
156 See Valentin Mudimbe, *The Invention of Africa: Gnosis, Philosophy and the Order of Knowledge* (Bloomington: Indiana University Press, 1988).
157 Kathy E. Ferguson, *The Man Question: Visions of Subjectivity in Feminist Theory* (Berkeley: University of California Press, 1993), 100.
158 Ibid., 101.
159 Ibid., 97.
160 Ibid., 99.
161 Ibid., 111. For a critical analysis of the consumerist logic of New Age primitivism, also see di Leonardo, *Exotics.* Di Leonardo is quite critical of Torgovnick's *Gone Primitive* for its facile treatment of anthropologists and the discipline of anthropology.
162 Torgovnick, *Primitive Passions,* 176.
163 Ibid., 164.
164 Ibid.
165 Ibid., 174.
166 Ibid., 188.
167 Ibid., 187.
168 Ibid.
169 Ibid., 186.

170 Ibid.
171 Ibid., 207.
172 Ibid., 205.
173 Torgovnick, *Gone Primitive*, 34.
174 Ibid., 9.
175 Benn Michaels, 'The New Modernism,' 265.
176 Ibid., 266.
177 Torgovnick, *Gone Primitive*, 83.
178 Torgovnick, *Primitive Passions*, 4.
179 Torgovnick, *Gone Primitive*, 246.
180 Ibid., 247.
181 Ibid., 247–8.
182 Torgovnick, *Primitive Passions*, 8.
183 Ibid., 19.
184 Ibid., 218–19.
185 Torgovnick, *Gone Primitive*, 20.
186 Ibid., 22.
187 Ibid., 12.
188 Ibid., 81.
189 Ibid., 124.
190 Torgovnick, *Primitive Passions*, 181.
191 Torgovnick, *Gone Primitive*, 220.
192 Ibid., 221, 220, 222.
193 Ibid., 241.
194 Peter C. van Wyck, *Primitives in the Wilderness: Deep Ecology and the Missing Human Subject* (Albany: SUNY Press, 1997), 93.
195 Torgovnick, *Primitive Passions*, 19.
196 Ibid., 212.
197 Torgovnick, *Gone Primitive*, 222.

3. Culture

1 Spivak, *Critique*, 355.
2 Robert Borofsky, 'When: A Conversation about Culture,' *American Anthropologist* 103, no. 2 (2001): 433.
3 Marshall Sahlins, *Islands of History* (Chicago: University of Chicago Press, 1985), 148.
4 William H. Sewell Jr, 'Geertz, Cultural Systems, and History: From Synchrony to Transformation,' *Representations* 59 (1997): 51n1.

5 Marshall Sahlins, *Historical Metaphors and Mythical Realities: Structure in the Early History of the Sandwhich Islands Kingdom* (Ann Arbor: University of Michigan Press, 1981), 19.
6 Ibid., 20.
7 Sahlins, *Islands*, 127.
8 Ibid.
9 Sahlins, *Historical Metaphors*, 10–12.
10 Sahlins, *Islands*, 128.
11 Ibid., 106.
12 Ibid.
13 Ibid.
14 Jonathan Friedman, 'No History Is an Island,' *Critique of Anthropology* 8, no. 3 (1988).
15 See Steen Bergendorff, Ulla Hasager, and Peter Henriques, 'Mythopraxis and History: On the Interpretation of the Makahiki,' *Journal of the Polynesian Society* 97 (1988).
16 See Marshall Sahlins, 'Deserted Islands of History: A Reply to Jonathan Friedman,' *Critique of Anthropology* 8, no. 3 (1988); also see Marshall Sahlins, 'Captain Cook at Hawaii,' *Journal of the Polynesian Society* 98 (1989).
17 Rod Edmond, *Representing the South Pacific: Colonial Discourse from Cook to Gauguin* (Cambridge: Cambridge University Press, 1997), 52.
18 Gananath Obeyesekere, *The Apotheosis of Captain Cook: European Mythmaking in the Pacific*, 2nd. ed. (Princeton, NJ: Princeton University Press, 1997), 177.
19 See Robert Borofsky, 'Cook, Lono, Obeyesekere, and Sahlins,' *Current Anthropology* 38, no. 2 (1997).
20 Sahlins, *Natives*, ix.
21 Ibid., 9.
22 David Scott, 'Culture in Political Theory,' *Political Theory* 31, no. 1 (2003): 106.
23 See Clifford Geertz, 'Culture War,' *New York Review of Books*, 30 Nov. 1995, and Ian Hacking, 'Aloha, Aloha,' *London Review of Books*, 7 Sept. 1995.
24 Geertz, 'Culture War,' 4.
25 Sahlins, *Natives*, ix.
26 Ibid., 9.
27 Obeyesekere, *Apotheosis*, 232.
28 Ibid., 233.
29 Lila Abu-Lughod, 'Writing against Culture,' in *Recapturing Anthropology: Working in the Present*, ed. Richard G. Fox (Santa Fe: School of American Research Press, 1991), 143.
30 Stocking, *Victorian*, 302.

31 McGrane, *Beyond Anthropology*, 113.
32 Abu-Lughod, 'Writing,' 144.
33 Sahlins, *Natives*, 12.
34 Ibid., 11–12.
35 Cited in Brian Whitton, 'Herder's Critique of Enlightenment: Cultural Community versus Cosmopolitan Rationalism,' *History and Theory* 27, no. 2 (1988): 153.
36 Ibid., 154.
37 Cited ibid.
38 Cited in Sahlins, *Natives*, 12.
39 Ibid.
40 Cited ibid.
41 Ibid., 13.
42 Ibid.
43 Ibid., 13–14.
44 Ibid., 14.
45 Ibid.
46 Ibid.
47 Ibid.
48 Marshall Sahlins, *Culture and Practical Reason* (Chicago: University of Chicago Press, 1976), 55.
49 Ibid., viii.
50 Ibid., 57.
51 Gananath Obeyesekere, *The Work of Culture* (Chicago: University of Chicago Press, 1990), 93.
52 Ibid., 94.
53 Ibid., 101.
54 Ibid., 105.
55 Ibid., 103.
56 Ibid., 103–4.
57 Obeyesekere, *Apotheosis*, 19.
58 Ibid., 21.
59 Ibid., 230.
60 Sahlins, *Natives*, 151.
61 Ibid., 150.
62 Ibid.
63 Ibid., 149n1. Sahlins refers to the chapters entitled 'The Impact of the Concept of Culture on the Concept of Man' and 'The Growth of Culture and the Evolution of Mind' in Geertz, *Interpretation.*
64 Sahlins, *Natives*, 149.

65 Ibid., 155.
66 Ibid., 8.
67 Ibid., 7.
68 Christopher Herbert, *Culture and Anomie: Ethnographic Imagination in the Nineteenth Century* (Chicago: University of Chicago Press, 1991), 5.
69 Cited in Michele M. Moody-Adams, *Fieldwork in Familiar Places: Morality, Culture, and Philosophy* (Cambridge, Mass.: Harvard University Press, 1997), 45.
70 Geertz, *Interpretation*, 17.
71 Ibid., 5.
72 Ibid., 452.
73 Ibid.
74 Ibid., 449–50.
75 Cited in Herbert, *Culture and Anomie*, 6.
76 Sahlins, *Culture*, 206.
77 Ibid.
78 Sahlins, *Islands*, 148.
79 Ibid., 109.
80 Sahlins, *Natives*, 65. See also *Islands*, 121.
81 Sahlins, *Natives*, 65.
82 Ibid., 65–6.
83 Ibid., 3.
84 Sahlins, 'Captain,' 412–13.
85 Obeyesekere, *Apotheosis*, 168.
86 Sahlins, *Natives*, 251.
87 For some recent critiques of the concept of cultural holism see, for example: Abu-Lughod, 'Writing'; Mary Margaret Steedly, 'What Is Culture? Does It Matter?' in *Field Work: Sites in Literary and Cultural Studies*, ed. Marjorie Garber, Paul B. Franklin, and Rebecca L. Walkowitz (New York: Routledge, 1996); Akhil Gupta and James Ferguson, 'Beyond "Culture": Space, Identity, and the Politics of Difference,' *Cultural Anthropology* 7, no. 1 (1992); Moody-Adams, *Fieldwork*; James Clifford, *The Predicament of Culture: Twentieth-Century Ethnography, Literature, and Art* (Cambridge, Mass.: Harvard University Press, 1988); and Arjun Appadurai, 'Putting Hierarchy in Its Place,' in *Rereading Cultural Anthropology*, ed. George E. Marcus (Durham: Duke University Press, 1992).
88 Marshall Sahlins, 'Goodbye to *Tristes Tropes*: Ethnography in the Context of Modern World History,' *Journal of Modern History* 65 (1993): 15.
89 Sahlins, 'Reply to Borofsky,' 273.
90 The anthropologist and ethnographer of Fijian divine kingship, A.M. Hocart, who is praised by Sahlins as 'a structuralist before the letter.' See Sahlins, *Islands*, xv.

91 Talal Asad, 'Anthropology and the Analysis of Ideology,' *Man* 14, no. 4 (1979): 614.

92 Cited in Dan Sperber, *On Anthropological Knowledge: Three Essays* (Cambridge: Cambridge University Press, 1985).

93 Cited in Jean-Pierre Olivier de Sardan, 'Occultism and the Ethnographic "I": The Exoticizing of Magic from Durkheim to "Postmodern" Anthropology,' *Critique of Anthropology* 12 (1992): 12.

94 Sahlins, 'Reply,' 273.

95 Ibid.

96 Cited in Moody-Adams, *Fieldwork*, 78.

97 Cited in Sahlins, *Culture*, 84.

98 Sahlins, 'Goodbye,' 15.

99 Sahlins, 'Reply,' 273.

100 Abu-Lughod, 'Writing,' 154.

101 Ibid.

102 Steedly, 'What Is Culture?' 21.

103 Sahlins, *Natives*, 25.

104 Geertz, 'Culture War,' 6.

105 Borofsky, 'Cook,' 258.

106 Valerio Valeri, 'Review of Gananath Obeyesekere's *The Apotheosis of Captain Cook*,' *Pacific Studies* 17, no. 2 (1994): 126.

107 Sahlins, *Natives*, 83; *Islands*, 106.

108 Sahlins, *Natives*, 59.

109 Steven Webster, 'Structuralist Historicism and the History of Structuralism: Sahlins, the Hansons' *Counterpoint in Maori Culture*, and Postmodernist Ethnographic Form,' *Journal of the Polynesian Society* 96, no. 1 (1987): 43.

110 Obeyesekere, *Apotheosis*, 220.

111 Gananath Obeyesekere, 'Reweaving the Argument: A Response to Parker,' *Oceania* 65, no. 3 (1995): 271.

112 Obeyesekere, *Apotheosis*, 214.

113 Sahlins, *Natives*, 39.

114 Ibid., 76.

115 Ibid., 271–2.

116 Ibid., 76.

117 Ibid.

118 Ibid.

119 Obeyesekere, *Apotheosis*, 57.

120 Ibid., 253.

121 Sahlins, *Natives*, 273.

122 Ibid., 232.

123 Samuel Parker, 'The Revenge of Practical Reason? A Review Essay on

Gananath Obeyesekere's *The Apotheosis of Captain Cook*,' *Oceania* 65, no. 3 (1995): 263.
124 Sahlins, *Natives*, 205; my emphasis.
125 Ibid., 149.
126 Ibid., 184–5.
127 Ibid., 42.
128 Sahlins, *Islands*, 122.
129 See Obeyesekere, *Apotheosis*, 55.
130 Sahlins, *Natives*, 246.
131 Ibid., 247.
132 Ibid., 248–9; *Islands*, 145.
133 Sahlins, *Islands*, 138.
134 Sahlins, *Historical Metaphors*, 67.
135 Friedman, 'No History,' 12.
136 Sahlins, 'Deserted,' 42.
137 Ibid., 43.
138 Sahlins, *Islands*, xiv.
139 Also see Adam Kuper, *Culture: The Anthropologists' Account* (Cambridge, Mass.: Harvard University Press, 1999). Commenting on the Friedman-Sahlins debate, Kuper agrees with Friedman's account of Sahlins as a cultural determinist.
140 Sahlins, 'Deserted,' 46.
141 Ibid., 47.
142 Sahlins, *Islands*, 146.
143 Sahlins, 'Deserted,' 45; emphasis added.
144 Sahlins, *Historical Metaphors*, 8.
145 Sahlins, *Islands*, x.
146 Ibid.
147 Sahlins, *Natives*, 248–9.
148 Ibid., 251.
149 Ibid.
150 Ibid. Also see Marshall Sahlins, 'The Sadness of Sweetness,' *Current Anthropology* 37, no. 3 (1996): 395–428.
151 Sahlins, *Historical Metaphors*, 72.
152 Ibid.
153 Friedman, 'No History,' 9.
154 Sahlins, *Islands*, 145.
155 Ibid., 144; emphasis in original.
156 Ibid., 153.
157 Ibid., 155.

158 Ibid., 153.
159 Ibid., xv.
160 Ibid., 156.
161 Ibid., 155.
162 For a similar critique of Sahlins's Hegelian interpretation of culture, see Friedman, 'No History,' 33.
163 Sahlins, 'Goodbye,' 3.
164 Ibid., 40.
165 Ibid., 4.
166 Ibid., 5.
167 Ibid., 7.
168 Ibid., 4.
169 Sahlins, 'Deserted,' 49.
170 Ibid., 48.
171 Sally Falk Moore, 'Explaining the Present: Theoretical Dilemmas in Processual Anthropology,' *American Ethnologist* 14, no. 4 (1987): 729.
172 Sahlins, 'Goodbye,' 8. See also Marshall Sahlins, *Waiting for Foucault* (Cambridge: Prickly Pear Press, 1993), 8.
173 Sahlins, 'Goodbye,' 19.
174 Ibid., 17.
175 Ibid., 20–21.
176 Ibid., 19.
177 Ibid., 21.
178 Ibid.
179 Ibid., 19.
180 Ibid., 20.
181 Ibid., 21.
182 Nicholas Thomas, *In Oceania: Visions, Artifacts, Histories* (Durham: Duke University Press, 1997), 43.
183 Nicholas Thomas, 'Beggars Can Be Choosers,' *American Ethnologist* 20, no. 4 (1993): 875.
184 Geertz, 'Culture War,' 5.
185 Martin Hollis and Steven Lukes, 'Introduction,' in *Rationality and Relativism*, ed. Martin Hollis and Steven Lukes (Cambridge, Mass.: MIT Press, 1982), 7.
186 Sahlins, *Natives*, 169, 179.
187 Ibid., 14.
188 Sahlins, *Islands*, 146.
189 Sahlins, *Natives*, 155.
190 Sahlins, *Islands*, 145.

191 Obeyesekere, *Apotheosis,* 60.
192 Sahlins, *Natives,* 149–50.
193 Sahlins, *Islands,* 144.
194 Sahlins, *Natives,* 120.
195 Ibid., 121.
196 Ibid.
197 Ibid., 169.
198 Sahlins, 'Reply,' 274.
199 Cited in Sahlins, *Islands,* 146.
200 Sahlins, 'Reply,' 274.
201 Sahlins, *Natives,* 169.
202 Ibid., 184.
203 Ibid.
204 Ibid., 149.
205 Ibid., 179.
206 Ibid., 180.
207 Ibid., 185.
208 Margaret Archer, *Culture and Agency: The Place of Culture in Social Theory* (Cambridge: Cambridge University Press, 1988), 9.
209 Thomas, *Oceania,* 38.
210 Sahlins, *Natives,* 158.
211 Michel Foucault, *The Order of Things: An Archaeology of the Human Sciences* (London: Tavistock Publications, 1970), xv; also cited in Sahlins, *Natives,* 163. Keith Windschuttle, in a scathing critique of Sahlins, argues that 'there is no Chinese encyclopedia that has ever described animals under the classifications listed by Foucault ... The taxonomy is fictitious.' He goes on to declare rather petulantly: 'This revelation, of course, would in no way disturb the assumptions of the typical postmodern thinker who believes that the distinction between fact and fiction is arbitrary anyway ... That a piece of fiction can be seriously deployed to make a case in history or anthropology indicates how low debate has sunk in the postmodern era.' Windschuttle's ill-tempered generalization not only promotes a caricature of so-called postmodern thought but also fails to engage seriously with the cogent criticisms postmodernism directs against the West's will to power. Thus, though often astute, his critique of Sahlins's cultural relativism is unfortunately marred by a rather problematic confidence in the truth of Western thought and method as his conclusion clearly reveals: 'This book has been designed to demonstrate and to reassert that the best method for gaining [access to the truth about the past] ... is through the tools refined by the discipline of history. Just as Western science is open to everyone,

Western historical method is available to the people of any culture to understand their past and their relations with other people.' See Keith Windschuttle, *The Killing of History: How Literary Critics and Social Theorists Are Murdering Our Past* (New York: The Free Press, 1997), 255, 281. The chapter in which Windschuttle attacks Sahlins is entitled 'The Return of Tribalism.' It could just as well have been called 'The Return of Western Triumphalism.' It is also interesting to note that Obeyesekere calls Windschuttle's book a 'highly polemical critique of the bleaker forms of postmodernism' and states that Windschuttle unfortunately 'overdoes his case without recognizing that one can have responsible social theories emphasizing nomological thought that have been both influenced by and critical of poststructuralist and postmodern thought' (Obeyesekere, *Apotheosis*, 294–5n42). Obeyesekere's critical distancing is no doubt caused by his alarm over Windschuttle's Eurocentric confidence. Windschuttle is of course mistaken in placing Sahlins in the postmodernist camp; Sahlins, as a cultural holist, is no friend of postmodernism.

212 Sahlins, *Natives*, 163.

213 Ibid., 159.

214 Ibid.

215 Hefner, 'Baudrillard,' 110.

216 Sahlins, *Natives*, 162n15.

217 L. Wittgenstein, *Remarks on Frazier's Golden Bough* (Atlantic Highlands, NJ: Humanities Press, 1979).

218 John R. Bowlin and Peter G. Stromberg, 'Representation and Reality in the Study of Culture,' *American Anthropologist* 99, no. 1 (1997): 132.

219 Sahlins, *Natives*, 118.

220 Ibid., 119.

221 Ibid., 62.

222 De Sardan, 'Occultism,' 20.

223 Nicholas Thomas, 'Against Ethnography,' *Cultural Anthropology* 6, no. 3 (1991): 309.

224 Clifford Geertz, 'Distinguished Lecture: Anti-Anti-Relativism,' *American Anthropologist* 86 (1984): 275.

225 Ibid., 276.

226 Roger Keesing, 'Exotic Readings of Cultural Texts,' *Current Anthropology* 30, no. 4 (1989): 459–60.

227 Sahlins, *Islands*, xi.

228 Sahlins, *Natives*, 163.

229 Moody-Adams, *Fieldwork*, 80.

230 Thomas, 'Against,' 310.

231 Sahlins, *Natives,* 171.
232 Jonathan Friedman, 'Review of How "Natives" Think,' *American Ethnologist* 24, no. 1 (1997): 262.
233 David Scott, 'Criticism and Culture: Theory and Post-Colonial Claims on Anthropological Disciplinarity,' *Critique of Anthropology* 12, no. 4 (1992): 387.
234 Gupta and Ferguson, 'Beyond "Culture,"' 13–14.
235 Thomas, 'Against,' 310–11.
236 Lila Abu-Lughod, 'The Interpretation of Culture(s) after Television,' *Representations* 59 (1997): 121.
237 Stolcke, 'Talking Culture,' 12.
238 James Suzman, 'Comment on Adam Kuper's "The Return of the Native,"' *Current Anthropology* 44, no. 3 (2003).
239 Sahlins, *Natives,* 25.
240 Sahlins, *Waiting,* 16.
241 Sahlins, *Culture,* 74.
242 Ibid., 75.
243 Sahlins, *Waiting,* 17.
244 Sahlins, *Culture,* 74.
245 Janet Dolgin, David Kennitzer, and David Schneider, eds., *Symbolic Anthropology: A Reader in the Study of Symbols and Meaning* (New York: Columbia University Press, 1977), 34.
246 Sahlins, *Islands,* 146.
247 Ibid., 154.
248 Sahlins, *Natives,* 188.
249 Ibid., 187.
250 Appadurai, 'Hierarchy,' 35.
251 Sahlins, 'Sadness,' 395.
252 Ibid., 415.
253 Sahlins, *Islands,* 146.
254 Sahlins, 'Reply,' 276.
255 Sahlins, 'Sadness,' 425.
256 Sahlins, *Islands,* 155.
257 Sahlins, 'Sadness,' 425.
258 Sahlins, *Waiting,* 10.
259 Hollis and Lukes, 'Introduction,' 11.
260 Sahlins, 'Reply,' 276.
261 Ibid., 273.
262 Ibid., 273–4.
263 Cited ibid., 274.

264 Ibid.; emphasis added.
265 Ibid.
266 Sahlins, *Natives*, 62.
267 Sahlins, 'Reply,' 275.
268 Ibid., 273.
269 Cited in Moody-Adams, *Fieldwork*, 78.
270 McGrane, *Beyond Anthropology*, 121.
271 Sahlins, 'Reply,' 276.
272 Ibid., 273.
273 Sahlins, *Natives*, 14.
274 The only explicit reference (that I know of) to the influence of Hegel on Sahlins's work appears in Friedman, 'No History.'
275 Charles Taylor, *Hegel* (Cambridge: Cambridge University Press, 1975), 118.
276 Ibid., 90.
277 Ibid., 91.
278 Ibid., 118.
279 Sahlins, 'Reply,' 273.
280 Ibid.
281 Sahlins, 'Goodbye,' 19.
282 Sahlins, *Natives*, 14.
283 Ibid.
284 Nicholas Dirks, 'Postcolonialism and Its Discontents: History, Anthropology, and Postcolonial Critique,' in *Schools of Thought: Twenty-Five Years of Interpretive Social Science*, ed. Joan W. Scott and Debra Keates (Princeton: Princeton University Press, 2002), 233.

4. Modernity

1 Jürgen Habermas, *Autonomy and Solidarity: Interviews with Jürgen Habermas*, ed. Peter Dews (London: Verso, 1986), 96.
2 Habermas, *Philosophical Discourse*, 121.
3 Ibid., 129.
4 Jürgen Habermas, *The Postnational Constellation: Political Essays*, ed. and trans. Max Pensky (Cambridge, Mass.: MIT Press, 2001), 132.
5 Ibid.
6 Ibid., 136.
7 Habermas, *Philosophical Discourse*, 310.
8 Ibid., 102.
9 Ibid., 102 and 307.
10 Diana Coole, 'Habermas and the Question of Alterity,' in *Habermas and the*

Unfinished Project of Modernity, ed. Maurizio Passerin d'Entreves and Seyla Benhabib (Cambridge, Mass.: MIT Press, 1997), 223.

11 Habermas, *Autonomy*, 203.

12 Coole, 'Habermas,' 223.

13 Richard J. Bernstein, ed., *Habermas and Modernity* (Cambridge, Mass.: MIT Press, 1985), 17.

14 Habermas, *Appendix*, 314.

15 Jürgen Habermas, *Communication and the Evolution of Society*, trans. Thomas McCarthy (Boston: Beacon Press, 1979), 1.

16 Ibid.

17 Ibid., 2.

18 Ibid., 2–3.

19 Ibid., 28–9; *Philosophical Discourse*, 313; Habermas, *Theory*, vol. 1: 99.

20 Habermas, *Communication*, 28.

21 Habermas, *Theory*, vol. 1, 98–9.

22 Ibid., 287.

23 Ibid., 286–7.

24 Ibid., 390 and 392.

25 Arie Brand, *The Force of Reason: An Introduction to Habermas' Theory of Communicative Action* (Sydney: Allen and Unwin, 1990), 11.

26 Jürgen Habermas, *The Theory of Communicative Action: Lifeworld and System*, ed. Peter Dews, trans. Thomas McCarthy, vol. 2 (Boston: Beacon Press, 1987), 96.

27 Habermas, *Theory*, vol. 1, 287.

28 Habermas, *Philosophical Discourse*, 311.

29 Jürgen Habermas, *Moral Consciousness and Communicative Action*, trans. C. Lenhardt and S.W. Nicholson (Cambridge, Mass.: MIT Press, 1991), 163.

30 Seyla Benhabib, *Critique, Norm, and Utopia: A Study of the Foundation of Critical Theory* (New York: Columbia University Press, 1986), 393n36.

31 Axel Honneth and Hans Joas, *Social Action and Human Nature*, trans. Raymond Meyer (New York: Cambridge University Press, 1988), 7.

32 Jürgen Habermas, 'A Reply to My Critics,' in *Habermas: Critical Debates*, ed. John B Thompson and David Held (London: Macmillan, 1982), 253.

33 Habermas, *Communication*, 3.

34 Karl-Otto Apel, 'Openly Strategic Uses of Language: A Transcendental-Pragmatic Perspective (a Second Attempt to Think with Habermas against Habermas),' in *Habermas: A Critical Reader*, ed. Peter Dews (Oxford: Blackwell, 1999), 276; emphasis added.

35 Habermas, *Moral Consciousness*, 88–9.

36 Benhabib, *Critique*, 290.

37 Habermas, *Moral Consciousness*, 85.

38 Commenting on Adorno's 'negative dialectics' and Derrida's 'deconstruction,' Habermas states: 'The totalizing self-critique of reason gets caught in a performative contradiction since subject-centered reason can be convicted of being authoritarian in nature only by having recourse to its own tools' (Habermas, *Philosophical Discourse*, 185).

39 Cf. Dean Pickard, 'Applied Nietzsche: The Problem of Reflexivity in Habermas, a Postmodern Critique,' *Auslegung* 19, no. 1 (1993). '[The] procedural rules that Habermas is trying to show as the necessary conditions for the communicative process in arriving at consensus ... require fixity, but are required by themselves to be open to debate and hence, subject to change' (ibid., 10).

40 Michael Kelly, 'Macintyre, Habermas, and Philosophical Ethics,' *The Philosophical Forum* 21, nos. 1–2 (1989–90): 76.

41 Rolf Zimmerman, 'Emancipation and Rationality: Foundational Problems in the Theories of Marx and Habermas,' *Ratio* 26, no. 2 (1984): 155.

42 Ibid., 156; emphasis added.

43 Benhabib, *Critique*, 306.

44 Habermas, 'Reply,' 262.

45 Habermas, *Moral Consciousness*, 208.

46 Ibid.

47 Ibid., 203.

48 Maeve Cooke, *Language and Reason: A Study of Habermas' Pragmatics* (Cambridge, Mass.: MIT Press, 1994), 19. See also David M. Rasmussen, *Reading Habermas* (Cambridge, Mass.: Blackwell, 1990), 26n23.

49 Jürgen Habermas, 'Questions and Counterquestions,' in *Habermas and Modernity*, ed. Richard J. Bernstein (Cambridge, Mass.: MIT Press, 1985), 197.

50 Habermas, 'Reply,' 221. See also Habermas, *Communication*, 97.

51 Habermas, 'Reply,' 227. For discussion of Hegel's concept of the causality of fate, see Habermas, *Philosophical Discourse*, 28–9.

52 Cited in John B. Thompson, 'Universal Pragmatics,' in *Habermas: Critical Debates*, ed. John B. Thompson and David Held (London: Macmillan, 1982), 125.

53 Martin Jay, *Marxism and Totality: The Adventures of a Concept from Lukács to Habermas* (Berkeley: University of California Press, 1984), 497.

54 Habermas, *Communication*, 97.

55 Romand Coles, 'Identity and Difference in the Ethical Positions of Adorno and Habermas,' in *The Cambridge Companion to Habermas*, ed. Stephen K. White (Cambridge: Cambridge University Press, 1995), 25.

56 Habermas, *Theory*, vol. 2, 329–30.
57 Dieter Henrich, 'What Is Metaphysics – What Is Modernity? Twelve Theses against Jürgen Habermas,' in *Habermas: A Critical Reader*, ed. Peter Dews (Oxford: Blackwell, 1999), 314.
58 Ibid., 313; my emphasis.
59 Gianni Vattimo, *The Transparent Society*, trans. David Webb (Baltimore: Johns Hopkins University Press, 1992), 42.
60 Richard J. Bernstein, 'Introduction,' in *Habermas and Modernity*, ed. R.J. Bernstein (Cambridge, Mass.: MIT Press, 1985), 20.
61 Axel Honneth, *The Critique of Power: Reflective Stages in a Critical Social Theory*, trans. Kenneth Baynes (Cambridge, Mass.: MIT Press, 1993), 282.
62 Benhabib, *Critique*, 264.
63 Thomas McCarthy, *Ideals and Illusions: Reconstruction and Deconstruction in Critical Theory* (Cambridge, Mass.: MIT Press, 1991), 134–35.
64 Habermas, *Autonomy*, 184.
65 McCarthy, *Ideals*, 135.
66 Jean Baudrillard, 'Modernité,' in *Encylopaedia Universalis* (Paris: Encyclopaedia Universalis, 1989), 552.
67 Naoki Sakai, 'Modernity and Its Critique: The Problem of Universalism and Particularism,' *South Atlantic Quarterly* 87, no. 3 (1988): 475.
68 Charles Taylor, 'Inwardness and the Culture of Modernity,' in *Philosophical Interventions in the Unfinished Project of Enlightenment*, ed. Axel Honneth, Thomas McCarthy, and Albrecht Wellmer (Cambridge, Mass.: MIT Press, 1992), 89.
69 Ibid., 93.
70 Habermas, *Philosophical Discourse*, 7.
71 Theodor Adorno, *Negative Dialectics*, trans. E.B. Ashton (New York: Seabury Press, 1973), 320.
72 Rick Roderick, 'Review of Habermas's The Theory of Communicative Reason, Vol. 1,' *Political Theory* 14, no. 1 (1986): 155.
73 Habermas, *Theory*, vol. 1, 70. See also Habermas, *Philosophical Discourse*, 298.
74 Habermas, *Theory*, vol. 1, 163–4, 175–80, and 235–6.
75 Stephen K. White, *The Recent Work of Jürgen Habermas* (Cambridge: Cambridge University Press, 1988), 90.
76 See the essays 'Solidarity or Objectivity?' and 'On Ethnocentrism' in Richard Rorty, *Objectivity, Relativism and Truth: Philosophical Papers Volume 1* (Cambridge: Cambridge University Press, 1991). Also note Rorty's remark in 'Habermas and Lyotard on Postmodernity': '[W]hereas Habermas compli-

ments "bourgeois ideals" by reference to the "elements of reason" contained in them, it would be better just to compliment those untheoretical sorts of narrative discourse which make up the political speech of the Western democracies. It would be better to be frankly ethnocentric.' Richard Rorty, *Essays on Heidegger and Others: Philosophical Papers Volume 2* (Cambridge: Cambridge University Press, 1991), 168.

77 Habermas, *Philosophical Discourse,* 322.

78 Habermas, *Theory,* vol. 1, 44.

79 Ibid.

80 Moody-Adams, *Fieldwork,* 80.

81 Thomas, 'Against,' 310.

82 Habermas, *Philosophical Discourse,* 114–15; *Theory,* vol. 1, 45–52.

83 Habermas, *Theory,* vol. 1, 52.

84 Habermas, *Philosophical Discourse,* 115.

85 Habermas, *Theory,* vol. 1, 44–5.

86 E.E. Evans-Pritchard, *Witchcraft, Oracles, and Magic among the Azande* (Oxford: Oxford University Press, 1937), 194–5. Cited in Moody-Adams, *Fieldwork,* 45.

87 Habermas, *Theory,* vol. 1, 60.

88 Ibid.

89 Peter Winch, 'Understanding a Primitive Society,' in *Rationality,* ed. Brian Wilson (Oxford: Oxford University Press, 1970), 93. Cited in Habermas, *Theory,* vol. 1, 60.

90 Habermas, *Theory,* vol. 1, 61.

91 See Robin Horton, 'African Traditional Thought and Western Science,' in *Rationality,* ed. Brian Wilson (Oxford: Oxford University Press, 1970).

92 Habermas, *Theory,* vol. 1, 64–5.

93 Ibid., 66.

94 Robert Wuthnow, 'Rationality and the Limits of Rational Theory: A Sociological Critique,' in *Habermas, Modernity and Public Theology,* ed. Don S. Browning and Francis Schüssler Fiorenza (New York: Crossroad, 1992), 212–13.

95 Habermas, *Theory,* vol. 1, 45.

96 Ibid., 46.

97 Ibid., 48–50.

98 On the rigidity of the premodern and modern divide and on Habermas's lack of empirical evidence, see Bruno Latour, *We Have Never Been Modern,* trans. Catherine Porter (Cambridge, Mass.: Harvard University Press, 1993), 60–1.

99 Moody-Adams, *Fieldwork,* 50.

100 Raul Pertierra, 'The Rationality Problematique: An Anthropological Review of Habermas' Theory of Communicative Action,' *Social Analysis* 23 (1988): 75.

101 For this example I am indebted to Tania Li, who has carried out extensive fieldwork among the Lauje of Sulawesi.

102 Stanley Jeyaraja Tambiah, *Magic, Science, Religion, and the Scope of Rationality* (Cambridge: Cambridge University Press, 1990), 136.

103 Ibid., 137.

104 Maurice Godelier, cited in Habermas, *Theory*, vol. 1, 46.

105 James Carrier, 'Occidentalism: The World Turned Upside-Down,' *American Ethnologist* 19, no. 2 (1992): 200.

106 Cited ibid.

107 Mauss, cited ibid.

108 Ibid.

109 Habermas, *Theory*, vol. 2, 163.

110 Carrier, 'Occidentalism,' 203.

111 Habermas, *Theory*, vol. 2, 86.

112 Kuper, *Invention*, 240.

113 Habermas, *Theory*, vol. 1, 44.

114 Habermas, *Theory*, vol. 2, 77.

115 Ibid., 87; emphasis mine.

116 Habermas's thought experiment with a primordial 'totally integrated society' resembles Lyotard's view of the Cashinahua as belonging to 'a very large scale integrated culture,' Sahlins's belief in the cultural holism of pre-contact Hawaiians, and Torgovnick's longing for the undifferentiated unity of the oceanic.

117 Fitzpatrick, *Mytholology*, ix–x and 63.

118 Ibid., 202.

119 Ibid., 138.

120 Ibid., 144.

121 Burrow, *Evolution*, 194, 219.

122 Habermas, *Communication*, 141.

123 Ibid., 141–3.

124 Habermas, *Moral Consciousness*, 168.

125 Habermas, *Autonomy*, 168.

126 Piet Strydom, 'Sociocultural Evolution or the Social Evolution of Practical Reason?: Eder's Critique of Habermas,' *Praxis International* 13, no. 3 (1993): 308.

127 Honneth and Joas, *Social Action*, 165.

128 Piet Strydom, 'The Ontogenetic Fallacy: The Immanent Critique of

Habermas's Developmental Logical Theory of Evolution,' *Theory, Culture and Society* 9, no. 3 (1992): 78.

129 Michael Schmid, 'Habermas's Theory of Social Evolution,' in *Habermas: Critical Debates*, ed. John B. Thompson and David Held (London: Macmillan, 1982), 173.

130 Benhabib, *Critique*, 276–7.

131 Habermas, *Communication*, 140.

132 Habermas, *Moral Consciousness*, 166–7, table 4.

133 Ibid., 156.

134 Strydom, 'Sociocultural,' 313.

135 Habermas, *Communication*, 120.

136 Strydom, 'Sociocultural,' 313.

137 For a comprehensive discussion of the lack of concrete historical and sociological analyses in Habermas's genetic-structural approach to evolution and history, see Donald A. Nielsen, 'A Theory of Communicative Action or a Sociology of Civilizations? A Critique of Jürgen Habermas,' *International Journal of Politics, Culture, and Society* 1, no. 1 (1987). Michael Kelly has also pointed to the lack of historical substantiation in Habermas's theory of the developmental logic of communicative rationality. See Michael Kelly, 'The Gadamer/Habermas Debate Revisited: The Question of Ethics,' in *Universalism vs. Communitarianism: Contemporary Debates in Ethics*, ed. David Rasmussen (Cambridge, Mass.: MIT Press, 1990), 148–50.

138 Thomas McCarthy, 'Rationality and Relativism: Habermas's "Overcoming" of Hermeneutics,' in *Habermas: Critical Debates*, ed. John B. Thompson and David Held (London: Macmillan, 1982), 64.

139 Strydom, 'Sociocultural,' 314.

140 Cited in Kelly, 'Gadamer,' 150.

141 Benhabib, *Critique*, 255.

142 Alessandro Ferrara, 'Universalisms: Procedural, Contextualist and Prudential,' in *Universalism vs. Communitarianism: Contemporary Debates in Ethics*, ed. David Rasmussen (Cambridge, Mass.: MIT Press, 1990), 18.

143 Habermas, *Moral Consciousness*, 168.

144 Ibid., 169.

145 McCarthy, *Ideals*, 139. McCarthy's strictures on Habermas's use of Piaget's and Kohlberg's ontogenetic studies are shared by Anthony Giddens, 'Reason without Revolution? Habermas's Theorie des Kommunikativen Handelns,' in *Habermas and Modernity*, ed. Richard J. Bernstein (Cambridge, Mass.: MIT Press, 1985), 117–19, and David Ingram, *Habermas and the Dialectic of Reason* (New Haven: Yale University Press, 1987), 132–4. See Gustav Jahoda, *Psychology and Anthropology: A Psychological Perspective* (Lon-

don: Academic Press, 1982) and Richard A. Shweder, 'On Savages and Other Children,' *American Anthropologist* 84, no. 2 (1982) for incisive criticisms of the Piagetian model of ontogenetic development and its extremely problematic application to so-called primitives and primitive societies by the anthropologist C.R. Hallpike in *The Foundations of Primitive Thought* (New York: Oxford University Press, 1979). Jahoda's and Shweder's criticisms of the application of ontogenetic development models to actual human societies can, *mutatis mutandis*, be directed also at Habermas's theory of sociocultural evolution.

146 Strydom, 'Sociocultural,' 315.

147 Ibid., 316.

148 Anthony Giddens, 'Jürgen Habermas,' in *The Return of Grand Theory in the Human Sciences*, ed. Quentin Skinner (Cambridge: Cambridge University Press, 1985), 133.

149 Habermas, *Inclusion*, xxxv.

150 Jürgen Habermas, *Postmetaphysical Thinking*, trans. W.M. Hohengarten (Cambridge, Mass.: MIT Press, 1992), 137–8.

151 Ibid., 138.

152 Ibid.

153 Ibid.

154 Habermas, *Inclusion*, 40.

155 Habermas, *Postmetaphysical*, 138.

156 Habermas, *Theory*, vol. 1, 115–16.

157 Bernard Flynn, *Political Philosophy at the Closure of Metaphysics* (Atlantic Highlands, NJ: Humanities Press, 1992), 61.

158 Habermas, *Moral Consciousness*, 30.

159 Ibid., 31.

160 Habermas, *Theory*, vol. 1, 116–17.

161 I owe this way of posing the question to Bernard Flynn, whose own example is that of an encounter between an anthropologist from Ames, Iowa, and a tribesman from the Amazon Basin. See Flynn, *Political Philosophy*, 62. Flynn offers one of the most cogent critiques of Habermas's inability to escape from metaphysics.

162 Habermas, *Postmetaphysical*, 138.

163 Habermas, *Theory*, vol. 1, 117.

164 Ibid.

165 Flynn, *Political Philosophy*, 62–3.

166 Brian J. Shaw, 'Habermas and Religious Inclusion: Lessons from Kant's Moral Theology,' *Political Theory* 27, no. 5 (1999): 645. Shaw argues that Habermas's conditions for discourse would in fact preclude not just primi-

tive tribesmen but also Habermas's religious contemporaries who have embraced theological dogma.

167 Jürgen Habermas, *Justice and Application: Remarks on Discourse Ethics*, trans. Ciaran Cronin (Cambridge, Mass.: MIT Press, 1993), 157; emphasis mine.

168 Dipesh Chakrabarty, 'Radical Histories and Question of Enlightenment Rationalism: Some Recent Critiques of Subaltern Studies,' in *Mapping Subaltern Studies and the Postcolonial*, ed. Vinayak Chaturvedi (London: Verso, 2000), 273.

169 Coole, 'Habermas,' 226.

170 Fitzpatrick, *Mytholology*, 41.

171 Frantz Fanon, *The Wretched of the Earth*, trans. Constance Farrington (Harmondsworth: Penguin, 1967), 81.

172 Flynn, *Political Philosophy*, 66.

173 Jacques Derrida, *Margins of Philosophy*, trans. Alan Bass (Chicago: University of Chicago Press, 1982), 213.

174 Don DeLillo, *White Noise* (New York: Penguin, 1986), 319.

175 Habermas, *Theory*, vol. 1, 65.

176 Horton, 'African Traditional Thought,' 179. Cited in Habermas, *Theory*, vol. 1, 65.

177 Habermas, *Theory*, vol. 2, 400.

178 Habermas, *Theory*, vol. 1, 66.

179 Ibid.

180 Bernstein, 'Introduction,' 23.

181 Habermas, *Philosophical Discourse*, 298.

182 Habermas, *Theory*, vol. 2, 124–6.

183 Habermas, *Philosophical Discourse*, 298. See also *Moral Consciousness*, 135.

184 Habermas, *Moral Consciousness*, 136–8.

185 Habermas, *Philosophical Discourse*, 326; *Theory*, vol. 1, 70.

186 Habermas, *Theory*, vol. 1, 70.

187 Ibid.

188 Ibid.

189 Habermas, 'Reply,' 224.

190 Habermas, *Theory*, vol. 2, 157.

191 Ibid., 156.

192 Benhabib, *Critique*, 242.

193 Habermas, *Theory*, vol. 2, 145.

194 Habermas, 'Reply,' 224. See also Habermas, *Philosophical Discourse*, 344–5, and *Theory*, vol. 2, 146.

195 Habermas, *Moral Consciousness*, 135.

196 Stephen Crook, *Modernist Radicalism and Its Aftermath: Foundationalism and*

Anti-Foundationalism in Radical Social Theory (London: Routledge, 1991), 119.

197 Habermas, *Moral Consciousness*, 126–7.

198 J.M. Bernstein, *Recovering Ethical Life: Jürgen Habermas and the Future of Critical Theory* (London: Routledge, 1995), 116.

199 Habermas, *Justice and Application*, 120.

200 Habermas, *Philosophical Discourse*, 321.

201 J.M. Bernstein, *Adorno: Disenchantment and Ethics* (Cambridge: Cambridge University Press, 2001), 81.

202 Cooke, *Language and Reason*, 16.

203 Habermas, 'Questions,' 215.

204 White, *Recent*, 103.

205 Habermas, *Theory*, vol. 2, 400.

206 Ibid., 400–1; my emphases.

207 Fred Dallmayr, *Polis and Praxis: Essays in Contemporary Political Theory* (Cambridge, Mass.: MIT Press, 1985), 247.

208 Habermas, *Theory*, vol. 2, 108.

209 Habermas, *Moral Consciousness*, 207; my emphasis.

210 Ibid., 109.

211 Bernstein, *Adorno*, 83.

212 Jürgen Habermas, 'Justice and Solidarity: On the Discussion Concerning Stage 6,' in *The Moral Domain: Essays in the Ongoing Discussion between Philosophy and the Social Sciences*, ed. Thomas E. Wren (Cambridge, Mass.: MIT Press, 1990), 244.

213 Ibid., 246.

214 Ibid., 245.

215 Ibid., 246.

216 Habermas, *Moral Consciousness*, 18.

217 White, *Recent*, 135.

218 Habermas, *Theory*, vol. 1, 65.

219 Habermas, *Autonomy*, 125.

220 Habermas, *Justice and Application*, 75–76. My emphasis.

221 Habermas, *Moral Consciousness*, 163.

222 Habermas, 'Reply,' 227.

223 Cooke, *Language and Reason*, 17.

224 Jürgen Habermas, 'Consciousness-Raising or Redemptive Criticism – the Contemporaneity of Walter Benjamin,' *New German Critique* 17 (1979): 58–9.

225 Ibid., 57.

226 Ingram, *Habermas*, 175.

227 Habermas, *Theory*, vol. 2, 77.

228 Donald Jay Rothberg, 'Rationality and Religion in Habermas' Recent Work: Some Remarks on the Relation between Critical Theory and the Phenomenology of Religion,' *Philosophy and Social Criticism* 11, no. 3 (1986): 233.

229 Peter Dews, *The Limits of Disenchantment: Essays on Contemporary European Philosophy* (London: Verso, 1995), 9.

230 Habermas, *Postmetaphysical*, 51.

231 Jürgen Habermas, *Between Facts and Norms: Contributions to a Discourse Theory of Law and Democracy*, trans. William Rehg (Cambridge, Mass.: MIT Press, 1996), 490.

232 Habermas, *Autonomy*, 203.

233 For further examples of Habermas's view of religion as both antithesis and supplement to rational discourse, see 'To Seek to Salvage an Unconditional Meaning without God Is a Futile Undertaking: Reflections on a Remark of Max Horkheimer,' in Habermas, *Justice and Application*. See also 'Israel or Athens: Where Does Anamnestic Reason Belong?' in *The Liberating Power of Symbols: Philosophical Essays*, ed. Jürgen Habermas (Cambridge, Mass.: MIT Press, 2001) and 'Transcendence from Within, Transcendence in This World,' in *Habermas, Modernity and Public Theology*, ed. Don S. Browning and Francis Schüssler Fiorenza (New York: Crossroad, 1992). All of these essays have now been collected in Habermas, *Religion and Rationality*.

234 Dews, *Limits*, 210.

235 Habermas, *Philosophical Discourse*, 130.

236 Ibid.

237 Agamben, *Homo Sacer*, 7.

238 Peter Fitzpatrick, *Modernism and the Grounds of Law* (Cambridge: Cambridge University Press, 2001), 63–4.

239 Bernstein, *Recovering*, 191.

240 Hartmut and Gernot Böhme's phrase, cited in Habermas, *Philosophical Discourse*, 307.

241 Jürgen Habermas, 'Fundamentalism and Terror: A Dialogue with Jürgen Habermas,' in *Philosophy in a Time of Terror: Dialogues with Jürgen Habermas and Jacques Derrida*, ed. Giovanna Borradori (Chicago: University of Chicago Press, 2003), 32.

242 Ibid., 33.

243 Jürgen Habermas, *The Future of Human Nature* (Cambridge: Polity, 2003), 111; emphasis mine.

Conclusion

1 Michel de Certeau, cited in Josette Féral, 'The Powers of Difference,' in *The Future of Difference*, ed. Hester Eisenstein and Alice Jardine (Boston: G.K. Hall, 1980), 88. Féral does not give the source of de Certeau's remark.
2 Will Self, 'Understanding the Ur-Bororo,' in *The Quantity Theory of Insanity: Together with Five Supporting Propositions* (London: Bloomsbury, 1991), 82.
3 Ibid., 80.
4 Ibid., 86.
5 Ibid., 91.
6 Ibid., 81, 85.
7 Ibid., 86.
8 Ibid., 87.
9 Geertz, 'Anti-Anti-Relativism,' 276.
10 Self, 'Understanding the Ur-Bororo,' 84.
11 Ibid., 69.
12 Ibid., 75.
13 Ibid., 76.
14 Ibid., 94.
15 Ibid., 69.
16 Dipesh Chakrabarty, *Habitations of Modernity: Essays in the Wake of Subaltern Studies* (Chicago: University of Chicago Press, 2002), 36.
17 I owe this formulation to Robert Bernasconi's illuminating discussion of Merleau-Ponty and Levinas in his 'One-Way Traffic: The Ontology of Decolonization and Its Ethics,' in *Ontology and Alterity in Merleau-Ponty*, ed. Galen A. Johnson and Michael B. Smith (Evanston, Ill.: Northwestern University Press, 1990), 79. For a related critique of the Eurocentric generosity of Levinas's thought, see Bernasconi, 'Who Is My Neighbor? Who Is the Other? Questioning "the Generosity of Western Thought,"' in *Ethics and Responsibility in the Phenomenological Tradition* (Pittsburgh: Dusquesne University, Simon Silverman Phenomenology Center, 1992), 1–31.
18 Jacques Rancière, *The Philosopher and His Poor*, ed. Andrew Parker, trans. John Drury, Corinne Oster, and Andrew Parker (Durham: Duke University Press, 2002), 203.
19 Levinas in Raoul Mortley, *French Philosophers in Conversation* (London: Routledge, 1991), 18.
20 Emmanuel Levinas, 'Intention, Ereignis und der Andere. Gesprach Zwischen Emmanuel Levinas und Christoph von Wolzogen am 20. Dezember 1985 in Paris,' in *Humanismus des Anderen Menschen*, ed. Christophe von

Wolzogen (Hamburg: Felix Meiner, 1989), 140. Cited in Bernasconi, 'Neighbor,' 14.

21 Emmanuel Levinas, *Collected Philosophical Papers*, ed. Alphonso Lingis (Dordrecht: Martinus Nijhoff, 1987), 101. Cited in Bernasconi, 'One-Way,' 78.

22 Sahlins, *Natives*, 62.

23 Adam Kuper, 'The Return of the Native,' *Current Anthropology* 44, no. 3 (2003): 395.

24 Baudrillard, *Transparency*, 174; emphasis mine.

25 Dipesh Chakrabarty, *Provincializing Europe: Postcolonial Thought and Historical Difference* (Princeton: Princeton University Press, 2000), 254.

26 Cited ibid., 105.

27 Ibid., 104.

28 Ibid., 254.

29 Rodolphe Gasché, *Of Minimal Things: Studies on the Notion of Relation* (Stanford: Stanford University Press, 1999), 370n7.

References

Abu-Lughod, Lila. 'The Interpretation of Culture(s) after Television.' *Representations* 59 (1997): 109–34.

– 'Writing against Culture.' In *Recapturing Anthropology: Working in the Present*, edited by Richard G. Fox, 137–62. Santa Fe: School of American Research Press, 1991.

Adorno, Theodor. *Negative Dialectics.* Translated by E.B. Ashton. New York: Seabury Press, 1973.

Agamben, Giorgio. *Homo Sacer: Sovereign Power and Bare Life.* Translated by Daniel Heller-Roazen. Stanford: Stanford University Press, 1998.

Alonzo, Carlos J. *The Burden of Modernity: The Rhetoric of Cultural Discourse in Spanish America.* New York: Oxford University Press, 1998.

Apel, Karl-Otto. 'Openly Strategic Uses of Language: A Transcendental-Pragmatic Perspective (a Second Attempt to Think with Habermas against Habermas).' In *Habermas: A Critical Reader*, edited by Peter Dews, 272–90. Oxford: Blackwell, 1999.

Appadurai, Arjun. 'Putting Hierarchy in Its Place.' In *Rereading Cultural Anthropology*, edited by George E. Marcus, 34–47. Durham: Duke University Press, 1992.

Archer, Margaret. *Culture and Agency: The Place of Culture in Social Theory.* Cambridge: Cambridge University Press, 1988.

Asad, Talal. 'Anthropology and the Analysis of Ideology.' *Man* 14, no. 4 (1979): 607–27.

Barkan, Elazar, and Ronald Bush. *Prehistories of the Future: The Primitivist Project and the Culture of Modernism.* Stanford: Stanford University Press, 1995.

Barthes, Roland. *Empire of Signs.* Translated by Richard Howard. New York: Hill and Wang, 1982.

Baudrillard, Jean. *America.* Translated by Chris Turner. London: Verso, 1988.

– *The Ecstasy of Communication.* Translated by Sheila Faria Fraser. Edited by Sylvère Lotringer. New York: Semiotext(e), 1988.

– 'An Interview with Jean Baudrillard.' By Monica Sassatelli. *European Journal of Social Theory* 5, no. 4 (2002): 521–30.

– *The Mirror of Production.* Translated by Mark Poster. St Louis: Telos Press, 1975.

– 'Modernité.' In *Encylopaedia Universalis*, 552–3. Paris: Encylopaedia Universalis, 1989.

– *The Perfect Crime.* Translated by Chris Turner. London: Verso, 1996.

– *Simulations.* Translated by Paul Foss et al. New York: Semiotext(e), 1983.

– *Symbolic Exchange and Death.* Translated by Iain Hamilton Grant. London: Sage Publications, 1993.

– *The Transparency of Evil: Essays on Extreme Phenomena.* Translated by James Benedict. London: Verso, 1993.

Benhabib, Seyla. *Critique, Norm, and Utopia: A Study of the Foundation of Critical Theory.* New York: Columbia University Press, 1986.

– 'Epistemologies of Postmodernism: A Rejoinder to Jean-François Lyotard.' In *Feminism/Postmodernism*, edited by Linda J. Nicholson, 107–30. New York: Routledge, 1990.

Benn Michaels, Walter. 'The New Modernism.' *ELH* 59, no. 1 (1992): 257–67.

Bergendorff, Steen, Ulla Hasager, and Peter Henriques. 'Mythopraxis and History: On the Interpretation of the Makahiki.' *Journal of the Polynesian Society* 97 (1988): 391–408.

Bernasconi, Robert. 'One-Way Traffic: The Ontology of Decolonization and Its Ethics.' In *Ontology and Alterity in Merleau-Ponty*, edited by Galen A. Johnson and Michael B. Smith, 67–80. Evanston, Ill.: Northwestern University Press, 1990.

– 'Who Is My Neighbor? Who Is the Other? Questioning the Generosity of Western Thought.' In *Ethics and Responsibility in the Phenomenological Tradition*, 1–31. Pittsburgh: Simon Silverman Phenomenology Center, Dusquesne University, 1992.

Bernstein, J.M. *Adorno: Disenchantment and Ethics.* Cambridge: Cambridge University Press, 2001.

– *Recovering Ethical Life: Jürgen Habermas and the Future of Critical Theory.* London: Routledge, 1995.

Bernstein, Richard J. 'Introduction.' In *Habermas and Modernity*, edited by Richard J. Bernstein, 1–32. Cambridge, Mass.: MIT Press, 1985.

Bernstein, Richard J., ed. *Habermas and Modernity.* Cambridge, Mass.: MIT Press, 1985.

Blanchot, Maurice. *Friendship.* Translated by Elizabeth Rottenberg. Stanford: Stanford University Press, 1997.

Borofsky, Robert. 'Cook, Lono, Obeyesekere, and Sahlins.' *Current Anthropology* 38, no. 2 (1997): 255–65.

– 'When: A Conversation about Culture.' *American Anthropologist* 103, no. 2 (2001): 432–46.

Bowlin, John R., and Peter G. Stromberg. 'Representation and Reality in the Study of Culture.' *American Anthropologist* 99, no. 1 (1997): 123–34.

Brand, Arie. *The Force of Reason: An Introduction to Habermas' Theory of Communicative Action.* Sydney: Allen and Unwin, 1990.

Browning, Don S., and Francis Schüssler Fiorenza, eds. *Habermas, Modernity and Public Theology.* New York: Crossroad, 1992.

Burrow, J.W. *Evolution and Society: A Study in Victorian Social Theory.* Cambridge: Cambridge University Press, 1966.

Burton, John W. 'Disappearing Savages? Thoughts on the Construction of an Anthropological Conundrum.' *Journal of Asian and African Studies* 34, no. 2 (1999): 199–209.

Carr, Helen. *Inventing the American Primitive: Politics, Gender, and the Representation of Native American Literary Traditions, 1789–1936.* New York: New York University Press, 1996.

Carrier, James. 'Occidentalism: The World Turned Upside-Down.' *American Ethnologist* 19, no. 2 (1992): 195–212.

Chakrabarty, Dipesh. *Habitations of Modernity: Essays in the Wake of Subaltern Studies.* Chicago: University of Chicago Press, 2002.

– *Provincializing Europe: Postcolonial Thought and Historical Difference.* Princeton: Princeton University Press, 2000.

– 'Radical Histories and Question of Enlightenment Rationalism: Some Recent Critiques of Subaltern Studies.' In *Mapping Subaltern Studies and the Postcolonial,* edited by Vinayak Chaturvedi, 256–80. London: Verso, 2000.

Chernela, Janet M. 'The "Ideal Speech Moment": Women and Narrative Performance in the Brazilian Amazon.' *Feminist Studies* 23, no. 1 (1997): 73–96.

Chow, Rey. 'How (the) Inscrutable Chinese Led to Globalized Theory.' *PMLA* 116, no. 1 (2001): 69–74.

– 'The Interruption of Referentiality: Poststructuralism and the Conundrum of Critical Multiculturalism.' *South Atlantic Quarterly* 101, no. 1 (2002): 171–86.

– *Primitive Passions: Visuality, Sexuality, Ethnography, and Contemporary Chinese Cinema.* New York: Columbia University Press, 1995.

– *Writing Diaspora: Tactics of Intervention in Contemporary Cultural Studies.* Bloomington: Indiana University Press, 1993.

Clifford, James. *The Predicament of Culture: Twentieth-Century Ethnography, Literature, and Art.* Cambridge, Mass.: Harvard University Press, 1988.

Coles, Romand. 'Identity and Difference in the Ethical Positions of Adorno and

Habermas.' In *The Cambridge Companion to Habermas*, edited by Stephen K. White, 19–45. Cambridge: Cambridge University Press, 1995.

Cooke, Maeve. *Language and Reason: A Study of Habermas' Pragmatics*. Cambridge, Mass.: MIT Press, 1994.

Coole, Diana. 'Habermas and the Question of Alterity.' In *Habermas and the Unfinished Project of Modernity*, edited by Maurizio Passerin d'Entreves and Seyla Benhabib, 221–44. Cambridge, Mass.: MIT Press, 1997.

Crook, Stephen. *Modernist Radicalism and Its Aftermath: Foundationalism and Anti-Foundationalism in Radical Social Theory*. London: Routledge, 1991.

'Culture Shock.' *Globe and Mail*, 2 August 2003, D12.

Dallmayr, Fred. *Polis and Praxis: Essays in Contemporary Political Theory*. Cambridge, Mass.: MIT Press, 1985.

d'Ans, André-Marcel. *Le Dit des Vrais Hommes: Myths, Contes, Légendes et Traditions des Indiens Cashinahua*. Paris: Union Générale d'Éditions, 1978.

de Certeau, Michel. *Heterologies: Discourse on the Other*. Translated by Brian Massumi. Minneapolis: University of Minnesota Press, 1986.

DeLillo, Don. *White Noise*. New York: Penguin, 1986.

Derrida, Jacques. *Margins of Philosophy*. Translated by Alan Bass. Chicago: University of Chicago Press, 1982.

– *Specters of Marx: The State of the Debt, the Work of Mourning, and the New International*. Translated by Peggy Kamuf. New York: Routledge, 1994.

de Sardan, Jean-Pierre Olivier. 'Occultism and the Ethnographic "I": The Exoticizing of Magic from Durkheim to "Postmodern" Anthropology.' *Critique of Anthropology* 12 (1992): 5–25.

Dews, Peter. *The Limits of Disenchantment: Essays on Contemporary European Philosophy*. London: Verso, 1995.

Diamond, Stanley. *In Search of the Primitive: A Critique of Civilization*. New Brunswick, NJ: Transaction Publishers, 1974.

di Leonardo, Micaela. *Exotics at Home: Anthropologies, Others, American Modernity*. Chicago: University of Chicago Press, 1998.

Dirks, Nicholas. 'Postcolonialism and Its Discontents: History, Anthropology, and Postcolonial Critique.' In *Schools of Thought: Twenty-Five Years of Interpretive Social Science*, edited by Joan W. Scott and Debra Keates, 227–51. Princeton: Princeton University Press, 2002.

Dolgin, Janet, David Kennitzer, and David Schneider, eds. *Symbolic Anthropology: A Reader in the Study of Symbols and Meaning*. New York: Columbia University Press, 1977.

Dozier, Edward P. 'The Concepts of "Primitive" and "Native" in Anthropology.' In *The Concept of the Primitive*, edited by Ashley Montagu, 228–56. New York: Free Press, 1968.

Dumont, Jean-Paul. 'The Tasaday, Which and Whose?: Toward the Political Economy of an Ethnographic Sign.' *Cultural Anthropology* 3, no. 3 (1988): 261–75.

Dunn, Allen. 'A Tyranny of Justice: The Ethics of Lyotard's Differend.' *boundary 2* 20, no. 1 (1993): 192–220.

Edmond, Rod. *Representing the South Pacific: Colonial Discourse from Cook to Gauguin.* Cambridge: Cambridge University Press, 1997.

Errington, Shelly. *The Death of Authentic Primitive Art and Other Tales of Progress.* Berkeley: University of California Press, 1998.

Evans-Pritchard, E.E. *Witchcraft, Oracles, and Magic among the Azande.* Oxford: Oxford University Press, 1937.

Fabian, Johannes. *Time and the Other: How Anthropology Makes Its Objects.* New York: Columbia University Press, 1983.

Fanon, Frantz. *The Wretched of the Earth.* Translated by Constance Farrington. Harmondsworth: Penguin, 1967.

Féral, Josette. 'The Powers of Difference.' In *The Future of Difference,* edited by Hester Eisenstein and Alice Jardine, 88–94. Boston: G.K. Hall, 1980.

Ferguson, Kathy E. *The Man Question: Visions of Subjectivity in Feminist Theory.* Berkeley: University of California Press, 1993.

Ferrara, Alessandro. 'Universalisms: Procedural, Contextualist and Prudential.' In *Universalism vs. Communitarianism: Contemporary Debates in Ethics,* edited by David Rasmussen, 11–37. Cambridge, Mass.: MIT Press, 1990.

Fiedler, Leslie A. *The Return of the Vanishing American.* London: Jonathan Cape, 1968.

Fitzpatrick, Peter. *Modernism and the Grounds of Law.* Cambridge: Cambridge University Press, 2001.

– *The Mythology of Modern Law.* London: Routledge, 1992.

Flynn, Bernard. *Political Philosophy at the Closure of Metaphysics.* Atlantic Highlands, NJ: Humanities Press, 1992.

Foster, Hal. *Recodings: Art, Spectacle, Cultural Politics.* Edited by Hal Foster. Port Townsend, Wash.: Bay Press, 1985.

Foucault, Michel. *The Order of Things: An Archaeology of the Human Sciences.* London: Tavistock Publications, 1970.

Friedman, Jonathan. 'No History Is an Island.' *Critique of Anthropology* 8, no. 3 (1988): 7–39.

– 'Review of *How "Natives" Think.*' *American Ethnologist* 24, no. 1 (1997): 261–2.

Gane, Mike. *Baudrillard: Critical and Fatal Theory.* London: Routledge, 1991.

Gasché, Rodolphe. *Inventions of Difference: On Jacques Derrida.* Cambridge, Mass.: Harvard University Press, 1994.

– *Of Minimal Things: Studies on the Notion of Relation.* Stanford: Stanford University Press, 1999.

Geertz, Clifford. 'Culture War.' *New York Review of Books*, 30 Nov. 1995, 4–6.

– 'Distinguished Lecture: Anti-Anti-Relativism.' *American Anthropologist* 86 (1984): 263–78.

– *The Interpretation of Cultures*. New York: Basic Books, 1973.

Genosko, Gary. *Baudrillard and Signs: Signification Ablaze*. London: Routledge, 1994.

Giddens, Anthony. 'Jürgen Habermas.' In *The Return of Grand Theory in the Human Sciences*, edited by Quentin Skinner, 121–39. Cambridge: Cambridge University Press, 1985.

– 'Reason without Revolution? Habermas's Theorie des Kommunikativen Handelns.' In *Habermas and Modernity*, edited by Richard J. Bernstein, 95–121. Cambridge, Mass.: MIT Press, 1985.

Gilroy, Paul. *Against Race: Imagining Political Culture Beyond the Color Line*. Cambridge, Mass.: Harvard University Press, 2000.

Gupta, Akhil, and James Ferguson. 'Beyond "Culture": Space, Identity, and the Politics of Difference.' *Cultural Anthropology* 7, no. 1 (1992): 6–23.

Habermas, Jürgen. 'Appendix.' In *Knowledge and Human Interests*. Translated by Jeremy J. Shapiro. 2nd ed. London: Heinemann, 1978.

– *Autonomy and Solidarity: Interviews with Jürgen Habermas*. Edited by Peter Dews. London: Verso, 1986.

– *Between Facts and Norms: Contributions to a Discourse Theory of Law and Democracy*. Translated by William Rehg. Cambridge, Mass.: MIT Press, 1996.

– *Communication and the Evolution of Society*. Translated by Thomas McCarthy. Boston: Beacon Press, 1979.

– 'Consciousness-Raising or Redemptive Criticism – the Contemporaneity of Walter Benjamin.' *New German Critique* 17 (1979): 30–59.

– 'Fundamentalism and Terror: A Dialogue with Jürgen Habermas.' In *Philosophy in a Time of Terror: Dialogues with Jürgen Habermas and Jacques Derrida*, edited by Giovanna Borradori. Chicago: University of Chicago Press, 2003.

– *The Future of Human Nature*. Cambridge: Polity, 2003.

– *The Inclusion of the Other: Studies in Political Theory*. Edited by Ciaran Cronin and Pablo De Greiff. Cambridge, Mass.: MIT Press, 1998.

– *Justice and Application: Remarks on Discourse Ethics*. Translated by Ciaran Cronin. Cambridge, Mass.: MIT Press, 1993.

– 'Justice and Solidarity: On the Discussion Concerning Stage 6.' In *The Moral Domain: Essays in the Ongoing Discussion between Philosophy and the Social Sciences*, edited by Thomas E. Wren. Cambridge, Mass.: MIT Press, 1990.

– *The Liberating Power of Symbols: Philosophical Essays*. Cambridge, Mass.: MIT Press, 2001.

– *Moral Consciousness and Communicative Action.* Translated by C. Lenhardt and S.W. Nicholson. Cambridge, Mass.: MIT Press, 1991.
– *The Philosophical Discourse of Modernity: Twelve Lectures.* Translated by Frederick Lawrence. Cambridge, Mass.: MIT Press, 1987.
– *Postmetaphysical Thinking.* Translated by W.M. Hohengarten. Cambridge, Mass.: MIT Press, 1992.
– *The Postnational Constellation: Political Essays.* Translated and edited by Max Pensky. Cambridge, Mass.: MIT Press, 2001.
– 'Questions and Counterquestions.' In *Habermas and Modernity*, edited by Richard J. Bernstein. Cambridge, Mass.: MIT Press, 1985.
– *Religion and Rationality: Essays on Reason, God, and Modernity.* Edited by Eduardo Mendieta. Cambridge: Polity Press, 2002.
– 'A Reply to My Critics.' In *Habermas: Critical Debates*, edited by John B. Thompson and David Held. London: Macmillan, 1982.
– *The Theory of Communicative Action: Lifeworld and System.* Translated by Thomas McCarthy. Vol. 2. Boston: Beacon Press, 1987.
– *The Theory of Communicative Action: Reason and the Rationalization of Society.* Translated by Thomas McCarthy. Vol. 1. Boston: Beacon, 1984.
Hacking, Ian. 'Aloha, Aloha.' *London Review of Books*, 7 Sept. 1995, 6–9.
Hallpike, C.R. *The Foundations of Primitive Thought.* New York: Oxford University Press, 1979.
Hallward, Peter. *Absolutely Postcolonial: Writing between the Singular and the Specific.* Manchester: Manchester University Press, 2001.
Hefner, Robert. 'Baudrillard's Noble Anthropology: The Image of Symbolic Exchange in Political Economy.' *Sub-Stance* 17 (1977): 105–13.
Hénaff, Marcel. *Claude Lévi-Strauss and the Making of Structural Anthropology.* Translated by Mary Barker. Minneapolis: University of Minnesota Press, 1998.
Henrich, Dieter. 'What Is Metaphysics – What Is Modernity? Twelve Theses against Jürgen Habermas.' In *Habermas: A Critical Reader*, edited by Peter Dews, 291–319. Oxford: Blackwell, 1999.
Herbert, Christopher. *Culture and Anomie: Ethnographic Imagination in the Nineteenth Century.* Chicago: University of Chicago Press, 1991.
Hollis, Martin, and Steven Lukes. 'Introduction.' In *Rationality and Relativism*, edited by Martin Hollis and Steven Lukes, 1–20. Cambridge, Mass.: MIT Press, 1982.
Honneth, Axel. *The Critique of Power: Reflective Stages in a Critical Social Theory.* Translated by Kenneth Baynes. Cambridge, Mass.: MIT Press, 1993.
Honneth, Axel, and Hans Joas. *Social Action and Human Nature.* Translated by Raymond Meyer. New York: Cambridge University Press, 1988.

Horkheimer, Max, and Theodore W. Adorno. *Dialectic of Enlightenment.* Translated by John Cumming. London: Allen Lane, 1973 [1944]

Horton, Robin. 'African Traditional Thought and Western Science.' In *Rationality,* edited by Brian Wilson, 131–71. Oxford: Oxford University Press, 1970.

Ingram, David. *Habermas and the Dialectic of Reason.* New Haven: Yale University Press, 1987.

Ivy, Marilyn. *Discourses of the Vanishing: Modernity, Phantasm, Japan.* Chicago: University of Chicago Press, 1995.

Jahoda, Gustav. *Psychology and Anthropology: A Psychological Perspective.* London: Academic Press, 1982.

Jameson, Fredric. *Postmodernism, or, the Cultural Logic of Late Capitalism.* Durham: Duke University Press, 1991.

Jay, Martin. *Marxism and Totality: The Adventures of a Concept from Lukács to Habermas.* Berkeley: University of California Press, 1984.

Keesing, Roger. 'Exotic Readings of Cultural Texts.' *Current Anthropology* 30, no. 4 (1989): 459–69.

Kellner, Douglas. *Jean Baudrillard: From Marxism to Postmodernism and Beyond.* Cambridge: Polity Press, 1989.

Kelly, Michael. 'The Gadamer/Habermas Debate Revisited: The Question of Ethics.' In *Universalism vs. Communitarianism: Contemporary Debates in Ethics,* edited by David Rasmussen, 139–59. Cambridge, Mass.: MIT Press, 1990.

– 'Macintyre, Habermas, and Philosophical Ethics.' *The Philosophical Forum* 21, no. 1–2 (1989–90): 70–93.

Klein, Kerwin Lee. 'In Search of Narrative Mastery: Postmodernism and the People without History.' *History and Theory* 34, no. 4 (1995): 275–98.

Kuklick, Henrika. *The Savage Within: The Social History of British Anthropology, 1885–1945.* Cambridge: Cambridge University Press, 1991.

Kuper, Adam. *Culture: The Anthropologists' Account.* Cambridge, Mass.: Harvard University Press, 1999.

– *The Invention of Primitive Society: Transformations of an Illusion.* London: Routledge, 1988.

– 'The Return of the Native.' *Current Anthropology* 44, no. 3 (2003): 389–402.

Latour, Bruno. *We Have Never Been Modern.* Translated by Catherine Porter. Cambridge, Mass.: Harvard University Press, 1993.

Lawrence, D.H. *Studies in Classic American Literature.* Harmondsworth: Penguin, 1971 [1924].

Lemke, Sieglinde. *Primitivist Modernism: Black Culture and the Origins of Transatlantic Modernism.* Oxford: Oxford University Press, 1998.

Lerner, Bettina. 'The Lost Tribe.' *Nova/Horizon.* 1989.

Levin, Charles. *Jean Baudrillard: A Study in Cultural Metaphysics*. Hemel Hempstead: Prentice Hall, 1996.

Levinas, Emmanuel. *Collected Philosophical Papers*. Edited by Alphonso Lingis. Dordrecht: Martinus Nijhoff, 1987.

– 'Intention, Ereignis und der Andere. Gesprach Zwischen Emmanuel Levinas und Christoph von Wolzogen am 20. Dezember 1985 in Paris.' In *Humanismus des Anderen Menschen*, edited by Christophe von Wolzogen, 140. Hamburg: Felix Meiner, 1989.

Lévi-Strauss, Claude. *Tristes Tropiques*. Translated by John Weightman and Doreen Weightman. Harmondsworth: Penguin, 1976 [1955].

Lyotard, Jean-François. *The Differend: Phrases in Dispute*. Translated by Georges van den Abbeele. Minneapolis: University of Minnesota Press, 1988.

– *The Inhuman: Reflections on Time*. Translated by Geoffrey Bennington and Rachel Bowlby. Stanford: Standford University Press, 1991.

– 'An Interview with Jean-François Lyotard.' *Theory, Culture and Society* 5, no. 2–3 (1988): 277–309.

– *Libidinal Economy*. Translated by Iain Hamilton Grant. Bloomington: Indiana University Press, 1993.

– 'Missive on Universal History.' In *The Postmodern Explained: Correspondence 1982–1985*, edited by Julian Pefanis and Morgan Thomas, 23–37. Minneapolis: University of Minnesota Press, 1992.

– *Political Writings*. Edited by Bill Readings and Kevin Paul Geiman. Minneapolis: University of Minnesota Press, 1993.

– *The Postmodern Condition: A Report on Knowledge*. Translated by Geoffrey Bennington and Brian Massumi. Minneapolis: University of Minnesota Press, 1984.

– *The Postmodern Explained: Correspondence 1982–1985*. Translated by Don Barry et al. Edited by Julian Pefanis and Morgan Thomas. Minneapolis: University of Minnesota Press, 1993.

Lyotard, Jean-François, and Jean-Loup Thébaud. *Just Gaming*. Translated by Wlad Godzich. Minneapolis: University of Minnesota Press, 1985.

Maranhao, Tullio. 'Invitation to an Anthropology Party.' *L'Esprit Créateur* 31, no. 1 (1991): 131–43.

Marcus, George E., and Michael M.J. Fischer. *Anthropology as Critique: An Experimental Moment in the Human Sciences*. Chicago: University of Chicago Press, 1986.

Masuzawa, Tomoko. *In Search of Dreamtime: The Quest for the Origin of Religion*. Chicago: University of Chicago Press, 1993.

McCarthy, Thomas. *Ideals and Illusions: Reconstruction and Deconstruction in Critical Theory*. Cambridge, Mass.: MIT Press, 1991.

– 'Rationality and Relativism: Habermas's "Overcoming" of Hermeneutics.'

In *Habermas: Critical Debates*, edited by John B. Thompson and David Held, 57–78. London: Macmillan, 1982.

McGowan, John. *Postmodernism and Its Critics*. Ithaca: Cornell University Press, 1991.

McGrane, Bernard. *Beyond Anthropology: Society and the Other*. New York: Columbia University Press, 1989.

Montagu, Ashley. 'The Concept of "Primitive" and Related Anthropological Terms: A Study in the Systematics of Confusion.' In *The Concept of the Primitive*, edited by Ashley Montagu, 148–68. New York: Free Press, 1968.

Moody-Adams, Michele M. *Fieldwork in Familiar Places: Morality, Culture, and Philosophy*. Cambridge, Mass.: Harvard University Press, 1997.

Moore, Sally Falk. 'Explaining the Present: Theoretical Dilemmas in Processual Anthropology.' *American Ethnologist* 14, no. 4 (1987): 727–36.

Mortley, Raoul. *French Philosophers in Conversation*. London: Routledge, 1991.

Mudimbe, Valentin. *The Invention of Africa: Gnosis, Philosophy and the Order of Knowledge*. Bloomington: Indiana University Press, 1988.

Nielsen, Donald A. 'A Theory of Communicative Action or a Sociology of Civilizations? A Critique of Jürgen Habermas.' *International Journal of Politics, Culture, and Society* 1, no. 1 (1987): 159–88.

Obeyesekere, Gananath. *The Apotheosis of Captain Cook: European Mythmaking in the Pacific*. 2nd ed. Princeton: Princeton University Press, 1997.

– 'Reweaving the Argument: A Response to Parker.' *Oceania* 65, no. 3 (1995): 268–73.

– *The Work of Culture*. Chicago: University of Chicago Press, 1990.

Parker, Samuel. 'The Revenge of Practical Reason? A Review Essay on Gananath Obeyesekere's *The Apotheosis of Captain Cook*.' *Oceania* 65, no. 3 (1995): 257–67.

Pefanis, Julian. *Heterology and the Postmodern: Bataille, Baudrillard, and Lyotard*. Durham: Duke University Press, 1991.

Pertierra, Raul. 'The Rationality Problematique: An Anthropological Review of Habermas' Theory of Communicative Action.' *Social Analysis* 23 (1988): 72–88.

Pickard, Dean. 'Applied Nietzsche: The Problem of Reflexivity in Habermas, a Postmodern Critique.' *Auslegung* 19, no. 1 (1993): 1–21.

Poster, Mark. 'Postmodernism and the Politics of Multiculturalism: The Lyotard-Habermas Debate over Social Theory.' *Modern Fiction Studies* 38, no. 3 (1992): 567–80.

Povinelli, Elizabeth A. *The Cunning of Recognition: Indigenous Alterities and the Making of Australian Multiculturalism*. Durham: Duke University Press, 2002.

Prior, Colin. *Living Tribes*. Toronto: Firefly Books, 2003.

Rancière, Jacques. *The Philosopher and His Poor*. Translated by John Drury, Corinne Oster, and Andrew Parker. Edited by Andrew Parker. Durham: Duke University Press, 2002.

Rasmussen, David M. *Reading Habermas.* Cambridge, Mass.: Blackwell, 1990.

Readings, Bill. 'Foreword: The End of the Political.' In Lyotard, *Political Writings,* xiii–xxvi. Minneapolis: University of Minnesota Press, 1993.

– *Introducing Lyotard: Art and Politics.* London: Routledge, 1991.

– 'Pagans, Perverts or Primitives? Experimental Justice in the Empire of Capital.' In *Judging Lyotard,* edited by Andrew Benjamin, 168–91. London: Routledge, 1992.

Richman, Michèle H. *Sacred Revolutions: Durkheim and the Collège de Sociologie.* Minneapolis: University of Minnesota Press, 2002.

Roderick, Rick. 'Review of Habermas's The Theory of Communicative Reason, Vol. 1.' *Political Theory* 14, no. 1 (1986): 152–6.

Rorty, Richard. *Philosophical Papers.* Volume 1. *Objectivity, Relativism and Truth.* Cambridge: Cambridge University Press, 1991.

– *Philosophical Papers.* Volume 2. *Essays on Heidegger and Others.* Cambridge: Cambridge University Press, 1991.

Rothberg, Donald Jay. 'Rationality and Religion in Habermas' Recent Work: Some Remarks on the Relation between Critical Theory and the Phenomenology of Religion.' *Philosophy and Social Criticism* 11, no. 3 (1986): 221–43.

Sahlins, Marshall. 'Captain Cook at Hawaii.' *Journal of the Polynesian Society* 98 (1989): 371–423.

– *Culture and Practical Reason.* Chicago: University of Chicago Press, 1976.

– 'Deserted Islands of History: A Reply to Jonathan Friedman.' *Critique of Anthropology* 8, no. 3 (1988): 41–51.

– 'Goodbye to *Tristes Tropes*: Ethnography in the Context of Modern World History.' *Journal of Modern History* 65 (1993): 1–25.

– *Historical Metaphors and Mythical Realities: Structure in the Early History of the Sandwich Islands Kingdom.* Ann Arbor: University of Michigan Press, 1981.

– *How 'Natives' Think: About Captain Cook, for Example.* Chicago: University of Chicago Press, 1995.

– *Islands of History.* Chicago: University of Chicago Press, 1985.

– 'Reply to Borofsky.' *Current Anthropology* 38, no. 2 (1997): 272–6.

– 'The Sadness of Sweetness.' *Current Anthropology* 37, no. 3 (1996): 395–428.

– *Waiting for Foucault.* Cambridge: Prickly Pear Press, 1993.

Sakai, Naoki. 'Modernity and Its Critique: The Problem of Universalism and Particularism.' *South Atlantic Quarterly* 87, no. 3 (1988): 475–504.

Sapir, Edward. 'Culture, Genuine and Spurious.' In *Culture, Language and Personality: Selected Essays,* edited by David G. Mandelbaum, 78–119. Berkeley: University of California Press, 1966.

Schmid, Michael. 'Habermas's Theory of Social Evolution.' In *Habermas: Critical*

Debates, edited by John B. Thompson and David Held, 162–80. London: Macmillan, 1982.

Scott, David. 'Criticism and Culture: Theory and Post-Colonial Claims on Anthropological Disciplinarity.' *Critique of Anthropology* 12, no. 4 (1992): 371–94.

– 'Culture in Political Theory.' *Political Theory* 31, no. 1 (2003): 92–115.

Self, Will. 'Understanding the Ur-Bororo.' In *The Quantity Theory of Insanity: Together with Five Supporting Propositions*, 69–94. London: Bloomsbury, 1991.

Sewell, William H., Jr. 'Geertz, Cultural Systems, and History: From Synchrony to Transformation.' *Representations* 59 (1997): 35–55.

Sharpe, Jenny, and Gayatri Chakravorty Spivak. 'A Conversation with Gayatri Chakravorty Spivak: Politics and the Imagination.' *Signs* 28, no. 2 (2002): 609–24.

Shaw, Brian J. 'Habermas and Religious Inclusion: Lessons from Kant's Moral Theology.' *Political Theory* 27, no. 5 (1999): 634–66.

Shweder, Richard A. 'On Savages and Other Children.' *American Anthropologist* 84, no. 2 (1982): 354–66.

Snyder, Jon R. 'Translator's Introduction.' In Gianni Vattimo, *The End of Modernity: Nihilism and Hermeneutics in Postmodern Culture*, vi–lviii. Baltimore: Johns Hopkins University Press, 1988.

Sperber, Dan. *On Anthropological Knowledge: Three Essays*. Cambridge: Cambridge University Press, 1985.

Spivak, Gayatri Chakravorty. 'Can the Subaltern Speak?' In *Colonial Discourse and Post-Colonial Theory: A Reader*, edited by Patrick Williams and Laura Chrisman, 66–111. New York: Columbia University Press, 1994.

– *A Critique of Postcolonial Reason: Toward a History of the Vanishing Present*. Cambridge, Mass.: Harvard University Press, 1999.

– *In Other Worlds: Essays in Cultural Politics*. London: Methuen, 1987.

– *The Post-Colonial Critic: Interviews, Strategies, Dialogues*. Edited by Sarah Harasym. New York: Routledge, 1990.

– 'Supplementing Marxism.' In *Whither Marxism? Global Crises in International Perspective*, edited by Bernd Magnus and Stephen Cullenberg, 109–19. New York: Routledge, 1995.

Steedly, Mary Margaret. 'What Is Culture? Does It Matter?' In *Field Work: Sites in Literary and Cultural Studies*, edited by Marjorie Garber, Paul B. Franklin and Rebecca L. Walkowitz, 18–25. New York: Routledge, 1996.

Stewart, Susan. *On Longing: Narratives of the Miniature, the Gigantic, the Souvenir, the Collection*. Durham: Duke University Press, 1993.

Stocking, George W., Jr. 'The Ethnographic Sensibility of the 1920s and the Dualism of the Anthropological Tradition.' In *Romantic Motives: Essays on*

Anthropological Sensibility, edited by George W. Stocking Jr, 208–76. Madison: University of Wisconsin Press, 1989.

– *Race, Culture, and Evolution: Essays in the History of Anthropology*. New York: Free Press, 1968.

– *Victorian Anthropology*. New York: Free Press, 1987.

Stolcke, Verena. 'Talking Culture: New Boundaries, New Rhetorics of Exclusion in Europe.' *Current Anthropology* 36, no. 1 (1995): 1–24.

Strydom, Piet. 'The Ontogenetic Fallacy: The Immanent Critique of Habermas's Developmental Logical Theory of Evolution.' *Theory, Culture and Society* 9, no. 3 (1992): 65–93.

– 'Sociocultural Evolution or the Social Evolution of Practical Reason?: Eder's Critique of Habermas.' *Praxis International* 13, no. 3 (1993): 304–22.

Suzman, James. 'Comment on Adam Kuper's "The Return of the Native."' *Current Anthropology* 44, no. 3 (2003): 399–400.

Taguieff, Pierre-André. *The Force of Prejudice*. Minneapolis: University of Minnesota Press, 2001.

Tambiah, Stanley Jeyaraja. *Magic, Science, Religion, and the Scope of Rationality*. Cambridge: Cambridge University Press, 1990.

Taylor, Charles. *Hegel*. Cambridge: Cambridge University Press, 1975.

– 'Inwardness and the Culture of Modernity.' In *Philosophical Interventions in the Unfinished Project of Enlightenment*, edited by Axel Honneth, Thomas McCarthy, and Albrecht Wellmer, 88–110. Cambridge, Mass.: MIT Press, 1992.

Thomas, Nicholas. 'Against Ethnography.' *Cultural Anthropology* 6, no. 3 (1991): 306–22.

– 'Beggars Can Be Choosers.' *American Ethnologist* 20, no. 4 (1993): 868–76.

– *Colonialism's Culture: Anthropology, Travel and Government*. Cambridge: Polity, 1994.

– *In Oceania: Visions, Artifacts, Histories*. Durham: Duke University Press, 1997.

Thompson, John B. 'Universal Pragmatics.' In *Habermas: Critical Debates*, edited by John B. Thompson and David Held, 116–33. London: Macmillan, 1982.

Torgovnick, Marianna. *Gone Primitive: Savage Intellects, Modern Lives*. Chicago: University of Chicago Press, 1990.

– *Primitive Passions: Men, Women, and the Quest for Ecstasy*. New York: Knopf, 1997.

Trouillot, Michel-Rolph. 'Anthropology and the Savage Slot: The Poetics and Politics of Otherness.' In *Recapturing Anthropology: Working in the Present*, edited by Richard G. Fox, 17–44. Santa Fe: School of American Research Press, 1991.

Valeri, Valerio. 'Review of Gananath Obeyesekere's *The Apotheosis of Captain Cook*.' *Pacific Studies* 17, no. 2 (1994): 124–36.

van Wyck, Peter C. *Primitives in the Wilderness: Deep Ecology and the Missing Human Subject*. Albany: SUNY Press, 1997.

Vattimo, Gianni. *The End of Modernity: Nihilism and Hermeneutics in Postmodern Culture.* Translated by Jon R. Snyder. Baltimore: Johns Hopkins University Press, 1988.

– *The Transparent Society.* Translated by David Webb. Baltimore: Johns Hopkins University Press, 1992.

Wearne, Phillip. *Return of the Indian: Conquest and Revival in the Americas.* London: Cassell, 1996.

Webster, Steven. 'Structuralist Historicism and the History of Structuralism: Sahlins, the Hansons' *Counterpoint in Maori Culture,* and Postmodernist Ethnographic Form.' *Journal of the Polynesian Society* 96, no. 1 (1987): 27–65.

White, Stephen K. *The Recent Work of Jürgen Habermas.* Cambridge: Cambridge University Press, 1988.

Whitton, Brian. 'Herder's Critique of Enlightenment: Cultural Community versus Cosmopolitan Rationalism.' *History and Theory* 27, no. 2 (1988): 146–68.

Winch, Peter. 'Understanding a Primitive Society.' In *Rationality,* edited by Brian Wilson, 78–111. Oxford: Oxford University Press, 1970.

Windschuttle, Keith. *The Killing of History: How Literary Critics and Social Theorists Are Murdering Our Past.* New York: Free Press, 1997.

Wittgenstein, L. *Remarks on Frazier's Golden Bough.* Atlantic Highlands, NJ: Humanities Press, 1979.

Wolf, Eric R. 'Foreword.' In Stanley Diamond, *In Search of the Primitive: A Critique of Civilization,* xi–xiii. New Brunswick, NJ: Transaction Publishers, 1974.

Wuthnow, Robert. 'Rationality and the Limits of Rational Theory: A Sociological Critique.' In *Habermas, Modernity and Public Theology,* edited by Don S. Browning and Francis Schüssler Fiorenza, 206–25. New York: Crossroad, 1992.

Zimmerman, Rolf. 'Emancipation and Rationality: Foundational Problems in the Theories of Marx and Habermas.' *Ratio* 26, no. 2 (1984): 143–65.

Index

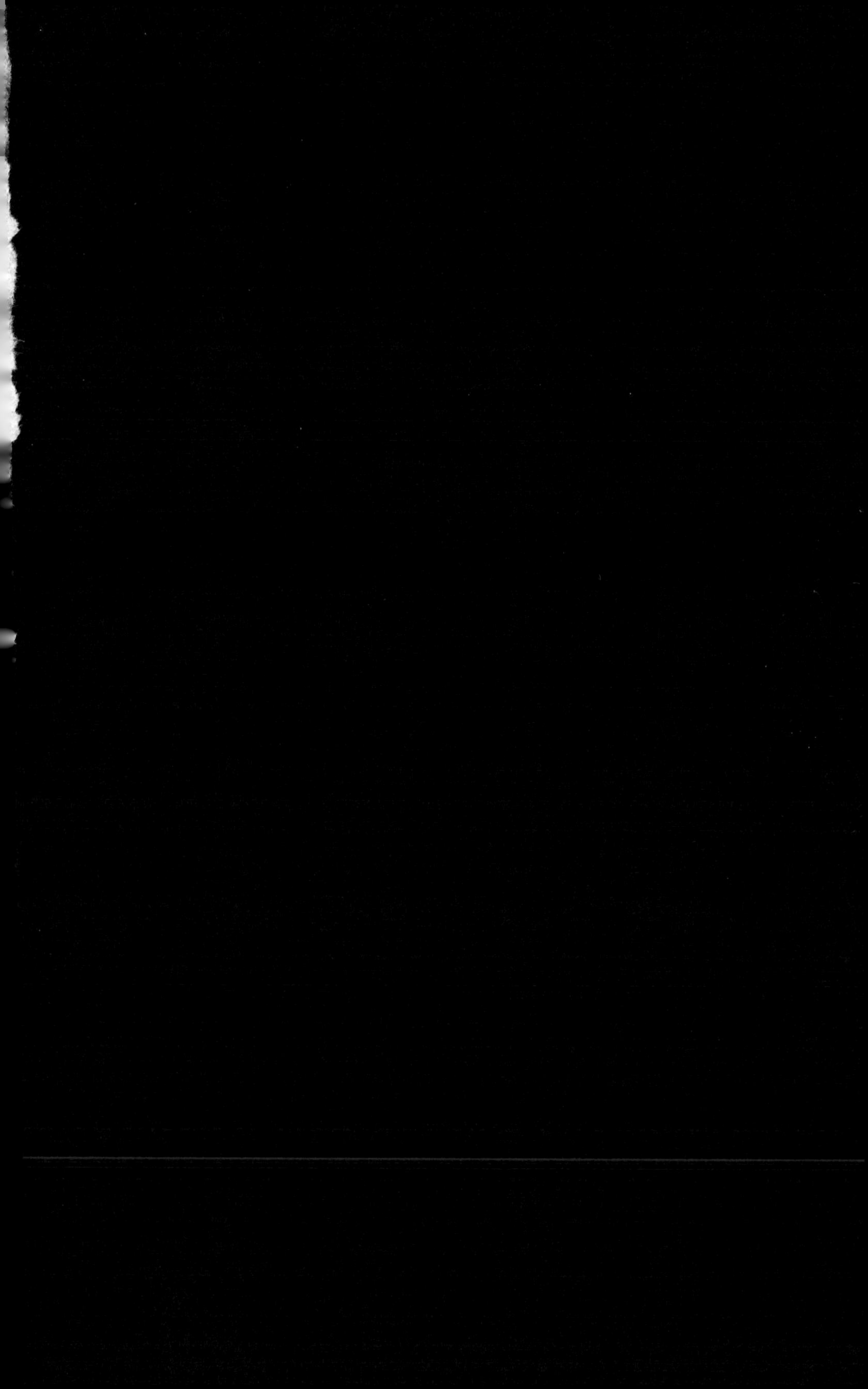